Lesson Plans

AMERICAN LITERATURE

The McGraw-Hill Companies

 Glencoe

Send all inquiries to:
Glencoe/McGraw-Hill
8787 Orion Place
Columbus, OH 43240-4027

ISBN-13: 978-0-07-891141-5
ISBN-10: 0-07-891141-9

Printed in the United States of America.
2 3 4 5 6 7 8 9 ROV 12 11 10

Table of Contents

Table of Contents

UNIT THREE

UNIT FOUR

Table of Contents

UNIT SEVEN

Table of Contents

Lesson Plans

The lesson plans address all selections and workshops in the *Glencoe Literature* Student Edition, including the Essential Course of Study—a curriculum designed to teach objectives that students commonly encounter on standardized tests. The selections in the Essential Course of Study are taken from the Student Edition and are also included in the *Read and Write* worktexts, which are available in three levels: English Learners, Approaching, and On-Level.

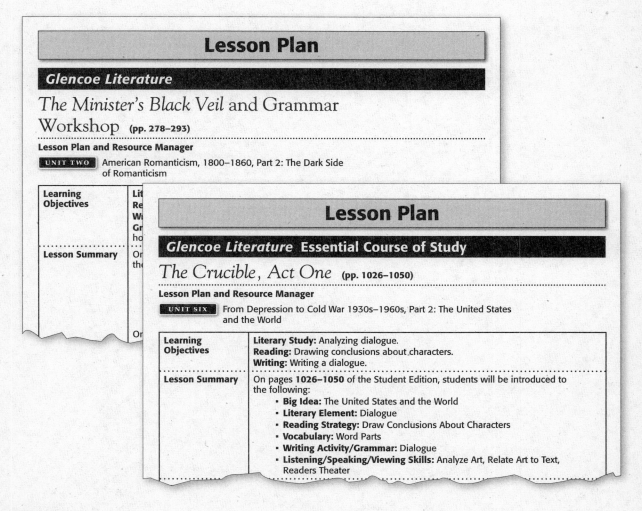

Lesson Plan

Glencoe Literature

The Minister's Black Veil and Grammar Workshop (pp. 278–293)

Lesson Plan and Resource Manager

UNIT TWO American Romanticism, 1800–1860, Part 2: The Dark Side of Romanticism

Learning Objectives	Lit... Re... W... Gr... ho...
Lesson Summary	Or... th...
	Or...

Lesson Plan

Glencoe Literature **Essential Course of Study**

The Crucible, Act One (pp. 1026–1050)

Lesson Plan and Resource Manager

UNIT SIX From Depression to Cold War 1930s–1960s, Part 2: The United States and the World

Learning Objectives	**Literary Study:** Analyzing dialogue. **Reading:** Drawing conclusions about characters. **Writing:** Writing a dialogue.
Lesson Summary	On pages **1026–1050** of the Student Edition, students will be introduced to the following: • **Big Idea:** The United States and the World • **Literary Element:** Dialogue • **Reading Strategy:** Draw Conclusions About Characters • **Vocabulary:** Word Parts • **Writing Activity/Grammar:** Dialogue • **Listening/Speaking/Viewing Skills:** Analyze Art, Relate Art to Text, Readers Theater

ICON KEY

TE Teacher Edition	📁 Black Line Master	📓 Workbook	🔥 Transparency
SE Student Edition	📖 Print Resource	💿 CD-ROM/DVD-ROM/DVD	▶ Internet Resource

Lesson Plan

Glencoe Literature

Unit 1 Introduction (pp. 4–18)

Lesson Plan and Resource Manager

UNIT ONE Early America, Beginnings–1800

Learning Objectives	**Literary Studies:** Analyzing literary periods. Analyzing literary genres. Evaluating historical influences.
Unit Summary	In this unit, students will be introduced to the following: • **Big Ideas:** The Sacred Earth and the Power of Storytelling, Life in the New World, The Road to Independence • **Reading Strategies:** Analyze Graphic Information, Analyze Cause and Effect, Evaluate, Draw Conclusions, Support the Main Idea • **Writing Activities/Grammar:** Essay, Graph • **Study Skills/Research/Assessment:** Use Timelines, Organize Ideas • **Listening/Speaking/Viewing Skill:** Analyze Art • **Vocabulary:** Phrases, Determine Precise Meanings
Lesson Duration	Two 45–50 minute sessions
Focus	**SE/TE** pp. 4–5 Daily Language Practice Transparency 1 Literature Launchers: Pre-Reading Videos DVD, Unit 1 Launcher Literature Launchers Teacher Guide
Teach	**SE/TE** pp. 6–17 Unit 1 Teaching Resources, Unit Introduction, pp. 1–2 Unit 1 Teaching Resources, Big Idea Foldable, pp. 3–4 Unit 1 Teaching Resources, Big Idea School-to-Home Connection, p. 5 Unit 1 Teaching Resources, Unit Challenge Planner, pp. 12–15 Unit 1 Teaching Resources: Academic Vocabulary Development, pp. 16–17 Classroom Presentation Toolkit CD-ROM TeacherWorks Plus CD-ROM
Assess	**SE/TE** p. 18 Assessment Resources, Unit 1 Diagnostic Assessment, pp. 1–8 ACT/SAT Preparation and Practice SE/ATE ExamView Assessment Suite CD-ROM Progress Reporter Online Assessment
Differentiated Instruction: English Learners	**TE** English Learner Activities, pp. 4–18 Unit 1 Teaching Resources, Big Idea School-to-Home Connections: English, Spanish, Vietnamese, Tagalog, Cantonese, Haitian Creole, and Hmong, pp. 6–11
Differentiated Instruction: Approaching Level	**TE** Approaching Level Activities, pp. 4–18 Skill Level Up! A Skills-Based Language Arts Game CD-ROM
Differentiated Instruction: Advanced/Pre-AP	Novel Companion SE, pp. 7–74 Novel Companion TG, pp. 10–20 Literature Classics, High School CD-ROM Skill Level Up! A Skills-Based Language Arts Game CD-ROM

Extension	◼ Grammar and Language Workbook SE
	◼ Grammar and Language Workbook TAE
	🗀 Revising with Style
	◼ Spelling Power SE
	◼ Spelling Power TAE
Daily Writing	**TE** p. 8
	SE/TE p. 18
Interdisciplinary Connections	**SE/TE** View the Art, pp. 4–5, 9, 13, 15
	TE Cultural History, pp. 6, 8, 11, 12
	TE Literary History, pp. 14, 17
	TE Political History, p. 16
	▶ glencoe.com
Independent Reading	💿 BookLink K–12 CD-ROM
	📖 Ethnic Anthologies
	📖 Glencoe Literature Library
	💿 Glencoe Literature Library Teacher Resources CD-ROM
	📖 inTIME magazine
	💿▶ Literature Classics, High School CD-ROM
Technology and Additional Resources	**Planning and Instruction:**
	💿 TeacherWorks Plus CD-ROM
	💿 Classroom Presentation Toolkit CD-ROM
	▶ Literature Online at **glencoe.com** (QuickPass Code: **GLA9879u1T**)
	Students Tools:
	💿 StudentWorks Plus CD-ROM or DVD-ROM
	▶ Online Student Edition at **glencoe.com**
	▶ Literature Online at **glencoe.com** (QuickPass Code: **GLA9800u1**)

Glencoe Literature

Part 1 Opener, Literary History: Native American Mythology, *How the World Was Made*, and Cultural Perspective: from *The Way to Rainy Mountain* (pp. 19–32)

Lesson Plan and Resource Manager

UNIT ONE Early America, Beginnings–1800, Part 1: The Sacred Earth and the Power of Storytelling

Learning Objectives	**Literary Study:** Analyzing literary periods. Analyzing literary genres. Analyzing archetype. Analyzing cultural traditions. **Reading:** Analyzing sequence. **Writing:** Writing a story.
Lesson Summary	On pages **19–32** of the Student Edition, students will be introduced to the following: • **Big Idea:** The Sacred Earth and the Power of Storytelling • **Literary Elements:** Archetype, Metaphor • **Reading Strategies:** Identify Sequence, Analyze Cultural Traditions • **Vocabulary:** Synonyms • **Writing Activities/Grammar:** Creation Myth, Description
Lesson Duration	Two 45–50 minute sessions
Readability Scores	"How the World Was Made" Dale-Chall: 5.9 DRP: 57 Lexile: 1250 Cultural Perspective Dale-Chall: 5.5 DRP: 61 Lexile: 1000
Focus	**SE/TE** pp. 20, 22–23, 27 🎞 Selection Focus Transparency 1 🎞 Daily Language Practice Transparencies 2–3
Teach	**SE/TE** pp. 20–21, 24–25, 28–32 📁 Unit 1 Teaching Resources, Literary History, pp. 19–20 📁 Unit 1 Teaching Resources, Literary Element, p. 28 📁 Unit 1 Teaching Resources, Reading Strategy, pp. 29, 30 🎞 Literary Elements Transparency 11 💿 Classroom Presentation Toolkit CD-ROM 💿 Listening Library CD, Selection Audio 💿 TeacherWorks Plus CD-ROM 💿 Vocabulary PuzzleMaker CD-ROM
Assess	**SE/TE** pp. 21, 26, 32 📁 Unit 1 Teaching Resources, Selection Quick Check, p. 31 📁 Unit 1 Teaching Resources, Selection Quick Check (Spanish), p. 32 📁 Assessment Resources, Selection Test, pp. 59–60 📁 Assessment Resources, Selection Test, pp. 61–62 💿 ExamView Assessment Suite CD-ROM 💿 Progress Reporter Online Assessment

Differentiated Instruction: English Learners	**TE** English Learner Activities, pp. 19–32 📁 Unit 1 Teaching Resources, English Language Coach, p. 21 📁 Unit 1 Teaching Resources, Selection Summaries: English, Spanish, Vietnamese, Tagalog, Cantonese, Haitian Creole, and Hmong, pp. 22–27 📁 Unit 1 Teaching Resources, Selection Quick Check (Spanish), p. 32 📁 English Language Coach 💿 Glencoe Interactive Vocabulary CD-ROM 💿 Listening Library Audio CD 📁 Listening Library Sourcebook: Strategies and Activities
Differentiated Instruction: Approaching Level	**TE** Approaching Level Activities, pp. 19–32 💿 Glencoe Interactive Vocabulary CD-ROM 💿 Listening Library Audio CD 📁 Listening Library Sourcebook: Strategies and Activities 💿 Skill Level Up! A Skills-Based Language Arts Game CD-ROM
Differentiated Instruction: Advanced/Pre-AP	📘 Novel Companion SE, pp. 7–74 📘 Novel Companion TG, pp. 10–20 💿 Literature Classics, High School CD-ROM 💿 Skill Level Up! A Skills-Based Language Arts Game CD-ROM
Extension	📘 Grammar and Language Workbook SE 📘 Grammar and Language Workbook TAE 📁 Revising with Style 📘 Spelling Power SE 📘 Spelling Power TAE
Daily Writing	**SE/TE** pp. 26, 30
Interdisciplinary Connections	**SE/TE** View the Art, pp. 19, 21, 31 **TE** Political History, p. 22 **TE** Cultural History, pp. 25, 28 **TE** Language History, p. 27 **SE/TE** View the Map, p. 29 ▶ glencoe.com
Independent Reading	💿 BookLink K–12 CD-ROM 📖 Ethnic Anthologies 📖 Glencoe Literature Library 💿 Glencoe Literature Library Teacher Resources CD-ROM 📖 *inTIME* magazine 💿 Literature Classics, High School CD-ROM
Technology and Additional Resources	**Planning and Instruction:** 💿 TeacherWorks Plus CD-ROM 💿 Classroom Presentation Toolkit CD-ROM ▶ Literature Online at **glencoe.com** (QuickPass Code: **GLA9879u1T**) **Students Tools:** 💿 StudentWorks Plus CD-ROM or DVD-ROM ▶ Online Student Edition at **glencoe.com** ▶ Literature Online at **glencoe.com** (QuickPass Code: **GLA9800u1**)

Lesson Plan

Comparing Literature: *The Sky Tree, How the Leopard Got His Claws*, and *Prayer to the Pacific* (pp. 33–46)

Lesson Plan and Resource Manager

UNIT ONE Early America, Beginnings–1800, Part 1: The Sacred Earth and the Power of Storytelling

Learning Objectives	**Literary Study:** Comparing cultural context.
Lesson Summary	On pages **33–46** of the Student Edition, students will be introduced to the following: • **Big Idea:** The Sacred Earth and the Power of Storytelling • **Literary Element:** Oral Tradition • **Reading Strategy:** Question • **Writing Activities/Grammar:** Dialogue, Essay • **Study Skills/Research/Assessment:** Notetaking, Research Cultures • **Listening/Speaking/Viewing Skills:** Analyze Art, Storytelling
Lesson Duration	Two to five 45–50 minute sessions
Readability Scores	"The Sky Tree" Dale-Chall: 3.6 DRP: 48 Lexile: 740 "How the Leopard Got His Claws" Dale-Chall: 3.2 DRP: 46 Lexile: 540
Focus	**SE/TE** pp. 33–34, 38, 44 🔖 Selection Focus Transparency 2 🔖 Daily Language Practice Transparency 4 ⊙ Literature Launchers: Pre-Reading Videos DVD, Selection Launcher 📁 Literature Launchers Teacher Guide
Teach	**SE/TE** pp. 35–36, 39–43, 45 📕 Interactive Read and Write SE/TE, pp. 1–16 📁 Unit 1 Teaching Resources, Compare Literature Graphic Organizer, p. 33 📁 Unit 1 Teaching Resources, Literary Element, p. 40 📁 Unit 1 Teaching Resources, Reading Strategy, p. 41 📁 Unit 1 Teaching Resources, Grammar Practice, p. 42 🔖 Literary Elements Transparency 71 ⊙ Classroom Presentation Toolkit CD-ROM ⊙ Listening Library CD, Selection Audio ⊙ TeacherWorks Plus CD-ROM ⊙ ⊙ Vocabulary PuzzleMaker CD-ROM
Assess	**SE/TE** pp. 37, 43, 45–46 📁 Unit 1 Teaching Resources, Selection Quick Check, p. 43 📁 Unit 1 Teaching Resources, Selection Quick Check (Spanish), p. 44 📁 Assessment Resources, Selection Test, pp. 63–64 ⊙ ExamView Assessment Suite CD-ROM ⊙ Progress Reporter Online Assessment

Differentiated Instruction: English Learners	**TE** English Learner Activities, pp. 33–46 Interactive Read and Write (EL) SE/TE, pp. 1–16 Unit 1 Teaching Resources, English Language Coach, p. 21 Unit 1 Teaching Resources, Selection Summaries: English, Spanish, Vietnamese, Tagalog, Cantonese, Haitian Creole, and Hmong, pp. 34–39 Unit 1 Teaching Resources, Selection Quick Check (Spanish), p. 44 English Language Coach Glencoe Interactive Vocabulary CD-ROM Listening Library Audio CD Listening Library Sourcebook: Strategies and Activities
Differentiated Instruction: Approaching Level	**TE** Approaching Level Activities, pp. 33–46 Interactive Read and Write (Approaching) SE/TE, pp. 1–16 Glencoe Interactive Vocabulary CD-ROM Listening Library Audio CD Listening Library Sourcebook: Strategies and Activities Skill Level Up! A Skills-Based Language Arts Game CD-ROM
Differentiated Instruction: Advanced/Pre-AP	Novel Companion SE, pp. 7–74 Novel Companion TG, pp. 10–20 Literature Classics, High School CD-ROM Skill Level Up! A Skills-Based Language Arts Game CD-ROM
Extension	Grammar and Language Workbook SE Grammar and Language Workbook TAE Revising with Style Spelling Power SE Spelling Power TAE
Daily Writing	**SE/TE** pp. 37, 46
Interdisciplinary Connections	**TE** Literary History, pp. 34, 38 **SE/TE** View the Art, pp. 36, 40, 42, 44 **TE** Cultural History, p. 45 glencoe.com
Independent Reading	BookLink K–12 CD-ROM Ethnic Anthologies Glencoe Literature Library Glencoe Literature Library Teacher Resources CD-ROM *inTIME* magazine Literature Classics, High School CD-ROM
Technology and Additional Resources	**Planning and Instruction:** TeacherWorks Plus CD-ROM Classroom Presentation Toolkit CD-ROM Literature Online at **glencoe.com** (QuickPass Code: **GLA9879u1T**) **Students Tools:** StudentWorks Plus CD-ROM or DVD-ROM Online Student Edition at **glencoe.com** Literature Online at **glencoe.com** (QuickPass Code: **GLA9800u1**)

Lesson Plan

Glencoe Literature

from *The Iroquois Constitution* and Vocabulary Workshop (pp. 47–54)

Lesson Plan and Resource Manager

UNIT ONE Early America, Beginnings–1800, Part 1: The Sacred Earth and the Power of Storytelling

Learning Objectives	**Literary Study:** Analyzing author's purpose. **Reading:** Drawing conclusions about culture. **Writing:** Writing a summary. **Vocabulary:** Understanding academic vocabulary. Using context clues to determine the meanings of words with multiple meanings.
Lesson Summary	On pages **47–52** of the Student Edition, students will be introduced to the following: • **Big Idea:** The Sacred Earth and the Power of Storytelling • **Literary Element:** Author's Purpose • **Reading Strategy:** Draw Conclusions About Culture • **Vocabulary:** Synonyms • **Writing:** Letter • **Listening/Speaking/Viewing Skill:** Analyze Art On pages **53–54** of the Student Edition, students will be introduced to the following: • **Vocabulary Workshop:** Academic Vocabulary
Lesson Duration	One 45–50 minute session
Readability Scores	Dale-Chall: 8.2 DRP: 63 Lexile: 1440
Focus	**SE/TE** pp. 47–48, 53 ✎ Selection Focus Transparency 3 ✎ Daily Language Practice Transparency 5
Teach	**SE/TE** pp. 49–50, 53–54 📁 Unit 1 Teaching Resources, Literary Element, p. 51 📁 Unit 1 Teaching Resources, Reading Strategy, p. 52 📁 Unit 1 Teaching Resources, Vocabulary Strategy, p. 53–54 📁 Unit 1 Teaching Resources, Grammar Practice, p. 55 ✎ Literary Elements Transparency 14 💿 Classroom Presentation Toolkit CD-ROM 💿 Listening Library CD, Selection Audio 💿 TeacherWorks Plus CD-ROM 💿 Vocabulary PuzzleMaker CD-ROM
Assess	**SE/TE** pp. 52, 54 📁 Unit 1 Teaching Resources, Selection Quick Check, p. 56 📁 Unit 1 Teaching Resources, Selection Quick Check (Spanish), p. 57 📁 Assessment Resources, Selection Test, pp. 65–66 💿 ExamView Assessment Suite CD-ROM ▶ Progress Reporter Online Assessment

Differentiated Instruction: English Learners	**TE** English Learner Activities, pp. 47–54 📁 Unit 1 Teaching Resources, English Language Coach, p. 21 📁 Unit 1 Teaching Resources, Selection Summaries: English, Spanish, Vietnamese, Tagalog, Cantonese, Haitian Creole, and Hmong, pp. 45–50 📁 Unit 1 Teaching Resources, Selection Quick Check (Spanish), p. 57 📁 English Language Coach 💿 Glencoe Interactive Vocabulary CD-ROM 💿 Listening Library Audio CD 📁 Listening Library Sourcebook: Strategies and Activities
Differentiated Instruction: Approaching Level	**TE** Approaching Level Activities, pp. 47–54 💿 Glencoe Interactive Vocabulary CD-ROM 💿 Listening Library Audio CD 📁 Listening Library Sourcebook: Strategies and Activities 💿 Skill Level Up! A Skills-Based Language Arts Game CD-ROM
Differentiated Instruction: Advanced/Pre-AP	📘 Novel Companion SE, pp. 7–74 📘 Novel Companion TG, pp. 10–20 💿 ▶ Literature Classics, High School CD-ROM 💿 Skill Level Up! A Skills-Based Language Arts Game CD-ROM
Extension	📘 Grammar and Language Workbook SE 📘 Grammar and Language Workbook TAE 📁 Revising with Style 📘 Spelling Power SE 📘 Spelling Power TAE
Daily Writing	**SE/TE** p. 52
Interdisciplinary Connections	**TE** Literary History, pp. 47, 51 **TE** Political History, p. 50 **SE/TE** View the Photograph, p. 51 ▶ glencoe.com
Independent Reading	💿 BookLink K–12 CD-ROM 📖 Ethnic Anthologies 📖 Glencoe Literature Library 💿 Glencoe Literature Library Teacher Resources CD-ROM 📖 inTIME magazine 💿 ▶ Literature Classics, High School CD-ROM
Technology and Additional Resources	**Planning and Instruction:** 💿 TeacherWorks Plus CD-ROM 💿 Classroom Presentation Toolkit CD-ROM ▶ Literature Online at **glencoe.com** (QuickPass Code: **GLA9879u1T**) **Students Tools:** 💿 StudentWorks Plus CD-ROM or DVD-ROM ▶ Online Student Edition at **glencoe.com** ▶ Literature Online at **glencoe.com** (QuickPass Code: **GLA9800u1**)

Lesson Plan

Part 2 Opener and from *La Relación* (pp. 55–61)

Lesson Plan and Resource Manager

UNIT ONE Early America, Beginnings–1800, Part 2: Life in the New World

Learning Objectives	**Literary Study:** Analyzing point of view. **Reading:** Recognizing bias. **Writing:** Writing a story.
Lesson Summary	On pages **56–61** of the Student Edition, students will be introduced to the following: • **Big Idea:** Life in the New World • **Literary Element:** Point of View • **Reading Strategy:** Recognize Bias • **Vocabulary:** Practice with Synonyms, Words with Many Uses • **Writing Activity:** Write a Story • **Listening/Speaking/Viewing Skill:** Analyze Art
Lesson Duration	One 45–50 minute session
Readability Scores	Dale-Chall: 6.1 DRP: 55 Lexile: 1100
Focus	**SE/TE** pp. 55–57 Selection Focus Transparency 4 Daily Language Practice Transparency 6
Teach	**SE/TE** pp. 58–60 Unit 1 Teaching Resources, Literary Element, p. 66 Unit 1 Teaching Resources, Reading Strategy, p. 67 Unit 1 Teaching Resources, Selection Vocabulary Practice, p. 68 Unit 1 Teaching Resources, Vocabulary Strategy, p. 69 Unit 1 Teaching Resources, Grammar Practice, p. 70 Literary Elements Transparency 80 Classroom Presentation Toolkit CD-ROM Listening Library CD, Selection Audio TeacherWorks Plus CD-ROM Vocabulary PuzzleMaker CD-ROM
Assess	**SE/TE** p. 61 Unit 1 Teaching Resources, Selection Quick Check, p. 71 Unit 1 Teaching Resources, Selection Quick Check (Spanish), p. 72 Assessment Resources, Selection Test, pp. 67–68 ExamView Assessment Suite CD-ROM Progress Reporter Online Assessment
Differentiated Instruction: English Learners	**TE** English Learner Activities, pp. 56–61 Unit 1 Teaching Resources, English Language Coach, p. 59 Unit 1 Teaching Resources, Selection Summaries: English, Spanish, Vietnamese, Tagalog, Cantonese, Haitian Creole, and Hmong, pp. 60–65 Unit 1 Teaching Resources, Selection Quick Check (Spanish), p. 72

Differentiated Instruction: English Learners *(continued)*	📁 English Language Coach 💿 Glencoe Interactive Vocabulary CD-ROM 💿 Listening Library Audio CD 📁 Listening Library Sourcebook: Strategies and Activities
Differentiated Instruction: Approaching Level	**TE** Approaching Level Activities, pp. 55–61 💿 Glencoe Interactive Vocabulary CD-ROM 💿 Listening Library Audio CD 📁 Listening Library Sourcebook: Strategies and Activities 💿 Skill Level Up! A Skills-Based Language Arts Game CD-ROM
Differentiated Instruction: Advanced/Pre-AP	**TE** Advanced Learner Activities, pp. 55–61 📖 Novel Companion SE, pp. 7–74 📖 Novel Companion TG, pp. 10–20 💿 ▶ Literature Classics, High School CD-ROM 💿 Skill Level Up! A Skills-Based Language Arts Game CD-ROM
Extension	📖 Grammar and Language Workbook SE 📖 Grammar and Language Workbook TAE 📁 Revising with Style 📖 Spelling Power SE 📖 Spelling Power TAE
Daily Writing	**SE/TE** p. 61
Interdisciplinary Connections	**SE/TE** View the Art, pp. 55, 60 ▶ glencoe.com
Independent Reading	💿 BookLink K–12 CD-ROM 📚 Ethnic Anthologies 📚 Glencoe Literature Library 💿 Glencoe Literature Library Teacher Resources CD-ROM 📚 inTIME magazine 💿 ▶ Literature Classics, High School CD-ROM
Technology and Additional Resources	**Planning and Instruction:** 💿 TeacherWorks Plus CD-ROM 💿 Classroom Presentation Toolkit CD-ROM ▶ Literature Online at **glencoe.com** (QuickPass Code: **GLA9879u1T**) **Students Tools:** 💿 StudentWorks Plus CD-ROM or DVD-ROM ▶ Online Student Edition at **glencoe.com** ▶ Literature Online at **glencoe.com** (QuickPass Code: **GLA9800u1**)

Lesson Plan

from *Of Plymouth Plantation* (pp. 62–68)

Lesson Plan and Resource Manager

UNIT ONE Early America, Beginnings–1800, Part 2: Life in the New World

Learning Objectives	**Literary Study:** Analyzing diction. **Reading:** Monitoring comprehension by breaking down sentences. **Writing:** Writing a letter.
Lesson Summary	On pages **62–68** of the Student Edition, students will be introduced to the following: ▪ **Big Idea:** Life in the New World ▪ **Literary Element:** Diction ▪ **Reading Strategy:** Monitor Comprehension ▪ **Vocabulary:** Context Clues ▪ **Writing Activity/Grammar:** Letter
Lesson Duration	One 45–50 minute session
Readability Scores	Dale-Chall: 11.6　　DRP: 62　　Lexile: 1430
Focus	**SE/TE** pp. 62–63 📖 Selection Focus Transparency 5 📖 Daily Language Practice Transparency 7
Teach	**SE/TE** pp. 64–67 📁 Unit 1 Teaching Resources, Literary Element, p. 79 📁 Unit 1 Teaching Resources, Reading Strategy, p. 80 📁 Unit 1 Teaching Resources, Selection Vocabulary Practice, p. 81 📁 Unit 1 Teaching Resources, Vocabulary Strategy, p. 82 📁 Unit 1 Teaching Resources, Grammar Practice, p. 83 📖 Read Aloud, Think Aloud Transparencies 1–4 📖 Literary Elements Transparency 27 💿 Classroom Presentation Toolkit CD-ROM 💿 Listening Library CD, Selection Audio 💿 TeacherWorks Plus CD-ROM 💿 ▶ Vocabulary PuzzleMaker CD-ROM
Assess	**SE/TE** p. 68 📁 Unit 1 Teaching Resources, Selection Quick Check, p. 84 📁 Unit 1 Teaching Resources, Selection Quick Check (Spanish), p. 85 📁 Assessment Resources, Selection Test, pp. 69–70 💿 ExamView Assessment Suite CD-ROM ▶ Progress Reporter Online Assessment
Differentiated Instruction: English Learners	**TE** English Learner Activities, pp. 62–68 📁 Unit 1 Teaching Resources, English Language Coach, p. 59 📁 Unit 1 Teaching Resources, Selection Summaries: English, Spanish, Vietnamese, Tagalog, Cantonese, Haitian Creole, and Hmong, pp. 73–78 📁 Unit 1 Teaching Resources, Selection Quick Check (Spanish), p. 85

Differentiated Instruction: English Learners *(continued)*	📁 English Language Coach 💿 Glencoe Interactive Vocabulary CD-ROM 💿 Listening Library Audio CD 📁 Listening Library Sourcebook: Strategies and Activities
Differentiated Instruction: Approaching Level	**TE** Approaching Level Activities, pp. 62–68 💿 Glencoe Interactive Vocabulary CD-ROM 💿 Listening Library Audio CD 📁 Listening Library Sourcebook: Strategies and Activities 💿 Skill Level Up! A Skills-Based Language Arts Game CD-ROM
Differentiated Instruction: Advanced/Pre-AP	📘 Novel Companion SE, pp. 7–74 📘 Novel Companion TG, pp. 10–20 💿 ▶ Literature Classics, High School CD-ROM 💿 Skill Level Up! A Skills-Based Language Arts Game CD-ROM
Extension	📘 Grammar and Language Workbook SE 📘 Grammar and Language Workbook TAE 📁 Revising with Style 📘 Spelling Power SE 📘 Spelling Power TAE
Daily Writing	**SE/TE** p. 68
Interdisciplinary Connections	**TE** Cultural History, pp. 62, 64 **SE/TE** View the Art, p. 66 ▶ glencoe.com
Independent Reading	💿 BookLink K–12 CD-ROM 📖 Ethnic Anthologies 📖 Glencoe Literature Library 💿 Glencoe Literature Library Teacher Resources CD-ROM 📖 *inTIME* magazine 💿 ▶ Literature Classics, High School CD-ROM
Technology and Additional Resources	**Planning and Instruction:** 💿 TeacherWorks Plus CD-ROM 💿 Classroom Presentation Toolkit CD-ROM ▶ Literature Online at **glencoe.com** (QuickPass Code: **GLA9879u1T**) **Students Tools:** 💿 StudentWorks Plus CD-ROM or DVD-ROM ▶ Online Student Edition at **glencoe.com** ▶ Literature Online at **glencoe.com** (QuickPass Code: **GLA9800u1**)

Lesson Plan

Glencoe Literature

from the *Life of Olaudah Equiano* (pp. 69–79)

Lesson Plan and Resource Manager

UNIT ONE Early America, Beginnings–1800, Part 2: Life in the New World

Learning Objectives	**Literary Study:** Analyzing autobiography. **Reading:** Responding to events. **Writing:** Writing a summary. **Grammar:** Understanding parts of speech.
Lesson Summary	On pages **69–79** of the Student Edition, students will be introduced to the following: 　▪ **Big Idea:** Life in the New World 　▪ **Literary Element:** Slave Narrative 　▪ **Reading Strategy:** Respond 　▪ **Vocabulary:** Academic Vocabulary, Word Origins 　▪ **Writing Activities/Grammar:** Summary, Parts of Speech 　▪ **Listening/Speaking/Viewing Skill:** Analyze Art
Lesson Duration	One 45–50 minute session
Readability Scores	Dale-Chall: 7.6　　　　DRP: 59　　　　Lexile: 1250
Focus	**SE/TE** pp. 69–70 　Selection Focus Transparency 6 　Daily Language Practice Transparency 8
Teach	**SE/TE** pp. 71–76 　Unit 1 Teaching Resources, Literary Element, p. 92 　Unit 1 Teaching Resources, Reading Strategy, p. 93 　Unit 1 Teaching Resources, Selection Vocabulary Practice, p. 94 　Unit 1 Teaching Resources, Vocabulary Strategy, p. 95 　Unit 1 Teaching Resources, Grammar Practice, p. 96 　Literary Elements Transparency 102 　Classroom Presentation Toolkit CD-ROM 　Listening Library CD, Selection Audio 　TeacherWorks Plus CD-ROM 　Vocabulary PuzzleMaker CD-ROM
Assess	**SE/TE** pp. 77–79 　Unit 1 Teaching Resources, Selection Quick Check, p. 97 　Unit 1 Teaching Resources, Selection Quick Check (Spanish), p. 98 　Assessment Resources, Selection Test, pp. 71–72 　ExamView Assessment Suite CD-ROM 　Progress Reporter Online Assessment
Differentiated Instruction: English Learners	**TE** English Learner Activities, pp. 69–79 　Unit 1 Teaching Resources, English Language Coach, p. 59 　Unit 1 Teaching Resources, Selection Summaries: English, Spanish, Vietnamese, Tagalog, Cantonese, Haitian Creole, and Hmong, pp. 86–91

Differentiated Instruction: English Learners (continued)	📁 Unit 1 Teaching Resources, Selection Quick Check (Spanish), p. 98 📁 English Language Coach 💿 Glencoe Interactive Vocabulary CD-ROM 💿 Listening Library Audio CD 📁 Listening Library Sourcebook: Strategies and Activities
Differentiated Instruction: Approaching Level	**TE** Approaching Level Activities, pp. 69–79 💿 Glencoe Interactive Vocabulary CD-ROM 💿 Listening Library Audio CD 📁 Listening Library Sourcebook: Strategies and Activities 💿 Skill Level Up! A Skills-Based Language Arts Game CD-ROM
Differentiated Instruction: Advanced/Pre-AP	**TE** Advanced Learner Activities, pp. 69–79 📘 Novel Companion SE, pp. 7–74 📘 Novel Companion TG, pp. 10–20 💿 ▶ Literature Classics, High School CD-ROM 💿 Skill Level Up! A Skills-Based Language Arts Game CD-ROM
Extension	📘 Grammar and Language Workbook SE 📘 Grammar and Language Workbook TAE 📁 Revising with Style 📘 Spelling Power SE 📘 Spelling Power TAE
Daily Writing	**SE/TE** p. 79
Interdisciplinary Connections	**TE** Cultural History, p. 69 **SE/TE** View the Art, pp. 72, 74 ▶ **glencoe.com**
Independent Reading	💿 BookLink K–12 CD-ROM 📖 Ethnic Anthologies 📖 Glencoe Literature Library 💿 Glencoe Literature Library Teacher Resources CD-ROM 📖 inTIME magazine 💿 ▶ Literature Classics, High School CD-ROM
Technology and Additional Resources	**Planning and Instruction:** 💿 TeacherWorks Plus CD-ROM 💿 Classroom Presentation Toolkit CD-ROM ▶ Literature Online at **glencoe.com** (QuickPass Code: **GLA9879u1T**) **Students Tools:** 💿 StudentWorks Plus CD-ROM or DVD-ROM ▶ Online Student Edition at **glencoe.com** ▶ Literature Online at **glencoe.com** (QuickPass Code: **GLA9800u1**)

Lesson Plan

from *A Narrative of the Captivity and Restoration of Mrs. Mary Rowlandson* and Grammar Workshop (pp. 80–88)

Lesson Plan and Resource Manager

UNIT ONE Early America, Beginnings–1800, Part 2: Life in the New World

Learning Objectives	**Literary Study:** Analyzing text structure. **Reading:** Analyzing historical content. **Writing:** Writing a list. **Grammar:** Recognizing the function of phrases, conjunctions, and clauses in sentence combining. Combining sentences using a variety of techniques.

Lesson Summary	On pages **80–86** of the Student Edition, students will be introduced to the following:
	    ▪ **Big Idea:** Life in the New World
	    ▪ **Literary Element:** Allusion
	    ▪ **Reading Strategy:** Analyze Historical Context
	    ▪ **Vocabulary:** Word Usage
	    ▪ **Writing Activity/Grammar:** List
	On pages **87–88** of the Student Edition, students will be introduced to the following:
	    ▪ **Grammar Workshop:** Sentence Combining

Lesson Duration	One 45–50 minute session
Readability Scores	Dale-Chall: 7.9 DRP: 57 Lexile: 1030
Focus	**SE/TE** pp. 80–81, 87 📖 Selection Focus Transparency 7 📖 Daily Language Practice Transparency 9
Teach	**SE/TE** pp. 82–85, 87–88 📁 Unit 1 Teaching Resources, Literary Element, p. 105 📁 Unit 1 Teaching Resources, Reading Strategy, p. 106 📁 Unit 1 Teaching Resources, Selection Vocabulary Practice, p. 107 📁 Unit 1 Teaching Resources, Vocabulary Strategy, p. 108 📁 Unit 1 Teaching Resources, Grammar Practice, p. 109 📖 Grammar and Language Transparencies 29, 35 📖 Literary Elements Transparency 3 💿 Classroom Presentation Toolkit CD-ROM 💿 Listening Library CD, Selection Audio 💿 TeacherWorks Plus CD-ROM 💿 ▶ Vocabulary PuzzleMaker CD-ROM
Assess	**SE/TE** p. 86, 88 📁 Unit 1 Teaching Resources, Selection Quick Check, p. 110 📁 Unit 1 Teaching Resources, Selection Quick Check (Spanish), p. 111 📁 Assessment Resources, Selection Test, pp. 73–74 💿 ExamView Assessment Suite CD-ROM ▶ Progress Reporter Online Assessment

Differentiated Instruction: English Learners	**TE** English Learner Activities, pp. 80–88 📁 Unit 1 Teaching Resources, English Language Coach, p. 59 📁 Unit 1 Teaching Resources, Selection Summaries: English, Spanish, Vietnamese, Tagalog, Cantonese, Haitian Creole, and Hmong, pp. 99–104 📁 Unit 1 Teaching Resources, Selection Quick Check (Spanish), p. 111 📁 English Language Coach 💿 Glencoe Interactive Vocabulary CD-ROM 💿 Listening Library Audio CD 📁 Listening Library Sourcebook: Strategies and Activities
Differentiated Instruction: Approaching Level	**TE** Approaching Level Activities, pp. 80–88 💿 Glencoe Interactive Vocabulary CD-ROM 💿 Listening Library Audio CD 📁 Listening Library Sourcebook: Strategies and Activities 💿 Skill Level Up! A Skills-Based Language Arts Game CD-ROM
Differentiated Instruction: Advanced/Pre-AP	**TE** Advanced Learner Activities, pp. 80–88 📖 Novel Companion SE, pp. 7–74 📖 Novel Companion TG, pp. 10–20 💿▶ Literature Classics, High School CD-ROM 💿 Skill Level Up! A Skills-Based Language Arts Game CD-ROM
Extension	📖 Grammar and Language Workbook SE 📖 Grammar and Language Workbook TAE 📁 Revising with Style 📖 Spelling Power SE 📖 Spelling Power TAE
Daily Writing	**SE/TE** p. 86
Interdisciplinary Connections	**TE** Literary History, pp. 80, 85 **TE** Political History, p. 83 ▶ glencoe.com
Independent Reading	💿 BookLink K–12 CD-ROM 📖 Ethnic Anthologies 📖 Glencoe Literature Library 💿 Glencoe Literature Library Teacher Resources CD-ROM 📖 inTIME magazine 💿▶ Literature Classics, High School CD-ROM
Technology and Additional Resources	**Planning and Instruction:** 💿 TeacherWorks Plus CD-ROM 💿 Classroom Presentation Toolkit CD-ROM ▶ Literature Online at **glencoe.com** (QuickPass Code: **GLA9879u1T**) **Students Tools:** 💿 StudentWorks Plus CD-ROM or DVD-ROM ▶ Online Student Edition at **glencoe.com** ▶ Literature Online at **glencoe.com** (QuickPass Code: **GLA9800u1**)

Lesson Plan

Glencoe Literature Essential Course of Study

Upon the Burning of Our House and To My Dear and Loving Husband (pp. 89–94)

Lesson Plan and Resource Manager

UNIT ONE Early America, Beginnings–1800, Part 2: Life in the New World

Learning Objectives	**Literary Study:** Analyzing metaphor. **Reading:** Drawing conclusions about author's beliefs. **Writing:** Applying extended metaphor in a poem.

Lesson Summary	On pages **89–94** of the Student Edition, students will be introduced to the following:
	  • **Big Idea:** Life in the New World
	  • **Literary Element:** Metaphor
	  • **Reading Strategy:** Draw Conclusions About Author's Beliefs
	  • **Vocabulary:** Synonyms, Academic Vocabulary
	  • **Writing Activity/Grammar:** Extended Metaphor
	  • **Study Skill/Research/Assessment:** Short Response
	  • **Listening/Viewing/Speaking Skill:** Analyze Art

Lesson Duration	One 45–50 minute session
Readability Scores	Dale-Chall: N/A DRP: N/A Lexile: N/A
Focus	**SE/TE** pp. 89–90 Selection Focus Transparency 8 Daily Language Practice Transparency 10 Literature Launchers: Pre-Reading Videos DVD, Selection Launcher Literature Launchers Teacher Guide
Teach	**SE/TE** pp. 91–92 Interactive Read and Write SE/TE, pp. 17–24 Unit 1 Teaching Resources, Literary Element, p. 119 Unit 1 Teaching Resources, Reading Strategy, p. 120 Unit 1 Teaching Resources, Vocabulary Strategy, p. 121 Literary Elements Transparency 60 Classroom Presentation Toolkit CD-ROM Listening Library CD, Selection Audio TeacherWorks Plus CD-ROM Vocabulary PuzzleMaker CD-ROM
Assess	**SE/TE** pp. 93–94 Unit 1 Teaching Resources, Selection Quick Check, p. 122 Unit 1 Teaching Resources, Selection Quick Check (Spanish), p. 123 Assessment Resources, Selection Test, pp. 75–76 ExamView Assessment Suite CD-ROM Progress Reporter Online Assessment

Differentiated Instruction: English Learners	📕 Interactive Read and Write (EL) SE/TE, pp. 17–24 📁 Unit 1 Teaching Resources, English Language Coach, p. 59 📁 Unit 1 Teaching Resources, Selection Summaries: English, Spanish, Vietnamese, Tagalog, Cantonese, Haitian Creole, and Hmong, pp. 113–118 📁 Unit 1 Teaching Resources, Selection Quick Check (Spanish), p. 123 📁 English Language Coach 💿 Glencoe Interactive Vocabulary CD-ROM 💿 Listening Library Audio CD 📁 Listening Library Sourcebook: Strategies and Activities
Differentiated Instruction: Approaching Level	**TE** Approaching Level Activities, pp. 89–94 📕 Interactive Read and Write (Approaching) SE/TE, pp. 17–24 💿 Glencoe Interactive Vocabulary CD-ROM 💿 Listening Library Audio CD 📁 Listening Library Sourcebook: Strategies and Activities 💿 Skill Level Up! A Skills-Based Language Arts Game CD-ROM
Differentiated Instruction: Advanced/Pre-AP	📕 Novel Companion SE, pp. 7–74 📕 Novel Companion TG, pp. 10–20 💿 ▶ Literature Classics, High School CD-ROM 💿 Skill Level Up! A Skills-Based Language Arts Game CD-ROM
Extension	📕 Grammar and Language Workbook SE 📕 Grammar and Language Workbook TAE 📁 Revising with Style 📕 Spelling Power SE 📕 Spelling Power TAE
Daily Writing	**SE/TE** p. 94
Interdisciplinary Connections	**TE** Language History, p. 89 **SE/TE** View the Art, p. 92 ▶ **glencoe.com**
Independent Reading	💿 BookLink K–12 CD-ROM 📖 Ethnic Anthologies 📖 Glencoe Literature Library 💿 Glencoe Literature Library Teacher Resources CD-ROM 📖 *inTIME* magazine 💿 ▶ Literature Classics, High School CD-ROM
Technology and Additional Resources	**Planning and Instruction:** 💿 TeacherWorks Plus CD-ROM 💿 Classroom Presentation Toolkit CD-ROM ▶ Literature Online at **glencoe.com** (QuickPass Code: **GLA9879u1T**) **Students Tools:** 💿 StudentWorks Plus CD-ROM or DVD-ROM ▶ Online Student Edition at **glencoe.com** ▶ Literature Online at **glencoe.com** (QuickPass Code: **GLA9800u1**)

Lesson Plan

from *Sinners in the Hands of an Angry God* and Vocabulary Workshop (pp. 95–102)

Lesson Plan and Resource Manager

UNIT ONE Early America, Beginnings–1800, Part 2: Life in the New World

Learning Objectives	**Literary Study:** Analyzing imagery. **Reading:** Examining connotation. **Writing:** Applying diction in a persuasive essay. **Vocabulary:** Understanding multiple-meaning words. Understanding language resources.
Lesson Summary	On pages **95–101** of the Student Edition, students will be introduced to the following: • **Big Idea:** Life in the New World • **Literary Element:** Imagery • **Reading Strategy:** Examine Connotation • **Vocabulary:** Word Origins, Academic Vocabulary • **Writing Activity/Grammar:** Apply Diction • **Listening/Speaking/Viewing Skill:** Analyze Art On page **102** of the Student Edition, students will be introduced to the following: • **Vocabulary Workshop:** Dictionary Use
Lesson Duration	One 45–50 minute session
Readability Scores	Dale-Chall: 7.3 DRP: 61 Lexile: 1280
Focus	**SE/TE** pp. 95–96, 102 📖 Selection Focus Transparency 9 📖 Daily Language Practice Transparency 11
Teach	**SE/TE** pp. 97–99, 102 📁 Unit 1 Teaching Resources, Literary Element, p. 130 📁 Unit 1 Teaching Resources, Reading Strategy, p. 131 📁 Unit 1 Teaching Resources, Selection Vocabulary Practice, p. 132 📁 Unit 1 Teaching Resources, Vocabulary Strategy, p. 133 📁 Unit 1 Teaching Resources, Grammar Practice, p. 134 📖 Literary Elements Transparency 52 💿 Classroom Presentation Toolkit CD-ROM 💿 Listening Library CD, Selection Audio 💿 TeacherWorks Plus CD-ROM 💿 Vocabulary PuzzleMaker CD-ROM
Assess	**SE/TE** pp. 100–101 📁 Unit 1 Teaching Resources, Selection Quick Check, p. 135 📁 Unit 1 Teaching Resources, Selection Quick Check (Spanish), p. 136 📁 Assessment Resources, Selection Test, pp. 77–78 💿 ExamView Assessment Suite CD-ROM 💿 Progress Reporter Online Assessment

Differentiated Instruction: English Learners	**TE** English Learner Activities, pp. 95–102 📁 Unit 1 Teaching Resources, English Language Coach, p. 59 📁 Unit 1 Teaching Resources, Selection Summaries: English, Spanish, Vietnamese, Tagalog, Cantonese, Haitian Creole, and Hmong, pp. 124–129 📁 Unit 1 Teaching Resources, Selection Quick Check (Spanish), p. 136 📁 English Language Coach 💿 Glencoe Interactive Vocabulary CD-ROM 💿 Listening Library Audio CD 📁 Listening Library Sourcebook: Strategies and Activities
Differentiated Instruction: Approaching Level	**TE** Approaching Level Activities, pp. 95–102 💿 Glencoe Interactive Vocabulary CD-ROM 💿 Listening Library Audio CD 📁 Listening Library Sourcebook: Strategies and Activities 💿 Skill Level Up! A Skills-Based Language Arts Game CD-ROM
Differentiated Instruction: Advanced/Pre-AP	**TE** Advanced Learner Activities, pp. 95–102 📘 Novel Companion SE, pp. 7–74 📘 Novel Companion TG, pp. 10–20 💿 Literature Classics, High School CD-ROM 💿 Skill Level Up! A Skills-Based Language Arts Game CD-ROM
Extension	📘 Grammar and Language Workbook SE 📘 Grammar and Language Workbook TAE 📁 Revising with Style 📘 Spelling Power SE 📘 Spelling Power TAE
Daily Writing	**SE/TE** p. 101
Interdisciplinary Connections	**SE/TE** View the Art, p. 98 **TE** Cultural History, pp. 95, 97 💿 glencoe.com
Independent Reading	💿 BookLink K–12 CD-ROM 📖 Ethnic Anthologies 📖 Glencoe Literature Library 💿 Glencoe Literature Library Teacher Resources CD-ROM 📖 inTIME magazine 💿 Literature Classics, High School CD-ROM
Technology and Additional Resources	**Planning and Instruction:** 💿 TeacherWorks Plus CD-ROM 💿 Classroom Presentation Toolkit CD-ROM ▶ Literature Online at **glencoe.com** (QuickPass Code: **GLA9879u1T**) **Students Tools:** 💿 StudentWorks Plus CD-ROM or DVD-ROM ▶ Online Student Edition at **glencoe.com** ▶ Literature Online at **glencoe.com** (QuickPass Code: **GLA9800u1**)

Lesson Plan

Glencoe Literature

Part 3 Opener, from the *Autobiography of Benjamin Franklin*, and from *Poor Richard's Almanack* (pp. 103–111)

Lesson Plan and Resource Manager

UNIT ONE Early America, Beginnings–1800, Part 3: The Road to Independence

Learning Objectives	**Literary Study:** Analyzing autobiography. Analyzing aphorism. **Reading:** Analyzing voice. Connecting to personal experience. **Writing:** Writing a journal entry. Writing an article.
Lesson Summary	On pages **103–111** of the Student Edition, students will be introduced to the following: ▪ **Big Idea:** The Road to Independence ▪ **Literary Elements:** Autobiography, Aphorism ▪ **Reading Strategies:** Analyze Voice, Connect ▪ **Vocabulary:** Word Parts ▪ **Writing Activity/Grammar:** Article ▪ **Listening/Speaking/Viewing Skill:** Analyze Art
Lesson Duration	One 45–50 minute session
Readability Scores	Dale-Chall: 7.0 DRP: 59 Lexile: 1170
Focus	**SE/TE** pp. 104–105, 110 🔖 Selection Focus Transparency 10 🔖 Daily Language Practice Transparency 12
Teach	**SE/TE** pp. 106–108, 110 📁 Unit 1 Teaching Resources, Literary Element, pp. 145, 158 📁 Unit 1 Teaching Resources, Reading Strategy, pp. 146, 159 📁 Unit 1 Teaching Resources, Selection Vocabulary Practice, p. 147 📁 Unit 1 Teaching Resources, Vocabulary Strategy, p. 148 📁 Unit 1 Teaching Resources, Grammar Practice, pp. 149, 160 🔖 Literary Elements Transparencies 8, 16 💿 Classroom Presentation Toolkit CD-ROM 💿 Listening Library CD, Selection Audio 💿 TeacherWorks Plus CD-ROM 💿 Vocabulary PuzzleMaker CD-ROM
Assess	**SE/TE** pp. 109, 111 📁 Unit 1 Teaching Resources, Selection Quick Check, pp. 150, 161 📁 Unit 1 Teaching Resources, Selection Quick Check (Spanish), pp. 151, 162 📁 Assessment Resources, Selection Test, pp. 79–80, 81–82 💿 ExamView Assessment Suite CD-ROM 💿 Progress Reporter Online Assessment

Differentiated Instruction: English Learners	**TE** English Learner Activities, pp. 103–111
	📁 Unit 1 Teaching Resources, English Language Coach, p. 138
	📁 Unit 1 Teaching Resources, Selection Summaries: English, Spanish, Vietnamese, Tagalog, Cantonese, Haitian Creole, and Hmong, pp. 139–144, 152–157
	📁 Unit 1 Teaching Resources, Selection Quick Check (Spanish), pp. 151, 162
	📁 English Language Coach
	💿 Glencoe Interactive Vocabulary CD-ROM
	💿 Listening Library Audio CD
	📁 Listening Library Sourcebook: Strategies and Activities
Differentiated Instruction: Approaching Level	**TE** Approaching Level Activities, pp. 103–111
	💿 Glencoe Interactive Vocabulary CD-ROM
	💿 Listening Library Audio CD
	📁 Listening Library Sourcebook: Strategies and Activities
	💿 Skill Level Up! A Skills-Based Language Arts Game CD-ROM
Differentiated Instruction: Advanced/Pre-AP	📘 Novel Companion SE, pp. 7–74
	📘 Novel Companion TG, pp. 10–20
	💿 Literature Classics, High School CD-ROM
	💿 Skill Level Up! A Skills-Based Language Arts Game CD-ROM
Extension	📘 Grammar and Language Workbook SE
	📘 Grammar and Language Workbook TAE
	📁 Revising with Style
	📘 Spelling Power SE
	📘 Spelling Power TAE
Daily Writing	**SE/TE** p. 111
Interdisciplinary Connections	**SE/TE** View the Art, pp. 103, 107
	TE Cultural History, p. 108
	▶ glencoe.com
Independent Reading	📖 BookLink K–12 CD-ROM
	📖 Ethnic Anthologies
	📖 Glencoe Literature Library
	💿 Glencoe Literature Library Teacher Resources CD-ROM
	📖 *inTIME* magazine
	💿 Literature Classics, High School CD-ROM
Technology and Additional Resources	**Planning and Instruction:**
	💿 TeacherWorks Plus CD-ROM
	💿 Classroom Presentation Toolkit CD-ROM
	▶ Literature Online at **glencoe.com** (QuickPass Code: **GLA9879u1T**)
	Students Tools:
	💿 StudentWorks Plus CD-ROM or DVD-ROM
	▶ Online Student Edition at **glencoe.com**
	▶ Literature Online at **glencoe.com** (QuickPass Code: **GLA9800u1**)

Lesson Plan

Glencoe Literature

Literary History: The Rhetoric of Revolution and *Speech to the Second Virginia Convention* (pp. 112–119)

Lesson Plan and Resource Manager

UNIT ONE Early America, Beginnings–1800, Part 3: The Road to Independence

Learning Objectives	**Literary Study:** Analyzing literary periods. Evaluating historical influences. Analyzing rhetorical question. **Reading:** Analyzing figures of speech. **Writing:** Writing a speech.
Lesson Summary	On pages **112–119** of the Student Edition, students will be introduced to the following: • **Big Idea:** The Road to Independence • **Literary Elements:** Rhetorical Devices, Rhetorical Question • **Reading Strategy:** Analyze Figures of Speech • **Vocabulary:** Antonyms • **Writing Activity/Grammar:** Speech • **Listening/Speaking/Viewing Skill:** Reasoning and Propositions
Lesson Duration	One 45–50 minute session
Readability Scores	Dale-Chall: 8.4 DRP: 60 Lexile: 930
Focus	SE/TE pp. 112, 114–115 📖 Selection Focus Transparency 11 📖 Daily Language Practice Transparencies 13–14
Teach	SE/TE pp. 112–113, 116–118 📁 Unit 1 Teaching Resources, Literary Element, p. 171 📁 Unit 1 Teaching Resources, Reading Strategy, p. 172 📁 Unit 1 Teaching Resources, Selection Vocabulary Practice, p. 173 📁 Unit 1 Teaching Resources, Vocabulary Strategy, p. 174 📁 Unit 1 Teaching Resources, Grammar Practice, p. 175 📖 Literary Elements Transparency 87 💿 Classroom Presentation Toolkit CD-ROM 💿 Listening Library CD, Selection Audio 💿 TeacherWorks Plus CD-ROM 💿 Vocabulary PuzzleMaker CD-ROM
Assess	SE/TE pp. 113, 119 📁 Unit 1 Teaching Resources, Selection Quick Check, p. 176 📁 Unit 1 Teaching Resources, Selection Quick Check (Spanish), p. 177 📁 Assessment Resources, Selection Test, pp. 83–84 💿 ExamView Assessment Suite CD-ROM 💿 Progress Reporter Online Assessment

Differentiated Instruction: English Learners	**TE** English Learner Activities, pp. 112–119 📁 Unit 1 Teaching Resources, English Language Coach, p. 134 📁 Unit 1 Teaching Resources, Selection Summaries: English, Spanish, Vietnamese, Tagalog, Cantonese, Haitian Creole, and Hmong, pp. 165–170 📁 Unit 1 Teaching Resources, Selection Quick Check (Spanish), p. 177 📁 English Language Coach 💿 Glencoe Interactive Vocabulary CD-ROM 💿 Listening Library Audio CD 📁 Listening Library Sourcebook: Strategies and Activities
Differentiated Instruction: Approaching Level	**TE** Approaching Level Activities, pp. 112–119 💿 Glencoe Interactive Vocabulary CD-ROM 💿 Listening Library Audio CD 📁 Listening Library Sourcebook: Strategies and Activities 💿 Skill Level Up! A Skills-Based Language Arts Game CD-ROM
Differentiated Instruction: Advanced/Pre-AP	📘 Novel Companion SE, pp. 7–74 📘 Novel Companion TG, pp. 10–20 💿 Literature Classics, High School CD-ROM 💿 Skill Level Up! A Skills-Based Language Arts Game CD-ROM
Extension	📘 Grammar and Language Workbook SE 📘 Grammar and Language Workbook TAE 📁 Revising with Style 📘 Spelling Power SE 📘 Spelling Power TAE
Daily Writing	**SE/TE** p. 119
Interdisciplinary Connections	**SE/TE** View the Art, pp. 112, 113, 116 🌐 glencoe.com
Independent Reading	💿 BookLink K–12 CD-ROM 📖 Ethnic Anthologies 📖 Glencoe Literature Library 💿 Glencoe Literature Library Teacher Resources CD-ROM 📖 inTIME magazine 💿 Literature Classics, High School CD-ROM
Technology and Additional Resources	**Planning and Instruction:** 💿 TeacherWorks Plus CD-ROM 💿 Classroom Presentation Toolkit CD-ROM 🌐 Literature Online at **glencoe.com** (QuickPass Code: **GLA9879u1T**) **Students Tools:** 💿 StudentWorks Plus CD-ROM or DVD-ROM 🌐 Online Student Edition at **glencoe.com** 🌐 Literature Online at **glencoe.com** (QuickPass Code: **GLA9800u1**)

Lesson Plan

Declaration of Independence (pp. 120–127)

Lesson Plan and Resource Manager

UNIT ONE Early America, Beginnings–1800, Part 3: The Road to Independence

Learning Objectives	**Literary Study:** Analyzing text structure. **Reading:** Evaluating argument. **Writing:** Write a persuasive essay. **Grammar:** Citing source information correctly.
Lesson Summary	On pages **120–127** of the Student Edition, students will be introduced to the following: • **Big Idea:** The Road to Independence • **Literary Element:** Text Structure • **Reading Strategy:** Evaluate Argument • **Vocabulary:** Context Clues, Academic Vocabulary • **Writing Activities/Grammar:** Persuasive Essay, Parentheses • **Listening/Speaking/Viewing Skill:** Analyze Art
Lesson Duration	One 45–50 minute session
Readability Scores	Dale-Chall: 12.6 DRP: 71 Lexile: 1360

Focus	SE/TE pp. 120–121
	  Selection Focus Transparency 12
	  Daily Language Practice Transparency 15

Teach	SE/TE pp. 122–124
	  Unit 1 Teaching Resources, Literary Element, p. 184
	  Unit 1 Teaching Resources, Reading Strategy, p. 185
	  Unit 1 Teaching Resources, Selection Vocabulary Practice, p. 186
	  Unit 1 Teaching Resources, Vocabulary Strategy, p. 187
	  Unit 1 Teaching Resources, Grammar Practice, p. 188
	  Literary Elements Transparency 101
	  Classroom Presentation Toolkit CD-ROM
	  Listening Library CD, Selection Audio
	  TeacherWorks Plus CD-ROM
	  Vocabulary PuzzleMaker CD-ROM

Assess	SE/TE pp. 125–127
	  Unit 1 Teaching Resources, Selection Quick Check, p. 189
	  Unit 1 Teaching Resources, Selection Quick Check (Spanish), p. 190
	  Assessment Resources, Selection Test, pp. 85–86
	  ExamView Assessment Suite CD-ROM
	  Progress Reporter Online Assessment

Differentiated Instruction: English Learners	**TE** English Learner Activities, pp. 120–127 📁 Unit 1 Teaching Resources, English Language Coach, p. 138 📁 Unit 1 Teaching Resources, Selection Summaries: English, Spanish, Vietnamese, Tagalog, Cantonese, Haitian Creole, and Hmong, pp. 178–183 📁 Unit 1 Teaching Resources, Selection Quick Check (Spanish), p. 190 📁 English Language Coach 💿 Glencoe Interactive Vocabulary CD-ROM 💿 Listening Library Audio CD 📁 Listening Library Sourcebook: Strategies and Activities
Differentiated Instruction: Approaching Level	**TE** Approaching Level Activities, pp. 120–127 💿 Glencoe Interactive Vocabulary CD-ROM 💿 Listening Library Audio CD 📁 Listening Library Sourcebook: Strategies and Activities 💿 Skill Level Up! A Skills-Based Language Arts Game CD-ROM
Differentiated Instruction: Advanced/Pre-AP	**TE** Advanced Learner Activities, pp. 120–127 📕 Novel Companion SE, pp. 7–74 📕 Novel Companion TG, pp. 10–20 💿▶ Literature Classics, High School CD-ROM 💿 Skill Level Up! A Skills-Based Language Arts Game CD-ROM
Extension	📕 Grammar and Language Workbook SE 📕 Grammar and Language Workbook TAE 📁 Revising with Style 📕 Spelling Power SE 📕 Spelling Power TAE
Daily Writing	**SE/TE** p. 127
Interdisciplinary Connections	**TE** Political History, p. 122 **SE/TE** View the Art, p. 123 ▶ **glencoe.com**
Independent Reading	💿 BookLink K–12 CD-ROM 📖 Ethnic Anthologies 📖 Glencoe Literature Library 💿 Glencoe Literature Library Teacher Resources CD-ROM 📖 *inTIME* magazine 💿▶ Literature Classics, High School CD-ROM
Technology and Additional Resources	**Planning and Instruction:** 💿 TeacherWorks Plus CD-ROM 💿 Classroom Presentation Toolkit CD-ROM ▶ Literature Online at **glencoe.com** (QuickPass Code: **GLA9879u1T**) **Students Tools:** 💿 StudentWorks Plus CD-ROM or DVD-ROM ▶ Online Student Edition at **glencoe.com** ▶ Literature Online at **glencoe.com** (QuickPass Code: **GLA9800u1**)

Lesson Plan

Glencoe Literature Essential Course of Study

TIME: *How They Chose These Words* and Vocabulary Workshop (pp. 128–131)

Lesson Plan and Resource Manager

UNIT ONE Early America, Beginnings–1800, Part 3: The Road to Independence

Learning Objectives	**Literary Study:** Analyzing informational text. Determining main idea and supporting details. **Vocabulary:** Understanding multiple-meaning words. Understanding language resources.
Lesson Summary	On pages **128–130** of the Student Edition, students will be introduced to the following: • **Big Idea:** The Road to Independence • **Reading Strategy:** Determine Main Idea and Supporting Details • **Writing Activity:** Draft and Revise On page **131** of the Student Edition, students will be introduced to the following: • **Vocabulary Workshop:** Word Origins
Lesson Duration	One 45–50 minute session
Readability Scores	Dale-Chall: 7.9 DRP: 68 Lexile: 1200
Focus	**SE/TE** pp. 128, 131 Literature Launchers: Pre-Reading Videos DVD, Selection Launcher Literature Launchers Teacher Guide
Teach	**SE/TE** pp. 128–129, 131 Interactive Read and Write SE/TE, pp. 25–36 Unit 1 Teaching Resources, Reading Strategy, p. 197 Classroom Presentation Toolkit CD-ROM Listening Library CD, Selection Audio TeacherWorks Plus CD-ROM Vocabulary PuzzleMaker CD-ROM
Assess	**SE/TE** pp. 130, 131 Unit 1 Teaching Resources, Selection Quick Check, p. 198 Unit 1 Teaching Resources, Selection Quick Check (Spanish), p. 199 Assessment Resources, Selection Test, pp. 87–88 ExamView Assessment Suite CD-ROM Progress Reporter Online Assessment
Differentiated Instruction: English Learners	**TE** English Learner Activities, pp. 128–131 Interactive Read and Write (EL) SE/TE, pp. 25–36 Unit 1 Teaching Resources, English Language Coach, p. 138 Unit 1 Teaching Resources, Selection Summaries: English, Spanish, Vietnamese, Tagalog, Cantonese, Haitian Creole, and Hmong, pp. 191–196 Unit 1 Teaching Resources, Selection Quick Check (Spanish), p. 199 English Language Coach Glencoe Interactive Vocabulary CD-ROM Listening Library Audio CD Listening Library Sourcebook: Strategies and Activities

Differentiated Instruction: Approaching Level	**TE** Approaching Level Activities, pp. 128–131 📘 Interactive Read and Write (Approaching) SE/TE, pp. 25–36 💿 Glencoe Interactive Vocabulary CD-ROM 💿 Listening Library Audio CD 📁 Listening Library Sourcebook: Strategies and Activities 💿 Skill Level Up! A Skills-Based Language Arts Game CD-ROM
Differentiated Instruction: Advanced/Pre-AP	📘 Novel Companion SE, pp. 7–74 📘 Novel Companion TG, pp. 10–20 💿 ▶ Literature Classics, High School CD-ROM 💿 Skill Level Up! A Skills-Based Language Arts Game CD-ROM
Extension	📘 Grammar and Language Workbook SE 📘 Grammar and Language Workbook TAE 📁 Revising with Style 📘 Spelling Power SE 📘 Spelling Power TAE
Daily Writing	**SE/TE** p. 128
Interdisciplinary Connections	💿 glencoe.com
Independent Reading	💿 BookLink K–12 CD-ROM 📖 Ethnic Anthologies 📖 Glencoe Literature Library 💿 Glencoe Literature Library Teacher Resources CD-ROM 📖 inTIME magazine 💿 ▶ Literature Classics, High School CD-ROM
Technology and Additional Resources	**Planning and Instruction:** 💿 TeacherWorks Plus CD-ROM 💿 Classroom Presentation Toolkit CD-ROM ▶ Literature Online at **glencoe.com** (QuickPass Code: **GLA9879u1T**) **Students Tools:** 💿 StudentWorks Plus CD-ROM or DVD-ROM ▶ Online Student Edition at **glencoe.com** ▶ Literature Online at **glencoe.com** (QuickPass Code: **GLA9800u1**)

Lesson Plan

Glencoe Literature

from *The Crisis, No. 1* (pp. 132–138)

Lesson Plan and Resource Manager

UNIT ONE Early America, Beginnings–1800, Part 3: The Road to Independence

Learning Objectives	**Literary Study:** Analyzing tone. **Reading:** Summarizing. **Writing:** Applying tone.
Lesson Summary	On pages **132–138** of the Student Edition, students will be introduced to the following: • **Big Idea:** The Road to Independence • **Literary Element:** Tone • **Reading Strategy:** Summarize • **Vocabulary:** Denotation and Connotation, Academic Vocabulary • **Writing Activity/Grammar:** Apply Tone • **Listening/Speaking/Viewing Skills:** Analyze Art, Presentation
Lesson Duration	One 45–50 minute session
Readability Scores	Dale-Chall: 8.8 DRP: 62 Lexile: 1050
Focus	SE/TE pp. 132–133 📖 Selection Focus Transparency 13 📖 Daily Language Practice Transparency 16
Teach	SE/TE pp. 134–136 📁 Unit 1 Teaching Resources, Literary Element, p. 206 📁 Unit 1 Teaching Resources, Reading Strategy, p. 207 📁 Unit 1 Teaching Resources, Selection Vocabulary Practice, p. 208 📁 Unit 1 Teaching Resources, Vocabulary Strategy, p. 209 📁 Unit 1 Teaching Resources, Grammar Practice, p. 210 📖 Literary Elements Transparency 105 💿 Classroom Presentation Toolkit CD-ROM 💿 Listening Library CD, Selection Audio 💿 TeacherWorks Plus CD-ROM 💿 Vocabulary PuzzleMaker CD-ROM
Assess	SE/TE pp. 137–138 📁 Unit 1 Teaching Resources, Selection Quick Check, p. 211 📁 Unit 1 Teaching Resources, Selection Quick Check (Spanish), p. 212 📁 Assessment Resources, Selection Test, pp. 89–90 💿 ExamView Assessment Suite CD-ROM 💿 Progress Reporter Online Assessment
Differentiated Instruction: English Learners	TE English Learner Activities, pp. 132–138 📁 Unit 1 Teaching Resources, English Language Coach, p. 138 📁 Unit 1 Teaching Resources, Selection Summaries: English, Spanish, Vietnamese, Tagalog, Cantonese, Haitian Creole, and Hmong, pp. 200–205 📁 Unit 1 Teaching Resources, Selection Quick Check (Spanish), p. 212

Differentiated Instruction: English Learners (*continued*)	📁 English Language Coach 🔵 Glencoe Interactive Vocabulary CD-ROM 🔵 Listening Library Audio CD 📁 Listening Library Sourcebook: Strategies and Activities
Differentiated Instruction: Approaching Level	**TE** Approaching Level Activities, pp. 132–138 🔵 Glencoe Interactive Vocabulary CD-ROM 🔵 Listening Library Audio CD 📁 Listening Library Sourcebook: Strategies and Activities 🔵 Skill Level Up! A Skills-Based Language Arts Game CD-ROM
Differentiated Instruction: Advanced/Pre-AP	**TE** Advanced Learner Activities, pp. 132–138 📘 Novel Companion SE, pp. 7–74 📘 Novel Companion TG, pp. 10–20 🔵 ▶ Literature Classics, High School CD-ROM 🔵 Skill Level Up! A Skills-Based Language Arts Game CD-ROM
Extension	📘 Grammar and Language Workbook SE 📘 Grammar and Language Workbook TAE 📁 Revising with Style 📘 Spelling Power SE 📘 Spelling Power TAE
Daily Writing	**SE/TE** p. 130
Interdisciplinary Connections	**SE/TE** View the Art, p. 136 **TE** Political History, pp. 134, 135 ▶ glencoe.com
Independent Reading	🔵 BookLink K–12 CD-ROM 📖 Ethnic Anthologies 📖 Glencoe Literature Library 🔵 Glencoe Literature Library Teacher Resources CD-ROM 📖 *inTIME* magazine 🔵 ▶ Literature Classics, High School CD-ROM
Technology and Additional Resources	**Planning and Instruction:** 🔵 TeacherWorks Plus CD-ROM 🔵 Classroom Presentation Toolkit CD-ROM ▶ Literature Online at **glencoe.com** (QuickPass Code: **GLA9879u1T**) **Students Tools:** 🔵 StudentWorks Plus CD-ROM or DVD-ROM ▶ Online Student Edition at **glencoe.com** ▶ Literature Online at **glencoe.com** (QuickPass Code: **GLA9800u1**)

Lesson Plan

To His Excellency, General Washington; Letter to John Adams; and Grammar Workshop (pp. 139–149)

Lesson Plan and Resource Manager

UNIT ONE Early America, Beginnings–1800, Part 3: The Road to Independence

Learning Objectives	**Literary Study:** Analyzing couplets. Analyzing description. **Reading:** Analyzing structure. Recognizing author's purpose. **Writing:** Writing a poem. **Grammar:** Understanding how to use clauses as modifiers. Punctuating subordinate clauses.
Lesson Summary	On pages **139–149** of the Student Edition, students will be introduced to the following: • **Big Idea:** The Road to Independence • **Literary Elements:** Couplet, Description • **Reading Strategies:** Analyze Structure, Recognize Author's Purpose • **Vocabulary:** Academic Vocabulary, Analogies • **Writing:** Poem, Letter • **Viewing Skill:** View Art • **Grammar Workshop:** Clauses as Modifiers
Lesson Duration	One to five 45–50 minute sessions
Readability Scores	Dale-Chall: 8.8　　　DRP: 62　　　Lexile: 1350
Focus	**SE/TE** pp. 139–140, 144–145, 149 🔖 Selection Focus Transparencies 14–15 🔖 Daily Language Practice Transparencies 17–18 ⊙ Literature Launchers: Pre-Reading Videos DVD, Selection Launcher 🗀 Literature Launchers Teacher Guide
Teach	**SE/TE** pp. 141–142, 146–147, 149 ▌Interactive Read and Write SE/TE, pp. 37–44 🗀 Unit 1 Teaching Resources, Literary Element, pp. 219, 229 🗀 Unit 1 Teaching Resources, Reading Strategy, pp. 220, 230 🗀 Unit 1 Teaching Resources, Selection Vocabulary Practice, p. 231 🗀 Unit 1 Teaching Resources, Vocabulary Strategy, p. 232 🗀 Unit 1 Teaching Resources, Grammar Practice, p. 233 🗀 Unit 1 Teaching Resources, Grammar Workshop, p. 236 🔖 Read Aloud, Think Aloud Transparencies 5–7 🔖 Grammar and Language Transparencies 2, 29, 32, 34 🗀 Literary Elements Transparencies 23, 24 ⊙ Classroom Presentation Toolkit CD-ROM; Listening Library CD, Selection Audio ⊙ TeacherWorks Plus CD-ROM ⊙ ⊙ Vocabulary PuzzleMaker CD-ROM

Assess	**SE/TE** pp. 143, 148, 149
	📁 Unit 1 Teaching Resources, Selection Quick Check, pp. 221, 234
	📁 Unit 1 Teaching Resources, Selection Quick Check (Spanish), pp. 222, 235
	📁 Assessment Resources, Selection Test, pp. 91–92, 93–94
	💿 ExamView Assessment Suite CD-ROM
	▶ Progress Reporter Online Assessment
Differentiated Instruction: English Learners	**TE** English Learner Activities, pp. 139–149
	📘 Interactive Read and Write (EL) SE/TE, pp. 37–44
	📁 Unit 1 Teaching Resources, English Language Coach, p. 138
	📁 Unit 1 Teaching Resources, Selection Summaries: English, Spanish, Vietnamese, Tagalog, Cantonese, Haitian Creole, and Hmong, pp. 213–218, 223–228
	📁 Unit 1 Teaching Resources, Selection Quick Check (Spanish), pp. 222, 235
	📁 English Language Coach
	💿 Glencoe Interactive Vocabulary CD-ROM
	💿 Listening Library Audio CD
	📁 Listening Library Sourcebook: Strategies and Activities
Differentiated Instruction: Approaching Level	**TE** Approaching Level Activities, pp. 133–149
	📘 Interactive Read and Write (Approaching) SE/TE, pp. 37–44
	💿 Glencoe Interactive Vocabulary CD-ROM
	💿 Listening Library Audio CD
	📁 Listening Library Sourcebook: Strategies and Activities
	💿 Skill Level Up! A Skills-Based Language Arts Game CD-ROM
Differentiated Instruction: Advanced/Pre-AP	**TE** Advanced Learner Activities, pp. 139–149
	📘 Novel Companion SE, pp. 7–74
	📘 Novel Companion TG, pp. 10–20
	💿 ▶ Literature Classics, High School CD-ROM
	💿 Skill Level Up! A Skills-Based Language Arts Game CD-ROM
Extension	📘 Grammar and Language Workbook SE
	📘 Grammar and Language Workbook TAE
	📁 Revising with Style
	📘 Spelling Power SE
	📘 Spelling Power TAE
Daily Writing	**SE/TE** p. 143
Interdisciplinary Connections	**SE/TE** View the Art, p. 146
	▶ glencoe.com
Independent Reading	💿 BookLink K–12 CD-ROM
	📖 Ethnic Anthologies
	📖 Glencoe Literature Library
	💿 Glencoe Literature Library Teacher Resources CD-ROM
	📖 *inTIME* magazine
	💿 ▶ Literature Classics, High School CD-ROM
Technology and Additional Resources	**Planning and Instruction:**
	💿 TeacherWorks Plus CD-ROM; Classroom Presentation Toolkit CD-ROM
	▶ Literature Online at **glencoe.com** (QuickPass Code: **GLA9879u1T**)
	Students Tools:
	💿 StudentWorks Plus CD-ROM or DVD-ROM
	▶ Online Student Edition at **glencoe.com**
	▶ Literature Online at **glencoe.com** (QuickPass Code: **GLA9800u1**)

Lesson Plan

Historical Perspective: from *John Adams* (pp. 150–153)

Lesson Plan and Resource Manager

UNIT ONE Early America, Beginnings–1800, Part 3: The Road to Independence

Learning Objectives	**Reading:** Analyzing informational text. Analyzing biographical narrative.
Lesson Summary	On pages **150–153** of the Student Edition, students will be introduced to the following: • **Big Idea:** The Road to Independence • **Literary Element:** Description • **Reading Strategy:** Analyze a Biographical Narrative • **Writing:** Summary
Lesson Duration	One 45–50 minute session
Readability Scores	Dale-Chall: 9.9 DRP: 64 Lexile: 1270
Focus	**SE/TE** p. 150
Teach	**SE/TE** pp. 150–153 📁 Unit 1 Teaching Resources, Reading Strategy, p. 243 💿 Classroom Presentation Toolkit CD-ROM 💿 Listening Library CD, Selection Audio 💿 TeacherWorks Plus CD-ROM 💿▶ Vocabulary PuzzleMaker CD-ROM
Assess	**SE/TE** p. 153 📁 Unit 1 Teaching Resources, Selection Quick Check, p. 244 📁 Unit 1 Teaching Resources, Selection Quick Check (Spanish), p. 245 📁 Assessment Resources, Selection Test, pp. 95–96 💿 ExamView Assessment Suite CD-ROM ▶ Progress Reporter Online Assessment
Differentiated Instruction: English Learners	**TE** English Learner Activities, pp. 150–153 📁 Unit 1 Teaching Resources, English Language Coach, p. 138 📁 Unit 1 Teaching Resources, Selection Summaries: English, Spanish, Vietnamese, Tagalog, Cantonese, Haitian Creole, and Hmong, pp. 237–242 📁 Unit 1 Teaching Resources, Selection Quick Check (Spanish), p. 245 📁 English Language Coach 💿 Glencoe Interactive Vocabulary CD-ROM 💿 Listening Library Audio CD 📁 Listening Library Sourcebook: Strategies and Activities
Differentiated Instruction: Approaching Level	**TE** Approaching Level Activities, pp. 150–153 💿 Glencoe Interactive Vocabulary CD-ROM 💿 Listening Library Audio CD 📁 Listening Library Sourcebook: Strategies and Activities 💿 Skill Level Up! A Skills-Based Language Arts Game CD-ROM

Differentiated Instruction: Advanced/Pre-AP	**TE** Advanced Learner Activities, pp. 150–153 Novel Companion SE, pp. 7–74 Novel Companion TG, pp. 10–20 Literature Classics, High School CD-ROM Skill Level Up! A Skills-Based Language Arts Game CD-ROM
Extension	Grammar and Language Workbook SE Grammar and Language Workbook TAE Revising with Style Spelling Power SE Spelling Power TAE
Daily Writing	**SE/TE** p. 152
Interdisciplinary Connections	**TE** Cultural History, pp. 151, 153 glencoe.com
Independent Reading	BookLink K–12 CD-ROM Ethnic Anthologies Glencoe Literature Library Glencoe Literature Library Teacher Resources CD-ROM *inTIME* magazine Literature Classics, High School CD-ROM
Technology and Additional Resources	**Planning and Instruction:** TeacherWorks Plus CD-ROM Classroom Presentation Toolkit CD-ROM Literature Online at **glencoe.com** (QuickPass Code: **GLA9879u1T**) **Students Tools:** StudentWorks Plus CD-ROM or DVD-ROM Online Student Edition at **glencoe.com** Literature Online at **glencoe.com** (QuickPass Code: **GLA9800u1**)

Lesson Plan

Writing Workshop: Persuasive Speech (pp. 154–161)

Lesson Plan and Resource Manager

UNIT ONE Early America, Beginnings–1800

Learning Objectives	**Writing:** Writing a persuasive speech as an instrument for change in your community or the world, including a clearly stated opinion supported by relevant evidence.
Lesson Duration	Two 45–50 minute sessions
Writing Prompt	Write a persuasive speech of at least 1,500 words about a situation in your school or community that you wish to change. As you work, keep your audience and purpose in mind.
Focus	**SE/TE** p. 154
Teach	**SE/TE** pp. 155–161 📁 Writing Resources: Writing Process Strategies 1–23 📁 Writing Resources: Persuasive Writing 1–17 🎞 Writing Workshop Transparencies 6–10 📁 Unit 1 Teaching Resources, Writing Workshop Persuasive Speech, p. 247
Assess	📁 Unit 1 Teaching Resources, Writing Workshop Rubric, pp. 248–249 📁 Rubrics for Assessing Writing, Listening and Speaking, High School, pp. 20–21 ◉ Glencoe Online Essay Grader at **glencoewriting.com**
Differentiated Instruction: English Learners	**TE** English Learner Activities, pp. 154–161
Differentiated Instruction: Approaching Level	**TE** Approaching Level Activities, pp. 154–161
Differentiated Instruction: Advanced/Pre-AP	**TE** Advanced Learner Activities, pp. 154–161
Extension	📖 Grammar and Language Workbook SE 📖 Grammar and Language Workbook TAE 📁 Revising with Style 📖 Spelling Power SE 📖 Spelling Power TAE
Daily Writing	**SE/TE** pp. 156, 161
Interdisciplinary Connections	**TE** Political History, p. 155 ◉ glencoe.com

| Technology and Additional Resources | **Planning and Instruction:**
📖 Grammar and Composition Handbook
📁 Success in Writing: Research and Reports
📁 Writing Constructed Responses
💿 TeacherWorks Plus CD-ROM
💿 Classroom Presentation Toolkit CD-ROM
▶ Glencoe Online Essay Grader at **glencoewriting.com**
▶ Literature Online at **glencoe.com** (QuickPass Code: **GLA9879u1T**)
Students Tools:
💿 StudentWorks Plus CD-ROM or DVD-ROM
▶ Online Student Edition at **glencoe.com**
▶ Glencoe Online Essay Grader at **glencoewriting.com**
▶ Literature Online at **glencoe.com** (QuickPass Code: **GLA9800u1**) |

Lesson Plan

Speaking, Listening, and Viewing Workshop: Persuasive Speech (pp. 162–163)

Lesson Plan and Resource Manager

UNIT ONE Early America, Beginnings–1800

Learning Objectives	**Speaking and Listening:** Delivering a persuasive presentation that develops a logical argument. Providing feedback on a presentation. Using visual media to support an oral presentation.
Lesson Summary	One 45–50 minute session
Assignment	Deliver your persuasive speech to an audience.
Focus	**SE/TE** p. 162
Teach	**SE/TE** pp. 162–163 📁 Unit 1 Teaching Resources, SLV Activity, pp. 250–251 💿 TeacherWorks Plus CD-ROM 💿 Classroom Presentation Toolkit CD-ROM 💿 Student Presentation Builder on StudentWorks Plus CD-ROM or DVD-ROM
Assess	📁 Unit 1 Teaching Resources, SLV Rubrics, pp. 252–253 📁 Rubrics for Assessing Writing, Listening, and Speaking, pp. 42–43
Differentiated Instruction: Approaching Level	**TE** Approaching Level Activities, pp. 162–163
Extension	📕 Grammar and Language Workbook SE 📕 Grammar and Language Workbook TAE 📁 Revising with Style 📕 Spelling Power SE 📕 Spelling Power TAE
Daily Writing	**SE/TE** p. 162
Interdisciplinary Connections	▶ glencoe.com
Technology and Additional Resources	**Planning and Instruction:** 💿 TeacherWorks Plus CD-ROM 💿 Classroom Presentation Toolkit CD-ROM ▶ Glencoe Online Essay Grader at **glencoewriting.com** ▶ Literature Online at **glencoe.com** (QuickPass Code: **GLA9879u1T**) **Students Tools:** 💿 Student Presentation Builder on StudentWorks Plus CD-ROM or DVD-ROM 💿 StudentWorks Plus CD-ROM or DVD-ROM ▶ Online Student Edition at **glencoe.com** ▶ Glencoe Online Essay Grader at **glencoewriting.com** ▶ Literature Online at **glencoe.com** (QuickPass Code: **GLA9800u1**)

Lesson Plan

Glencoe Literature

Unit 1 Wrap-Up (pp. 164–171)

Lesson Plan and Resource Manager

UNIT ONE Early America, Beginnings–1800

Lesson Summary	On pages **164–171** of the Student Edition, students will: • Read independently • Complete the end-of-unit assessment
Lesson Duration	Two 45–50 minute sessions
Focus	**TE** pp. 164, 166
Teach	**TE** pp. 165, 166
Assess	**TE** pp. 167–171 📁 Assessment Resources, Unit 1 Summative Assessment, pp. 331–332 📘 ACT/SAT Preparation and Practice SE/ATE 💿 ExamView Assessment Suite CD-ROM ▶ Progress Reporter Online Assessment
Differentiated Instruction: English Learners	**TE** English Learner Activities, pp. 164–171
Differentiated Instruction: Approaching Level	**TE** Approaching Level Activities, pp. 164–171
Differentiated Instruction: Advanced/Pre-AP	📘 Novel Companion SE, pp. 7–74/TG, pp. 10–20 💿 Literature Classics, High School CD-ROM
Extension	📘 Grammar and Language Workbook SE/TAE; Spelling Power SE/TAE 📁 Revising with Style
Daily Writing	**SE/TE** pp. 164, 170
Interdisciplinary Connections	**TE** Cultural History, p. 165
Independent Reading	**SE/TE** pp. 164–165 💿 BookLink K–12 CD-ROM; Glencoe Literature Library Teacher Resources CD-ROM 📖 Ethnic Anthologies; Glencoe Literature Library; *inTIME* magazine 💿 ▶ Literature Classics, High School CD-ROM
Technology and Additional Resources	**Planning and Instruction:** 💿 TeacherWorks Plus CD-ROM; Classroom Presentation Toolkit CD-ROM ▶ Literature Online at **glencoe.com** (QuickPass Code: **GLA9879u1T**) **Students Tools:** 💿 StudentWorks Plus CD-ROM or DVD-ROM ▶ Online Student Edition at **glencoe.com**; Glencoe Online Essay Grader at **glencoewriting.com**; Literature Online at **glencoe.com** (QuickPass Code: **GLA9800u1**)

Lesson Plan

Unit 2 Introduction (pp. 172–186)

Lesson Plan and Resource Manager

UNIT TWO American Romanticism, 1800–1860

Learning Objectives	**Literary Studies:** Analyzing literary periods. Analyzing literary genres. Evaluating historical influences. Connecting to the literature.

Unit Summary	In this unit, students will be introduced to the following:
	• **Big Ideas:** Part 1: Optimism and Individualism
	        Part 2: Kinship with Nature
	        Part 3: The Power of Darkness
	• **Reading Skills:** Analyze Graphic Information, Analyze Cause and Effect, Interpret, Compare and Contrast
	• **Writing Activity:** Write an Essay
	• **Speaking/Listening Skill:** Create a Presentation
	• **Study Skill:** Take Notes

Lesson Duration	Two 45–50 minute sessions
Focus	**SE/TE** pp. 172–173 Daily Language Practice Transparency 19 Literature Launchers: Pre-Reading Videos DVD, Unit 2 Launcher Literature Launchers Teacher Guide
Teach	**SE/TE** pp. 174–185 Unit 2 Teaching Resources, Unit Introduction, pp. 1–2 Unit 2 Teaching Resources, Big Idea Foldable, pp. 3–4 Unit 2 Teaching Resources, Big Idea School-to-Home Connection, p. 5 Unit 2 Teaching Resources, Unit Challenge Planner, pp. 12–15 Unit 2 Teaching Resources: Academic Vocabulary Development, pp. 16–17 Classroom Presentation Toolkit CD-ROM TeacherWorks Plus CD-ROM
Assess	**SE/TE** p. 186 Assessment Resources, Unit 2 Diagnostic Assessment, pp. 9–16 ACT/SAT Preparation and Practice SE/ATE ExamView Assessment Suite CD-ROM Progress Reporter Online Assessment
Differentiated Instruction: English Learners	**TE** English Learner Activities, pp. 172–186 Unit 2 Teaching Resources, Big Idea School-to-Home Connections: English, Spanish, Vietnamese, Tagalog, Cantonese, Haitian Creole, and Hmong, pp. 6–11 English Language Coach
Differentiated Instruction: Approaching Level	**TE** Approaching Level Activities, pp. 172–186 Skill Level Up! A Skills-Based Language Arts Game CD-ROM

Differentiated Instruction: Advanced/Pre-AP	**TE** Advanced Learner Activities, pp. 172–186 ■ Novel Companion SE, pp. 75–118 ■ Novel Companion TG, pp. 21–28 ◉ ▶ Literature Classics, High School CD-ROM ◉ Skill Level Up! A Skills-Based Language Arts Game CD-ROM
Extension	■ Grammar and Language Workbook SE ■ Grammar and Language Workbook TAE 🗀 Revising with Style ■ Spelling Power SE ■ Spelling Power TAE
Daily Writing	**TE** p. 182 **SE/TE** p. 186
Interdisciplinary Connections	**TE** Language History: Rise of American English, p. 174 **TE** Literary History: *Uncle Tom's Cabin*, p. 175 **TE** Political History: Log Cabin Election, p. 176 **TE** Literary History: American Gothic, p. 179 **SE/TE** View the Art, pp. 172–173, 177, 181, 183, 185 **TE** Literary History: The Influence of Thoreau, p. 182 ▶ glencoe.com
Independent Reading	◉ BookLink K–12 CD-ROM 📖 Ethnic Anthologies 📖 Glencoe Literature Library ◉ Glencoe Literature Library Teacher Resources CD-ROM 📖 *inTIME* magazine ◉ ▶ Literature Classics, High School CD-ROM
Technology and Additional Resources	**Planning and Instruction:** ◉ TeacherWorks Plus CD-ROM ◉ Classroom Presentation Toolkit CD-ROM ▶ Literature Online at **glencoe.com** (QuickPass Code: **GLA9879u2T**) **Students Tools:** ◉ StudentWorks Plus CD-ROM or DVD-ROM ▶ Online Student Edition at **glencoe.com** ▶ Literature Online at **glencoe.com** (QuickPass Code: **GLA9800u2**)

Lesson Plan

Part 1 Opener, from *Nature*, and from *Self-Reliance* (pp. 187–197)

Lesson Plan and Resource Manager

UNIT TWO American Romanticism, 1800–1860, Part 1: Individualism and Nature

Learning Objectives	**Literary Study:** Analyzing theme. **Reading:** Recognize author's purpose. **Writing:** Writing a journal entry.
Lesson Summary	On pages **187–193** of the Student Edition, students will be introduced to the following: • **Big Idea:** Kinship with Nature • **Literary Element:** Theme • **Reading Strategy:** Recognize Author's Purpose • **Vocabulary:** Word Usage • **Writing Activity:** Write a Journal Entry On pages **194–197** of the Student Edition, students will be introduced to the following: • **Big Idea:** Optimism and Individualism • **Literary Element:** Figurative Language • **Reading Strategy:** Draw Conclusions • **Vocabulary:** Context Clues, Academic Vocabulary • **Speaking/Listening Skill:** Deliver a Persuasive Speech
Lesson Duration	Two 45–50 minute sessions
Readability Scores	from "Nature"　　　　Dale-Chall: 8.9　　　DRP: 61　　　Lexile: 960 from "Self-Reliance"　Dale-Chall: 10.2　　DRP: 64　　　Lexile: 1030
Focus	**SE/TE** pp. 188–189, 194 📖 Daily Language Practice Transparency 20
Teach	**SE/TE** pp. 190–192, 194–195 📁 Unit 2 Teaching Resources, Literary Element, pp. 26, 39 📁 Unit 2 Teaching Resources, Reading Strategy, pp. 27, 40 📁 Unit 2 Teaching Resources, Selection Vocabulary Practice, pp. 28, 41 📁 Unit 2 Teaching Resources, Vocabulary Strategy, pp. 29, 42 📁 Unit 2 Teaching Resources, Grammar Practice, pp. 30, 43 📖 Read Aloud, Think Aloud Transparencies 8–10 📖 Literary Elements Transparencies 41, 103 💿 Classroom Presentation Toolkit CD-ROM 💿 Listening Library CD, Selection Audio 💿 TeacherWorks Plus CD-ROM 💿 Vocabulary PuzzleMaker CD-ROM

Assess	**SE/TE** pp. 193, 196
	📁 Unit 2 Teaching Resources, Selection Quick Check, pp. 31, 44
	📁 Unit 2 Teaching Resources, Selection Quick Check (Spanish), pp. 32, 45
	📁 Assessment Resources, Selection Test, pp. 97–98, 99–100
	💿 ExamView Assessment Suite CD-ROM
	▶ Progress Reporter Online Assessment
Differentiated Instruction: English Learners	**TE** English Learner Activities, pp. 187–197
	📁 Unit 2 Teaching Resources, English Language Coach, p. 19
	📁 Unit 2 Teaching Resources, Selection Summaries: English, Spanish, Vietnamese, Tagalog, Cantonese, Haitian Creole, and Hmong, pp. 20–25, 33–38
	📁 Unit 2 Teaching Resources, Selection Quick Check (Spanish), pp. 32, 45
	📁 English Language Coach
	💿 Glencoe Interactive Vocabulary CD-ROM
	💿 Listening Library Audio CD
	📁 Listening Library Sourcebook: Strategies and Activities
Differentiated Instruction: Approaching Level	**TE** Approaching Level Activities, pp. 187–197
	💿 Glencoe Interactive Vocabulary CD-ROM
	💿 Listening Library Audio CD
	📁 Listening Library Sourcebook: Strategies and Activities
	💿 Skill Level Up! A Skills-Based Language Arts Game CD-ROM
Differentiated Instruction: Advanced/Pre-AP	**TE** Advanced Learner Activities, pp. 187–197
	📘 Novel Companion SE, pp. 75–118
	📘 Novel Companion TG, pp. 21–28
	💿 ▶ Literature Classics, High School CD-ROM
	💿 Skill Level Up! A Skills-Based Language Arts Game CD-ROM
Extension	📘 Grammar and Language Workbook SE
	📘 Grammar and Language Workbook TAE
	📁 Revising with Style
	📘 Spelling Power SE
	📘 Spelling Power TAE
Daily Writing	**SE/TE** pp. 193, 197
Interdisciplinary Connections	**SE/TE** View the Art, pp. 187, 190
	▶ glencoe.com
Independent Reading	💿 BookLink K–12 CD-ROM
	📖 Ethnic Anthologies
	📖 Glencoe Literature Library
	💿 Glencoe Literature Library Teacher Resources CD-ROM
	📖 inTIME magazine
	💿 ▶ Literature Classics, High School CD-ROM
Technology and Additional Resources	**Planning and Instruction:**
	💿 TeacherWorks Plus CD-ROM
	💿 Classroom Presentation Toolkit CD-ROM
	▶ Literature Online at **glencoe.com** (QuickPass Code: **GLA9879u2T**)
	Students Tools:
	💿 StudentWorks Plus CD-ROM or DVD-ROM
	▶ Online Student Edition at **glencoe.com**
	▶ Literature Online at **glencoe.com** (QuickPass Code: **GLA9800u2**)

Lesson Plan

Glencoe Literature

TIME: *The Biology of Joy* (pp. 198–202)

Lesson Plan and Resource Manager

UNIT TWO American Romanticism, 1800–1860, Part 1: Individualism and Nature

Learning Objectives	**Reading:** Analyzing informational text. Analyzing cause-and-effect relationships.
Lesson Summary	On pages **198–202** of the Student Edition, students will be introduced to the following: • **Big Idea:** Optimism and Individualism • **Reading Strategy:** Analyze Cause-and-Effect Relationships
Lesson Duration	One 45–50 minute session
Readability Scores	Dale-Chall: 11.9　　　DRP: 68　　　Lexile: 1110
Focus	SE/TE p. 198
Teach	SE/TE pp. 198–202 📁 Unit 2 Teaching Resources, Reading Strategy, p. 52 💿 Classroom Presentation Toolkit CD-ROM 💿 Listening Library CD, Selection Audio 💿 TeacherWorks Plus CD-ROM 💿▶ Vocabulary PuzzleMaker CD-ROM
Assess	SE/TE p. 202 📁 Unit 2 Teaching Resources, Selection Quick Check, p. 53 📁 Unit 2 Teaching Resources, Selection Quick Check (Spanish), p. 54 📁 Assessment Resources, Selection Test, pp. 101–102 💿 ExamView Assessment Suite CD-ROM ▶ Progress Reporter Online Assessment
Differentiated Instruction: English Learners	TE English Learner Activities, pp. 198–202 📁 Unit 2 Teaching Resources, English Language Coach, p. 19 📁 Unit 2 Teaching Resources, Selection Summaries: English, Spanish, Vietnamese, Tagalog, Cantonese, Haitian Creole, and Hmong, pp. 46–51 📁 Unit 2 Teaching Resources, Selection Quick Check (Spanish), p. 54 📁 English Language Coach 💿 Glencoe Interactive Vocabulary CD-ROM 💿 Listening Library Audio CD 📁 Listening Library Sourcebook: Strategies and Activities
Differentiated Instruction: Approaching Level	TE Approaching Level Activities, pp. 198–202 💿 Glencoe Interactive Vocabulary CD-ROM 💿 Listening Library Audio CD 📁 Listening Library Sourcebook: Strategies and Activities 💿 Skill Level Up! A Skills-Based Language Arts Game CD-ROM
Differentiated Instruction: Advanced/Pre-AP	📖 Novel Companion SE, pp. 75–118 📖 Novel Companion TG, pp. 21–28 💿▶ Literature Classics, High School CD-ROM 💿 Skill Level Up! A Skills-Based Language Arts Game CD-ROM

Extension	▪ Grammar and Language Workbook SE ▪ Grammar and Language Workbook TAE 📁 Revising with Style ▪ Spelling Power SE ▪ Spelling Power TAE
Daily Writing	**SE/TE** p. 202
Interdisciplinary Connections	**TE** Cultural History: Buddhism, p. 199 **TE** Cultural History: Pavlov's Dogs, p. 200 🌐 glencoe.com
Independent Reading	💿 BookLink K–12 CD-ROM 📖 Ethnic Anthologies 📖 Glencoe Literature Library 💿 Glencoe Literature Library Teacher Resources CD-ROM 📖 *inTIME* magazine 💿▶ Literature Classics, High School CD-ROM
Technology and Additional Resources	**Planning and Instruction:** 💿 TeacherWorks Plus CD-ROM 💿 Classroom Presentation Toolkit CD-ROM ▶ Literature Online at **glencoe.com** (QuickPass Code: **GLA9879u2T**) **Students Tools:** 💿 StudentWorks Plus CD-ROM or DVD-ROM 💿 Online Student Edition at **glencoe.com** ▶ Literature Online at **glencoe.com** (QuickPass Code: **GLA9800u2**)

Lesson Plan

from *Woman in the Nineteenth Century* (pp. 203–209)

Lesson Plan and Resource Manager

UNIT TWO American Romanticism, 1800–1860, Part 1: Individualism and Nature

Learning Objectives	**Literary Study:** Analyzing thesis. **Reading:** Summarizing. **Writing:** Writing a letter.
Lesson Summary	On pages **203–209** of the Student Edition, students will be introduced to the following: • **Big Idea:** Optimism and Individualism • **Literary Element:** Thesis • **Reading Strategy:** Summarize • **Vocabulary:** Word Usage • **Writing Activity:** Write a Letter
Lesson Duration	One 45–50 minute session
Readability Scores	Dale-Chall: 8.2 DRP: 65 Lexile: 1340
Focus	**SE/TE** pp. 203–204 Daily Language Practice Transparency 21
Teach	**SE/TE** pp. 205–208 Unit 2 Teaching Resources, Literary Element, p. 61 Unit 2 Teaching Resources, Reading Strategy, p. 62 Unit 2 Teaching Resources, Selection Vocabulary Practice, p. 63 Unit 2 Teaching Resources, Vocabulary Strategy, p. 64 Unit 2 Teaching Resources, Grammar Practice, p. 65 Literary Elements Transparency 12 Classroom Presentation Toolkit CD-ROM Listening Library CD, Selection Audio TeacherWorks Plus CD-ROM Vocabulary PuzzleMaker CD-ROM
Assess	**SE/TE** p. 209 Unit 2 Teaching Resources, Selection Quick Check, p. 66 Unit 2 Teaching Resources, Selection Quick Check (Spanish), p. 67 Assessment Resources, Selection Test, pp. 103–104 ExamView Assessment Suite CD-ROM Progress Reporter Online Assessment
Differentiated Instruction: English Learners	**TE** English Learner Activities, pp. 203–209 Unit 2 Teaching Resources, English Language Coach, p. 19 Unit 2 Teaching Resources, Selection Summaries: English, Spanish, Vietnamese, Tagalog, Cantonese, Haitian Creole, and Hmong, pp. 55–60 Unit 2 Teaching Resources, Selection Quick Check (Spanish), p. 67 English Language Coach Glencoe Interactive Vocabulary CD-ROM Listening Library Audio CD Listening Library Sourcebook: Strategies and Activities

Differentiated Instruction: Approaching Level	**TE** Approaching Level Activities, pp. 203–209 ◉ Glencoe Interactive Vocabulary CD-ROM ◉ Listening Library Audio CD 📁 Listening Library Sourcebook: Strategies and Activities ◉ Skill Level Up! A Skills-Based Language Arts Game CD-ROM
Differentiated Instruction: Advanced/Pre-AP	**TE** Advanced Learner Activities, pp. 203–209 ▯ Novel Companion SE, pp. 75–118 ▯ Novel Companion TG, pp. 21–28 ◉ ▶ Literature Classics, High School CD-ROM ◉ Skill Level Up! A Skills-Based Language Arts Game CD-ROM
Extension	▯ Grammar and Language Workbook SE ▯ Grammar and Language Workbook TAE 📁 Revising with Style ▯ Spelling Power SE ▯ Spelling Power TAE
Daily Writing	**SE/TE** p. 209
Interdisciplinary Connections	**TE** Literary History: Summer on the Lakes, in 1843, p. 203 **SE/TE** View the Art, pp. 205, 206 **TE** Cultural History: Women's Rights, p. 207 ▶ glencoe.com
Independent Reading	◉ BookLink K–12 CD-ROM 📖 Ethnic Anthologies 📖 Glencoe Literature Library ◉ Glencoe Literature Library Teacher Resources CD-ROM 📖 *inTIME* magazine ◉ ▶ Literature Classics, High School CD-ROM
Technology and Additional Resources	**Planning and Instruction:** ◉ TeacherWorks Plus CD-ROM ◉ Classroom Presentation Toolkit CD-ROM ▶ Literature Online at **glencoe.com** (QuickPass Code: **GLA9879u2T**) **Students Tools:** ◉ StudentWorks Plus CD-ROM or DVD-ROM ▶ Online Student Edition at **glencoe.com** ▶ Literature Online at **glencoe.com** (QuickPass Code: **GLA9800u2**)

Lesson Plan

Literary History: The Fireside Poets (pp. 210–211)

Lesson Plan and Resource Manager

UNIT TWO American Romanticism, 1800–1860, Part 1: Individualism and Nature

Learning Objectives	**Literary Study:** Analyzing literary periods. Analyzing literary genres.
Lesson Summary	On pages **210–211** of the Student Edition, students will be introduced to the following: • **Big Idea:** Kinship with Nature • **Literary Element:** Poetry
Lesson Duration	One 45–50 minute session
Focus	**SE/TE** p. 210 🔖 Daily Language Practice Transparency 22
Teach	**SE/TE** p. 210 📁 Unit 2 Teaching Resources, Literary History: The Fireside Poets, pp. 68–69 🔖 Literary Elements Transparency 60 💿 Classroom Presentation Toolkit CD-ROM 💿 Listening Library CD, Selection Audio 💿 TeacherWorks Plus CD-ROM 💿 ▶ Vocabulary PuzzleMaker CD-ROM
Assess	**SE/TE** p. 211 💿 ExamView Assessment Suite CD-ROM ▶ Progress Reporter Online Assessment
Differentiated Instruction: English Learners	**TE** English Learner Activities, pp. 210–211 📁 English Language Coach 💿 Glencoe Interactive Vocabulary CD-ROM 💿 Listening Library Audio CD 📁 Listening Library Sourcebook: Strategies and Activities
Differentiated Instruction: Approaching Level	**TE** Approaching Level Activities, pp. 210–211 💿 Glencoe Interactive Vocabulary CD-ROM 💿 Listening Library Audio CD 📁 Listening Library Sourcebook: Strategies and Activities 💿 Skill Level Up! A Skills-Based Language Arts Game CD-ROM
Differentiated Instruction: Advanced/Pre-AP	📕 Novel Companion SE, pp. 75–118 📕 Novel Companion TG, pp. 21–28 💿 ▶ Literature Classics, High School CD-ROM 💿 Skill Level Up! A Skills-Based Language Arts Game CD-ROM
Extension	📕 Grammar and Language Workbook SE 📕 Grammar and Language Workbook TAE 📁 Revising with Style 📕 Spelling Power SE 📕 Spelling Power TAE
Daily Writing	**SE/TE** p. 210

Interdisciplinary Connections	**SE/TE** View the Art, p. 210 ▶ **glencoe.com**
Independent Reading	● BookLink K–12 CD-ROM ▯ Ethnic Anthologies ▯ Glencoe Literature Library ● Glencoe Literature Library Teacher Resources CD-ROM ▯ *inTIME* magazine ● ▶ Literature Classics, High School CD-ROM
Technology and Additional Resources	**Planning and Instruction:** ● TeacherWorks Plus CD-ROM ● Classroom Presentation Toolkit CD-ROM ▶ Literature Online at **glencoe.com** (QuickPass Code: **GLA9879u2T**) **Students Tools:** ● StudentWorks Plus CD-ROM or DVD-ROM ▶ Online Student Edition at **glencoe.com** ▶ Literature Online at **glencoe.com** (QuickPass Code: **GLA9800u2**)

Lesson Plan

Glencoe Literature

from *Walden* (pp. 212–219)

Lesson Plan and Resource Manager

UNIT TWO American Romanticism, 1800–1860, Part 1: Individualism and Nature

Learning Objectives	**Literary Study:** Analyzing metaphor. **Reading:** Connecting to personal experience. **Writing:** Writing a speech.
Lesson Summary	On pages **212–219** of the Student Edition, students will be introduced to the following: • **Big Idea:** Kinship with Nature • **Literary Elements:** Metaphor, Tone • **Reading Strategies:** Connect, Vary Reading Rate • **Vocabulary:** Context Clues, Modifiers • **Writing Activities/Grammar:** Compare Literature, Summarize • **Listening/Speaking/Viewing Skill:** Analyze Art
Lesson Duration	One 45–50 minute session
Readability Scores	Dale-Chall: 6.3 DRP: 58 Lexile: 1260
Focus	**SE/TE** pp. 212–213 📖 Selection Focus Transparency 16 📖 Daily Language Practice Transparency 23
Teach	**SE/TE** pp. 214–218 📁 Unit 2 Teaching Resources, Literary Element, p. 76 📁 Unit 2 Teaching Resources, Reading Strategy, p. 77 📁 Unit 2 Teaching Resources, Selection Vocabulary Practice, p. 78 📁 Unit 2 Teaching Resources, Vocabulary Strategy, p. 79 📁 Unit 2 Teaching Resources, Grammar Practice, p. 80 📖 Literary Elements Transparency 60 💿 Classroom Presentation Toolkit CD-ROM 💿 Listening Library CD, Selection Audio 💿 TeacherWorks Plus CD-ROM 💿 Vocabulary PuzzleMaker CD-ROM
Assess	**SE/TE** p. 219 📁 Unit 2 Teaching Resources, Selection Quick Check, p. 81 📁 Unit 2 Teaching Resources, Selection Quick Check (Spanish), p. 82 📁 Assessment Resources, Selection Test, pp. 105–106 💿 ExamView Assessment Suite CD-ROM 💿 Progress Reporter Online Assessment

Differentiated Instruction: English Learners	**TE** English Learner Activities, pp. 212–219
	📁 Unit 2 Teaching Resources, Selection Summaries: English, Spanish, Vietnamese, Tagalog, Cantonese, Haitian Creole, and Hmong, pp. 70–75
	📁 Unit 2 Teaching Resources, Selection Quick Check (Spanish), p. 82
	📁 English Language Coach
	💿 Glencoe Interactive Vocabulary CD-ROM
	💿 Listening Library Audio CD
	📁 Listening Library Sourcebook: Strategies and Activities
Differentiated Instruction: Approaching Level	**TE** Approaching Level Activities, pp. 212–219
	💿 Glencoe Interactive Vocabulary CD-ROM
	💿 Listening Library Audio CD
	📁 Listening Library Sourcebook: Strategies and Activities
	💿 Skill Level Up! A Skills-Based Language Arts Game CD-ROM
Differentiated Instruction: Advanced/Pre-AP	**TE** Advanced Learner Activities, pp. 212–219
	📘 Novel Companion SE, pp. 75–118
	📘 Novel Companion TG, pp. 21–28
	💿 ▶ Literature Classics, High School CD-ROM
	💿 Skill Level Up! A Skills-Based Language Arts Game CD-ROM
Extension	📘 Grammar and Language Workbook SE
	📘 Grammar and Language Workbook TAE
	📁 Revising with Style
	📘 Spelling Power SE
	📘 Spelling Power TAE
Daily Writing	**TE** p. 214
Interdisciplinary Connections	**SE/TE** View the Art, p. 216
	TE Literary History: Beyond Nature, p. 212
	▶ glencoe.com
Independent Reading	💿 BookLink K–12 CD-ROM
	📖 Ethnic Anthologies
	📖 Glencoe Literature Library
	💿 Glencoe Literature Library Teacher Resources CD-ROM
	📖 *inTIME* magazine
	💿 ▶ Literature Classics, High School CD-ROM
Technology and Additional Resources	**Planning and Instruction:**
	💿 TeacherWorks Plus CD-ROM
	💿 Classroom Presentation Toolkit CD-ROM
	▶ Literature Online at **glencoe.com** (QuickPass Code: **GLA9879u2T**)
	Students Tools:
	💿 StudentWorks Plus CD-ROM or DVD-ROM
	▶ Online Student Edition at **glencoe.com**
	▶ Literature Online at **glencoe.com** (QuickPass Code: **GLA9800u2**)

Lesson Plan

Glencoe Literature Essential Course of Study

Comparing Literature: from *Civil Disobedience*, On *the Eve of Historic Dandi March*, and from *Long Walk to Freedom* (pp. 220–236)

Lesson Plan and Resource Manager

UNIT TWO American Romanticism, 1800–1860, Part 1: Individualism and Nature

Learning Objectives	**Literary Study:** Comparing cultural context. Comparing themes. Analyzing argument.
Lesson Summary	On pages **220–236** of the Student Edition, students will be introduced to the following: • **Big Idea:** Optimism and Individualism • **Literary Element:** Argument • **Reading Strategies:** Evaluate Evidence, Compare Persuasive Messages, Compare Cultures • **Vocabulary:** Antonyms • **Writing Activities:** Write a Summary, Write an Essay
Lesson Duration	Two to five 45–50 minute sessions
Readability Scores	from "Civil Disobedience" Dale-Chall: 7.7 DRP: 63 Lexile: 1110 "On the Eve of Historic Dandi March" Dale-Chall: 6.8 DRP: 59 Lexile: 950 from "Long Walk to Freedom" Dale-Chall: 6.8 DRP: 59 Lexile: 950
Focus	**SE/TE** pp. 220–221, 229, 231 Daily Language Practice Transparency 24 Literature Launchers: Pre-Reading Video DVD, Selection Launcher Literature Launchers Teacher Guide
Teach	**SE/TE** pp. 222–227, 230, 232–235 Interactive Read and Write SE/TE, pp. 45–78 Unit 2 Teaching Resources, Comparing Literature Graphic Organizer, p. 83 Unit 2 Teaching Resources, Literary Element, p. 90 Unit 2 Teaching Resources, Reading Strategy, p. 91 Unit 2 Teaching Resources, Selection Vocabulary Practice, p. 92 Unit 2 Teaching Resources, Vocabulary Strategy, p. 93 Unit 2 Teaching Resources, Grammar Practice, p. 94 Literary Elements Transparency 12 Classroom Presentation Toolkit CD-ROM Listening Library CD, Selection Audio TeacherWorks Plus CD-ROM Vocabulary PuzzleMaker CD-ROM
Assess	**SE/TE** pp. 228, 236 Unit 2 Teaching Resources, Selection Quick Check, p. 95 Unit 2 Teaching Resources, Selection Quick Check (Spanish), p. 96 Assessment Resources, Selection Test, pp. 107–108 ExamView Assessment Suite CD-ROM Progress Reporter Online Assessment

Copyright © by The McGraw-Hill Companies, Inc.

Differentiated Instruction: English Learners	**TE** English Learner Activities, pp. 220–236
	Interactive Read and Write (EL) SE/TE, pp. 45–78
	Unit 2 Teaching Resources, English Language Coach, p. 19
	Unit 2 Teaching Resources, Selection Summaries: English, Spanish, Vietnamese, Tagalog, Cantonese, Haitian Creole, and Hmong, pp. 84–89
	Unit 2 Teaching Resources, Selection Quick Check (Spanish), p. 96
	English Language Coach
	Glencoe Interactive Vocabulary CD-ROM
	Listening Library Audio CD
	Listening Library Sourcebook: Strategies and Activities
Differentiated Instruction: Approaching Level	**TE** Approaching Level Activities, pp. 220–236
	Interactive Read and Write (AL) SE/TE, pp. 45–78
	Glencoe Interactive Vocabulary CD-ROM
	Listening Library Audio CD
	Listening Library Sourcebook: Strategies and Activities
	Skill Level Up! A Skills-Based Language Arts Game CD-ROM
Differentiated Instruction: Advanced/Pre-AP	**TE** Advanced Learner Activities, pp. 220–236
	Novel Companion SE, pp. 75–118
	Novel Companion TG, pp. 21–28
	Literature Classics, High School CD-ROM
	Skill Level Up! A Skills-Based Language Arts Game CD-ROM
Extension	Grammar and Language Workbook SE/TAE
	Revising with Style
	Spelling Power SE/TAE
Daily Writing	**SE/TE** pp. 230, 236
Interdisciplinary Connections	**SE/TE** View the Art, p. 225
	TE Political History: Manifest Destiny, p. 223
	TE Literary History: Publishing Background, p. 227
	TE Political History: Civil Disobedience, p. 229
	TE Cultural History: An Epic Speech, p. 230
	TE Political History: Establishment of Apartheid, p. 231
	TE Political History: Apartheid Laws, p. 232
	TE Cultural History: Mandela's Retirement, p. 234
	TE Cultural History: The ANC, p. 235
	glencoe.com
Independent Reading	BookLink K–12 CD-ROM
	Ethnic Anthologies; Glencoe Literature Library; *inTIME* magazine
	Glencoe Literature Library Teacher Resources CD-ROM
	Literature Classics, High School CD-ROM
Technology and Additional Resources	**Planning and Instruction:**
	TeacherWorks Plus CD-ROM
	Classroom Presentation Toolkit CD-ROM
	Literature Online at **glencoe.com** (QuickPass Code: **GLA9879u2T**)
	Students Tools:
	StudentWorks Plus CD-ROM or DVD-ROM
	Online Student Edition at **glencoe.com**
	Literature Online at **glencoe.com** (QuickPass Code: **GLA9800u2**)

Lesson Plan

Part 2 Opener, Literary History: American Short Stories, and *The Devil and Tom Walker* (pp. 237–253)

Lesson Plan and Resource Manager

UNIT TWO American Romanticism, 1800–1860, Part 2: The Dark Side of Romanticism

Learning Objectives	**Literary Study:** Analyzing literary periods. Analyzing literary genres. Analyzing characterization (direct and indirect). **Reading:** Making and verifying predictions about plot. **Writing:** Writing a summary. **Grammar:** Using verb tenses.
Lesson Summary	On pages **237–253** of the Student Edition, students will be introduced to the following: ▪ **Big Idea:** The Power of Darkness ▪ **Literary Element:** Characterization ▪ **Reading Strategy:** Make and Verify Predictions ▪ **Vocabulary:** Analogies, Academic Vocabulary ▪ **Writing Activity/Grammar:** Report Story Events, Verb Tenses
Lesson Duration	Two 45–50 minute sessions
Readability Scores	"The Devil and Tom Walker" Dale-Chall: 8.4 DRP: 64 Lexile: 1220
Focus	**SE/TE** pp. 238, 240–241 Selection Focus Transparency 17 Daily Language Practice Transparencies 25, 26
Teach	**SE/TE** pp. 23, 242–250 Unit 2 Teaching Resources, Literary History: American Short Stories, pp. 98–99 Unit 2 Teaching Resources, Literary Element, p. 107 Unit 2 Teaching Resources, Reading Strategy, p. 108 Unit 2 Teaching Resources, Selection Vocabulary Practice, p. 109 Unit 2 Teaching Resources, Vocabulary Strategy, p. 110 Unit 2 Teaching Resources, Grammar Practice, p. 111 Literary Elements Transparency 21 Classroom Presentation Toolkit CD-ROM Listening Library CD, Selection Audio TeacherWorks Plus CD-ROM Vocabulary PuzzleMaker CD-ROM
Assess	**SE/TE** pp. 238, 251–253 Unit 2 Teaching Resources, Selection Quick Check, p. 112 Unit 2 Teaching Resources, Selection Quick Check (Spanish), p. 113 Assessment Resources, Selection Test, pp. 109–110 ExamView Assessment Suite CD-ROM Progress Reporter Online Assessment

Differentiated Instruction: English Learners	**TE** English Learner Activities, pp. 237–253
	📁 Unit 2 Teaching Resources, English Language Coach, p. 100
	📁 Unit 2 Teaching Resources, Selection Summaries: English, Spanish, Vietnamese, Tagalog, Cantonese, Haitian Creole, and Hmong, pp. 101–106
	📁 Unit 2 Teaching Resources, Selection Quick Check (Spanish), p. 113
	📁 English Language Coach
	💿 Glencoe Interactive Vocabulary CD-ROM
	💿 Listening Library Audio CD
	📁 Listening Library Sourcebook: Strategies and Activities
Differentiated Instruction: Approaching Level	**TE** Approaching Level Activities, pp. 237–253
	💿 Listening Library Audio CD
	📁 Listening Library Sourcebook: Strategies and Activities
	💿 Skill Level Up! A Skills-Based Language Arts Game CD-ROM
Differentiated Instruction: Advanced/Pre-AP	📘 Novel Companion SE, pp. 75–118
	📘 Novel Companion TG, pp. 21–28
	💿 ▶ Literature Classics, High School CD-ROM
	💿 Skill Level Up! A Skills-Based Language Arts Game CD-ROM
Extension	📘 Grammar and Language Workbook SE
	📘 Grammar and Language Workbook TAE
	📁 Revising with Style
	📘 Spelling Power SE
	📘 Spelling Power TAE
Daily Writing	**TE** p. 238
	SE/TE p. 253
Interdisciplinary Connections	**SE/TE** View the Art, pp. 237, 238, 245, 247, 250
	TE Literary History: Captain Kidd, p. 242
	▶ glencoe.com
Independent Reading	💿 BookLink K–12 CD-ROM
	📖 Ethnic Anthologies
	📖 Glencoe Literature Library
	💿 Glencoe Literature Library Teacher Resources CD-ROM
	📖 inTIME magazine
	💿 ▶ Literature Classics, High School CD-ROM
Technology and Additional Resources	**Planning and Instruction:**
	💿 TeacherWorks Plus CD-ROM
	💿 Classroom Presentation Toolkit CD-ROM
	▶ Literature Online at **glencoe.com** (QuickPass Code: **GLA9879u2T**)
	Students Tools:
	💿 StudentWorks Plus CD-ROM or DVD-ROM
	▶ Online Student Edition at **glencoe.com**
	▶ Literature Online at **glencoe.com** (QuickPass Code: **GLA9800u2**)

Lesson Plan

The Raven (pp. 254–261)

Lesson Plan and Resource Manager

UNIT TWO American Romanticism, 1800–1860, Part 2: The Dark Side of Romanticism

Learning Objectives	**Literary Study:** Analyzing narrative poetry. Analyzing sound devices. **Writing:** Writing a summary.
Lesson Summary	On pages **254–261** of the Student Edition, students will be introduced to the following: • **Big Idea:** The Power of Darkness • **Literary Element:** Narrative Poem • **Reading Strategy:** Analyze Sound Devices • **Vocabulary:** Synonyms • **Writing Activity:** Write a Summary
Lesson Duration	One 45–50 minute session
Readability Scores	Dale-Chall: N/A DRP: N/A Lexile: N/A
Focus	**SE/TE** pp. 254–255 Selection Focus Transparency 18 Daily Language Practice Transparency 27
Teach	**SE/TE** pp. 256–260 Unit 2 Teaching Resources, Literary Element, p. 120 Unit 2 Teaching Resources, Reading Strategy, p. 121 Unit 2 Teaching Resources, Selection Vocabulary Practice, p. 122 Unit 2 Teaching Resources, Vocabulary Strategy, p. 123 Literary Elements Transparency 66 Classroom Presentation Toolkit CD-ROM Listening Library CD, Selection Audio TeacherWorks Plus CD-ROM Vocabulary PuzzleMaker CD-ROM
Assess	**SE/TE** p. 261 Unit 2 Teaching Resources, Selection Quick Check, p. 124 Unit 2 Teaching Resources, Selection Quick Check (Spanish), p. 125 Assessment Resources, Selection Test, pp. 111–112 ExamView Assessment Suite CD-ROM Progress Reporter Online Assessment
Differentiated Instruction: English Learners	**TE** English Learner Activities, pp. 254–261 Unit 2 Teaching Resources, English Language Coach, p. 100 Unit 2 Teaching Resources, Selection Summaries: English, Spanish, Vietnamese, Tagalog, Cantonese, Haitian Creole, and Hmong, pp. 114–119 Unit 2 Teaching Resources, Selection Quick Check (Spanish), p. 125 English Language Coach Glencoe Interactive Vocabulary CD-ROM Listening Library Audio CD Listening Library Sourcebook: Strategies and Activities

Differentiated Instruction: Approaching Level	**TE** Approaching Level Activities, pp. 254–261
	Glencoe Interactive Vocabulary CD-ROM
	Listening Library Audio CD
	Listening Library Sourcebook: Strategies and Activities
	Skill Level Up! A Skills-Based Language Arts Game CD-ROM
Differentiated Instruction: Advanced/Pre-AP	**TE** Advanced Learner Activities, pp. 254–261
	Novel Companion SE, pp. 75–118
	Novel Companion TG, pp. 21–28
	Literature Classics, High School CD-ROM
	Skill Level Up! A Skills-Based Language Arts Game CD-ROM
Extension	Grammar and Language Workbook SE
	Grammar and Language Workbook TAE
	Revising with Style
	Spelling Power SE
	Spelling Power TAE
Daily Writing	**SE/TE** p. 261
Interdisciplinary Connections	**TE** Literary History: Ravens, p. 256
	TE Cultural History: Athena, p. 258
	TE Language History: Biblical Allusions, p. 260
	glencoe.com
Independent Reading	BookLink K–12 CD-ROM
	Ethnic Anthologies
	Glencoe Literature Library
	Glencoe Literature Library Teacher Resources CD-ROM
	inTIME magazine
	Literature Classics, High School CD-ROM
Technology and Additional Resources	**Planning and Instruction:**
	TeacherWorks Plus CD-ROM
	Classroom Presentation Toolkit CD-ROM
	Literature Online at **glencoe.com** (QuickPass Code: **GLA9879u2T**)
	Students Tools:
	StudentWorks Plus CD-ROM or DVD-ROM
	Online Student Edition at **glencoe.com**
	Literature Online at **glencoe.com** (QuickPass Code: **GLA9800u2**)

Lesson Plan

The Pit and the Pendulum and Vocabulary Workshop (pp. 262–277)

Lesson Plan and Resource Manager

UNIT TWO American Romanticism, 1800–1860, Part 2: The Dark Side of Romanticism

Learning Objectives	**Literary Study:** Analyzing sequence. **Reading:** Identifying sequence. **Writing:** Writing an expository essay. **Grammar:** Understanding apostrophes. **Vocabulary:** Inferring meaning from context clues.
Lesson Summary	On pages **262–276** of the Student Edition, students will be introduced to the following: • **Big Idea:** The Power of Darkness • **Literary Element:** Suspense • **Reading Strategy:** Identify Sequence • **Vocabulary:** Word Origins, Academic Vocabulary • **Writing Activity/Grammar:** Expository Essay, Apostrophes On page **277** of the Student Edition, students will be introduced to the following: • **Vocabulary Workshop:** Context Clues
Lesson Duration	Two to five 45–50 minute sessions
Readability Scores	"The Pit and the Pendulum" Dale-Chall: 9.0 DRP: 65 Lexile: 1010
Focus	**SE/TE** pp. 262, 277 Selection Focus Transparency 18 Daily Language Practice Transparency 27 Literature Launchers: Pre-Reading Videos DVD, Selection Launcher Literature Launchers Teacher Guide
Teach	**SE/TE** pp. 263–273, 277 Interactive Read and Write SE/TE, pp. 79–98 Unit 2 Teaching Resources, Literary Element, p. 132 Unit 2 Teaching Resources, Reading Strategy, p. 133 Unit 2 Teaching Resources, Selection Vocabulary Practice, p. 134 Unit 2 Teaching Resources, Vocabulary Strategy, p. 135 Unit 2 Teaching Resources, Grammar Practice, p. 136 Literary Elements Transparency 99 Classroom Presentation Toolkit CD-ROM Listening Library CD, Selection Audio TeacherWorks Plus CD-ROM Vocabulary PuzzleMaker CD-ROM
Assess	**SE/TE** pp. 274–276, 277 Unit 2 Teaching Resources, Selection Quick Check, p. 137 Unit 2 Teaching Resources, Selection Quick Check (Spanish), p. 138 Assessment Resources, Selection Test, pp. 113–114

Assess *(continued)*	● ExamView Assessment Suite CD-ROM ▶ Progress Reporter Online Assessment
Differentiated Instruction: English Learners	**TE** English Learner Activities, pp. 262–277 ▌ Interactive Read and Write (EL) SE/TE, pp. 79–98 🗀 Unit 2 Teaching Resources, English Language Coach, p. 100 🗀 Unit 2 Teaching Resources, Selection Summaries: English, Spanish, Vietnamese, Tagalog, Cantonese, Haitian Creole, and Hmong, pp. 126–131 🗀 Unit 2 Teaching Resources, Selection Quick Check (Spanish), p. 138 🗀 English Language Coach ● Glencoe Interactive Vocabulary CD-ROM ● Listening Library Audio CD 🗀 Listening Library Sourcebook: Strategies and Activities
Differentiated Instruction: Approaching Level	**TE** Approaching Level Activities, pp. 262–277 ▌ Interactive Read and Write (AL) SE/TE, pp. 79–98 ● Glencoe Interactive Vocabulary CD-ROM ● Listening Library Audio CD 🗀 Listening Library Sourcebook: Strategies and Activities ● Skill Level Up! A Skills-Based Language Arts Game CD-ROM
Differentiated Instruction: Advanced/Pre-AP	**TE** Advanced Learner Activities, pp. 262–277 ▌ Novel Companion SE, pp. 75–118 ▌ Novel Companion TG, pp. 21–28 ● ▶ Literature Classics, High School CD-ROM ● Skill Level Up! A Skills-Based Language Arts Game CD-ROM
Extension	▌ Grammar and Language Workbook SE ▌ Grammar and Language Workbook TAE 🗀 Revising with Style ▌ Spelling Power SE ▌ Spelling Power TAE
Daily Writing	**TE** p. 266 **SE/TE** p. 276
Interdisciplinary Connections	**SE/TE** View the Art, pp. 263, 266, 270 **TE** Literary History: The Gothic Tradition, p. 264 **TE** Literary History: The Detective Story, p. 268 ▶ glencoe.com
Independent Reading	● BookLink K–12 CD-ROM 📖 Ethnic Anthologies 📖 Glencoe Literature Library ● Glencoe Literature Library Teacher Resources CD-ROM 📖 *inTIME* magazine ● ▶ Literature Classics, High School CD-ROM
Technology and Additional Resources	**Planning and Instruction:** ● TeacherWorks Plus CD-ROM ● Classroom Presentation Toolkit CD-ROM ▶ Literature Online at **glencoe.com** (QuickPass Code: **GLA9879u2T**) **Students Tools:** ● StudentWorks Plus CD-ROM or DVD-ROM ▶ Online Student Edition at **glencoe.com** ▶ Literature Online at **glencoe.com** (QuickPass Code: **GLA9800u2**)

Lesson Plan

Glencoe Literature

The Minister's Black Veil and Grammar Workshop (pp. 278–293)

Lesson Plan and Resource Manager

UNIT TWO American Romanticism, 1800–1860, Part 2: The Dark Side of Romanticism

Learning Objectives	**Literary Study:** Analyzing symbols. **Reading:** Making inferences about theme. **Writing:** Writing an expository essay. **Grammar:** Using comparative and superlative forms of modifiers. Understanding how to avoid misplaced and dangling modifiers.

Lesson Summary	On pages **278–292** of the Student Edition, students will be introduced to the following:
	    ▪ **Big Idea:** The Power of Darkness
	    ▪ **Literary Element:** Symbol
	    ▪ **Reading Strategy:** Make Inferences
	    ▪ **Vocabulary:** Synonyms, Academic Vocabulary
	    ▪ **Writing Activity/Grammar:** Expository Essay, Degrees of Comparison
	On page **293** of the Student Edition, students will be introduced to the following:
	    ▪ **Grammar Workshop:** Misplaced and Dangling Modifiers

Lesson Duration	Two 45–50 minute sessions
Readability Scores	"The Minister's Black Veil" Dale-Chall: 8.0 DRP: 66 Lexile: 1240

Focus	**SE/TE** pp. 278–279, 293
	  Selection Focus Transparency 19
	  Daily Language Practice Transparency 28

Teach	**SE/TE** pp. 280–289, 293
	  Unit 2 Teaching Resources, Literary Element, p. 145
	  Unit 2 Teaching Resources, Reading Strategy, p. 146
	  Unit 2 Teaching Resources, Selection Vocabulary Practice, p. 147
	  Unit 2 Teaching Resources, Vocabulary Strategy, p. 148
	  Unit 2 Teaching Resources, Grammar Practice, p. 149
	  Literary Elements Transparency 100
	  Classroom Presentation Toolkit CD-ROM
	  Listening Library CD, Selection Audio
	  TeacherWorks Plus CD-ROM
	  Vocabulary PuzzleMaker CD-ROM

Assess	**SE/TE** pp. 290–292, 293
	  Unit 2 Teaching Resources, Selection Quick Check, p. 150
	  Unit 2 Teaching Resources, Selection Quick Check (Spanish), p. 151
	  Assessment Resources, Selection Test, pp. 115–116
	  ExamView Assessment Suite CD-ROM
	  Progress Reporter Online Assessment

Copyright © by The McGraw-Hill Companies, Inc.

Differentiated Instruction: English Learners	**TE** English Learner Activities, pp. 278–293 📁 Unit 2 Teaching Resources, English Language Coach, p. 100 📁 Unit 2 Teaching Resources, Selection Summaries: English, Spanish, Vietnamese, Tagalog, Cantonese, Haitian Creole, and Hmong, pp. 139–144 📁 Unit 2 Teaching Resources, Selection Quick Check (Spanish), p. 151 📁 English Language Coach 💿 Glencoe Interactive Vocabulary CD-ROM 💿 Listening Library Audio CD 📁 Listening Library Sourcebook: Strategies and Activities
Differentiated Instruction: Approaching Level	**TE** Approaching Level Activities, pp. 278–293 💿 Glencoe Interactive Vocabulary CD-ROM 💿 Listening Library Audio CD 📁 Listening Library Sourcebook: Strategies and Activities 💿 Skill Level Up! A Skills-Based Language Arts Game CD-ROM
Differentiated Instruction: Advanced/Pre-AP	**TE** Advanced Learner Activities, pp. 278–293 📖 Novel Companion SE, pp. 75–118 📖 Novel Companion TG, pp. 21–28 💿 ▶ Literature Classics, High School CD-ROM 💿 Skill Level Up! A Skills-Based Language Arts Game CD-ROM
Extension	📖 Grammar and Language Workbook SE 📖 Grammar and Language Workbook TAE 📁 Revising with Style 📖 Spelling Power SE 📖 Spelling Power TAE
Daily Writing	**TE** p. 288 **SE/TE** p. 292
Interdisciplinary Connections	**SE/TE** View the Art, pp. 283, 287 **TE** Cultural History: Architecture, p. 280 **TE** Literary History: Hawthorne and Original Sin, p. 282 **TE** Cultural History: Early Puritanism, p. 285 **TE** Literary History: Hawthorne's Sources, p. 286 ▶ glencoe.com
Independent Reading	💿 BookLink K–12 CD-ROM 📖 Ethnic Anthologies 📖 Glencoe Literature Library 💿 Glencoe Literature Library Teacher Resources CD-ROM 📖 inTIME magazine 💿 ▶ Literature Classics, High School CD-ROM
Technology and Additional Resources	**Planning and Instruction:** 💿 TeacherWorks Plus CD-ROM 💿 Classroom Presentation Toolkit CD-ROM ▶ Literature Online at **glencoe.com** (QuickPass Code: **GLA9879u2T**) **Students Tools:** 💿 StudentWorks Plus CD-ROM or DVD-ROM ▶ Online Student Edition at **glencoe.com** ▶ Literature Online at **glencoe.com** (QuickPass Code: **GLA9800u2**)

Lesson Plan

Glencoe Literature

from *Moby-Dick* (pp. 294–305)

Lesson Plan and Resource Manager

UNIT TWO American Romanticism, 1800–1860, Part 2: The Dark Side of Romanticism

Learning Objectives	**Literary Study:** Analyzing motivation. **Reading:** Monitoring comprehension. **Writing:** Writing a literary critical response.
Lesson Summary	On pages **294–305** of the Student Edition, students will be introduced to the following: ▪ **Big Idea:** The Power of Darkness ▪ **Literary Element:** Motivation ▪ **Reading Strategies:** Monitor Comprehension, Preview ▪ **Vocabulary:** Antonyms ▪ **Writing Activities/Grammar:** Literary Criticism, Character Sketch ▪ **Listening/Speaking/Viewing Skills:** Analyze Art, Dramatic Presentation
Lesson Duration	One 45–50 minute session
Readability Scores	Dale-Chall: 9.0 DRP: 67 Lexile: 1150
Focus	**SE/TE** pp. 294–295 ⬛ Daily Language Practice Transparency 29
Teach	**SE/TE** pp. 296–303 📁 Unit 2 Teaching Resources, Literary Element, p. 159 📁 Unit 2 Teaching Resources, Reading Strategy, p. 160 📁 Unit 2 Teaching Resources, Selection Vocabulary Practice, p. 161 📁 Unit 2 Teaching Resources, Vocabulary Strategy, p. 162 📁 Unit 2 Teaching Resources, Grammar Practice, p. 163 ⬛ Read Aloud, Think Aloud Transparencies 11–14 ⬛ Literary Elements Transparency 65 💿 Classroom Presentation Toolkit CD-ROM 💿 Listening Library CD, Selection Audio 💿 TeacherWorks Plus CD-ROM 💿 Vocabulary PuzzleMaker CD-ROM
Assess	**SE/TE** pp. 304–305 📁 Unit 2 Teaching Resources, Selection Quick Check, p. 164 📁 Unit 2 Teaching Resources, Selection Quick Check (Spanish), p. 165 📁 Assessment Resources, Selection Test, pp. 117–118 💿 ExamView Assessment Suite CD-ROM 💿 Progress Reporter Online Assessment
Differentiated Instruction: English Learners	**TE** English Learner Activities, pp. 294–305 📁 Unit 2 Teaching Resources, Selection Summaries: English, Spanish, Vietnamese, Tagalog, Cantonese, Haitian Creole, and Hmong, pp. 153–158 📁 Unit 2 Teaching Resources, Selection Quick Check (Spanish), p. 165 📁 English Language Coach

Copyright © by The McGraw-Hill Companies, Inc.

Differentiated Instruction: English Learners *(continued)*	💿 Glencoe Interactive Vocabulary CD-ROM 💿 Listening Library Audio CD 📁 Listening Library Sourcebook: Strategies and Activities
Differentiated Instruction: Approaching Level	**TE** Approaching Level Activities, pp. 294–305 💿 Glencoe Interactive Vocabulary CD-ROM 💿 Listening Library Audio CD 📁 Listening Library Sourcebook: Strategies and Activities 💿 Skill Level Up! A Skills-Based Language Arts Game CD-ROM
Differentiated Instruction: Advanced/Pre-AP	**TE** Advanced Learner Activities, pp. 294–305 📘 Novel Companion SE, pp. 75–118 📘 Novel Companion TG, pp. 21–28 💿 ▶ Literature Classics, High School CD-ROM 💿 Skill Level Up! A Skills-Based Language Arts Game CD-ROM
Extension	📘 Grammar and Language Workbook SE 📘 Grammar and Language Workbook TAE 📁 Revising with Style 📘 Spelling Power SE 📘 Spelling Power TAE
Daily Writing	**TE** p. 298
Interdisciplinary Connections	**SE/TE** View the Art, p. 300 **TE** Cultural History: Ship's Captain, p. 297 **TE** Literary History: The Pequod, p. 298 **TE** Cultural History: Movies, p. 303 **TE** Cultural History, p. 309 ▶ glencoe.com
Independent Reading	💿 BookLink K–12 CD-ROM 📖 Ethnic Anthologies 📖 Glencoe Literature Library 💿 Glencoe Literature Library Teacher Resources CD-ROM 📖 *inTIME* magazine 💿 ▶ Literature Classics, High School CD-ROM
Technology and Additional Resources	**Planning and Instruction:** 💿 TeacherWorks Plus CD-ROM 💿 Classroom Presentation Toolkit CD-ROM ▶ Literature Online at **glencoe.com** (QuickPass Code: **GLA9879u2T**) **Students Tools:** 💿 StudentWorks Plus CD-ROM or DVD-ROM ▶ Online Student Edition at **glencoe.com** ▶ Literature Online at **glencoe.com** (QuickPass Code: **GLA9800u2**)

Lesson Plan

Glencoe Literature

Historical Perspective: from *In the Heart of the Sea* (pp. 306–309)

Lesson Plan and Resource Manager

UNIT TWO American Romanticism, 1800–1860, Part 2: The Dark Side of Romanticism

Learning Objectives	**Literary Study:** Analyzing historical context. **Reading:** Analyzing informational text.

Lesson Summary	On pages **306–309** of the Student Edition, students will be introduced to the following:
	  • **Big Idea:** The Power of Darkness
	  • **Reading Strategy:** Analyze Historical Context

Lesson Duration	One 45–50 minute session
Readability Scores	Dale-Chall: 9.0 DRP: 67 Lexile: 1150
Focus	SE/TE p. 306
Teach	SE/TE pp. 306–309 📁 Unit 2 Teaching Resources, Reading Strategy, p. 172 🎙 Read Aloud, Think Aloud Transparencies 11–14 🎙 Literary Elements Transparency 65 💿 Classroom Presentation Toolkit CD-ROM 💿 Listening Library CD, Selection Audio 💿 TeacherWorks Plus CD-ROM 💿 ▶ Vocabulary PuzzleMaker CD-ROM
Assess	SE/TE p. 309 📁 Unit 2 Teaching Resources, Selection Quick Check, p. 173 📁 Unit 2 Teaching Resources, Selection Quick Check (Spanish), p. 174 📁 Assessment Resources, Selection Test, pp. 119–120 💿 ExamView Assessment Suite CD-ROM ▶ Progress Reporter Online Assessment
Differentiated Instruction: English Learners	TE English Learner Activities, pp. 306–309 📁 Unit 2 Teaching Resources, Selection Summaries: English, Spanish, Vietnamese, Tagalog, Cantonese, Haitian Creole, and Hmong, pp. 166–171 📁 Unit 2 Teaching Resources, Selection Quick Check (Spanish), p. 174 📁 English Language Coach 💿 Glencoe Interactive Vocabulary CD-ROM 💿 Listening Library Audio CD 📁 Listening Library Sourcebook: Strategies and Activities
Differentiated Instruction: Approaching Level	TE Approaching Level Activities, pp. 306–309 💿 Glencoe Interactive Vocabulary CD-ROM 💿 Listening Library Audio CD 📁 Listening Library Sourcebook: Strategies and Activities 💿 Skill Level Up! A Skills-Based Language Arts Game CD-ROM

Differentiated Instruction: Advanced/Pre-AP	▮ Novel Companion SE, pp. 75–118
	▮ Novel Companion TG, pp. 21–28
	◉ ▶ Literature Classics, High School CD-ROM
	◉ Skill Level Up! A Skills-Based Language Arts Game CD-ROM
Extension	▮ Grammar and Language Workbook SE
	▮ Grammar and Language Workbook TAE
	▭ Revising with Style
	▮ Spelling Power SE
	▮ Spelling Power TAE
Daily Writing	**TE** p. 308
Interdisciplinary Connections	**SE/TE** View the Art, p. 307
	TE Cross-Curricular Link: Biology, p. 308
	TE Cultural History, p. 309
	▶ glencoe.com
Independent Reading	◉ BookLink K–12 CD-ROM
	▯ Ethnic Anthologies
	▯ Glencoe Literature Library
	◉ Glencoe Literature Library Teacher Resources CD-ROM
	▯ *inTIME* magazine
	◉ ▶ Literature Classics, High School CD-ROM
Technology and Additional Resources	**Planning and Instruction:**
	◉ TeacherWorks Plus CD-ROM
	◉ Classroom Presentation Toolkit CD-ROM
	▶ Literature Online at **glencoe.com** (QuickPass Code: **GLA9879u2T**)
	Students Tools:
	◉ StudentWorks Plus CD-ROM or DVD-ROM
	▶ Online Student Edition at **glencoe.com**
	▶ Literature Online at **glencoe.com** (QuickPass Code: **GLA9800u2**)

Lesson Plan

Glencoe Literature

Writing Workshop: Reflective Essay (pp. 310–317)

Lesson Plan and Resource Manager

UNIT TWO American Romanticism, 1800–1860

Learning Objectives	**Writing:** Writing a reflective essay using the writing process.
Lesson Duration	Two 45–50 minute sessions
Writing Prompt	Write a reflective essay of about 1,500 words that describes one of your experiences and expresses the insight you gained. As you work, keep your audience and purpose in mind.
Focus	**SE/TE** p. 310
Teach	**SE/TE** pp. 311–317 Writing Resources: Writing Process Strategies 1–23 Writing Workshop Transparencies 11–15 Unit 2 Teaching Resources, Writing Workshop Activity, p. 176
Assess	Unit 2 Teaching Resources, Writing Workshop Rubric, pp. 177–178 Rubrics for Assessing Writing, Listening and Speaking, High School, Reflective Essay, pp. 10–11 Glencoe Online Essay Grader at **glencoewriting.com**
Differentiated Instruction: English Learners	**TE** English Learner Activities, pp. 310–317
Differentiated Instruction: Approaching Level	**TE** Approaching Level Activities, pp. 310–317
Differentiated Instruction: Advanced/Pre-AP	Novel Companion SE, pp. 75–118 Novel Companion TG, pp. 21–28
Extension	Grammar and Language Workbook SE Grammar and Language Workbook TAE Revising with Style Spelling Power SE Spelling Power TAE
Daily Writing	**SE/TE** pp. 314, 317
Interdisciplinary Connections	**TE** Cross-Curricular Link: Biology, p. 312 glencoe.com

Technology and Additional Resources	**Planning and Instruction:**
	📖 Grammar and Composition Handbook
	📁 Success in Writing: Research and Reports
	📁 Writing Constructed Responses
	💿 TeacherWorks Plus CD-ROM
	💿 Classroom Presentation Toolkit CD-ROM
	▶ Glencoe Online Essay Grader at **glencoewriting.com**
	▶ Literature Online at **glencoe.com** (QuickPass Code: **GLA9879u2T**)
	Students Tools:
	💿 StudentWorks Plus CD-ROM or DVD-ROM
	▶ Online Student Edition at **glencoe.com**
	▶ Glencoe Online Essay Grader at **glencoewriting.com**
	▶ Literature Online at **glencoe.com** (QuickPass Code: **GLA9800u2**)

Lesson Plan

Speaking, Listening, and Viewing Workshop: Reflective Presentation (pp. 318–319)

Lesson Plan and Resource Manager

UNIT TWO American Romanticism, 1800–1860

Learning Objectives	**Speaking and Listening:** Delivering a reflective presentation.
Lesson Duration	One 45–50 minute session
Assignment	Present your reflective essay to the class.
Focus	**SE/TE** p. 318
Teach	**SE/TE** pp. 318–319 Unit 2 Teaching Resources, SLV Activity, pp. 179–180 TeacherWorks Plus CD-ROM Classroom Presentation Toolkit CD-ROM Student Presentation Builder on StudentWorks Plus CD-ROM or DVD-ROM
Assess	Unit 2 Teaching Resources, SLV Rubrics, pp. 181–182 Rubrics for Assessing Writing, Listening, and Speaking, Presenting a Reflection, pp. 30–31
Differentiated Instruction: English Learners	**TE** English Learner Activities, pp. 318–319
Differentiated Instruction: Approaching Level	**TE** Approaching Level Activities, pp. 318–319
Differentiated Instruction: Advanced/Pre-AP	Novel Companion SE, pp. 75–118 Novel Companion TG, pp. 21–28
Daily Writing	**SE/TE** p. 318
Interdisciplinary Connections	glencoe.com
Technology and Additional Resources	**Planning and Instruction:** TeacherWorks Plus CD-ROM Classroom Presentation Toolkit CD-ROM Glencoe Online Essay Grader at **glencoewriting.com** Literature Online at **glencoe.com** (QuickPass Code: **GLA9879u2T**) **Students Tools:** Student Presentation Builder on StudentWorks Plus CD-ROM or DVD-ROM StudentWorks Plus CD-ROM or DVD-ROM Online Student Edition at **glencoe.com** Glencoe Online Essay Grader at **glencoewriting.com** Literature Online at **glencoe.com** (QuickPass Code: **GLA9800u2**)

Lesson Plan

Glencoe Literature

Unit 2 Wrap-Up (pp. 320–327)

Lesson Plan and Resource Manager

UNIT TWO American Romanticism, 1800–1860

Lesson Summary	On pages **164–171** of the Student Edition, students will be introduced to the following: • Read independently • Complete the end-of-unit assessment
Lesson Duration	Independent Reading: One 45–50 minute session Assessment: One 45–50 minute session
Focus	**SE/TE** Independent Reading, p. 320 **SE/TE** Assessment, p. 322
Teach	**SE/TE** Independent Reading, pp. 320–321 **SE/TE** Assessment, p. 322
Assess	**SE/TE** Assessment, pp. 323–327 📁 Assessment Resources, Unit 2 Summative Assessment, pp. 333–334 📕 ACT/SAT Preparation and Practice SE/ATE ⊙ ExamView Assessment Suite CD-ROM ▶ Progress Reporter Online Assessment
Differentiated Instruction: English Learners	**TE** English Learner Activities, pp. 320–327
Differentiated Instruction: Advanced/Pre-AP	📕 Novel Companion SE, pp. 75–118 📕 Novel Companion TG, pp. 21–28 ⊙ ▶ Literature Classics, High School CD-ROM
Daily Writing	**SE/TE** pp. 321, 327
Interdisciplinary Connections	**TE** Literary History: Clarissa, p. 320
Independent Reading	**TE** pp. 320–321 ⊙ BookLink K–12 CD-ROM; Glencoe Literature Library Teacher Resources CD-ROM 📖 Ethnic Anthologies; Glencoe Literature Library; *inTIME* magazine ⊙ ▶ Literature Classics, High School CD-ROM
Technology and Additional Resources	**Planning and Instruction:** ⊙ TeacherWorks Plus CD-ROM ⊙ Classroom Presentation Toolkit CD-ROM ▶ Literature Online at **glencoe.com** (QuickPass Code: **GLA9879u2T**) **Students Tools:** ⊙ StudentWorks Plus CD-ROM or DVD-ROM ▶ Online Student Edition at **glencoe.com** ▶ Glencoe Online Essay Grader at **glencoewriting.com** ▶ Literature Online at **glencoe.com** (QuickPass Code: **GLA9800u2**)

Lesson Plan

Unit 3 Introduction (pp. 328–342)

Lesson Plan and Resource Manager

UNIT THREE The Civil War Era, 1850–1880

Learning Objectives	**Literary Studies:** Analyzing literary periods. Evaluating historical influences. **Reading:** Connecting to the literature.

Unit Summary	In this unit, students will be introduced to the following:
	• **Big Ideas:** Part 1: Resistance to Slavery
	      Part 2: A Nation Divided
	      Part 3: A Poetic Revolution
	• **Reading Strategies:** Analyze Graphic Information, Analyze Author's Purpose, Summarize Main Idea, Analyze Imagery and Metaphor, Analyze Cause and Effect, Use Bar Graphs
	• **Literary Elements:** Imagery, Metaphor, Allusion, Poetic Language
	• **Writing Activities:** Summarize, Write an Essay
	• **Listening/Speaking/Viewing Skills:** Give an Oral Interpretation, Create a Timeline, Analyze Art

Lesson Duration	Two 45–50 minute sessions
Focus	**SE/TE** pp. 328–329 📖 Daily Language Practice Transparency 30 ⦿ Literature Launchers: Pre-Reading Videos DVD, Unit 3 Launcher 🗂 Literature Launchers Teacher Guide
Teach	**SE/TE** pp. 330–341 🗂 Unit 3 Teaching Resources, Unit Introduction, pp. 1–2 🗂 Unit 3 Teaching Resources, Big Idea Foldable, pp. 3–4 🗂 Unit 3 Teaching Resources, Big Idea School-to-Home Connection, p. 5 🗂 Unit 3 Teaching Resources, Unit Challenge Planner, pp. 12–15 🗂 Unit 3 Teaching Resources: Academic Vocabulary Development, pp. 16–17 ⦿ Classroom Presentation Toolkit CD-ROM ⦿ TeacherWorks Plus CD-ROM
Assess	**SE/TE** p. 342 🗂 Assessment Resources, Unit 3 Diagnostic Assessment, pp. 17–24 📕 ACT/SAT Preparation and Practice SE/ATE ⦿ ExamView Assessment Suite CD-ROM ⦿ Progress Reporter Online Assessment
Differentiated Instruction: English Learners	**TE** English Learner Activities, pp. 328–342 🗂 Unit 3 Teaching Resources, Big Idea School-to-Home Connections: English, Spanish, Vietnamese, Tagalog, Cantonese, Haitian Creole, and Hmong, pp. 6–11
Differentiated Instruction: Approaching Level	**TE** Approaching Level Activities, pp. 328–342 ⦿ Skill Level Up! A Skills-Based Language Arts Game CD-ROM

Differentiated Instruction: Advanced/Pre-AP	**TE** Advanced Learner Activities, pp. 328–342 Novel Companion SE, pp. 119–162 Novel Companion TG, pp. 29–36 Literature Classics, High School CD-ROM Skill Level Up! A Skills-Based Language Arts Game CD-ROM
Extension	Grammar and Language Workbook SE Grammar and Language Workbook TAE Revising with Style Spelling Power SE Spelling Power TAE
Daily Writing	**TE** pp. 334, 338
Interdisciplinary Connections	**TE** Literary History, pp. 330, 331, 340 **TE** Political History: Economy and War, pp. 332, 335, 338 **SE/TE** View the Art, pp. 328, 333, 337, 341 **SE/TE** View the Photograph, pp. 334, 339 glencoe.com
Independent Reading	BookLink K–12 CD-ROM Ethnic Anthologies Glencoe Literature Library Glencoe Literature Library Teacher Resources CD-ROM *inTIME* magazine Literature Classics, High School CD-ROM
Technology and Additional Resources	**Planning and Instruction:** TeacherWorks Plus CD-ROM Classroom Presentation Toolkit CD-ROM Literature Online at **glencoe.com** (QuickPass Code: **GLA9879u3T**) **Students Tools:** StudentWorks Plus CD-ROM or DVD-ROM Online Student Edition at **glencoe.com** Literature Online at **glencoe.com** (QuickPass Code: **GLA9800u3**)

Lesson Plan

Glencoe Literature

Part 1 Opener and Three Spirituals: *Swing Low, Sweet Chariot; Go Down, Moses;* and *Keep Your Hand on the Plow* (pp. 343–349)

Lesson Plan and Resource Manager

UNIT THREE The Civil War Era 1850–1880, Part 1: Resistance to Slavery

Learning Objectives	**Literary Study:** Analyzing repetition. **Reading:** Author's historical context. **Writing:** Writing a list.
Lesson Summary	On pages **343–349** of the Student Edition, students will be introduced to the following: • **Big Idea:** Resistance to Slavery • **Literary Element:** Refrain • **Reading Strategy:** Analyze Historical Context • **Vocabulary:** Academic Vocabulary • **Writing Activity:** Write a List • **Listening/Speaking/Viewing Skill:** Analyze Art
Lesson Duration	One 45–50 minute session
Readability Scores	Dale-Chall: N/A DRP: N/A Lexile: N/A
Focus	**SE/TE** pp. 344–345 Selection Focus Transparency 20 Daily Language Practice Transparency 31
Teach	**SE/TE** pp. 346–348 Unit 3 Teaching Resources, Literary Element, p. 26 Unit 3 Teaching Resources, Reading Strategy, p. 27 Literary Elements Transparency 83 Classroom Presentation Toolkit CD-ROM Listening Library CD, Selection Audio TeacherWorks Plus CD-ROM Vocabulary PuzzleMaker CD-ROM
Assess	**SE/TE** p. 349 Unit 3 Teaching Resources, Selection Quick Check, p. 28 Unit 3 Teaching Resources, Selection Quick Check (Spanish), p. 29 Assessment Resources, Selection Test, pp. 121–122 ExamView Assessment Suite CD-ROM Progress Reporter Online Assessment
Differentiated Instruction: English Learners	**TE** English Learner Activities, pp. 343–349 Unit 3 Teaching Resources, English Language Coach, p. 19 Unit 3 Teaching Resources, Selection Summaries: English, Spanish, Vietnamese, Tagalog, Cantonese, Haitian Creole, and Hmong, pp. 20–25 Unit 3 Teaching Resources, Selection Quick Check (Spanish), p. 29 English Language Coach

Differentiated Instruction: English Learners *(continued)*	• Glencoe Interactive Vocabulary CD-ROM • Listening Library Audio CD • Listening Library Sourcebook: Strategies and Activities
Differentiated Instruction: Approaching Level	**TE** Approaching Level Activities, pp. 343–349 • Glencoe Interactive Vocabulary CD-ROM • Listening Library Audio CD • Listening Library Sourcebook: Strategies and Activities • Skill Level Up! A Skills-Based Language Arts Game CD-ROM
Differentiated Instruction: Advanced/Pre-AP	• Novel Companion SE, pp. 119–162 • Novel Companion TG, pp. 29–36 • Literature Classics, High School CD-ROM • Skill Level Up! A Skills-Based Language Arts Game CD-ROM
Extension	• Grammar and Language Workbook SE • Grammar and Language Workbook TAE • Revising with Style • Spelling Power SE • Spelling Power TAE
Daily Writing	**SE/TE** p. 349
Interdisciplinary Connections	**TE** View the Art, pp. 343, 346, 347, 348 **TE** Literary History, p. 345 • glencoe.com
Independent Reading	• BookLink K–12 CD-ROM • Ethnic Anthologies • Glencoe Literature Library • Glencoe Literature Library Teacher Resources CD-ROM • *inTIME* magazine • Literature Classics, High School CD-ROM
Technology and Additional Resources	**Planning and Instruction:** • TeacherWorks Plus CD-ROM • Classroom Presentation Toolkit CD-ROM • Literature Online at **glencoe.com** (QuickPass Code: **GLA9879u3T**) **Students Tools:** • StudentWorks Plus CD-ROM or DVD-ROM • Online Student Edition at **glencoe.com** • Literature Online at **glencoe.com** (QuickPass Code: **GLA9800u3**)

Lesson Plan

Glencoe Literature Essential Course of Study

Comparing Literature: from *My Bondage and My Freedom*, *Frederick Douglass*, and *In Texas Grass* (pp. 350–361)

Lesson Plan and Resource Manager

UNIT THREE The Civil War Era 1850–1880, Part 1: Resistance to Slavery

Learning Objectives	**Literary Study:** Comparing cultural contexts. Comparing historical contexts.
Lesson Summary	On pages **350–361** of the Student Edition, students will be introduced to the following: • **Big Idea:** Resistance to Slavery • **Literary Element:** Autobiography • **Reading Strategy:** Analyze Cause and Effect • **Vocabulary:** Transitive Verbs, Connotation, Denotation • **Writing Activities:** Write a Dialogue, Write About Literature • **Listening/Speaking/Viewing Skill:** Analyze Art
Lesson Duration	Two to five 45–50 minute sessions
Readability Scores	"My Bondage and My Freedom" Dale-Chall: 6.6 DRP: 63 Lexile: 1160
Focus	**SE/TE** pp. 350–352, 359, 360 Selection Focus Transparency 21 Daily Language Practice Transparency 32 Literature Launchers: Pre-Reading Videos DVD, Selection Launcher Literature Launchers Teacher Guide
Teach	**SE/TE** pp. 353–357, 359, 360 Interactive Read and Write SE/TE, pp. 99–114 Unit 3 Teaching Resources, Comparing Literature: Graphic Organizer, p. 30 Unit 3 Teaching Resources, Literary Element, p. 37 Unit 3 Teaching Resources, Reading Strategy, p. 38 Unit 3 Teaching Resources, Selection Vocabulary Practice, p. 39 Unit 3 Teaching Resources, Vocabulary Strategy, p. 40 Unit 3 Teaching Resources, Grammar Practice, p. 41 Literary Elements Transparency 16 Classroom Presentation Toolkit CD-ROM Listening Library CD, Selection Audio TeacherWorks Plus CD-ROM Vocabulary PuzzleMaker CD-ROM
Assess	**SE/TE** pp. 358, 361 Unit 3 Teaching Resources, Selection Quick Check, p. 42 Unit 3 Teaching Resources, Selection Quick Check (Spanish), p. 43 Assessment Resources, Selection Test, pp. 123–124 ExamView Assessment Suite CD-ROM Progress Reporter Online Assessment

Differentiated Instruction: English Learners	**TE** English Learner Activities, pp. 350–361 ■ Interactive Read and Write (EL) SE/TE, pp. 99–114 📁 Unit 3 Teaching Resources, English Language Coach, p. 19 📁 Unit 3 Teaching Resources, Selection Summaries: English, Spanish, Vietnamese, Tagalog, Cantonese, Haitian Creole, and Hmong, pp. 31–36 📁 Unit 3 Teaching Resources, Selection Quick Check (Spanish), p. 43 📁 English Language Coach 💿 Glencoe Interactive Vocabulary CD-ROM 💿 Listening Library Audio CD 📁 Listening Library Sourcebook: Strategies and Activities
Differentiated Instruction: Approaching Level	**TE** Approaching Level Activities, pp. 350–361 ■ Interactive Read and Write (Approaching) SE/TE, pp. 99–114 💿 Glencoe Interactive Vocabulary CD-ROM 💿 Listening Library Audio CD 📁 Listening Library Sourcebook: Strategies and Activities 💿 Skill Level Up! A Skills-Based Language Arts Game CD-ROM
Differentiated Instruction: Advanced/Pre-AP	**TE** Advanced Learner Activities, pp. 350–361 ■ Novel Companion SE, pp. 119–162 ■ Novel Companion TG, pp. 29–36 💿 ▶ Literature Classics, High School CD-ROM 💿 Skill Level Up! A Skills-Based Language Arts Game CD-ROM
Extension	■ Grammar and Language Workbook SE ■ Grammar and Language Workbook TAE 📁 Revising with Style ■ Spelling Power SE ■ Spelling Power TAE
Daily Writing	**SE/TE** pp. 358, 361
Interdisciplinary Connections	**SE/TE** View the Art, pp. 355, 361 **TE** Political History, pp. 351, 357 **TE** Literary History, pp. 356, 359 💿 **glencoe.com**
Independent Reading	💿 BookLink K–12 CD-ROM 📖 Ethnic Anthologies 📖 Glencoe Literature Library 💿 Glencoe Literature Library Teacher Resources CD-ROM 📖 *inTIME* magazine 💿 ▶ Literature Classics, High School CD-ROM
Technology and Additional Resources	**Planning and Instruction:** 💿 TeacherWorks Plus CD-ROM 💿 Classroom Presentation Toolkit CD-ROM ▶ Literature Online at **glencoe.com** (QuickPass Code: **GLA9879u3T**) **Students Tools:** 💿 StudentWorks Plus CD-ROM or DVD-ROM ▶ Online Student Edition at **glencoe.com** ▶ Literature Online at **glencoe.com** (QuickPass Code: **GLA9800u3**)

Lesson Plan

Glencoe Literature

Literary History: Slave Narratives and Civil War Memoirs, Letters, and Diaries; and TIME: *Slavery Under Glass* (pp. 362–367)

Lesson Plan and Resource Manager

UNIT THREE The Civil War Era 1850–1880, Part 1: Resistance to Slavery

Learning Objectives	**Literary Study:** Analyzing literary periods. **Reading:** Evaluating historical influences. Analyzing and evaluating informational text. Connecting to contemporary issues.
Lesson Summary	On pages **362–367** of the Student Edition, students will be introduced to the following: ▪ **Big Idea:** Resistance to Slavery ▪ **Reading Strategies:** Question, Connect ▪ **Writing Activity:** Journal Entry
Lesson Duration	One 45–50 minute session
Readability Scores	Dale-Chall: 8.8 DRP: 68 Lexile: 1240
Focus	**SE/TE** pp. 362, 364 🖌 Daily Language Practice Transparency 33
Teach	**SE/TE** pp. 363, 365–366 📁 Unit 3 Teaching Resources, Literary History: Slave Narratives, pp. 44–45 📁 Unit 3 Teaching Resources, Reading Strategy, p. 52 💿 Classroom Presentation Toolkit CD-ROM 💿 Listening Library CD, Selection Audio 💿 TeacherWorks Plus CD-ROM 💿 ▶ Vocabulary PuzzleMaker CD-ROM
Assess	**SE/TE** pp. 363, 367 📁 Unit 3 Teaching Resources, Selection Quick Check, p. 53 📁 Unit 3 Teaching Resources, Selection Quick Check (Spanish), p. 54 📁 Assessment Resources, Selection Test, pp. 125–126 💿 ExamView Assessment Suite CD-ROM ▶ Progress Reporter Online Assessment
Differentiated Instruction: English Learners	📁 Unit 3 Teaching Resources, English Language Coach, p. 19 📁 Unit 3 Teaching Resources, Selection Summaries: English, Spanish, Vietnamese, Tagalog, Cantonese, Haitian Creole, and Hmong, pp. 46–51 📁 Unit 3 Teaching Resources, Selection Quick Check (Spanish), p. 54 💿 Glencoe Interactive Vocabulary CD-ROM 💿 Listening Library Audio CD 📁 Listening Library Sourcebook: Strategies and Activities

Differentiated Instruction: Approaching Level	TE Approaching Level Activities, pp. 362–367
	Glencoe Interactive Vocabulary CD-ROM
	Listening Library Audio CD
	Listening Library Sourcebook: Strategies and Activities
	Skill Level Up! A Skills-Based Language Arts Game CD-ROM
Differentiated Instruction: Advanced/Pre-AP	TE Advanced Learner Activities, pp. 362–367
	Novel Companion SE, pp. 119–162
	Novel Companion TG, pp. 29–36
	Literature Classics, High School CD-ROM
	Skill Level Up! A Skills-Based Language Arts Game CD-ROM
Extension	Grammar and Language Workbook SE
	Grammar and Language Workbook TAE
	Revising with Style
	Spelling Power SE
	Spelling Power TAE
Daily Writing	SE/TE p. 366
Interdisciplinary Connections	SE/TE View the Photograph, pp. 362, 363, 366
	TE Political History, p. 365
	glencoe.com
Independent Reading	BookLink K–12 CD-ROM
	Ethnic Anthologies
	Glencoe Literature Library
	Glencoe Literature Library Teacher Resources CD-ROM
	inTIME magazine
	Literature Classics, High School CD-ROM
Technology and Additional Resources	**Planning and Instruction:**
	TeacherWorks Plus CD-ROM
	Classroom Presentation Toolkit CD-ROM
	Literature Online at **glencoe.com** (QuickPass Code: **GLA9879u3T**)
	Students Tools:
	StudentWorks Plus CD-ROM or DVD-ROM
	Online Student Edition at **glencoe.com**
	Literature Online at **glencoe.com** (QuickPass Code: **GLA9800u3**)

Lesson Plan

Glencoe Literature

And Ain't I a Woman? and Vocabulary Workshop (pp. 368–372)

Lesson Plan and Resource Manager

UNIT THREE The Civil War Era 1850–1880, Part 1: Resistance to Slavery

Learning Objectives	**Literary Study:** Analyzing oratory. **Reading:** Evaluating argument. **Writing:** Writing a speech. **Vocabulary:** Understanding denotation and connotation.
Lesson Summary	On pages **368–372** of the Student Edition, students will be introduced to the following: ▪ **Big Idea:** Resistance to Slavery ▪ **Literary Element:** Oratory ▪ **Reading Strategy:** Evaluate Argument ▪ **Vocabulary:** Word Usage, Multiple Meanings, Denotation and Connotation ▪ **Writing Activity:** Persuasive Speech
Lesson Duration	One to five 45–50 minute sessions
Readability Scores	Dale-Chall: 3.7 DRP: 49 Lexile: 750
Focus	**SE/TE** pp. 368–369, 372 Selection Focus Transparency 22 Daily Language Practice Transparency 34 Literature Launchers: Pre-Reading Videos DVD, Selection Launcher Literature Launchers Teacher Guide
Teach	**SE/TE** pp. 370, 372 Interactive Read and Write SE/TE, pp. 115–122 Unit 3 Teaching Resources, Literary Element, p. 61 Unit 3 Teaching Resources, Reading Strategy, p. 62 Unit 3 Teaching Resources, Vocabulary Strategy, p. 63 Unit 3 Teaching Resources, Grammar Practice, p. 64 Read Aloud, Think Aloud Transparencies 15–16 Literary Elements Transparency 72 Classroom Presentation Toolkit CD-ROM Listening Library CD, Selection Audio TeacherWorks Plus CD-ROM Vocabulary PuzzleMaker CD-ROM
Assess	**SE/TE** pp. 371, 372 Unit 3 Teaching Resources, Selection Quick Check, p. 65 Unit 3 Teaching Resources, Selection Quick Check (Spanish), p. 66 Assessment Resources, Selection Test, pp. 127–128 ExamView Assessment Suite CD-ROM Progress Reporter Online Assessment

Differentiated Instruction: English Learners	**TE** English Learner Activities, pp. 368–372 📖 Interactive Read and Write (EL) SE/TE, pp. 115–122 📁 Unit 3 Teaching Resources, English Language Coach, p. 19 📁 Unit 3 Teaching Resources, Selection Summaries: English, Spanish, Vietnamese, Tagalog, Cantonese, Haitian Creole, and Hmong, pp. 55–60 📁 Unit 3 Teaching Resources, Selection Quick Check (Spanish), p. 66 📁 English Language Coach 💿 Glencoe Interactive Vocabulary CD-ROM 💿 Listening Library Audio CD 📁 Listening Library Sourcebook: Strategies and Activities
Differentiated Instruction: Approaching Level	📖 Interactive Read and Write (Approaching) SE/TE, pp. 115–122 💿 Glencoe Interactive Vocabulary CD-ROM 💿 Listening Library Audio CD 📁 Listening Library Sourcebook: Strategies and Activities 💿 Skill Level Up! A Skills-Based Language Arts Game CD-ROM
Differentiated Instruction: Advanced/Pre-AP	📖 Novel Companion SE, pp. 119–162 📖 Novel Companion TG, pp. 29–36 💿 ▶ Literature Classics, High School CD-ROM 💿 Skill Level Up! A Skills-Based Language Arts Game CD-ROM
Extension	📖 Grammar and Language Workbook SE 📖 Grammar and Language Workbook TAE 📁 Revising with Style 📖 Spelling Power SE 📖 Spelling Power TAE
Daily Writing	**SE/TE** p. 371
Interdisciplinary Connections	**TE** Literary History, p. 368 ▶ glencoe.com
Independent Reading	💿 BookLink K–12 CD-ROM 📙 Ethnic Anthologies 📙 Glencoe Literature Library 💿 Glencoe Literature Library Teacher Resources CD-ROM 📙 *inTIME* magazine 💿 ▶ Literature Classics, High School CD-ROM
Technology and Additional Resources	**Planning and Instruction:** 💿 TeacherWorks Plus CD-ROM 💿 Classroom Presentation Toolkit CD-ROM ▶ Literature Online at **glencoe.com** (QuickPass Code: **GLA9879u3T**) **Students Tools:** 💿 StudentWorks Plus CD-ROM or DVD-ROM ▶ Online Student Edition at **glencoe.com** ▶ Literature Online at **glencoe.com** (QuickPass Code: **GLA9800u3**)

Lesson Plan

Part 2 Opener, from *Mary Chesnut's Civil War*, and Grammar Workshop (pp. 373–381)

Lesson Plan and Resource Manager

UNIT THREE The Civil War Era 1850–1880, Part 2: The Civil War: A Nation Divided

Learning Objectives	**Literary Study:** Analyzing a journal. **Reading:** Distinguishing fact and opinion. **Grammar:** Using transitional expressions.
Lesson Summary	On pages **373–381** of the Student Edition, students will be introduced to the following: • **Big Idea:** A Nation Divided • **Literary Elements:** Journal, Point of View • **Reading Strategy:** Distinguish Fact and Opinion • **Writing Activities/Grammar:** Write a Memo, Use Transitional Expressions • **Vocabulary:** Context Clues, Latin Word Parts • **Listening/Speaking/Viewing Skill:** Analyze Art
Lesson Duration	One to five 45–50 minute sessions
Readability Scores	Dale-Chall: 6.9 DRP: 52 Lexile: 680
Focus	**SE/TE** pp. 374–375, 381 Selection Focus Transparency 23 Daily Language Practice Transparency 35 Literature Launchers: Pre-Reading Videos DVD, Selection Launcher Literature Launchers Teacher Guide
Teach	**SE/TE** pp. 376–379, 381 Interactive Read and Write SE/TE, pp. 123–132 Unit 3 Teaching Resources, Literary Element, p. 75 Unit 3 Teaching Resources, Reading Strategy, p. 76 Unit 3 Teaching Resources, Vocabulary Strategy, p. 77 Unit 3 Teaching Resources, Grammar Practice, p. 78 Grammar and Language Transparency 10 Literary Elements Transparency 55 Classroom Presentation Toolkit CD-ROM Listening Library CD, Selection Audio TeacherWorks Plus CD-ROM Vocabulary PuzzleMaker CD-ROM
Assess	**SE/TE** pp. 380, 381 Unit 3 Teaching Resources, Selection Quick Check, p. 79 Unit 3 Teaching Resources, Selection Quick Check (Spanish), p. 80 Assessment Resources, Selection Test, pp. 129–130 ExamView Assessment Suite CD-ROM Progress Reporter Online Assessment

Differentiated Instruction: English Learners	**TE** English Learner Activities, pp. 373–381 ▊ Interactive Read and Write (EL) SE/TE, pp. 123–132 🗀 Unit 3 Teaching Resources, English Language Coach, p. 68 🗀 Unit 3 Teaching Resources, Selection Summaries: English, Spanish, Vietnamese, Tagalog, Cantonese, Haitian Creole, and Hmong, pp. 69–74 🗀 Unit 3 Teaching Resources, Selection Quick Check (Spanish), p. 80 🗀 English Language Coach 💿 Glencoe Interactive Vocabulary CD-ROM 💿 Listening Library Audio CD 🗀 Listening Library Sourcebook: Strategies and Activities
Differentiated Instruction: Approaching Level	**TE** Approaching Level Activities, pp. 373–381 ▊ Interactive Read and Write (Approaching) SE/TE, pp. 123–132 💿 Glencoe Interactive Vocabulary CD-ROM 💿 Listening Library Audio CD 🗀 Listening Library Sourcebook: Strategies and Activities 💿 Skill Level Up! A Skills-Based Language Arts Game CD-ROM
Differentiated Instruction: Advanced/Pre-AP	**TE** Advanced Learner Activities, pp. 373–381 ▊ Novel Companion SE, pp. 119–162 ▊ Novel Companion TG, pp. 29–36 💿 ▶ Literature Classics, High School CD-ROM 💿 Skill Level Up! A Skills-Based Language Arts Game CD-ROM
Extension	▊ Grammar and Language Workbook SE ▊ Grammar and Language Workbook TAE 🗀 Revising with Style ▊ Spelling Power SE ▊ Spelling Power TAE
Daily Writing	**SE/TE** p. 380
Interdisciplinary Connections	**SE/TE** View the Art, pp. 373, 376, 379 **TE** Political History, p. 377 ▶ glencoe.com
Independent Reading	💿 BookLink K–12 CD-ROM 📖 Ethnic Anthologies 📖 Glencoe Literature Library 💿 Glencoe Literature Library Teacher Resources CD-ROM 📖 inTIME magazine 💿 ▶ Literature Classics, High School CD-ROM
Technology and Additional Resources	**Planning and Instruction:** 💿 TeacherWorks Plus CD-ROM 💿 Classroom Presentation Toolkit CD-ROM ▶ Literature Online at **glencoe.com** (QuickPass Code: **GLA9879u3T**) **Students Tools:** 💿 StudentWorks Plus CD-ROM or DVD-ROM ▶ Online Student Edition at **glencoe.com** ▶ Literature Online at **glencoe.com** (QuickPass Code: **GLA9800u3**)

Lesson Plan

Glencoe Literature

Letter to His Son (pp. 382–386)

Lesson Plan and Resource Manager

UNIT THREE The Civil War Era 1850–1880, Part 2: The Civil War: A Nation Divided

Learning Objectives	**Literary Study:** Analyzing diction. **Reading:** Determining main idea and supporting details.
Lesson Summary	On pages **382–386** of the Student Edition, students will be introduced to the following: • **Big Idea:** A Nation Divided • **Literary Element:** Diction • **Reading Strategy:** Determine Main Idea and Supporting Details • **Writing Activity:** Summary • **Vocabulary:** Word Parts, Diction
Lesson Duration	One 45–50 minute sessions
Readability Scores	Dale-Chall: 9.9 DRP: 64 Lexile: 1130
Focus	**SE/TE** pp. 382–383 Selection Focus Transparency 24 Daily Language Practice Transparency 36
Teach	**SE/TE** pp. 384–385 Unit 3 Teaching Resources, Literary Element, p. 89 Unit 3 Teaching Resources, Reading Strategy, p. 90 Unit 3 Teaching Resources, Selection Vocabulary Practice, p. 91 Unit 3 Teaching Resources, Vocabulary Strategy, p. 92 Unit 3 Teaching Resources, Grammar Practice, p. 93 Literary Elements Transparencies 27, 80 Classroom Presentation Toolkit CD-ROM Listening Library CD, Selection Audio TeacherWorks Plus CD-ROM Vocabulary PuzzleMaker CD-ROM
Assess	**SE/TE** p. 386 Unit 3 Teaching Resources, Selection Quick Check, p. 94 Unit 3 Teaching Resources, Selection Quick Check (Spanish), p. 95 Assessment Resources, Selection Test, pp. 131–132 ExamView Assessment Suite CD-ROM Progress Reporter Online Assessment

Differentiated Instruction: English Learners	**TE** English Learner Activities, pp. 382–386
	📁 Unit 3 Teaching Resources, Selection Summaries: English, Spanish, Vietnamese, Tagalog, Cantonese, Haitian Creole, and Hmong, pp. 83–88
	📁 Unit 3 Teaching Resources, Selection Quick Check (Spanish), p. 95
	💿 Glencoe Interactive Vocabulary CD-ROM
	💿 Listening Library Audio CD
	📁 Listening Library Sourcebook: Strategies and Activities
	📁 Unit 3 Teaching Resources, English Language Coach, p. 68
	📁 English Language Coach
Differentiated Instruction: Approaching Level	**TE** Approaching Level Activities, pp. 382–386
	💿 Glencoe Interactive Vocabulary CD-ROM
	💿 Listening Library Audio CD
	📁 Listening Library Sourcebook: Strategies and Activities
	💿 Skill Level Up! A Skills-Based Language Arts Game CD-ROM
Differentiated Instruction: Advanced/Pre-AP	📘 Novel Companion SE, pp. 119–162
	📘 Novel Companion TG, pp. 29–36
	📀 Literature Classics, High School CD-ROM
	💿 Skill Level Up! A Skills-Based Language Arts Game CD-ROM
Extension	📘 Grammar and Language Workbook SE
	📘 Grammar and Language Workbook TAE
	📁 Revising with Style
	📘 Spelling Power SE
	📘 Spelling Power TAE
Daily Writing	**SE/TE** p. 386
Interdisciplinary Connections	**TE** Political History, pp. 382, 384
	TE Literary History, p. 385
	📀 **glencoe.com**
Independent Reading	💿 BookLink K–12 CD-ROM
	📖 Ethnic Anthologies
	📖 Glencoe Literature Library
	💿 Glencoe Literature Library Teacher Resources CD-ROM
	📖 *inTIME* magazine
	📀 Literature Classics, High School CD-ROM
Technology and Additional Resources	**Planning and Instruction:**
	💿 TeacherWorks Plus CD-ROM
	💿 Classroom Presentation Toolkit CD-ROM
	📀 Literature Online at **glencoe.com** (QuickPass Code: **GLA9879u3T**)
	Students Tools:
	💿 StudentWorks Plus CD-ROM or DVD-ROM
	📀 Online Student Edition at **glencoe.com**
	📀 Literature Online at **glencoe.com** (QuickPass Code: **GLA9800u3**)

Lesson Plan

An Occurrence at Owl Creek Bridge (pp. 387–399)

Lesson Plan and Resource Manager

UNIT THREE The Civil War Era 1850–1880, Part 2: The Civil War: A Nation Divided

Learning Objectives	**Literary Study:** Analyzing point of view. **Reading:** Making and verifying predictions. **Writing:** Writing an expository essay. **Grammar:** Using conjunctions.
Lesson Summary	On pages **387–399** of the Student Edition, students will be introduced to the following: • **Big Idea:** A Nation Divided • **Literary Element:** Point of View • **Reading Strategies:** Make and Verify Predictions, Chronological Order, Identify Steps in a Process, Make Inferences • **Writing Activity/Grammar:** Expository Essay, Coordinating Conjunctions • **Vocabulary:** Pronunciation, Academic Vocabulary • **Listening/Speaking/Viewing Skills:** Analyze Art, Group Discussion
Lesson Duration	One 45–50 minute sessions
Readability Scores	Dale-Chall: 7.3 DRP: 63 Lexile: 1000
Focus	**SE/TE** pp. 387–388 Selection Focus Transparency 25 Daily Language Practice Transparencies 37
Teach	**SE/TE** pp. 389–396 Unit 3 Teaching Resources, Literary Element, p. 102 Unit 3 Teaching Resources, Reading Strategy, p. 103 Unit 3 Teaching Resources, Selection Vocabulary Practice, p. 104 Unit 3 Teaching Resources, Vocabulary Strategy, p. 105 Unit 3 Teaching Resources, Grammar Practice, p. 106 Literary Elements Transparencies 27, 80 Classroom Presentation Toolkit CD-ROM Listening Library CD, Selection Audio TeacherWorks Plus CD-ROM Vocabulary PuzzleMaker CD-ROM
Assess	**SE/TE** pp. 397–399 Unit 3 Teaching Resources, Selection Quick Check, p. 107 Unit 3 Teaching Resources, Selection Quick Check (Spanish), p. 108 Assessment Resources, Selection Test, pp. 133–134 ExamView Assessment Suite CD-ROM Progress Reporter Online Assessment

Differentiated Instruction: English Learners	**TE** English Learner Activities, pp. 387–399
	📁 Unit 3 Teaching Resources, Selection Summaries: English, Spanish, Vietnamese, Tagalog, Cantonese, Haitian Creole, and Hmong, pp. 83, 96–101
	📁 Unit 3 Teaching Resources, Selection Quick Check (Spanish), p. 108
	📁 Unit 3 Teaching Resources, English Language Coach, p. 68
	📁 English Language Coach
	💿 Glencoe Interactive Vocabulary CD-ROM
	💿 Listening Library Audio CD
	📁 Listening Library Sourcebook: Strategies and Activities
Differentiated Instruction: Approaching Level	**TE** Approaching Level Activities, pp. 387–399
	💿 Glencoe Interactive Vocabulary CD-ROM
	💿 Listening Library Audio CD
	📁 Listening Library Sourcebook: Strategies and Activities
	💿 Skill Level Up! A Skills-Based Language Arts Game CD-ROM
Differentiated Instruction: Advanced/Pre-AP	**TE** Advanced Learner Activities, pp. 387–399
	📕 Novel Companion SE, pp. 119–162
	📕 Novel Companion TG, pp. 29–36
	💿 ▶ Literature Classics, High School CD-ROM
	💿 Skill Level Up! A Skills-Based Language Arts Game CD-ROM
Extension	📕 Grammar and Language Workbook SE
	📕 Grammar and Language Workbook TAE
	📁 Revising with Style
	📕 Spelling Power SE
	📕 Spelling Power TAE
Daily Writing	**SE/TE** p. 399
Interdisciplinary Connections	**SE/TE** View the Photograph, pp. 389, 396
	SE/TE View the Art, pp. 391, 394
	TE Cultural History, pp. 387, 393
	TE Language History, p. 395
	▶ glencoe.com
Independent Reading	💿 BookLink K–12 CD-ROM
	📖 Ethnic Anthologies
	📖 Glencoe Literature Library
	💿 Glencoe Literature Library Teacher Resources CD-ROM
	📖 inTIME magazine
	💿 ▶ Literature Classics, High School CD-ROM
Technology and Additional Resources	**Planning and Instruction:**
	💿 TeacherWorks Plus CD-ROM
	💿 Classroom Presentation Toolkit CD-ROM
	▶ Literature Online at **glencoe.com** (QuickPass Code: **GLA9879u3T**)
	Students Tools:
	💿 StudentWorks Plus CD-ROM or DVD-ROM
	▶ Online Student Edition at **glencoe.com**
	▶ Literature Online at **glencoe.com** (QuickPass Code: **GLA9800u3**)

Lesson Plan

Glencoe Literature

The Gettysburg Address (pp. 400–403)

Lesson Plan and Resource Manager

UNIT THREE The Civil War Era 1850–1880, Part 2: The Civil War: A Nation Divided

Learning Objectives	**Literary Study:** Analyzing parallelism. **Reading:** Analyzing style. **Writing:** Writing an interior monologue.
Lesson Summary	On pages **400–403** of the Student Edition, students will be introduced to the following: • **Big Idea:** A Nation Divided • **Literary Element:** Parallelism • **Reading Strategy:** Analyze Style • **Writing Activity:** Interior Monologue • **Vocabulary:** Synonyms
Lesson Duration	One 45–50 minute session
Readability Scores	Dale-Chall: 9.3 DRP: 62 Lexile: 1490
Focus	**SE/TE** pp. 400–401 Selection Focus Transparency 26 Daily Language Practice Transparency 38
Teach	**SE/TE** p. 402 Unit 3 Teaching Resources, Literary Element, p. 115 Unit 3 Teaching Resources, Reading Strategy, p. 116 Unit 3 Teaching Resources, Selection Vocabulary Practice, p. 117 Unit 3 Teaching Resources, Vocabulary Strategy, p. 118 Unit 3 Teaching Resources, Grammar Practice, p. 119 Read Aloud, Think Aloud Transparencies 17–18 Literary Elements Transparency 74 Classroom Presentation Toolkit CD-ROM Listening Library CD, Selection Audio TeacherWorks Plus CD-ROM Vocabulary PuzzleMaker CD-ROM
Assess	**SE/TE** p. 403 Unit 3 Teaching Resources, Selection Quick Check, p. 120 Unit 3 Teaching Resources, Selection Quick Check (Spanish), p. 121 Assessment Resources, Selection Test, pp. 135–136 ExamView Assessment Suite CD-ROM Progress Reporter Online Assessment

Differentiated Instruction: English Learners	**TE** English Learner Activities, pp. 400–403 📁 Unit 3 Teaching Resources, English Language Coach, p. 68 📁 English Language Coach 📁 Unit 3 Teaching Resources, Selection Summaries: English, Spanish, Vietnamese, Tagalog, Cantonese, Haitian Creole, and Hmong, pp. 109–114 📁 Unit 3 Teaching Resources, Selection Quick Check (Spanish), p. 121 💿 Glencoe Interactive Vocabulary CD-ROM 💿 Listening Library Audio CD 📁 Listening Library Sourcebook: Strategies and Activities
Differentiated Instruction: Approaching Level	**TE** Approaching Level Activities, pp. 400–403 💿 Glencoe Interactive Vocabulary CD-ROM 💿 Listening Library Audio CD 📁 Listening Library Sourcebook: Strategies and Activities 💿 Skill Level Up! A Skills-Based Language Arts Game CD-ROM
Differentiated Instruction: Advanced/Pre-AP	**TE** Advanced Learner Activities, pp. 400–403 📘 Novel Companion SE, pp. 119–162 📘 Novel Companion TG, pp. 29–36 💿 Literature Classics, High School CD-ROM 💿 Skill Level Up! A Skills-Based Language Arts Game CD-ROM
Extension	📘 Grammar and Language Workbook SE 📘 Grammar and Language Workbook TAE 📁 Revising with Style 📘 Spelling Power SE 📘 Spelling Power TAE
Daily Writing	**SE/TE** p. 403
Interdisciplinary Connections	**TE** Political History, p. 400 ▶ glencoe.com
Independent Reading	💿 BookLink K–12 CD-ROM 📖 Ethnic Anthologies 📖 Glencoe Literature Library 💿 Glencoe Literature Library Teacher Resources CD-ROM 📖 *inTIME* magazine 💿 Literature Classics, High School CD-ROM
Technology and Additional Resources	**Planning and Instruction:** 💿 TeacherWorks Plus CD-ROM 💿 Classroom Presentation Toolkit CD-ROM ▶ Literature Online at **glencoe.com** (QuickPass Code: **GLA9879u3T**) **Students Tools:** 💿 StudentWorks Plus CD-ROM or DVD-ROM ▶ Online Student Edition at **glencoe.com** ▶ Literature Online at **glencoe.com** (QuickPass Code: **GLA9800u3**)

Lesson Plan

Glencoe Literature

Political Perspective: from *Lincoln at Gettysburg: The Words that Remade America* (pp. 404–406)

Lesson Plan and Resource Manager

UNIT THREE The Civil War Era 1850–1880, Part 2: The Civil War: A Nation Divided

Learning Objectives	**Literary Study:** Making connections across literature. **Reading:** Analyzing informational text.
Lesson Summary	On pages **404–406** of the Student Edition, students will be introduced to the following: • **Big Idea:** A Nation Divided • **Reading Strategy:** Connect to Political Context • **Writing Activity:** Primary and Secondary Sources
Lesson Duration	One 45–50 minute session
Readability Scores	Dale-Chall: 10.4 DRP: 68 Lexile: 1250
Focus	**SE/TE** p. 404
Teach	**SE/TE** pp. 404–406 📁 Unit 3 Teaching Resources, Reading Strategy, p. 128 💿 Classroom Presentation Toolkit CD-ROM 💿 Listening Library CD, Selection Audio 💿 TeacherWorks Plus CD-ROM 💿 Vocabulary PuzzleMaker CD-ROM
Assess	**SE/TE** p. 406 📁 Unit 3 Teaching Resources, Selection Quick Check, p. 129 📁 Unit 3 Teaching Resources, Selection Quick Check (Spanish), p. 130 📁 Assessment Resources, Selection Test, pp. 137–138 💿 ExamView Assessment Suite CD-ROM 💿 Progress Reporter Online Assessment
Differentiated Instruction: English Learners	**TE** English Learner Activities, pp. 404–406 📁 Unit 3 Teaching Resources, English Language Coach, p. 68 📁 English Language Coach 📁 Unit 3 Teaching Resources, Selection Summaries: English, Spanish, Vietnamese, Tagalog, Cantonese, Haitian Creole, and Hmong, pp. 122–127 📁 Unit 3 Teaching Resources, Selection Quick Check (Spanish), p. 130 💿 Glencoe Interactive Vocabulary CD-ROM 💿 Listening Library Audio CD 📁 Listening Library Sourcebook: Strategies and Activities
Differentiated Instruction: Approaching Level	💿 Glencoe Interactive Vocabulary CD-ROM 💿 Listening Library Audio CD 📁 Listening Library Sourcebook: Strategies and Activities 💿 Skill Level Up! A Skills-Based Language Arts Game CD-ROM

Differentiated Instruction: Advanced/Pre-AP	▌ Novel Companion SE, pp. 119–162 ▌ Novel Companion TG, pp. 29–36 ◉ ◉ Literature Classics, High School CD-ROM ◉ Skill Level Up! A Skills-Based Language Arts Game CD-ROM
Extension	▌ Grammar and Language Workbook SE ▌ Grammar and Language Workbook TAE 🗀 Revising with Style ▌ Spelling Power SE ▌ Spelling Power TAE
Daily Writing	**SE/TE** p. 406
Interdisciplinary Connections	**TE** Political History, p. 406 ◉ glencoe.com
Independent Reading	◉ BookLink K–12 CD-ROM 📖 Ethnic Anthologies 📖 Glencoe Literature Library ◉ Glencoe Literature Library Teacher Resources CD-ROM 📖 inTIME magazine ◉ ◉ Literature Classics, High School CD-ROM
Technology and Additional Resources	**Planning and Instruction:** ◉ TeacherWorks Plus CD-ROM ◉ Classroom Presentation Toolkit CD-ROM ◉ Literature Online at **glencoe.com** (QuickPass Code: **GLA9879u3T**) **Students Tools:** ◉ StudentWorks Plus CD-ROM or DVD-ROM ◉ Online Student Edition at **glencoe.com** ◉ Literature Online at **glencoe.com** (QuickPass Code: **GLA9800u3**)

Lesson Plan

Part 3 Opener, *I Hear America Singing*, and *When I Heard the Learn'd Astronomer* (pp. 407–412)

Lesson Plan and Resource Manager

UNIT THREE The Civil War Era 1850–1880, Part 3: A Poetic Revolution

Learning Objectives	**Literary Study:** Analyzing free verse. Analyzing historical narratives. **Reading:** Paraphrasing. **Writing:** Writing a poem.
Lesson Summary	On pages **407–412** of the Student Edition, students will be introduced to the following: • **Big Idea:** A Poetic Revolution • **Literary Element:** Free Verse • **Reading Strategy:** Paraphrase • **Writing Activity/Grammar:** Write a Poem, Sentence Fragments • **Vocabulary:** Word Parts • **Listening/Speaking/Viewing Skill:** Analyze Art
Lesson Duration	One to five 45–50 minute sessions
Readability Scores	Dale-Chall: N/A DRP: N/A Lexile: N/A
Focus	**SE/TE** pp. 408–409 🖐 Daily Language Practice Transparency 39 💿 Literature Launchers: Pre-Reading Videos DVD, Selection Launcher 📁 Literature Launchers Teacher Guide
Teach	**SE/TE** pp. 410–411 📖 Interactive Read and Write SE, pp. 133–138 📖 Interactive Read and Write TE, pp. 133–138 📁 Unit 3 Teaching Resources, Literary Element, p. 139 📁 Unit 3 Teaching Resources, Reading Strategy, p. 140 🖐 Literary Elements Transparency 46 💿 Classroom Presentation Toolkit CD-ROM 💿 Listening Library CD, Selection Audio 💿 TeacherWorks Plus CD-ROM 💿 Vocabulary PuzzleMaker CD-ROM
Assess	**SE/TE** p. 412 📁 Unit 3 Teaching Resources, Selection Quick Check, p. 141 📁 Unit 3 Teaching Resources, Selection Quick Check (Spanish), p. 142 📁 Assessment Resources, Selection Test, pp. 139–140 💿 ExamView Assessment Suite CD-ROM 💿 Progress Reporter Online Assessment

Differentiated Instruction: English Learners	**TE** English Learner Activities, pp. 407–412 Interactive Read and Write (EL) SE, pp. 133–138 Interactive Read and Write (EL) TE, pp. 133–138 Unit 3 Teaching Resources, English Language Coach, p. 132 English Language Coach Unit 3 Teaching Resources, Selection Summaries: English, Spanish, Vietnamese, Tagalog, Cantonese, Haitian Creole, and Hmong, pp. 133–138 Unit 3 Teaching Resources, Selection Quick Check (Spanish), p. 142 Glencoe Interactive Vocabulary CD-ROM Listening Library Audio CD Listening Library Sourcebook: Strategies and Activities
Differentiated Instruction: Approaching Level	**TE** Approaching Level Activities, pp. 407–412 Interactive Read and Write (Approaching) SE, pp. 133–138 Interactive Read and Write (Approaching) TE, pp. 133–138 Glencoe Interactive Vocabulary CD-ROM Listening Library Audio CD Listening Library Sourcebook: Strategies and Activities Skill Level Up! A Skills-Based Language Arts Game CD-ROM
Differentiated Instruction: Advanced/Pre-AP	**TE** Advanced Learner Activities, pp. 407–412 Novel Companion SE, pp. 119–162 Novel Companion TG, pp. 29–36 Literature Classics, High School CD-ROM Skill Level Up! A Skills-Based Language Arts Game CD-ROM
Extension	Grammar and Language Workbook SE Grammar and Language Workbook TAE Revising with Style Spelling Power SE Spelling Power TAE
Daily Writing	**SE/TE** p. 412
Interdisciplinary Connections	**SE/TE** View the Art, pp. 407, 410, 411 **TE** Cultural History, p. 408 glencoe.com
Independent Reading	BookLink K–12 CD-ROM Ethnic Anthologies Glencoe Literature Library Glencoe Literature Library Teacher Resources CD-ROM *inTIME* magazine Literature Classics, High School CD-ROM
Technology and Additional Resources	**Planning and Instruction:** TeacherWorks Plus CD-ROM Classroom Presentation Toolkit CD-ROM Literature Online at **glencoe.com** (QuickPass Code: **GLA9879u3T**) **Students Tools:** StudentWorks Plus CD-ROM or DVD-ROM Online Student Edition at **glencoe.com** Literature Online at **glencoe.com** (QuickPass Code: **GLA9800u3**)

Lesson Plan

A Sight in Camp in the Daybreak Gray and Dim and Beat! Beat! Drums! (pp. 413–415)

Lesson Plan and Resource Manager

UNIT THREE The Civil War Era 1850–1880, Part 3: A Poetic Revolution

Learning Objectives	**Literary Study:** Analyzing free verse. Analyzing historical narratives. **Reading:** Paraphrasing. **Writing:** Writing an essay.
Lesson Summary	On pages **413–415** of the Student Edition, students will be introduced to the following: • **Big Idea:** A Poetic Revolution • **Literary Elements:** Alliteration, Free Verse • **Reading Strategies:** Interpret, Paraphrase • **Writing Activity/Grammar:** Write an Essay, Run-on Sentences
Lesson Duration	One 45–50 minute session
Readability Scores	Dale-Chall: N/A DRP: N/A Lexile: N/A
Focus	✍ Selection Focus Transparency 27
Teach	**SE/TE** pp. 413–414 📁 Unit 3 Teaching Resources, Literary Element, p. 149 📁 Unit 3 Teaching Resources, Reading Strategy, p. 150 ✍ Literary Elements Transparency 46 💿 Classroom Presentation Toolkit CD-ROM 💿 Listening Library CD, Selection Audio 💿 TeacherWorks Plus CD-ROM 💿 ▶ Vocabulary PuzzleMaker CD-ROM
Assess	**SE/TE** p. 415 📁 Unit 3 Teaching Resources, Selection Quick Check, p. 151 📁 Unit 3 Teaching Resources, Selection Quick Check (Spanish), p. 152 📁 Assessment Resources, Selection Test, pp. 141–142 💿 ExamView Assessment Suite CD-ROM ▶ Progress Reporter Online Assessment
Differentiated Instruction: English Learners	**TE** English Learner Activities, pp. 413–415 📁 Unit 3 Teaching Resources, English Language Coach, p. 132 📁 English Language Coach 📁 Unit 3 Teaching Resources, Selection Summaries: English, Spanish, Vietnamese, Tagalog, Cantonese, Haitian Creole, and Hmong, pp. 143–148 📁 Unit 3 Teaching Resources, Selection Quick Check (Spanish), p. 152 💿 Glencoe Interactive Vocabulary CD-ROM 💿 Listening Library Audio CD 📁 Listening Library Sourcebook: Strategies and Activities

Differentiated Instruction: Approaching Level	**TE** Approaching Level Activities, pp. 413–415 Glencoe Interactive Vocabulary CD-ROM Listening Library Audio CD Listening Library Sourcebook: Strategies and Activities Skill Level Up! A Skills-Based Language Arts Game CD-ROM
Differentiated Instruction: Advanced/Pre-AP	**TE** Advanced Learner Activities, pp. 413–415 Novel Companion SE, pp. 119–162 Novel Companion TG, pp. 29–36 Literature Classics, High School CD-ROM Skill Level Up! A Skills-Based Language Arts Game CD-ROM
Extension	Grammar and Language Workbook SE Grammar and Language Workbook TAE Revising with Style Spelling Power SE Spelling Power TAE
Daily Writing	**SE/TE** p. 415
Interdisciplinary Connections	**SE/TE** View the Art, p. 413 glencoe.com
Independent Reading	BookLink K–12 CD-ROM Ethnic Anthologies Glencoe Literature Library Glencoe Literature Library Teacher Resources CD-ROM *inTIME* magazine Literature Classics, High School CD-ROM
Technology and Additional Resources	**Planning and Instruction:** TeacherWorks Plus CD-ROM Classroom Presentation Toolkit CD-ROM Literature Online at **glencoe.com** (QuickPass Code: **GLA9879u3T**) **Students Tools:** StudentWorks Plus CD-ROM or DVD-ROM Online Student Edition at **glencoe.com** Literature Online at **glencoe.com** (QuickPass Code: **GLA9800u3**)

Lesson Plan

Glencoe Literature

from *Specimen Days* (pp. 416–419)

Lesson Plan and Resource Manager

UNIT THREE The Civil War Era 1850–1880, Part 3: A Poetic Revolution

Learning Objectives	**Literary Study:** Analyzing free verse. Analyzing historical narratives. **Reading:** Paraphrasing. **Writing:** Writing a journal entry.
Lesson Summary	On pages **416–419** of the Student Edition, students will be introduced to the following: • **Big Idea:** A Poetic Revolution • **Literary Element:** Historical Narrative • **Writing Activity/Grammar:** Journal Entry • **Vocabulary:** Academic Vocabulary • **Study Skill/Research/Assessment:** Text Aids • **Listening/Speaking/Viewing Skill:** Analyze Art
Lesson Duration	One 45–50 minute session
Readability Scores	Dale-Chall: 5.8 DRP: 62 Lexile: 1410
Focus	**SE/TE** p. 416
Teach	**SE/TE** pp. 416–418 📁 Unit 3 Teaching Resources, Literary Element, p. 159 📁 Unit 3 Teaching Resources, Selection Vocabulary Practice, p. 160 📁 Unit 3 Teaching Resources, Vocabulary Strategy, p. 161 📁 Unit 3 Teaching Resources, Grammar Practice, p. 162 📖 Literary Elements Transparency 49 💿 Classroom Presentation Toolkit CD-ROM 💿 Listening Library CD, Selection Audio 💿 TeacherWorks Plus CD-ROM 💿 ▶ Vocabulary PuzzleMaker CD-ROM
Assess	**SE/TE** p. 419 📁 Unit 3 Teaching Resources, Selection Quick Check, p. 163 📁 Unit 3 Teaching Resources, Selection Quick Check (Spanish), p. 164 📁 Assessment Resources, Selection Test, pp. 143–144 💿 ExamView Assessment Suite CD-ROM ▶ Progress Reporter Online Assessment
Differentiated Instruction: English Learners	**TE** English Learner Activities, pp. 416–419 📁 Unit 3 Teaching Resources, English Language Coach, p. 132 📁 English Language Coach 📁 Unit 3 Teaching Resources, Selection Summaries: English, Spanish, Vietnamese, Tagalog, Cantonese, Haitian Creole, and Hmong, pp. 153–158 📁 Unit 3 Teaching Resources, Selection Quick Check (Spanish), p. 164 💿 Glencoe Interactive Vocabulary CD-ROM 💿 Listening Library Audio CD 📁 Listening Library Sourcebook: Strategies and Activities

Differentiated Instruction: Approaching Level	⊙ Glencoe Interactive Vocabulary CD-ROM ⊙ Listening Library Audio CD 📁 Listening Library Sourcebook: Strategies and Activities ⊙ Skill Level Up! A Skills-Based Language Arts Game CD-ROM
Differentiated Instruction: Advanced/Pre-AP	**TE** Advanced Learner Activities, pp. 416–419 ▮ Novel Companion SE, pp. 119–162 ▮ Novel Companion TG, pp. 29–36 ⊙ ▶ Literature Classics, High School CD-ROM ⊙ Skill Level Up! A Skills-Based Language Arts Game CD-ROM
Extension	▮ Grammar and Language Workbook SE ▮ Grammar and Language Workbook TAE 📁 Revising with Style ▮ Spelling Power SE ▮ Spelling Power TAE
Daily Writing	**SE/TE** p. 419
Interdisciplinary Connections	**SE/TE** View the Art, p. 418 ▶ glencoe.com
Independent Reading	⊙ BookLink K–12 CD-ROM 📖 Ethnic Anthologies 📖 Glencoe Literature Library ⊙ Glencoe Literature Library Teacher Resources CD-ROM 📖 *inTIME* magazine ⊙ ▶ Literature Classics, High School CD-ROM
Technology and Additional Resources	**Planning and Instruction:** ⊙ TeacherWorks Plus CD-ROM ⊙ Classroom Presentation Toolkit CD-ROM ▶ Literature Online at **glencoe.com** (QuickPass Code: **GLA9879u3T**) **Students Tools:** ⊙ StudentWorks Plus CD-ROM or DVD-ROM ▶ Online Student Edition at **glencoe.com** ▶ Literature Online at **glencoe.com** (QuickPass Code: **GLA9800u3**)

Lesson Plan

Glencoe Literature Essential Course of Study

from *Song of Myself* (pp. 420–429)

Lesson Plan and Resource Manager

UNIT THREE The Civil War Era 1850–1880, Part 3: A Poetic Revolution

Learning Objectives	**Literary Study:** Analyzing voice. **Reading:** Drawing conclusions. **Writing:** Writing a reflective essay. **Grammar:** Using hyphens.
Lesson Summary	On pages **420–429** of the Student Edition, students will be introduced to the following: ▪ **Big Idea:** A Poetic Revolution ▪ **Literary Elements:** Voice, Author's Purpose, Parallelism ▪ **Reading Strategy:** Draw Conclusions ▪ **Writing Activities/Grammar:** Reflective Essay, Free Verse, Hyphens ▪ **Vocabulary:** Academic Vocabulary ▪ **Listening/Speaking/Viewing Skill:** Analyze Art
Lesson Duration	Two to five 45–50 minute sessions
Readability Scores	Dale-Chall: N/A　　DRP: N/A　　Lexile: N/A
Focus	**SE/TE** p. 420 Selection Focus Transparency 28 Literature Launchers: Pre-Reading Videos DVD, Selection Launcher Literature Launchers Teacher Guide
Teach	**SE/TE** pp. 421–426 Unit 3 Teaching Resources, Literary Element, p. 171 Unit 3 Teaching Resources, Reading Strategy, p. 172 Grammar and Language Transparency 71 Literary Elements Transparency 107 Classroom Presentation Toolkit CD-ROM Listening Library CD, Selection Audio TeacherWorks Plus CD-ROM Vocabulary PuzzleMaker CD-ROM
Assess	**SE/TE** pp. 427–429 Unit 3 Teaching Resources, Selection Quick Check, p. 173 Unit 3 Teaching Resources, Selection Quick Check (Spanish), p. 174 Assessment Resources, Selection Test, pp. 145–146 ExamView Assessment Suite CD-ROM Progress Reporter Online Assessment

Differentiated Instruction: English Learners	**TE** English Learner Activities, pp. 420–429 📁 Unit 3 Teaching Resources, English Language Coach, p. 132 📁 English Language Coach 📁 Unit 3 Teaching Resources, Selection Summaries: English, Spanish, Vietnamese, Tagalog, Cantonese, Haitian Creole, and Hmong, pp. 165–170 📁 Unit 3 Teaching Resources, Selection Quick Check (Spanish), p. 174 💿 Glencoe Interactive Vocabulary CD-ROM 💿 Listening Library Audio CD 📁 Listening Library Sourcebook: Strategies and Activities
Differentiated Instruction: Approaching Level	**TE** Approaching Level Activities, pp. 420–429 💿 Glencoe Interactive Vocabulary CD-ROM 💿 Listening Library Audio CD 📁 Listening Library Sourcebook: Strategies and Activities 💿 Skill Level Up! A Skills-Based Language Arts Game CD-ROM
Differentiated Instruction: Advanced/Pre-AP	📘 Novel Companion SE, pp. 119–162 📘 Novel Companion TG, pp. 29–36 💿 Literature Classics, High School CD-ROM 💿 Skill Level Up! A Skills-Based Language Arts Game CD-ROM
Extension	📘 Grammar and Language Workbook SE 📘 Grammar and Language Workbook TAE 📁 Revising with Style 📘 Spelling Power SE 📘 Spelling Power TAE
Daily Writing	**TE** p. 426 **SE/TE** p. 429
Interdisciplinary Connections	**SE/TE** View the Art, pp. 422, 426 **TE** Literary History, pp. 420, 421, 425 ▶ glencoe.com
Independent Reading	💿 BookLink K–12 CD-ROM 📖 Ethnic Anthologies 📖 Glencoe Literature Library 💿 Glencoe Literature Library Teacher Resources CD-ROM 📖 inTIME magazine 💿 Literature Classics, High School CD-ROM
Technology and Additional Resources	**Planning and Instruction:** 💿 TeacherWorks Plus CD-ROM 💿 Classroom Presentation Toolkit CD-ROM ▶ Literature Online at glencoe.com (QuickPass Code: GLA9879u3T) **Students Tools:** 💿 StudentWorks Plus CD-ROM or DVD-ROM ▶ Online Student Edition at glencoe.com ▶ Literature Online at glencoe.com (QuickPass Code: GLA9800u3)

Lesson Plan

Literary Perspective: from *Walt Whitman: A Life* (pp. 430–436)

Lesson Plan and Resource Manager

UNIT THREE The Civil War Era 1850–1880, Part 3: A Poetic Revolution

Learning Objectives	**Literary Study:** Making connections across literature. **Reading:** Analyzing informational text.
Lesson Summary	On pages **430–436** of the Student Edition, students will be introduced to the following: ▪ **Big Idea:** A Poetic Revolution ▪ **Reading Strategy:** Synthesize Information ▪ **Writing Activity/Grammar:** Research Allusions, Subject-Verb Agreement ▪ **Research Skill:** Citing Evidence
Lesson Duration	One 45–50 minute session
Readability Scores	Dale-Chall: 8.4 DRP: 68 Lexile: 1390
Focus	**SE/TE** p. 430
Teach	**SE/TE** pp. 430–435 📁 Unit 3 Teaching Resources, Reading Strategy, p. 181 💿 Classroom Presentation Toolkit CD-ROM 💿 Listening Library CD, Selection Audio 💿 TeacherWorks Plus CD-ROM 💿 ▶ Vocabulary PuzzleMaker CD-ROM
Assess	**SE/TE** p. 436 📁 Unit 3 Teaching Resources, Selection Quick Check, p. 182 📁 Unit 3 Teaching Resources, Selection Quick Check (Spanish), p. 183 📁 Assessment Resources, Selection Test, pp. 147–148 💿 ExamView Assessment Suite CD-ROM ▶ Progress Reporter Online Assessment
Differentiated Instruction: English Learners	**TE** English Learner Activities, pp. 430–436 📁 Unit 3 Teaching Resources, English Language Coach, p. 132 📁 English Language Coach 📁 Unit 3 Teaching Resources, Selection Summaries: English, Spanish, Vietnamese, Tagalog, Cantonese, Haitian Creole, and Hmong, pp. 175–180 📁 Unit 3 Teaching Resources, Selection Quick Check (Spanish), p. 183 💿 Glencoe Interactive Vocabulary CD-ROM 💿 Listening Library Audio CD 📁 Listening Library Sourcebook: Strategies and Activities
Differentiated Instruction: Approaching Level	**TE** Approaching Level Activities, pp. 430–436 💿 Glencoe Interactive Vocabulary CD-ROM 💿 Listening Library Audio CD 📁 Listening Library Sourcebook: Strategies and Activities 💿 Skill Level Up! A Skills-Based Language Arts Game CD-ROM

Differentiated Instruction: Advanced/Pre-AP	**TE** Advanced Learner Activities, pp. 430–436 Novel Companion SE, pp. 119–162 Novel Companion TG, pp. 29–36 Literature Classics, High School CD-ROM Skill Level Up! A Skills-Based Language Arts Game CD-ROM
Extension	Grammar and Language Workbook SE Grammar and Language Workbook TAE Revising with Style Spelling Power SE Spelling Power TAE
Daily Writing	**SE/TE** p. 432
Interdisciplinary Connections	glencoe.com
Independent Reading	BookLink K–12 CD-ROM Ethnic Anthologies Glencoe Literature Library Glencoe Literature Library Teacher Resources CD-ROM *inTIME* magazine Literature Classics, High School CD-ROM
Technology and Additional Resources	**Planning and Instruction:** TeacherWorks Plus CD-ROM Classroom Presentation Toolkit CD-ROM Literature Online at **glencoe.com** (QuickPass Code: **GLA9879u3T**) **Students Tools:** StudentWorks Plus CD-ROM or DVD-ROM Online Student Edition at **glencoe.com** Literature Online at **glencoe.com** (QuickPass Code: **GLA9800u3**)

Lesson Plan

If you were coming in the Fall, My life closed twice before its close, and *The Soul selects her own Society* (pp. 437–441)

Lesson Plan and Resource Manager

UNIT THREE The Civil War Era 1850–1880, Part 3: A Poetic Revolution

Learning Objectives	**Literary Study:** Analyzing rhyme. Analyzing personification. **Reading:** Analyzing sound devices. Clarifying meaning. **Writing:** Writing a journal entry.
Lesson Summary	On pages **437–441** of the Student Edition, students will be introduced to the following: ▪ **Big Idea:** A Poetic Revolution ▪ **Literary Element:** Rhyme ▪ **Reading Strategies:** Analyze Sound Devices, Read Poetic Lines ▪ **Writing Activity:** Journal Entry ▪ **Vocabulary:** Suffixes
Lesson Duration	One to five 45–50 minute sessions
Readability Scores	Dale-Chall: N/A DRP: N/A Lexile: N/A
Focus	**SE/TE** pp. 437–438 Selection Focus Transparency 29 Daily Language Practice Transparency 40 Literature Launchers: Pre-Reading Videos DVD, Selection Launcher Literature Launchers Teacher Guide
Teach	**SE/TE** pp. 439–440 Interactive Read and Write SE, pp. 139–146 Interactive Read and Write TE, pp. 139–146 Unit 3 Teaching Resources, Literary Element, p. 190 Unit 3 Teaching Resources, Reading Strategy, p. 191 Literary Elements Transparency 88 Classroom Presentation Toolkit CD-ROM Listening Library CD, Selection Audio TeacherWorks Plus CD-ROM Vocabulary PuzzleMaker CD-ROM
Assess	**SE/TE** Teacher Edition, p. 441 Unit 3 Teaching Resources, Selection Quick Check, p. 192 Unit 3 Teaching Resources, Selection Quick Check (Spanish), p. 193 Assessment Resources, Selection Test, pp. 149–150 ExamView Assessment Suite CD-ROM Progress Reporter Online Assessment

Differentiated Instruction: English Learners	**TE** English Learner Activities, pp. 437–441 📖 Interactive Read and Write (EL) SE, pp. 139–146 📖 Interactive Read and Write (EL) TE, pp. 139–146 📁 Unit 3 Teaching Resources, English Language Coach, p. 132 📁 English Language Coach 📁 Unit 3 Teaching Resources, Selection Summaries: English, Spanish, Vietnamese, Tagalog, Cantonese, Haitian Creole, and Hmong, pp. 184–189 📁 Unit 3 Teaching Resources, Selection Quick Check (Spanish), p. 193 💿 Glencoe Interactive Vocabulary CD-ROM 💿 Listening Library Audio CD 📁 Listening Library Sourcebook: Strategies and Activities
Differentiated Instruction: Approaching Level	**TE** Approaching Level Activities, pp. 437–441 📖 Interactive Read and Write (Approaching) SE, pp. 139–146 📖 Interactive Read and Write (Approaching) TE, pp. 139–146 💿 Glencoe Interactive Vocabulary CD-ROM 💿 Listening Library Audio CD 📁 Listening Library Sourcebook: Strategies and Activities 💿 Skill Level Up! A Skills-Based Language Arts Game CD-ROM
Differentiated Instruction: Advanced/Pre-AP	📖 Novel Companion SE, pp. 119–162 📖 Novel Companion TG, pp. 29–36 💿 Literature Classics, High School CD-ROM 💿 Skill Level Up! A Skills-Based Language Arts Game CD-ROM
Extension	📖 Grammar and Language Workbook SE 📖 Grammar and Language Workbook TAE 📁 Revising with Style 📖 Spelling Power SE 📖 Spelling Power TAE
Daily Writing	**SE/TE** p. 441
Interdisciplinary Connections	🔘 glencoe.com
Independent Reading	💿 BookLink K–12 CD-ROM 📚 Ethnic Anthologies 📚 Glencoe Literature Library 💿 Glencoe Literature Library Teacher Resources CD-ROM 📚 *inTIME* magazine 💿 Literature Classics, High School CD-ROM
Technology and Additional Resources	**Planning and Instruction:** 💿 TeacherWorks Plus CD-ROM 💿 Classroom Presentation Toolkit CD-ROM 🔘 Literature Online at **glencoe.com** (QuickPass Code: **GLA9879u3T**) **Students Tools:** 💿 StudentWorks Plus CD-ROM or DVD-ROM 🔘 Online Student Edition at **glencoe.com** 🔘 Literature Online at **glencoe.com** (QuickPass Code: **GLA9800u3**)

Lesson Plan

Glencoe Literature

Much Madness is divinest Sense and Success is counted sweetest (pp. 442–444)

Lesson Plan and Resource Manager

UNIT THREE The Civil War Era 1850–1880, Part 3: A Poetic Revolution

Learning Objectives	**Literary Study:** Analyzing rhyme. Analyzing personification. **Reading:** Analyzing sound devices. Clarifying meaning. **Writing:** Writing a poem.
Lesson Summary	On pages **442–444** of the Student Edition, students will be introduced to the following: ▪ **Big Idea:** A Poetic Revolution ▪ **Literary Elements:** Rhyme, Imagery ▪ **Reading Strategy:** Analyze Sound Devices ▪ **Writing Activity/Grammar:** Poem, Elliptical Constructions
Lesson Duration	One 45–50 minute session
Readability Scores	Dale-Chall: N/A DRP: N/A Lexile: N/A
Teach	**SE/TE** pp. 442–443 📂 Unit 3 Teaching Resources, Literary Element, p. 200 📂 Unit 3 Teaching Resources, Reading Strategy, p. 201 📖 Literary Elements Transparency 88 💿 Classroom Presentation Toolkit CD-ROM 💿 Listening Library CD, Selection Audio 💿 TeacherWorks Plus CD-ROM 💿 Vocabulary PuzzleMaker CD-ROM
Assess	**SE/TE** p. 444 📂 Unit 3 Teaching Resources, Selection Quick Check, p. 202 📂 Unit 3 Teaching Resources, Selection Quick Check (Spanish), p. 203 📂 Assessment Resources, Selection Test, pp. 151–152 💿 ExamView Assessment Suite CD-ROM 💿 Progress Reporter Online Assessment
Differentiated Instruction: English Learners	**TE** English Learner Activities, pp. 442–444 📂 Unit 3 Teaching Resources, English Language Coach, p. 132 📂 English Language Coach 📂 Unit 3 Teaching Resources, Selection Summaries: English, Spanish, Vietnamese, Tagalog, Cantonese, Haitian Creole, and Hmong, pp. 194–199 📂 Unit 3 Teaching Resources, Selection Quick Check (Spanish), p. 203 💿 Glencoe Interactive Vocabulary CD-ROM 💿 Listening Library Audio CD 📂 Listening Library Sourcebook: Strategies and Activities
Differentiated Instruction: Approaching Level	💿 Glencoe Interactive Vocabulary CD-ROM 💿 Listening Library Audio CD 📂 Listening Library Sourcebook: Strategies and Activities 💿 Skill Level Up! A Skills-Based Language Arts Game CD-ROM

Differentiated Instruction: Advanced/Pre-AP	▪ Novel Companion SE, pp. 119–162
	▪ Novel Companion TG, pp. 29–36
	⊙ ⊚ Literature Classics, High School CD-ROM
	⊙ Skill Level Up! A Skills-Based Language Arts Game CD-ROM
Extension	▪ Grammar and Language Workbook SE
	▪ Grammar and Language Workbook TAE
	▭ Revising with Style
	▪ Spelling Power SE
	▪ Spelling Power TAE
Daily Writing	**SE/TE** p. 444
Interdisciplinary Connections	**SE/TE** View the Art, p. 443
	⊙ **glencoe.com**
Independent Reading	⊛ BookLink K–12 CD-ROM
	▱ Ethnic Anthologies
	▱ Glencoe Literature Library
	⊙ Glencoe Literature Library Teacher Resources CD-ROM
	▱ *inTIME* magazine
	⊙ ⊚ Literature Classics, High School CD-ROM
Technology and Additional Resources	**Planning and Instruction:**
	⊛ TeacherWorks Plus CD-ROM
	⊛ Classroom Presentation Toolkit CD-ROM
	⊙ Literature Online at **glencoe.com** (QuickPass Code: **GLA9879u3T**)
	Students Tools:
	⊛ StudentWorks Plus CD-ROM or DVD-ROM
	⊙ Online Student Edition at **glencoe.com**
	⊙ Literature Online at **glencoe.com** (QuickPass Code: **GLA9800u3**)

Lesson Plan

Glencoe Literature

I heard a Fly buzz when I died and The Bustle in a House (pp. 445–447)

Lesson Plan and Resource Manager

UNIT THREE The Civil War Era 1850–1880, Part 3: A Poetic Revolution

Learning Objectives	**Literary Study:** Analyzing rhyme. Analyzing personification. **Reading:** Analyzing sound devices. Clarifying meaning. **Writing:** Writing an essay.
Lesson Summary	On pages **445–447** of the Student Edition, students will be introduced to the following: • **Big Idea:** A Poetic Revolution • **Literary Elements:** Rhyme, Irony • **Reading Strategies:** Analyze Sound Devices, Compare and Contrast • **Writing Activity:** Write an Essay
Lesson Duration	One 45–50 minute session
Readability Scores	Dale-Chall: N/A DRP: N/A Lexile: N/A
Teach	**SE/TE** pp. 445–446 📁 Unit 3 Teaching Resources, Literary Element, p. 210 📁 Unit 3 Teaching Resources, Reading Strategy, p. 211 🔖 Literary Elements Transparency 88 💿 Classroom Presentation Toolkit CD-ROM 💿 Listening Library CD, Selection Audio 💿 TeacherWorks Plus CD-ROM 💿 Vocabulary PuzzleMaker CD-ROM
Assess	**SE/TE** p. 447 📁 Unit 3 Teaching Resources, Selection Quick Check, p. 212 📁 Unit 3 Teaching Resources, Selection Quick Check (Spanish), p. 213 📁 Assessment Resources, Selection Test, pp. 153–154 💿 ExamView Assessment Suite CD-ROM 💿 Progress Reporter Online Assessment
Differentiated Instruction: English Learners	**TE** English Learner Activities, pp. 445–447 📁 Unit 3 Teaching Resources, English Language Coach, p. 132 📁 English Language Coach 📁 Unit 3 Teaching Resources, Selection Summaries: English, Spanish, Vietnamese, Tagalog, Cantonese, Haitian Creole, and Hmong, pp. 204–209 📁 Unit 3 Teaching Resources, Selection Quick Check (Spanish), p. 213 💿 Glencoe Interactive Vocabulary CD-ROM 💿 Listening Library Audio CD 📁 Listening Library Sourcebook: Strategies and Activities
Differentiated Instruction: Approaching Level	💿 Glencoe Interactive Vocabulary CD-ROM 💿 Listening Library Audio CD 📁 Listening Library Sourcebook: Strategies and Activities 💿 Skill Level Up! A Skills-Based Language Arts Game CD-ROM

Differentiated Instruction: Advanced/Pre-AP	Novel Companion SE, pp. 119–162 Novel Companion TG, pp. 29–36 Literature Classics, High School CD-ROM Skill Level Up! A Skills-Based Language Arts Game CD-ROM
Extension	Grammar and Language Workbook SE Grammar and Language Workbook TAE Revising with Style Spelling Power SE Spelling Power TAE
Daily Writing	**SE/TE** p. 447
Interdisciplinary Connections	**SE/TE** View the Art, pp. 445, 446 glencoe.com
Independent Reading	BookLink K–12 CD-ROM Ethnic Anthologies Glencoe Literature Library Glencoe Literature Library Teacher Resources CD-ROM *inTIME* magazine Literature Classics, High School CD-ROM
Technology and Additional Resources	**Planning and Instruction:** TeacherWorks Plus CD-ROM Classroom Presentation Toolkit CD-ROM Literature Online at **glencoe.com** (QuickPass Code: **GLA9879u3T**) **Students Tools:** StudentWorks Plus CD-ROM or DVD-ROM Online Student Edition at **glencoe.com** Literature Online at **glencoe.com** (QuickPass Code: **GLA9800u3**)

Lesson Plan

Glencoe Literature

Because I could not stop for Death (pp. 448–449)

Lesson Plan and Resource Manager

UNIT THREE The Civil War Era 1850–1880, Part 3: A Poetic Revolution

Learning Objectives	**Literary Study:** Analyzing rhyme. Analyzing personification. **Reading:** Analyzing sound devices. Clarifying meaning. **Writing:** Writing a paragraph.

Lesson Summary	On pages **448–449** of the Student Edition, students will be introduced to the following:
	     ▪ **Big Idea:** A Poetic Revolution
	     ▪ **Literary Element:** Personification
	     ▪ **Reading Strategy:** Clarify Meaning
	     ▪ **Vocabulary:** Explore Latin Roots
	     ▪ **Writing Activity:** Write a Paragraph

Lesson Duration	One 45–50 minute session
Readability Scores	Dale-Chall: N/A DRP: N/A Lexile: N/A
Teach	**SE/TE** p. 448 📁 Unit 3 Teaching Resources, Literary Element, p. 220 📁 Unit 3 Teaching Resources, Reading Strategy, p. 221 🖐 Literary Elements Transparency 77 💿 Classroom Presentation Toolkit CD-ROM 💿 Listening Library CD, Selection Audio 💿 TeacherWorks Plus CD-ROM 💿 ▶ Vocabulary PuzzleMaker CD-ROM
Assess	**SE/TE** p. 449 📁 Unit 3 Teaching Resources, Selection Quick Check, p. 222 📁 Unit 3 Teaching Resources, Selection Quick Check (Spanish), p. 223 📁 Assessment Resources, Selection Test, pp. 155–156 💿 ExamView Assessment Suite CD-ROM ▶ Progress Reporter Online Assessment
Differentiated Instruction: English Learners	**TE** English Learner Activities, pp. 448–449 📁 Unit 3 Teaching Resources, English Language Coach, p. 132 📁 Unit 3 Teaching Resources, Selection Summaries: English, Spanish, Vietnamese, Tagalog, Cantonese, Haitian Creole, and Hmong, pp. 214–219 📁 Unit 3 Teaching Resources, Selection Quick Check (Spanish), p. 223 💿 Glencoe Interactive Vocabulary CD-ROM 💿 Listening Library Audio CD 📁 Listening Library Sourcebook: Strategies and Activities
Differentiated Instruction: Approaching Level	💿 Glencoe Interactive Vocabulary CD-ROM 💿 Listening Library Audio CD 📁 Listening Library Sourcebook: Strategies and Activities 💿 Skill Level Up! A Skills-Based Language Arts Game CD-ROM

Differentiated Instruction: Advanced/Pre-AP	▮ Novel Companion SE, pp. 119–162 ▮ Novel Companion TG, pp. 29–36 ● ▶ Literature Classics, High School CD-ROM ● Skill Level Up! A Skills-Based Language Arts Game CD-ROM
Extension	▮ Grammar and Language Workbook SE ▮ Grammar and Language Workbook TAE 🗁 Revising with Style ▮ Spelling Power SE ▮ Spelling Power TAE
Daily Writing	**SE/TE** p. 449
Interdisciplinary Connections	**TE** Language History, p. 448 ● glencoe.com
Independent Reading	● BookLink K–12 CD-ROM 📖 Ethnic Anthologies 📖 Glencoe Literature Library ● Glencoe Literature Library Teacher Resources CD-ROM 📖 *inTIME* magazine ● ▶ Literature Classics, High School CD-ROM
Technology and Additional Resources	**Planning and Instruction:** ● TeacherWorks Plus CD-ROM ● Classroom Presentation Toolkit CD-ROM ▶ Literature Online at **glencoe.com** (QuickPass Code: **GLA9879u3T**) **Students Tools:** ● StudentWorks Plus CD-ROM or DVD-ROM ▶ Online Student Edition at **glencoe.com** ▶ Literature Online at **glencoe.com** (QuickPass Code: **GLA9800u3**)

Lesson Plan

Glencoe Literature

There's a certain Slant of light and *This is my letter to the World* (pp. 450–454)

Lesson Plan and Resource Manager

UNIT THREE The Civil War Era 1850–1880, Part 3: A Poetic Revolution

Learning Objectives	**Literary Study:** Analyzing rhyme. Analyzing personification. **Reading:** Analyzing sound devices. Clarifying meaning. **Writing:** Writing an expository essay. **Grammar:** Using dashes.
Lesson Summary	On pages **450–454** of the Student Edition, students will be introduced to the following: • **Big Idea:** A Poetic Revolution • **Literary Elements:** Rhyme, Personification • **Reading Strategy:** Analyze Sound Devices • **Writing Activity/Grammar:** Expository Essay, Dashes • **Vocabulary:** Academic Vocabulary
Lesson Duration	One 45–50 minute session
Readability Scores	Dale-Chall: N/A DRP: N/A Lexile: N/A
Teach	**SE/TE** pp. 450–451 📁 Unit 3 Teaching Resources, Literary Element, p. 230 📁 Unit 3 Teaching Resources, Reading Strategy, p. 231 📁 Unit 3 Teaching Resources, Selection Vocabulary Practice, p. 232 📁 Unit 3 Teaching Resources, Vocabulary Strategy, p. 233 📖 Grammar and Language Transparency 37 📖 Literary Elements Transparency 88 💿 Classroom Presentation Toolkit CD-ROM 💿 Listening Library CD, Selection Audio 💿 TeacherWorks Plus CD-ROM 💿 Vocabulary PuzzleMaker CD-ROM
Assess	**SE/TE** pp. 452–454 📁 Unit 3 Teaching Resources, Selection Quick Check, p. 234 📁 Unit 3 Teaching Resources, Selection Quick Check (Spanish), p. 235 📁 Assessment Resources, Selection Test, pp. 157–158 💿 ExamView Assessment Suite CD-ROM 💿 Progress Reporter Online Assessment
Differentiated Instruction: English Learners	**TE** English Learner Activities, pp. 450–454 📁 Unit 3 Teaching Resources, English Language Coach, p. 132 📁 English Language Coach 📁 Unit 3 Teaching Resources, Selection Summaries: English, Spanish, Vietnamese, Tagalog, Cantonese, Haitian Creole, and Hmong, pp. 224–229 📁 Unit 3 Teaching Resources, Selection Quick Check (Spanish), p. 235 📁 Glencoe Interactive Vocabulary CD-ROM 💿 Listening Library Audio CD 📁 Listening Library Sourcebook: Strategies and Activities

Differentiated Instruction: Approaching Level	⊚ Glencoe Interactive Vocabulary CD-ROM ⊚ Listening Library Audio CD 🗀 Listening Library Sourcebook: Strategies and Activities ⊚ Skill Level Up! A Skills-Based Language Arts Game CD-ROM
Differentiated Instruction: Advanced/Pre-AP	**TE** Advanced Learner Activities, pp. 450–454 ▉ Novel Companion SE, pp. 119–162 ▉ Novel Companion TG, pp. 29–36 ⊚ ▶ Literature Classics, High School CD-ROM ⊚ Skill Level Up! A Skills-Based Language Arts Game CD-ROM
Extension	▉ Grammar and Language Workbook SE ▉ Grammar and Language Workbook TAE 🗀 Revising with Style ▉ Spelling Power SE ▉ Spelling Power TAE
Daily Writing	**SE/TE** p. 454
Interdisciplinary Connections	**SE/TE** View the Art, p. 450 ▶ glencoe.com
Independent Reading	⊚ BookLink K–12 CD-ROM 📖 Ethnic Anthologies 📖 Glencoe Literature Library ⊚ Glencoe Literature Library Teacher Resources CD-ROM 📖 *inTIME* magazine ⊚ ▶ Literature Classics, High School CD-ROM
Technology and Additional Resources	**Planning and Instruction:** ⊚ TeacherWorks Plus CD-ROM ⊚ Classroom Presentation Toolkit CD-ROM ▶ Literature Online at **glencoe.com** (QuickPass Code: **GLA9879u3T**) **Students Tools:** ⊚ StudentWorks Plus CD-ROM or DVD-ROM ▶ Online Student Edition at **glencoe.com** ▶ Literature Online at **glencoe.com** (QuickPass Code: **GLA9800u3**)

Lesson Plan

Literary Perspective: *Emily Dickinson, An Introduction* (pp. 455–457)

Lesson Plan and Resource Manager

UNIT THREE The Civil War Era 1850–1880, Part 3: A Poetic Revolution

Learning Objectives	**Literary Study:** Making connections across literature. **Reading:** Analyzing informational text. Analyzing literary criticism.
Lesson Summary	On pages **455–457** of the Student Edition, students will be introduced to the following: • **Big Idea:** A Poetic Revolution • **Reading Strategies:** Analyze Literary Criticism, Set a Purpose for Reading • **Writing Activity:** Write a Summary
Lesson Duration	One 45–50 minute session
Readability Scores	Dale-Chall: 10.6 DRP: 66 Lexile: 1360
Focus	**SE/TE** p. 455
Teach	**SE/TE** pp. 455–457 Unit 3 Teaching Resources, Reading Strategy, p. 242 Classroom Presentation Toolkit CD-ROM Listening Library CD, Selection Audio TeacherWorks Plus CD-ROM Vocabulary PuzzleMaker CD-ROM
Assess	**SE/TE** p. 457 Unit 3 Teaching Resources, Selection Quick Check, p. 243 Unit 3 Teaching Resources, Selection Quick Check (Spanish), p. 244 Assessment Resources, Selection Test, pp. 159–160 ExamView Assessment Suite CD-ROM Progress Reporter Online Assessment
Differentiated Instruction: English Learners	Unit 3 Teaching Resources, English Language Coach, p. 132 English Language Coach Unit 3 Teaching Resources, Selection Summaries: English, Spanish, Vietnamese, Tagalog, Cantonese, Haitian Creole, and Hmong, pp. 236–241 Unit 3 Teaching Resources, Selection Quick Check (Spanish), p. 244 Glencoe Interactive Vocabulary CD-ROM Listening Library Audio CD Listening Library Sourcebook: Strategies and Activities
Differentiated Instruction: Approaching Level	**TE** Approaching Level Activities, pp. 455–457 Glencoe Interactive Vocabulary CD-ROM Listening Library Audio CD Listening Library Sourcebook: Strategies and Activities Skill Level Up! A Skills-Based Language Arts Game CD-ROM

Differentiated Instruction: Advanced/Pre-AP	▪ Novel Companion SE, pp. 119–162 ▪ Novel Companion TG, pp. 29–36 ◉ ▸ Literature Classics, High School CD-ROM ◉ Skill Level Up! A Skills-Based Language Arts Game CD-ROM
Extension	▪ Grammar and Language Workbook SE ▪ Grammar and Language Workbook TAE ▭ Revising with Style ▪ Spelling Power SE ▪ Spelling Power TAE
Daily Writing	**SE/TE** p. 457
Interdisciplinary Connections	**SE/TE** View the Photograph, p. 457 ◉ glencoe.com
Independent Reading	◉ BookLink K–12 CD-ROM ▯ Ethnic Anthologies ▯ Glencoe Literature Library ◉ Glencoe Literature Library Teacher Resources CD-ROM ▯ *inTIME* magazine ◉ ▸ Literature Classics, High School CD-ROM
Technology and Additional Resources	**Planning and Instruction:** ◉ TeacherWorks Plus CD-ROM ◉ Classroom Presentation Toolkit CD-ROM ▸ Literature Online at **glencoe.com** (QuickPass Code: **GLA9879u3T**) **Students Tools:** ◉ StudentWorks Plus CD-ROM or DVD-ROM ▸ Online Student Edition at **glencoe.com** ▸ Literature Online at **glencoe.com** (QuickPass Code: **GLA9800u3**)

Lesson Plan

Glencoe Literature

Writing Workshop: Research Report (pp. 458–467)

Lesson Plan and Resource Manager

UNIT THREE The Civil War Era 1850–1880

Learning Objectives	**Writing:** Write a historical research paper using the writing process.
Lesson Duration	Two 45–50 minute sessions
Writing Prompt	Write a Research Report: Write a research report of at least 1,500 words in which you synthesize information from a variety of sources, draw conclusions, and discuss related insights. As you write, keep your audience and purpose in mind.
Focus	**SE/TE** pp. 458, 460, 464, 466
Teach	**SE/TE** pp. 459, 461–463, 465, 467 📖 Writing Resources: Writing Process Strategies 1–23 ✎ Writing Workshop Transparencies 16–20 🗀 Unit 3 Teaching Resources, Writing Workshop Graphic Organizer, p. 246
Assess	🗀 Unit 3 Teaching Resources, Writing Workshop Rubric, pp. 247–248 🗀 Rubrics for Assessing Writing, Listening and Speaking, High School, Historical Research Paper, pp. 16–17 ▶ Glencoe Online Essay Grader at **glencoewriting.com**
Differentiated Instruction: English Learners	**TE** English Learner Activities, pp. 458–467
Differentiated Instruction: Approaching Level	**TE** Approaching Level Activities, pp. 458–467
Differentiated Instruction: Advanced/Pre-AP	**TE** Advanced Learner Activities, pp. 458–467
Extension	📕 Grammar and Language Workbook SE 📕 Grammar and Language Workbook TAE 🗀 Revising with Style 📕 Spelling Power SE 📕 Spelling Power TAE
Daily Writing	**SE/TE** pp. 459, 467
Interdisciplinary Connections	**TE** Cultural History, p. 459 **TE** Language History, p. 460 ▶ **glencoe.com**

Technology and Additional Resources	**Planning and Instruction:** 📘 Grammar and Composition Handbook 📁 Success in Writing: Research and Reports 📁 Writing Constructed Responses 💿 TeacherWorks Plus CD-ROM 💿 Classroom Presentation Toolkit CD-ROM ▶ Glencoe Online Essay Grader at **glencoewriting.com** ▶ Literature Online at **glencoe.com** (QuickPass Code: **GLA9879u3T**) **Students Tools:** 💿 StudentWorks Plus CD-ROM or DVD-ROM ▶ Online Student Edition at **glencoe.com** ▶ Glencoe Online Essay Grader at **glencoewriting.com** ▶ Literature Online at **glencoe.com** (QuickPass Code: **GLA9800u3**)

Lesson Plan

Speaking, Listening, and Viewing Workshop: Multimedia Presentation (pp. 468–471)

Lesson Plan and Resource Manager

UNIT THREE The Civil War Era 1850–1880

Learning Objectives	**Speaking and Listening:** Delivering a multimedia presentation
Lesson Duration	Two 45–50 minute sessions
Assignment	Plan and deliver a multimedia presentation of your historical investigation report. As you develop your presentation, keep your audience and purpose in mind.
Focus	**SE/TE** p. 468
Teach	**SE/TE** pp. 468–471 📁 Unit 3 Teaching Resources, SLV Activity, pp. 249–250 💿 TeacherWorks Plus CD-ROM 💿 Classroom Presentation Toolkit CD-ROM 💿 ▶ Student Presentation Builder on StudentWorks Plus CD-ROM or DVD-ROM
Assess	📁 Unit 3 Teaching Resources, SLV Rubrics, pp. 251–252 📁 Rubrics for Assessing Writing, Listening, and Speaking, pp. 38–39
Differentiated Instruction: English Learners	**TE** English Learner Activities, pp. 468–471
Differentiated Instruction: Approaching Level	**TE** Approaching Level Activities, pp. 468–471
Extension	📕 Grammar and Language Workbook SE/TAE 📁 Revising with Style 📕 Spelling Power SE/TAE
Daily Writing	**SE/TE** pp. 469, 470
Interdisciplinary Connections	▶ glencoe.com
Technology and Additional Resources	**Planning and Instruction:** 💿 TeacherWorks Plus CD-ROM 💿 Classroom Presentation Toolkit CD-ROM ▶ Literature Online at **glencoe.com** (QuickPass Code: **GLA9879u3T**) **Students Tools:** 💿 StudentWorks Plus CD-ROM or DVD-ROM ▶ Online Student Edition at **glencoe.com** ▶ Literature Online at **glencoe.com** (QuickPass Code: **GLA9800u3**)

Lesson Plan

Glencoe Literature

Unit 3 Wrap-Up (pp. 472–479)

Lesson Plan and Resource Manager

UNIT THREE The Civil War Era 1850–1880

Lesson Summary	On pages **472–479** of the Student Edition, students will: • Read independently • Complete the end-of-unit assessment
Lesson Duration	Two 45–50 minute sessions
Focus	**SE/TE** p. 472
Teach	**SE/TE** pp. 472–473
Assess	**SE/TE** pp. 475–479 📁 Assessment Resources, Unit 3 Summative Assessment, pp. 335–336 📕 ACT/SAT Preparation and Practice SE/ATE 💿 ExamView Assessment Suite CD-ROM ▶ Progress Reporter Online Assessment
Differentiated Instruction: English Learners	**TE** English Learner Activities, pp. 472–479
Differentiated Instruction: Approaching Level	**TE** Approaching Level Activities, pp. 472–479
Differentiated Instruction: Advanced/Pre-AP	📕 Novel Companion SE, pp. 119–162; TG, pp. 29–36 💿 ▶ Literature Classics, High School CD-ROM
Extension	📕 Grammar and Language Workbook SE/TAE; Spelling Power SE/TAE 📁 Revising with Style
Daily Writing	**SE/TE** pp. 473, 479
Interdisciplinary Connections	**TE** Literary History: Louisa May Alcott, pp. 472, 473
Independent Reading	💿 BookLink K–12 CD-ROM 📖 Ethnic Anthologies; Glencoe Literature Library; *inTIME* magazine 💿 Glencoe Literature Library Teacher Resources CD-ROM 💿 ▶ Literature Classics, High School CD-ROM
Technology and Additional Resources	**Planning and Instruction:** 💿 TeacherWorks Plus CD-ROM; Classroom Presentation Toolkit CD-ROM ▶ Literature Online at **glencoe.com** (QuickPass Code: **GLA9879u3T**) **Students Tools:** 💿 StudentWorks Plus CD-ROM or DVD-ROM ▶ Online Student Edition at **glencoe.com** ▶ Literature Online at **glencoe.com** (QuickPass Code: **GLA9800u3**)

Lesson Plan

Glencoe Literature

Unit 4 Introduction (pp. 480–494)

Lesson Plan and Resource Manager

UNIT FOUR Regionalism and Realism, 1880–1910

Learning Objectives	**Literary Studies:** Analyzing literary periods. Evaluating historical influences. **Reading:** Connecting to the literature.
Unit Summary	In this unit, students will be introduced to the following: • **Big Ideas:** Regionalism, Realism, and Naturalism • **Reading Strategies:** Analyze Graphic Information, Generalize, Cause and Effect, Compare and Contrast • **Literary Elements:** Dialect, Cultural Characteristics, Imagery, Relate to the Text • **Writing Skills/Grammar:** Contrast Literary Periods • **Listening/Speaking/Viewing Skills:** Analyze Art, Visual Literacy
Lesson Duration	Two 45–50 minute sessions
Focus	**SE/TE** pp. 480–481 Daily Language Practice Transparencies 41, 42 Literature Launchers: Pre-Reading Videos DVD, Unit 4 Launcher Literature Launchers Teacher Guide
Teach	**SE/TE** pp. 482–493 Unit 4 Teaching Resources, Unit Introduction, pp. 1–2 Unit 4 Teaching Resources, Big Idea Foldable, pp. 3–4 Unit 4 Teaching Resources, Big Idea School-to-Home Connection, p. 5 Unit 4 Teaching Resources, Unit Challenge Planner, pp. 12–15 Unit 4 Teaching Resources: Academic Vocabulary Development, pp. 16–17 Classroom Presentation Toolkit CD-ROM TeacherWorks Plus CD-ROM
Assess	**SE/TE** p. 494 Assessment Resources, Unit 4 Diagnostic Assessment, pp. 25–32 ACT/SAT Preparation and Practice SE/ATE ExamView Assessment Suite CD-ROM Progress Reporter Online Assessment
Differentiated Instruction: English Learners	**TE** English Learner Activities, pp. 480–494 Unit 4 Teaching Resources, Big Idea School-to-Home Connections: English, Spanish, Vietnamese, Tagalog, Cantonese, Haitian Creole, and Hmong, pp. 6–11 English Language Coach
Differentiated Instruction: Approaching Level	**TE** Approaching Level Activities, pp. 480–494 Skill Level Up! A Skills-Based Language Arts Game CD-ROM

Differentiated Instruction: Advanced/Pre-AP	**TE** Advanced Learner Activities, pp. 480–494 ■ Novel Companion SE, pp. 163–206 ■ Novel Companion TG, pp. 37–44 ● ▶ Literature Classics, High School CD-ROM ● Skill Level Up! A Skills-Based Language Arts Game CD-ROM
Extension	■ Grammar and Language Workbook SE ■ Grammar and Language Workbook TAE 📁 Revising with Style ■ Spelling Power SE ■ Spelling Power TAE
Daily Writing	**TE** pp. 484, 492 **SE/TE** p. 494
Interdisciplinary Connections	**TE** Cultural History: Railroads and Growth, p. 483 **TE** Cultural History: Moving Away from Romanticism, p. 490 **TE** Cultural History: Psychology, p. 492 **TE** Literary History: Realism and Naturalism, p. 487 **TE** Literary History: Children's Literature, p. 484 **TE** Literary History: Twain's Inspirations, p. 488 **SE/TE** View the Art, pp. 480–481, 486, 489, 491 **SE/TE** View the Photograph, pp. 485, 493 ● glencoe.com
Independent Reading	● BookLink K–12 CD-ROM 📖 Ethnic Anthologies 📖 Glencoe Literature Library ● Glencoe Literature Library Teacher Resources CD-ROM 📖 *inTIME* magazine ● ▶ Literature Classics, High School CD-ROM
Technology and Additional Resources	**Planning and Instruction:** ● TeacherWorks Plus CD-ROM ● Classroom Presentation Toolkit CD-ROM ▶ Literature Online at **glencoe.com** (QuickPass Code: **GLA9879u4T**) **Students Tools:** ● StudentWorks Plus CD-ROM or DVD-ROM ▶ Online Student Edition at **glencoe.com** ▶ Literature Online at **glencoe.com** (QuickPass Code: **GLA9800u4**)

Lesson Plan

Part 1 Opener and *The Celebrated Jumping Frog of Calaveras County* (pp. 495–503)

Lesson Plan and Resource Manager

UNIT FOUR Regionalism and Realism 1880–1910, Part 1: Regionalism and Local Color

Learning Objectives	**Literary Study:** Analyzing dialect. **Reading:** Analyzing comic devices. **Writing:** Writing a story.
Lesson Summary	On pages **495–503** of the Student Edition, students will be introduced to the following: • **Big Idea:** Regionalism • **Literary Element:** Dialect • **Reading Strategy:** Analyze Comic Devices • **Writing Skill/Grammar:** Write a Story • **Vocabulary:** Word Origins, Visual Vocabulary • **Listening/Speaking/Viewing Skill:** Analyze Art
Lesson Duration	One to five 45–50 minute sessions
Readability Scores	Dale-Chall: 10.2 DRP: 59 Lexile: 1410
Focus	SE/TE pp. 496–497 Selection Focus Transparency 30 Daily Language Practice Transparency 43 Literature Launchers: Pre-Reading Videos DVD, Selection Launcher Literature Launchers Teacher Guide
Teach	SE/TE pp. 498–502 Interactive Read and Write SE, pp. 147–158 Interactive Read and Write TE, pp. 147–158 Unit 4 Teaching Resources, Literary Element, p. 26 Unit 4 Teaching Resources, Reading Strategy, p. 27 Unit 4 Teaching Resources, Selection Vocabulary Practice, p. 28 Unit 4 Teaching Resources, Vocabulary Strategy, p. 29 Unit 4 Teaching Resources, Grammar Practice, p. 30 Literary Elements Transparency 25 Classroom Presentation Toolkit CD-ROM Listening Library CD, Selection Audio TeacherWorks Plus CD-ROM Vocabulary PuzzleMaker CD-ROM
Assess	SE/TE p. 503 Unit 4 Teaching Resources, Selection Quick Check, p. 31 Unit 4 Teaching Resources, Selection Quick Check (Spanish), p. 32 Assessment Resources, Selection Test, pp. 161–162 ExamView Assessment Suite CD-ROM Progress Reporter Online Assessment

Differentiated Instruction: English Learners	**TE** English Learner Activities, pp. 495–503
	▪ Interactive Read and Write (EL) SE, pp. 147–158
	▪ Interactive Read and Write (EL) TE, pp. 147–158
	📁 Unit 4 Teaching Resources, English Language Coach, p. 19
	📁 Unit 4 Teaching Resources, English Language Coach, English, Spanish, Vietnamese, Tagalog, Cantonese, Haitian Creole, and Hmong, pp. 20–25
	📁 Unit 4 Teaching Resources, Selection Quick Check (Spanish), p. 32
	📁 English Language Coach
	💿 Glencoe Interactive Vocabulary CD-ROM
	💿 Listening Library Audio CD
	📁 Listening Library Sourcebook: Strategies and Activities
Differentiated Instruction: Approaching Level	**TE** Approaching Level Activities, pp. 495–503
	▪ Interactive Read and Write (Approaching) SE, pp. 147–158
	▪ Interactive Read and Write (Approaching) TE, pp. 147–158
	💿 Glencoe Interactive Vocabulary CD-ROM
	💿 Listening Library Audio CD
	📁 Listening Library Sourcebook: Strategies and Activities
	💿 Skill Level Up! A Skills-Based Language Arts Game CD-ROM
Differentiated Instruction: Advanced/Pre-AP	**TE** Advanced Learner Activities, pp. 495–503
	▪ Novel Companion SE, pp. 163–206
	▪ Novel Companion TG, pp. 37–44
	💿 ▶ Literature Classics, High School CD-ROM
	💿 Skill Level Up! A Skills-Based Language Arts Game CD-ROM
Extension	▪ Grammar and Language Workbook SE
	▪ Grammar and Language Workbook TAE
	📁 Revising with Style
	▪ Spelling Power SE
	▪ Spelling Power TAE
Daily Writing	**SE/TE** p. 503
Interdisciplinary Connections	**SE/TE** View the Art, p. 495
	SE/TE View the Photograph, p. 501
	TE Political History: Andrew Jackson, p. 500
	▶ glencoe.com
Independent Reading	💿 BookLink K–12 CD-ROM
	📖 Ethnic Anthologies; Glencoe Literature Library; *inTIME* magazine
	💿 Glencoe Literature Library Teacher Resources CD-ROM
	💿 ▶ Literature Classics, High School CD-ROM
Technology and Additional Resources	**Planning and Instruction:**
	💿 TeacherWorks Plus CD-ROM
	💿 Classroom Presentation Toolkit CD-ROM
	▶ Literature Online at **glencoe.com** (QuickPass Code: **GLA9879u4T**)
	Students Tools:
	💿 StudentWorks Plus CD-ROM or DVD-ROM
	▶ Online Student Edition at **glencoe.com**
	▶ Literature Online at **glencoe.com** (QuickPass Code: **GLA9800u4**)

Lesson Plan

Glencoe Literature

from *Two Views of the River* and TIME: *Life Along the Mississippi* (pp. 504–513)

Lesson Plan and Resource Manager

UNIT FOUR Regionalism and Realism 1880–1910, Part 1: Regionalism and Local Color

Learning Objectives	**Literary Study:** Analyzing dialect. **Reading:** Analyzing comic devices. Clarifying meaning. Analyzing informational text. Using text features. **Writing:** Writing a story.
Lesson Summary	On pages **504–513** of the Student Edition, students will be introduced to the following: • **Big Idea:** Regionalism • **Literary Elements:** Analogy, Tone • **Reading Strategies:** Compare and Contrast Language, Clarify Meaning • **Writing Activities/Grammar:** Travel Brochure, Summary • **Vocabulary:** Academic Vocabulary
Lesson Duration	One 45–50 minute session
Readability Scores	"Two Views of the River" Dale-Chall: 7.7 DRP: 63 Lexile: 1130 TIME: "Life Along the Mississippi" Dale-Chall: 7.1 DRP: 62 Lexile: 1120
Focus	**SE/TE** pp. 504, 508 📖 Selection Focus Transparency 31
Teach	**SE/TE** pp. 504–505, 508–512 📁 Unit 4 Teaching Resources, Literary Element, p. 39 📁 Unit 4 Teaching Resources, Reading Strategy, pp. 40, 51 📁 Unit 4 Teaching Resources, Vocabulary Strategy, p. 41 📁 Unit 4 Teaching Resources, Grammar Practice, p. 42 📖 Literary Elements Transparency 4 💿 Classroom Presentation Toolkit CD-ROM 💿 Listening Library CD, Selection Audio 💿 TeacherWorks Plus CD-ROM 💿 Vocabulary PuzzleMaker CD-ROM
Assess	**SE/TE** pp. 506–507, 513 📁 Unit 4 Teaching Resources, Selection Quick Check, pp. 43, 52 📁 Unit 4 Teaching Resources, Selection Quick Check (Spanish), pp. 44, 53 📁 Assessment Resources, Selection Test, pp. 163–164, 165–166 💿 ExamView Assessment Suite CD-ROM 💿 Progress Reporter Online Assessment
Differentiated Instruction: English Learners	**TE** English Learner Activities, pp. 504–513 📁 Unit 4 Teaching Resources, English Language Coach, p. 19 📁 Unit 4 Teaching Resources, Selection Summaries: English, Spanish, Vietnamese, Tagalog, Cantonese, Haitian Creole, and Hmong pp. 33–38, 45–50 📁 Unit 4 Teaching Resources, Selection Quick Check (Spanish), pp. 44, 53 📁 English Language Coach

Differentiated Instruction: English Learners *(continued)*	● Glencoe Interactive Vocabulary CD-ROM ● Listening Library Audio CD 📁 Listening Library Sourcebook: Strategies and Activities
Differentiated Instruction: Approaching Level	**TE** Approaching Level Activities, pp. 504–513 ● Glencoe Interactive Vocabulary CD-ROM ● Listening Library Audio CD 📁 Listening Library Sourcebook: Strategies and Activities ● Skill Level Up! A Skills-Based Language Arts Game CD-ROM
Differentiated Instruction: Advanced/Pre-AP	**TE** Advanced Learner Activities, pp. 504–513 📘 Novel Companion SE, pp. 163–206 📘 Novel Companion TG, pp. 37–44 ● ▶ Literature Classics, High School CD-ROM ● Skill Level Up! A Skills-Based Language Arts Game CD-ROM
Extension	📘 Grammar and Language Workbook SE 📘 Grammar and Language Workbook TAE 📁 Revising with Style 📘 Spelling Power SE 📘 Spelling Power TAE
Daily Writing	**SE/TE** p. 507
Interdisciplinary Connections	**SE/TE** View the Art, p. 504 **SE/TE** View the Photograph, pp. 505, 511, 512 **TE** Cultural History: Two Wars, p. 509 **TE** Cultural History: Mississippi, p. 510 ▶ glencoe.com
Independent Reading	● BookLink K–12 CD-ROM 📖 Ethnic Anthologies 📖 Glencoe Literature Library ● Glencoe Literature Library Teacher Resources CD-ROM 📖 *inTIME* magazine ● ▶ Literature Classics, High School CD-ROM
Technology and Additional Resources	**Planning and Instruction:** ● TeacherWorks Plus CD-ROM ● Classroom Presentation Toolkit CD-ROM ▶ Literature Online at **glencoe.com** (QuickPass Code: **GLA9879u4T**) **Students Tools:** ● StudentWorks Plus CD-ROM or DVD-ROM ● Online Student Edition at **glencoe.com** ● Literature Online at **glencoe.com** (QuickPass Code: **GLA9800u4**)

Lesson Plan

Glencoe Literature

Lucinda Matlock and Fiddler Jones (pp. 514–518)

Lesson Plan and Resource Manager

UNIT FOUR Regionalism and Realism 1880–1910, Part 1: Regionalism and Local Color

Learning Objectives	**Literary Study:** Analyzing dramatic monologue. **Reading:** Drawing conclusions about characters. **Writing:** Writing a poem.
Lesson Summary	On pages **514–518** of the Student Edition, students will be introduced to the following: • **Big Idea:** Regionalism • **Literary Element:** Dramatic Monologue • **Reading Strategy:** Draw Conclusions About Characters • **Vocabulary:** Word Usage • **Writing Skill/Grammar:** Poem
Lesson Duration	One 45–50 minute session
Readability Scores	N/A
Focus	**SE/TE** pp. 514–515 ⬚ Selection Focus Transparency 32 ⬚ Daily Language Practice Transparency 44
Teach	**SE/TE** pp. 516–517 ⬚ Unit 4 Teaching Resources, Literary Element, p. 60 ⬚ Unit 4 Teaching Resources, Reading Strategy, p. 61 ⬚ Unit 4 Teaching Resources, Vocabulary Strategy, p. 62 ⬚ Grammar and Language Transparency 16 ⬚ Literary Elements Transparency 29 ⬚ Classroom Presentation Toolkit CD-ROM ⬚ Listening Library CD, Selection Audio ⬚ TeacherWorks Plus CD-ROM ⬚ Vocabulary PuzzleMaker CD-ROM
Assess	**SE/TE** p. 518 ⬚ Unit 4 Teaching Resources, Selection Quick Check, p. 63 ⬚ Unit 4 Teaching Resources, Selection Quick Check (Spanish), p. 64 ⬚ Assessment Resources, Selection Test, pp. 167–168 ⬚ ExamView Assessment Suite CD-ROM ⬚ Progress Reporter Online Assessment
Differentiated Instruction: English Learners	**TE** English Learner Activities, pp. 514–518 ⬚ Unit 4 Teaching Resources, English Language Coach, p. 19 ⬚ Unit 4 Teaching Resources, Selection Summaries: English, Spanish, Vietnamese, Tagalog, Cantonese, Haitian Creole, and Hmong, pp. 54–59 ⬚ Unit 4 Teaching Resources, Selection Quick Check (Spanish), p. 64 ⬚ English Language Coach ⬚ Glencoe Interactive Vocabulary CD-ROM ⬚ Listening Library Audio CD ⬚ Listening Library Sourcebook: Strategies and Activities

Differentiated Instruction: Approaching Level	**TE** Approaching Level Activities, pp. 514–518 Glencoe Interactive Vocabulary CD-ROM Listening Library Audio CD Listening Library Sourcebook: Strategies and Activities Skill Level Up! A Skills-Based Language Arts Game CD-ROM
Differentiated Instruction: Advanced/Pre-AP	Novel Companion SE, pp. 163–206 Novel Companion TG, pp. 37–44 Literature Classics, High School CD-ROM Skill Level Up! A Skills-Based Language Arts Game CD-ROM
Extension	Grammar and Language Workbook SE Grammar and Language Workbook TAE Revising with Style Spelling Power SE Spelling Power TAE
Daily Writing	**SE/TE** p. 518
Interdisciplinary Connections	**SE/TE** View the Art, pp. 516, 517 glencoe.com
Independent Reading	BookLink K–12 CD-ROM Ethnic Anthologies Glencoe Literature Library Glencoe Literature Library Teacher Resources CD-ROM *inTIME* magazine Literature Classics, High School CD-ROM
Technology and Additional Resources	**Planning and Instruction:** TeacherWorks Plus CD-ROM Classroom Presentation Toolkit CD-ROM Literature Online at **glencoe.com** (QuickPass Code: **GLA9879u4T**) **Students Tools:** StudentWorks Plus CD-ROM or DVD-ROM Online Student Edition at **glencoe.com** Literature Online at **glencoe.com** (QuickPass Code: **GLA9800u4**)

Lesson Plan

A Wagner Matinée and Grammar Workshop (pp. 519–530)

Lesson Plan and Resource Manager

UNIT FOUR Regionalism and Realism 1880–1910, Part 1: Regionalism and Local Color

Learning Objectives	**Literary Study:** Analyzing point of view. **Reading:** Identifying sequence. **Writing:** Writing a reflective essay. **Grammar:** Using absolute phrases. Distinguishing between essential and nonessential appositives. Using commas with nonessential elements.
Lesson Summary	On pages **519–529** of the Student Edition, students will be introduced to the following: • **Big Idea:** Regionalism • **Literary Elements:** Point of View, Voice • **Reading Strategy:** Identify Sequence • **Vocabulary:** Analogies, Academic Vocabulary • **Listening/Speaking/Viewing Skills:** Analyze Art, Analyze Music • **Writing Skill/Grammar:** Absolute Phrases • **Respond Through Writing:** Reflective Essay On pages **530** of the Student Edition, students will be introduced to the following: • **Grammar Workshop:** Appositives
Lesson Duration	Two to five 45–50 minute sessions
Readability Scores	Dale-Chall: 10.5 DRP: 63 Lexile: 1410
Focus	**SE/TE** pp. 519–520, 530 Selection Focus Transparency 33 Daily Language Practice Transparencies 45, 46 Literature Launchers: Pre-Reading Videos DVD, Selection Launcher Literature Launchers Teacher Guide
Teach	**SE/TE** pp. 521–526, 529, 530 Interactive Read and Write SE/TE, pp. 159–170 Unit 4 Teaching Resources, Literary Element, p. 71 Unit 4 Teaching Resources, Reading Strategy, p. 72 Unit 4 Teaching Resources, Selection Vocabulary Practice, p. 73 Unit 4 Teaching Resources, Vocabulary Strategy, p. 74 Unit 4 Teaching Resources, Grammar Practice, p. 75 Unit 4 Teaching Resources, Grammar Workshop, p. 78 Literary Elements Transparency 80 Classroom Presentation Toolkit CD-ROM Listening Library CD, Selection Audio TeacherWorks Plus CD-ROM Vocabulary PuzzleMaker CD-ROM
Assess	**SE/TE** pp. 527–528, 530 Unit 4 Teaching Resources, Selection Quick Check, p. 76 Unit 4 Teaching Resources, Selection Quick Check (Spanish), p. 77

Assess *(continued)*	📁 Assessment Resources, Selection Test, pp. 169–170
	💿 ExamView Assessment Suite CD-ROM
	▶️ Progress Reporter Online Assessment
Differentiated Instruction: English Learners	**TE** English Learner Activities, pp. 519–529
	📕 Interactive Read and Write (EL) SE/TE, pp. 159–170
	📁 Unit 4 Teaching Resources, English Language Coach, p. 19
	📁 Unit 4 Teaching Resources, Selection Summaries: English, Spanish, Vietnamese, Tagalog, Cantonese, Haitian Creole, and Hmong, pp. 65–70
	📁 Unit 4 Teaching Resources, Selection Quick Check (Spanish), p. 77
	📁 English Language Coach
	💿 Glencoe Interactive Vocabulary CD-ROM
	💿 Listening Library Audio CD
	📁 Listening Library Sourcebook: Strategies and Activities
Differentiated Instruction: Approaching Level	**TE** Approaching Level Activities, pp. 519–529
	📕 Interactive Read and Write (Approaching) SE/TE, pp. 159–170
	💿 Glencoe Interactive Vocabulary CD-ROM
	💿 Listening Library Audio CD
	📁 Listening Library Sourcebook: Strategies and Activities
	💿 Skill Level Up! A Skills-Based Language Arts Game CD-ROM
Differentiated Instruction: Advanced/Pre-AP	📕 Novel Companion SE, pp. 163–206
	📕 Novel Companion TG, pp. 37–44
	💿 ▶️ Literature Classics, High School CD-ROM
	💿 Skill Level Up! A Skills-Based Language Arts Game CD-ROM
Extension	📕 Grammar and Language Workbook SE
	📕 Grammar and Language Workbook TAE
	📁 Revising with Style
	📕 Spelling Power SE
	📕 Spelling Power TAE
Daily Writing	**TE** p. 522
	SE/TE p. 529
Interdisciplinary Connections	**SE/TE** View the Art, pp. 521, 523
	TE Cultural History: Richard Wagner, p. 524
	▶️ glencoe.com
Independent Reading	💿 BookLink K–12 CD-ROM
	📗 Ethnic Anthologies
	📗 Glencoe Literature Library
	💿 Glencoe Literature Library Teacher Resources CD-ROM
	📗 *inTIME* magazine
	💿 ▶️ Literature Classics, High School CD-ROM
Technology and Additional Resources	**Planning and Instruction:**
	💿 TeacherWorks Plus CD-ROM
	💿 Classroom Presentation Toolkit CD-ROM
	▶️ Literature Online at **glencoe.com** (QuickPass Code: **GLA9879u4T**)
	Students Tools:
	💿 StudentWorks Plus CD-ROM or DVD-ROM
	▶️ Online Student Edition at **glencoe.com**
	▶️ Literature Online at **glencoe.com** (QuickPass Code: **GLA9800u4**)

Lesson Plan

Glencoe Literature

I Will Fight No More Forever (pp. 531–534)

Lesson Plan and Resource Manager

UNIT FOUR Regionalism and Realism 1880–1910, Part 1: Regionalism and Local Color

Learning Objectives	**Literary Study:** Analyzing tone. **Reading:** Evaluating style. **Writing:** Writing a journal entry.
Lesson Summary	On pages **531–534** of the Student Edition, students will be introduced to the following: ▪ **Big Idea:** Regionalism ▪ **Literary Element:** Tone ▪ **Reading Skill:** Evaluate Style ▪ **Writing Skill/Grammar:** Journal Entry ▪ **Vocabulary:** Academic Vocabulary
Lesson Duration	One 45–50 minute session
Readability Scores	Dale-Chall: 3.0 DRP: 41 Lexile: 380
Focus	**SE/TE** pp. 531–532 🖴 Selection Focus Transparency 34 🖴 Daily Language Practice Transparency 47
Teach	**SE/TE** p. 533 📁 Unit 4 Teaching Resources, Literary Element, p. 85 📁 Unit 4 Teaching Resources, Reading Strategy, p. 86 📁 Unit 4 Teaching Resources, Vocabulary Strategy, p. 87 📁 Unit 4 Teaching Resources, Grammar Practice, p. 88 🖴 Read Aloud, Think Aloud Transparencies 19–21 🖴 Literary Elements Transparency 105 💿 Classroom Presentation Toolkit CD-ROM 💿 Listening Library CD, Selection Audio 💿 TeacherWorks Plus CD-ROM 💿 Vocabulary PuzzleMaker CD-ROM
Assess	**SE/TE** p. 534 📁 Unit 4 Teaching Resources, Selection Quick Check, p. 89 📁 Unit 4 Teaching Resources, Selection Quick Check (Spanish), p. 90 📁 Assessment Resources, Selection Test, pp. 171–172 💿 ExamView Assessment Suite CD-ROM 💿 Progress Reporter Online Assessment

Differentiated Instruction: English Learners	**TE** English Learner Activities, pp. 531–534
	📁 Unit 4 Teaching Resources, English Language Coach, p. 19
	📁 Unit 4 Teaching Resources, Selection Summaries: English, Spanish, Vietnamese, Tagalog, Cantonese, Haitian Creole, Hmong, pp. 79–84
	📁 Unit 4 Teaching Resources, Selection Quick Check (Spanish), p. 90
	📁 English Language Coach
	💿 Glencoe Interactive Vocabulary CD-ROM
	💿 Listening Library Audio CD
	📁 Listening Library Sourcebook: Strategies and Activities
Differentiated Instruction: Approaching Level	**TE** Approaching Level Activities, pp. 531–534
	💿 Glencoe Interactive Vocabulary CD-ROM
	💿 Listening Library Audio CD
	📁 Listening Library Sourcebook: Strategies and Activities
	💿 Skill Level Up! A Skills-Based Language Arts Game CD-ROM
Differentiated Instruction: Advanced/Pre-AP	📙 Novel Companion SE, pp. 163–206
	📙 Novel Companion TG, pp. 37–44
	💿 ▶ Literature Classics, High School CD-ROM
	💿 Skill Level Up! A Skills-Based Language Arts Game CD-ROM
Extension	📙 Grammar and Language Workbook SE
	📙 Grammar and Language Workbook TAE
	📁 Revising with Style
	📙 Spelling Power SE
	📙 Spelling Power TAE
Daily Writing	**SE/TE** p. 534
Interdisciplinary Connections	**SE/TE** View the Art, p. 533
	TE Cultural History, Media Influence, p. 532
	▶ glencoe.com
Independent Reading	💿 BookLink K–12 CD-ROM
	📖 Ethnic Anthologies
	📖 Glencoe Literature Library
	💿 Glencoe Literature Library Teacher Resources CD-ROM
	📖 inTIME magazine
	💿 ▶ Literature Classics, High School CD-ROM
Technology and Additional Resources	**Planning and Instruction:**
	💿 TeacherWorks Plus CD-ROM
	💿 Classroom Presentation Toolkit CD-ROM
	▶ Literature Online at **glencoe.com** (QuickPass Code: **GLA9879u4T**)
	Students Tools:
	💿 StudentWorks Plus CD-ROM or DVD-ROM
	▶ Online Student Edition at **glencoe.com**
	▶ Literature Online at **glencoe.com** (QuickPass Code: **GLA9800u4**)

Lesson Plan

Glencoe Literature

Part 2 Opener, Literary History: Urban America's Two Faces, *April Showers*, and Vocabulary Workshop (pp. 535–549)

Lesson Plan and Resource Manager

UNIT FOUR Regionalism and Realism 1880–1910, Part 2: Realism and Naturalism

Learning Objectives	**Literary Study:** Analyzing literary periods. Evaluating historical influences. Connecting to the literature. Analyzing flashback. **Reading:** Making and verifying predictions. **Writing:** Applying point of view in a brief narrative. **Vocabulary:** Understanding language resources.
Lesson Summary	On pages **535–549** of the Student Edition, students will be introduced to the following: • **Big Idea:** Realism • **Literary Elements:** Flashback, Characterization • **Reading Strategy:** Make and Verify Predictions • **Writing Skill/Grammar:** Apply Point of View • **Vocabulary:** Denotation and Connotation, Thesaurus Usage
Lesson Duration	Two 45–50 minute sessions
Readability Scores	Dale-Chall: 5.8 DRP: 60 Lexile: 1020
Focus	SE/TE pp. 536, 538–539, 549 📖 Daily Language Practice Transparencies 48, 49
Teach	SE/TE pp. 536–537, 540–546, 549 📁 Unit 4 Teaching Resources, Literary History: The Two Faces of Urban America, pp. 92–93 📁 Unit 4 Teaching Resources, Literary Element, p. 101 📁 Unit 4 Teaching Resources, Reading Strategy, p. 102 📁 Unit 4 Teaching Resources, Selection Vocabulary Practice, p. 103 📁 Unit 4 Teaching Resources, Vocabulary Strategy, p. 104 📁 Unit 4 Teaching Resources, Grammar Practice, p. 105 📖 Literary Elements Transparency 42 💿 Classroom Presentation Toolkit CD-ROM 💿 Listening Library CD, Selection Audio 💿 TeacherWorks Plus CD-ROM 💿 ▶ Vocabulary PuzzleMaker CD-ROM
Assess	SE/TE pp. 538, 547–548, 549 📁 Unit 4 Teaching Resources, Selection Quick Check, p. 106 📁 Unit 4 Teaching Resources, Selection Quick Check (Spanish), p. 107 📁 Assessment Resources, Selection Test, pp. 173–174 💿 ExamView Assessment Suite CD-ROM ▶ Progress Reporter Online Assessment

Differentiated Instruction: English Learners	**TE** English Learner Activities, pp. 535–549 📁 Unit 4 Teaching Resources, English Language Coach, p. 94 📁 Unit 4 Teaching Resources, Selection Summaries: English, Spanish, Vietnamese, Tagalog, Cantonese, Haitian Creole, and Hmong, pp. 95–100 📁 Unit 4 Teaching Resources, Selection Quick Check (Spanish), p. 107 📁 English Language Coach 💿 Glencoe Interactive Vocabulary CD-ROM 💿 Listening Library Audio CD 📁 Listening Library Sourcebook: Strategies and Activities
Differentiated Instruction: Approaching Level	**TE** Approaching Level Activities, pp. 535–549 💿 Glencoe Interactive Vocabulary CD-ROM 💿 Listening Library Audio CD 📁 Listening Library Sourcebook: Strategies and Activities 💿 Skill Level Up! A Skills-Based Language Arts Game CD-ROM
Differentiated Instruction: Advanced/Pre-AP	📘 Novel Companion SE, pp. 163–206 📘 Novel Companion TG, pp. 37–44 💿 ▶ Literature Classics, High School CD-ROM 💿 Skill Level Up! A Skills-Based Language Arts Game CD-ROM
Extension	📘 Grammar and Language Workbook SE 📘 Grammar and Language Workbook TAE 📁 Revising with Style 📘 Spelling Power SE 📘 Spelling Power TAE
Daily Writing	**SE/TE** pp. 537, 548
Interdisciplinary Connections	**SE/TE** View the Art, pp. 535, 537 **SE/TE** View the Photograph, p. 544 **TE** Language History, A-one, p. 540 **TE** Cultural History, Medicine in the Early 1900s, p. 542 **TE** Literary History, George Eliot, p. 541 ▶ **glencoe.com**
Independent Reading	💿 BookLink K–12 CD-ROM 📖 Ethnic Anthologies 📖 Glencoe Literature Library 💿 Glencoe Literature Library Teacher Resources CD-ROM 📖 inTIME magazine 💿 ▶ Literature Classics, High School CD-ROM
Technology and Additional Resources	**Planning and Instruction:** 💿 TeacherWorks Plus CD-ROM 💿 Classroom Presentation Toolkit CD-ROM ▶ Literature Online at **glencoe.com** (QuickPass Code: **GLA9879u4T**) **Students Tools:** 💿 StudentWorks Plus CD-ROM or DVD-ROM ▶ Online Student Edition at **glencoe.com** ▶ Literature Online at **glencoe.com** (QuickPass Code: **GLA9800u4**)

Copyright © by The McGraw-Hill Companies, Inc.

Copyright © by The McGraw-Hill Companies, Inc.

Lesson Plan

Glencoe Literature

Comparing Literature: *The Story of an Hour,* *The Darling,* and *Richness* (pp. 550–567)

Lesson Plan and Resource Manager

UNIT FOUR Regionalism and Realism 1880–1910, Part 2: Realism and Naturalism

Learning Objectives	**Literary Study:** Comparing cultural context. Comparing historical context.
Lesson Summary	On pages **550–567** of the Student Edition, students will be introduced to the following: • **Big Idea:** Realism • **Literary Elements:** Social Context, Conflict • **Reading Skills:** Compare and Contrast, Apply Background Knowledge • **Writing Skills/Grammar:** Interior Monologue, Short-Response Essay • **Vocabulary:** Word Usage • **Listening/Speaking/Viewing Skill:** Discussion
Lesson Duration	Three 45–50 minute sessions
Readability Scores	"The Story of an Hour" Dale-Chall: 7.3 DRP: 57 Lexile: 970 "The Darling" Dale-Chall: 7.3 DRP: 57 Lexile: 1100
Focus	**SE/TE** pp. 550–552, 557, 566 ✍ Selection Focus Transparency 35 ✍ Daily Language Practice Transparency 50
Teach	**SE/TE** pp. 553–555, 558–565, 566 📁 Unit 4 Teaching Resources, Comparing Literature Graphic Organizer, p. 108 📁 Unit 4 Teaching Resources, Literary Element, p. 115 📁 Unit 4 Teaching Resources, Reading Strategy, p. 116 📁 Unit 4 Teaching Resources, Selection Vocabulary Practice, p. 117 📁 Unit 4 Teaching Resources, Vocabulary Strategy, p. 118 📁 Unit 4 Teaching Resources, Grammar Practice, p. 119 ✍ Literary Elements Transparency 22 💿 Classroom Presentation Toolkit CD-ROM 💿 Listening Library CD, Selection Audio 💿 TeacherWorks Plus CD-ROM 💿 Vocabulary PuzzleMaker CD-ROM
Assess	**SE/TE** pp. 556, 567 📁 Unit 4 Teaching Resources, Selection Quick Check, p. 120 📁 Unit 4 Teaching Resources, Selection Quick Check (Spanish), p. 121 📁 Assessment Resources, Selection Test, pp. 175–176 💿 ExamView Assessment Suite CD-ROM 💿 Progress Reporter Online Assessment

Differentiated Instruction: English Learners	**TE** English Learner Activities, pp. 550–567
	🗁 Unit 4 Teaching Resources, English Language Coach, p. 94
	🗁 Unit 4 Teaching Resources, Selection Summaries: English, Spanish, Vietnamese, Tagalog, Cantonese, Haitian Creole, and Hmong, pp. 109–114
	🗁 Unit 4 Teaching Resources, Selection Quick Check (Spanish), p. 121
	🗁 English Language Coach
	💿 Glencoe Interactive Vocabulary CD-ROM
	💿 Listening Library Audio CD
	🗁 Listening Library Sourcebook: Strategies and Activities
Differentiated Instruction: Approaching Level	**TE** Approaching Level Activities, pp. 550–567
	💿 Glencoe Interactive Vocabulary CD-ROM
	💿 Listening Library Audio CD
	🗁 Listening Library Sourcebook: Strategies and Activities
	💿 Skill Level Up! A Skills-Based Language Arts Game CD-ROM
Differentiated Instruction: Advanced/Pre-AP	**TE** Advanced Learner Activities, pp. 550–567
	📗 Novel Companion SE, pp. 163–206
	📗 Novel Companion TG, pp. 37–44
	💿 ▶ Literature Classics, High School CD-ROM
	💿 Skill Level Up! A Skills-Based Language Arts Game CD-ROM
Extension	📗 Grammar and Language Workbook SE
	📗 Grammar and Language Workbook TAE
	🗁 Revising with Style
	📗 Spelling Power SE
	📗 Spelling Power TAE
Daily Writing	**TE** pp. 552, 554, 564
	SE/TE p. 567
Interdisciplinary Connections	**SE/TE** View the Art, pp. 553, 559, 562
	TE Cultural History, Women's Career Choices, p. 551
	TE Cultural History, Telegram, p. 554
	TE Cultural History, Nike, p. 555
	▶ **glencoe.com**
Independent Reading	💿 BookLink K–12 CD-ROM
	📖 Ethnic Anthologies; Glencoe Literature Library; *inTIME* magazine
	💿 Glencoe Literature Library Teacher Resources CD-ROM
	💿 ▶ Literature Classics, High School CD-ROM
Technology and Additional Resources	**Planning and Instruction:**
	💿 TeacherWorks Plus CD-ROM
	💿 Classroom Presentation Toolkit CD-ROM
	▶ Literature Online at **glencoe.com** (QuickPass Code: **GLA9879u4T**)
	Students Tools:
	💿 StudentWorks Plus CD-ROM or DVD-ROM
	▶ Online Student Edition at **glencoe.com**
	▶ Literature Online at **glencoe.com** (QuickPass Code: **GLA9800u4**)

Lesson Plan

Douglass and *We Wear the Mask* (pp. 568–572)

Lesson Plan and Resource Manager

UNIT FOUR Regionalism and Realism 1880–1910, Part 2: Realism and Naturalism

Learning Objectives	**Literary Study:** Analyzing rhyme scheme. **Reading:** Clarifying meaning. **Writing:** Writing a letter.
Lesson Summary	On pages **568–572** of the Student Edition, students will be introduced to the following: ▪ **Big Idea:** Naturalism ▪ **Literary Element:** Rhyme Scheme ▪ **Reading Skill:** Clarify Meaning ▪ **Writing Skill/Grammar:** Letter ▪ **Vocabulary:** Denotation and Connotation
Lesson Duration	One to five 45–50 minute sessions
Readability Scores	Dale-Chall: N/A DRP: N/A Lexile: N/A
Focus	**SE/TE** pp. 568–569 Selection Focus Transparency 36 Daily Language Practice Transparency 51 Literature Launchers: Pre-Reading Videos DVD, Selection Launcher Literature Launchers Teacher Guide
Teach	**SE/TE** pp. 570–571 Interactive Read and Write SE, pp. 171–178 Interactive Read and Write TE, pp. 171–178 Unit 4 Teaching Resources, Literary Element, p. 128 Unit 4 Teaching Resources, Reading Strategy, p. 129 Unit 4 Teaching Resources, Selection Vocabulary Practice, p. 130 Unit 4 Teaching Resources, Vocabulary Strategy, p. 131 Literary Elements Transparency 88 Classroom Presentation Toolkit CD-ROM Listening Library CD, Selection Audio TeacherWorks Plus CD-ROM Vocabulary PuzzleMaker CD-ROM
Assess	**SE/TE** p. 572 Unit 4 Teaching Resources, Selection Quick Check, p. 132 Unit 4 Teaching Resources, Selection Quick Check (Spanish), p. 133 Assessment Resources, Selection Test, pp. 177–178 ExamView Assessment Suite CD-ROM Progress Reporter Online Assessment

Differentiated Instruction: English Learners	**TE** English Learner Activities, pp. 568–572 ▮ Interactive Read and Write (EL) SE, pp. 171–178 ▮ Interactive Read and Write (EL) TE, pp. 171–178 🗀 Unit 4 Teaching Resources, English Language Coach, p. 94 🗀 Unit 4 Teaching Resources, Selection Summaries: English, Spanish, Vietnamese, Tagalog, Cantonese, Haitian Creole, and Hmong, pp. 122–127 🗀 Unit 4 Teaching Resources, Selection Quick Check (Spanish), p. 133 🗀 English Language Coach 💿 Glencoe Interactive Vocabulary CD-ROM 💿 Listening Library Audio CD 🗀 Listening Library Sourcebook: Strategies and Activities
Differentiated Instruction: Approaching Level	**TE** Approaching Level Activities, pp. 568–572 ▮ Interactive Read and Write (Approaching) SE, pp. 171–178 ▮ Interactive Read and Write (Approaching) TE, pp. 171–178 💿 Glencoe Interactive Vocabulary CD-ROM 💿 Listening Library Audio CD 🗀 Listening Library Sourcebook: Strategies and Activities 💿 Skill Level Up! A Skills-Based Language Arts Game CD-ROM
Differentiated Instruction: Advanced/Pre-AP	▮ Novel Companion SE, pp. 163–206 ▮ Novel Companion TG, pp. 37–44 💿 ▶ Literature Classics, High School CD-ROM 💿 Skill Level Up! A Skills-Based Language Arts Game CD-ROM
Extension	▮ Grammar and Language Workbook SE ▮ Grammar and Language Workbook TAE 🗀 Revising with Style ▮ Spelling Power SE ▮ Spelling Power TAE
Daily Writing	**SE/TE** p. 572
Interdisciplinary Connections	**SE/TE** View the Art, pp. 570, 571 ▶ **glencoe.com**
Independent Reading	💿 BookLink K–12 CD-ROM 📖 Ethnic Anthologies 📖 Glencoe Literature Library 💿 Glencoe Literature Library Teacher Resources CD-ROM 📖 *inTIME* magazine 💿 ▶ Literature Classics, High School CD-ROM
Technology and Additional Resources	**Planning and Instruction:** 💿 TeacherWorks Plus CD-ROM 💿 Classroom Presentation Toolkit CD-ROM ▶ Literature Online at **glencoe.com** (QuickPass Code: **GLA9879u4T**) **Students Tools:** 💿 StudentWorks Plus CD-ROM or DVD-ROM ▶ Online Student Edition at **glencoe.com** ▶ Literature Online at **glencoe.com** (QuickPass Code: **GLA9800u4**)

Lesson Plan

Glencoe Literature

Richard Cory and Miniver Cheevy (pp. 573–577)

Lesson Plan and Resource Manager

UNIT FOUR Regionalism and Realism 1880–1910, Part 2: Realism and Naturalism

Learning Objectives	**Literary Study:** Analyzing irony. **Reading:** Making inferences about characters. **Writing:** Writing a poem.
Lesson Summary	On pages **573–577** of the Student Edition, students will be introduced to the following: • **Big Idea:** Naturalism • **Literary Element:** Irony • **Reading Skill:** Make Inferences About Characters • **Writing Skill/Grammar:** Poem • **Vocabulary:** Denotation and Connotation
Lesson Duration	One 45–50 Minute Session
Readability Scores	N/A
Focus	**SE/TE** pp. 573–574 Selection Focus Transparency 37 Daily Language Practice Transparency 52
Teach	**SE/TE** pp. 575–576 Unit 4 Teaching Resources, Literary Element, p. 140 Unit 4 Teaching Resources, Reading Strategy, p. 141 Unit 4 Teaching Resources, Selection Vocabulary Practice, p. 142 Unit 4 Teaching Resources, Vocabulary Strategy, p. 143 Read Aloud, Think Aloud Transparencies 22–24 Literary Elements Transparency 54 Classroom Presentation Toolkit CD-ROM Listening Library CD, Selection Audio TeacherWorks Plus CD-ROM Vocabulary PuzzleMaker CD-ROM
Assess	**SE/TE** p. 577 Unit 4 Teaching Resources, Selection Quick Check, p. 144 Unit 4 Teaching Resources, Selection Quick Check (Spanish), p. 145 Assessment Resources, Selection Test, pp. 179–180 ExamView Assessment Suite CD-ROM Progress Reporter Online Assessment
Differentiated Instruction: English Learners	**TE** English Learner Activities, pp. 573–577 Unit 4 Teaching Resources, English Language Coach, p. 94 Unit 4 Teaching Resources, Selection Summaries: English, Spanish, Vietnamese, Tagalog, Cantonese, Haitian Creole, and Hmong, pp. 134–139 Unit 4 Teaching Resources, Selection Quick Check (Spanish), p. 145 English Language Coach

Differentiated Instruction: English Learners *(continued)*	● Glencoe Interactive Vocabulary CD-ROM ● Listening Library Audio CD 📁 Listening Library Sourcebook: Strategies and Activities
Differentiated Instruction: Approaching Level	**TE** Approaching Level Activities, pp. 573–577 ● Glencoe Interactive Vocabulary CD-ROM ● Listening Library Audio CD 📁 Listening Library Sourcebook: Strategies and Activities ● Skill Level Up! A Skills-Based Language Arts Game CD-ROM
Differentiated Instruction: Advanced/Pre-AP	📗 Novel Companion SE, pp. 163–206 📗 Novel Companion TG, pp. 37–44 ● ▶ Literature Classics, High School CD-ROM ● Skill Level Up! A Skills-Based Language Arts Game CD-ROM
Extension	📗 Grammar and Language Workbook SE 📗 Grammar and Language Workbook TAE 📁 Revising with Style 📗 Spelling Power SE 📗 Spelling Power TAE
Daily Writing	**SE/TE** p. 577
Interdisciplinary Connections	**SE/TE** View the Art, p. 575 ▶ glencoe.com
Independent Reading	● BookLink K–12 CD-ROM 📖 Ethnic Anthologies 📖 Glencoe Literature Library ● Glencoe Literature Library Teacher Resources CD-ROM 📖 *inTIME* magazine ● ▶ Literature Classics, High School CD-ROM
Technology and Additional Resources	**Planning and Instruction:** ● TeacherWorks Plus CD-ROM ● Classroom Presentation Toolkit CD-ROM ▶ Literature Online at **glencoe.com** (QuickPass Code: **GLA9879u4T**) **Students Tools:** ● StudentWorks Plus CD-ROM or DVD-ROM ▶ Online Student Edition at **glencoe.com** ▶ Literature Online at **glencoe.com** (QuickPass Code: **GLA9800u4**)

Lesson Plan

Glencoe Literature

The Open Boat (pp. 578–600)

Lesson Plan and Resource Manager

UNIT FOUR Regionalism and Realism 1880–1910, Part 2: Realism and Naturalism

Learning Objectives	**Literary Study:** Analyzing author's purpose. **Reading:** Summarizing. **Writing:** Writing a review.

Lesson Summary	On pages **578–600** of the Student Edition, students will be introduced to the following:
	   • **Big Idea:** Naturalism
	   • **Literary Elements:** Author's Purpose, Conflict
	   • **Reading Skill:** Summarize
	   • **Writing Skills/Grammar:** Story Review, Evaluate a Story
	   • **Vocabulary:** Context Clues, Academic Vocabuary

Lesson Duration	Three 45–50 minute sessions
Readability Scores	Dale-Chall: 7.6 DRP: 60 Lexile: 980

Focus	**SE/TE** pp. 578–579
	  Selection Focus Transparency 38
	  Daily Language Practice Transparency 53

Teach	**SE/TE** pp. 580–597
	  Unit 4 Teaching Resources, Literary Element, p. 152
	  Unit 4 Teaching Resources, Reading Strategy, p. 153
	  Unit 4 Teaching Resources, Selection Vocabulary Practice, p. 154
	  Unit 4 Teaching Resources, Vocabulary Strategy, p. 155
	  Unit 4 Teaching Resources, Grammar Practice, p. 156
	  Literary Elements Transparency 14
	  Classroom Presentation Toolkit CD-ROM
	  Listening Library CD, Selection Audio
	  TeacherWorks Plus CD-ROM
	  Vocabulary PuzzleMaker CD-ROM

Assess	**SE/TE** pp. 598–600
	  Unit 4 Teaching Resources, Selection Quick Check, p. 157
	  Unit 4 Teaching Resources, Selection Quick Check (Spanish), p. 158
	  Assessment Resources, Selection Test, pp. 181–182
	  ExamView Assessment Suite CD-ROM
	  Progress Reporter Online Assessment

Differentiated Instruction: English Learners	**TE** English Learner Activities, pp. 578–600
	  Unit 4 Teaching Resources, English Language Coach, p. 94
	  Unit 4 Teaching Resources, Selection Summaries: English, Spanish, Vietnamese, Tagalog, Cantonese, Haitian Creole, and Hmong, pp. 146–151

Differentiated Instruction: English Learners *(continued)*	📁 Unit 4 Teaching Resources, Selection Quick Check (Spanish), p. 158 📁 English Language Coach 💿 Glencoe Interactive Vocabulary CD-ROM 💿 Listening Library Audio CD 📁 Listening Library Sourcebook: Strategies and Activities
Differentiated Instruction: Approaching Level	**TE** Approaching Level Activities, pp. 578–600 💿 Glencoe Interactive Vocabulary CD-ROM 💿 Listening Library Audio CD 📁 Listening Library Sourcebook: Strategies and Activities 💿 Skill Level Up! A Skills-Based Language Arts Game CD-ROM
Differentiated Instruction: Advanced/Pre-AP	**TE** Advanced Learner Activities, pp. 578–600 📕 Novel Companion SE, pp. 163–206 📕 Novel Companion TG, pp. 37–44 💿 ▶ Literature Classics, High School CD-ROM 💿 Skill Level Up! A Skills-Based Language Arts Game CD-ROM
Extension	📕 Grammar and Language Workbook SE 📕 Grammar and Language Workbook TAE 📁 Revising with Style 📕 Spelling Power SE 📕 Spelling Power TAE
Daily Writing	**TE** pp. 588, 594, 596 **SE/TE** p. 600
Interdisciplinary Connections	**TE** Literary History, The Sinking of the Commodore, p. 580 **TE** Literary History, Author's Purpose, p. 584 **SE/TE** View the Art, pp. 583, 587, 590, 593, 597 **TE** Language History, Epithet, p. 587 **TE** Literary History, Misquotation of the Poem, p. 592 ▶ **glencoe.com**
Independent Reading	💿 BookLink K–12 CD-ROM 📖 Ethnic Anthologies; Glencoe Literature Library; *inTIME* magazine 💿 Glencoe Literature Library Teacher Resources CD-ROM 💿 ▶ Literature Classics, High School CD-ROM
Technology and Additional Resources	**Planning and Instruction:** 💿 TeacherWorks Plus CD-ROM 💿 Classroom Presentation Toolkit CD-ROM ▶ Literature Online at **glencoe.com** (QuickPass Code: **GLA9879u4T**) **Students Tools:** 💿 StudentWorks Plus CD-ROM or DVD-ROM ▶ Online Student Edition at **glencoe.com** ▶ Literature Online at **glencoe.com** (QuickPass Code: **GLA9800u4**)

Lesson Plan

Glencoe Literature

To Build a Fire (pp. 601–616)

Lesson Plan and Resource Manager

UNIT FOUR Regionalism and Realism 1880–1910, Part 2: Realism and Naturalism

Learning Objectives	**Literary Study:** Analyze setting. **Reading:** Analyzing cause-and-effect relationships. **Writing:** Applying imagery in a descriptive essay.
Lesson Summary	On pages **601–616** of the Student Edition, students will be introduced to the following: ▪ **Big Idea:** Naturalism ▪ **Literary Element:** Setting ▪ **Reading Strategy:** Analyze Cause-and-Effect Relationships ▪ **Writing Skill/Grammar:** Descriptive Essay ▪ **Vocabulary:** Word Origins, Academic Vocabulary ▪ **Study Skill/Research/Assessment:** Assessment
Lesson Duration	Two 45–50 minute sessions
Readability Scores	Dale-Chall: 6.1 DRP: 59 Lexile: 970
Focus	SE/TE pp. 601–602 📖 Selection Focus Transparency 39 📖 Daily Language Practice Transparency 54
Teach	SE/TE pp. 603–614 📁 Unit 4 Teaching Resources, Literary Element, p. 165 📁 Unit 4 Teaching Resources, Reading Strategy, p. 166 📁 Unit 4 Teaching Resources, Selection Vocabulary Practice, p. 167 📁 Unit 4 Teaching Resources, Vocabulary Strategy, p. 168 📁 Unit 4 Teaching Resources, Grammar Practice, p. 169 📖 Literary Elements Transparency 91 💿 Classroom Presentation Toolkit CD-ROM 💿 Listening Library CD, Selection Audio 💿 TeacherWorks Plus CD-ROM 💿 Vocabulary PuzzleMaker CD-ROM
Assess	SE/TE pp. 615–616 📁 Unit 4 Teaching Resources, Selection Quick Check, p. 170 📁 Unit 4 Teaching Resources, Selection Quick Check (Spanish), p. 171 📁 Assessment Resources, Selection Test, pp. 183–184 💿 ExamView Assessment Suite CD-ROM 💿 Progress Reporter Online Assessment
Differentiated Instruction: English Learners	TE English Learner Activities, pp. 601–616 📁 Unit 4 Teaching Resources, English Language Coach, p. 94 📁 Unit 4 Teaching Resources, Selection Summaries: English, Spanish, Vietnamese, Tagalog, Cantonese, Haitian Creole, and Hmong, pp. 159–164

Differentiated Instruction: English Learners *(continued)*	📁 Unit 4 Teaching Resources, Selection Quick Check (Spanish), p. 171 📁 English Language Coach 💿 Glencoe Interactive Vocabulary CD-ROM 💿 Listening Library Audio CD 📁 Listening Library Sourcebook: Strategies and Activities
Differentiated Instruction: Approaching Level	**TE** Approaching Level Activities, pp. 601–616 💿 Glencoe Interactive Vocabulary CD-ROM 💿 Listening Library Audio CD 📁 Listening Library Sourcebook: Strategies and Activities 💿 Skill Level Up! A Skills-Based Language Arts Game CD-ROM
Differentiated Instruction: Advanced/Pre-AP	**TE** Advanced Learner Activities, pp. 601–616 📕 Novel Companion SE, pp. 163–206 📕 Novel Companion TG, pp. 37–44 💿 ▶ Literature Classics, High School CD-ROM 💿 Skill Level Up! A Skills-Based Language Arts Game CD-ROM
Extension	📕 Grammar and Language Workbook SE 📕 Grammar and Language Workbook TAE 📁 Revising with Style 📕 Spelling Power SE 📕 Spelling Power TAE
Daily Writing	**TE** pp. 610, 612, 614 **SE/TE** p. 616
Interdisciplinary Connections	**SE/TE** View the Art, p. 607 **TE** Language History, Hypothermia, p. 613 ▶ glencoe.com
Independent Reading	💿 BookLink K–12 CD-ROM 📖 Ethnic Anthologies 📖 Glencoe Literature Library 💿 Glencoe Literature Library Teacher Resources CD-ROM 📖 *inTIME* magazine 💿 ▶ Literature Classics, High School CD-ROM
Technology and Additional Resources	**Planning and Instruction:** 💿 TeacherWorks Plus CD-ROM 💿 Classroom Presentation Toolkit CD-ROM ▶ Literature Online at **glencoe.com** (QuickPass Code: **GLA9879u4T**) **Students Tools:** 💿 StudentWorks Plus CD-ROM or DVD-ROM ▶ Online Student Edition at **glencoe.com** ▶ Literature Online at **glencoe.com** (QuickPass Code: **GLA9800u4**)

Lesson Plan

Geographic Perspective: from *Arctic Dreams: Imagination and Desire in a Northern Landscape* (pp. 617–623)

Lesson Plan and Resource Manager

UNIT FOUR Regionalism and Realism 1880–1910, Part 2: Realism and Naturalism

Learning Objectives	**Literary Study:** Making connections across literature. **Reading:** Analyzing relevance of setting. Analyzing informational text.
Lesson Summary	On pages **617–623** of the Student Edition, students will be introduced to the following: • Big Idea: Naturalism • Reading Skill: Analyze Relevance of Setting
Lesson Duration	One 45–50 minute session
Readability Scores	Dale-Chall: 8.0 DRP: 60 Lexile: 1130
Focus	**SE/TE** p. 617 🖋 Daily Language Practice Transparency 55
Teach	**SE/TE** pp. 617–623 📁 Unit 4 Teaching Resources, Reading Strategy, p. 178 💿 Classroom Presentation Toolkit CD-ROM 💿 Listening Library CD, Selection Audio 💿 TeacherWorks Plus CD-ROM 💿 Vocabulary PuzzleMaker CD-ROM
Assess	**SE/TE** p. 623 📁 Unit 4 Teaching Resources, Selection Quick Check, p. 179 📁 Unit 4 Teaching Resources, Selection Quick Check (Spanish), p. 180 📁 Assessment Resources, Selection Test, pp. 185–186 💿 ExamView Assessment Suite CD-ROM ▶ Progress Reporter Online Assessment
Differentiated Instruction: English Learners	**TE** English Learner Activities, pp. 617–623 📁 Unit 4 Teaching Resources, English Language Coach, p. 94 📁 Unit 4 Teaching Resources, Selection Summaries: English, Spanish, Vietnamese, Tagalog, Cantonese, Haitian Creole, and Hmong, pp. 172–177 📁 Unit 4 Teaching Resources, Selection Quick Check (Spanish), p. 180 📁 English Language Coach 💿 Glencoe Interactive Vocabulary CD-ROM 💿 Listening Library Audio CD 📁 Listening Library Sourcebook: Strategies and Activities
Differentiated Instruction: Approaching Level	**TE** Approaching Level Activities, pp. 617–623 💿 Glencoe Interactive Vocabulary CD-ROM 💿 Listening Library Audio CD 📁 Listening Library Sourcebook: Strategies and Activities 💿 Skill Level Up! A Skills-Based Language Arts Game CD-ROM

Differentiated Instruction: Advanced/Pre-AP	**TE** Advanced Learner Activities, pp. 617–623
	Novel Companion SE, pp. 163–206
	Novel Companion TG, pp. 37–44
	Literature Classics, High School CD-ROM
	Skill Level Up! A Skills-Based Language Arts Game CD-ROM
Extension	Grammar and Language Workbook SE
	Grammar and Language Workbook TAE
	Revising with Style
	Spelling Power SE
	Spelling Power TAE
Daily Writing	**TE** p. 620
	SE/TE p. 623
Interdisciplinary Connections	**SE/TE** View the Photograph, p. 619
	TE Political History: Exploration Chronology, p. 621
	TE Cultural History: Arctic Seal Hunting, p. 618
	TE Literary History: Writers Inspiring Other Writers, p. 622
	glencoe.com
Independent Reading	BookLink K–12 CD-ROM
	Ethnic Anthologies
	Glencoe Literature Library
	Glencoe Literature Library Teacher Resources CD-ROM
	inTIME magazine
	Literature Classics, High School CD-ROM
Technology and Additional Resources	**Planning and Instruction:**
	TeacherWorks Plus CD-ROM
	Classroom Presentation Toolkit CD-ROM
	Literature Online at **glencoe.com** (QuickPass Code: **GLA9879u4T**)
	Students Tools:
	StudentWorks Plus CD-ROM or DVD-ROM
	Online Student Edition at **glencoe.com**
	Literature Online at **glencoe.com** (QuickPass Code: **GLA9800u4**)

Lesson Plan

Glencoe Literature

Writing Workshop: Literary Analysis (pp. 624–633)

Lesson Plan and Resource Manager

UNIT FOUR Regionalism and Realism 1880–1910

Learning Objectives	**Writing:** Writing a literary analysis. **Grammar:** Maintaining subject-verb agreement.
Lesson Duration	Two 45–50 minute sessions
Writing Prompt	**Analyze a Short Story:** Write a literary analysis of about 1,500 words of a selection from the unit. Show how the author's language, characters, plot, setting, themes, or other elements of the text contribute to the story's meaning. As you work, keep your audience and purpose in mind.
Focus	**SE/TE** p. 624
Teach	**SE/TE** pp. 625–633 📖 Writing Resources: Writing Process Strategies 1–23 📖 Writing Resources: Response to Literary Text 1–13 📖 Writing Workshop Transparencies 21–25 📁 Unit 4 Teaching Resources, Writing Workshop Graphic Organizer, p. 182
Assess	📁 Unit 4 Teaching Resources, Writing Workshop Rubric, pp. 183–184 📁 Rubrics for Assessing Writing, Listening and Speaking, High School, Response to Literature, pp. 4–5 ▶ Glencoe Online Essay Grader at **glencoewriting.com**
Differentiated Instruction: English Learners	**TE** English Learner Activities, pp. 624–633
Differentiated Instruction: Approaching Level	**TE** Approaching Level Activities, pp. 624–633
Differentiated Instruction: Advanced/Pre-AP	**TE** Advanced Learner Activities, pp. 624–633
Extension	📕 Grammar and Language Workbook SE 📕 Grammar and Language Workbook TAE 📁 Revising with Style 📕 Spelling Power SE 📕 Spelling Power TAE
Daily Writing	**SE/TE** p. 632 **TE** p. 630
Interdisciplinary Connections	**TE** Literary History, Bettina L. Knapp, p. 625 **TE** Literary History, Word Origins, p. 627 **TE** Cultural History, Role of Critics, p. 631 **TE** Literary History, Literary Scholars, p. 633 ▶ **glencoe.com**

Technology and Additional Resources	**Planning and Instruction:**
	Grammar and Composition Handbook
	Success in Writing: Research and Reports
	Writing Constructed Responses
	TeacherWorks Plus CD-ROM
	Classroom Presentation Toolkit CD-ROM
	Glencoe Online Essay Grader at **glencoewriting.com**
	Literature Online at **glencoe.com** (QuickPass Code: **GLA9879u4T**)
	Students Tools:
	StudentWorks Plus CD-ROM or DVD-ROM
	Online Student Edition at **glencoe.com**
	Glencoe Online Essay Grader at **glencoewriting.com**
	Literature Online at **glencoe.com** (QuickPass Code: **GLA9800u4**)

Glencoe Literature

Speaking, Listening, and Viewing Workshop: Oral Response to Literature (pp. 634–635)

Lesson Plan and Resource Manager

UNIT FOUR Regionalism and Realism 1880–1910

Learning Objectives	**Listening and Speaking:** Delivering an oral response to literature. Listening to and evaluating a presentation.
Lesson Duration	One 45–50 Minute Session
Assignment	Working in groups, discuss and respond to the major themes in "To Build a Fire" or another literary work.
Focus	**SE/TE** p. 634
Teach	**SE/TE** pp. 634–635 📁 Unit 4 Teaching Resources, SLV Activity, pp. 185–186 💿 TeacherWorks Plus CD-ROM 💿 Classroom Presentation Toolkit CD-ROM 💿 Student Presentation Builder on StudentWorks Plus CD-ROM or DVD-ROM
Assess	📁 Unit 4 Teaching Resources, SLV Workshop Rubrics, pp. 187–188 📁 Rubrics for Assessing Writing, Listening, and Speaking: Presenting an oral Response to Literature, pp. 26–27
Differentiated Instruction: English Learners	**TE** English Learner Activities, pp. 634–635
Extension	📘 Grammar and Language Workbook SE 📘 Grammar and Language Workbook TAE 📁 Revising with Style 📘 Spelling Power SE 📘 Spelling Power TAE
Daily Writing	**SE/TE** p. 634
Interdisciplinary Connections	**TE** Cultural History, Ways of Listening, p. 635 ▶ glencoe.com
Technology and Additional Resources	**Planning and Instruction:** 💿 TeacherWorks Plus CD-ROM 💿 Classroom Presentation Toolkit CD-ROM ▶ Glencoe Online Essay Grader at **glencoewriting.com** ▶ Literature Online at **glencoe.com** (QuickPass Code: **GLA9879u4T**) **Students Tools:** 💿 Student Presentation Builder on StudentWorks Plus CD-ROM or DVD-ROM 💿 StudentWorks Plus CD-ROM or DVD-ROM ▶ Online Student Edition at **glencoe.com** ▶ Glencoe Online Essay Grader at **glencoewriting.com** ▶ Literature Online at **glencoe.com** (QuickPass Code: **GLA9800u4**)

Lesson Plan

Glencoe Literature

Unit 4 Wrap-Up (pp. 636–643)

Lesson Plan and Resource Manager

UNIT FOUR Regionalism and Realism 1880–1910

Lesson Summary	On pages **636–643** of the Student Edition, students will: • Read independently • Complete the end-of-unit assessment
Lesson Duration	Two 45–50 minute sessions
Focus	**SE/TE** Independent Reading, p. 636; Assessment, p. 638
Teach	**SE/TE** Independent Reading, pp. 636–637; Assessment, pp. 638–639
Assess	**SE/TE** Assessment, pp. 639–643 📁 Assessment Resources, Unit 4 Summative Assessment, pp. 337–338 📓 ACT/SAT Preparation and Practice SE/ATE 💿 ExamView Assessment Suite CD-ROM ▶ Progress Reporter Online Assessment
Differentiated Instruction: English Learners	**TE** English Learner Activities, pp. 636–643 📁 English Language Coach
Differentiated Instruction: Approaching Level	**TE** Approaching Level Activities, pp. 636–643
Differentiated Instruction: Advanced/Pre-AP	📓 Novel Companion SE, pp. 163–206 📓 Novel Companion TG, pp. 37–44 💿 ▶ Literature Classics, High School CD-ROM
Extension	📓 Grammar and Language Workbook SE/TAE; Spelling Power SE/TAE 📁 Revising with Style
Daily Writing	**SE/TE** pp. 637, 643
Interdisciplinary Connections	**TE** Literary History, pp. 636, 639 **TE** Cultural History, Censorship, p. 637
Independent Reading	**TE** pp. 636–637 💿 BookLink K–12 CD-ROM; Glencoe Literature Library Teacher Resources CD-ROM 📖 Ethnic Anthologies; Glencoe Literature Library; *inTIME* magazine 💿 ▶ Literature Classics, High School CD-ROM
Technology and Additional Resources	**Planning and Instruction:** 💿 TeacherWorks Plus CD-ROM; Classroom Presentation Toolkit CD-ROM ▶ Literature Online at **glencoe.com** (QuickPass Code: **GLA9879u4T**) **Students Tools:** 💿 StudentWorks Plus CD-ROM or DVD-ROM ▶ Online Student Edition at **glencoe.com** ▶ Glencoe Online Essay Grader at **glencoewriting.com** ▶ Literature Online at **glencoe.com** (QuickPass Code: **GLA9800u4**)

Lesson Plan

Unit 5 Introduction (pp. 644–658)

Lesson Plan and Resource Manager

UNIT FIVE Beginnings of the Modern Age 1910–1930s

Learning Objectives	**Literary Studies:** Analyzing literary periods. Analyzing literary genres. Evaluating historical influences. Connecting to the literature.
Unit Summary	In this unit, students will be introduced to the following: • **Big Ideas:** Part 1: New Poetics Part 2: Modern Fiction Part 3: The Harlem Renaissance • **Reading Strategies:** Analyze Graphic Information, Summarize, Analyze Cause and Effect, Use Graphic Organizers, Outline • **Writing Activities/Grammar:** Create a Graph, Organize Information • **Vocabulary:** Use Context Clues • **Listening/Speaking/Viewing Skills:** Give an Oral Interpretation, Analyze Art
Lesson Duration	Two 45–50 minute sessions
Focus	**SE/TE** pp. 644–645 Daily Language Practice Transparency 55 Literature Launchers: Pre-Reading Videos DVD, Unit 5 Launcher Literature Launchers Teacher Guide
Teach	**SE/TE** pp. 646–657 Unit 5 Teaching Resources, Unit Introduction, pp. 1–2 Unit 5 Teaching Resources, Big Idea Foldable, pp. 3–4 Unit 5 Teaching Resources, Big Idea School-to-Home Connection, p. 5 Unit 5 Teaching Resources, Unit Challenge Planner, pp. 12–15 Unit 5 Teaching Resources: Academic Vocabulary Development, pp. 16–18 Classroom Presentation Toolkit CD-ROM TeacherWorks Plus CD-ROM
Assess	**SE/TE** p. 658 Assessment Resources, Unit 5 Diagnostic Assessment, pp. 33–40 ACT/SAT Preparation and Practice SE/ATE ExamView Assessment Suite CD-ROM Progress Reporter Online Assessment
Differentiated Instruction: English Learners	**TE** English Learner Activities, pp. 644–658 Unit 5 Teaching Resources, Big Idea School-to-Home Connections: English, Spanish, Vietnamese, Tagalog, Cantonese, Haitian Creole, and Hmong, pp. 6–11
Differentiated Instruction: Approaching Level	**TE** Approaching Level Activities, pp. 644–658 Skill Level Up! A Skills-Based Language Arts Game CD-ROM

Differentiated Instruction: Advanced/Pre-AP	**TE** Advanced Learner Activities, pp. 644–658 Novel Companion SE, pp. 207–250 Novel Companion TG, pp. 45–53 Literature Classics, High School CD-ROM Skill Level Up! A Skills-Based Language Arts Game CD-ROM
Extension	Grammar and Language Workbook SE Grammar and Language Workbook TAE Revising with Style Spelling Power SE Spelling Power TAE
Daily Writing	**TE** pp. 648, 658
Interdisciplinary Connections	**TE** Political History, pp. 646, 656 **TE** Cultural History, pp. 647, 648, 650, 652 **TE** Literary History, p. 654 **SE/TE** View the Art, pp. 644–645, 653, 655, 657 **SE/TE** View the Photograph, pp. 649, 651 glencoe.com
Independent Reading	BookLink K–12 CD-ROM Ethnic Anthologies Glencoe Literature Library Glencoe Literature Library Teacher Resources CD-ROM *inTIME* magazine Literature Classics, High School CD-ROM
Technology and Additional Resources	**Planning and Instruction:** TeacherWorks Plus CD-ROM Classroom Presentation Toolkit CD-ROM Literature Online at **glencoe.com** (QuickPass Code: **GLA9879u5T**) **Students Tools:** StudentWorks Plus CD-ROM or DVD-ROM Online Student Edition at **glencoe.com** Literature Online at **glencoe.com** (QuickPass Code: **GLA9800u5**)

Lesson Plan

Glencoe Literature

Part 1 Opener, Literary History: Symbolist and Imagist Poetry, *In a Station of the Metro*, and *A Pact* (pp. 659–665)

Lesson Plan and Resource Manager

UNIT FIVE Beginnings of the Modern Age 1910–1930s, Part 1: Modern Poetry

Learning Objectives	**Literary Study:** Analyzing literary periods. Analyzing literary genres. Evaluating historical influences. Analyzing imagery. **Reading:** Connecting to the literature. Questioning. **Writing:** Writing a poem.
Lesson Summary	On pages **659–665** of the Student Edition, students will be introduced to the following: ▪ **Big Idea:** New Poetics ▪ **Literary Element:** Imagery ▪ **Reading Strategy:** Question ▪ **Writing Activity/Grammar:** Poem ▪ **Vocabulary:** Context Clues
Lesson Duration	Two 45–50 minute sessions
Readability Scores	Dale-Chall: N/A DRP: N/A Lexile: N/A
Focus	SE/TE pp. 660, 662–663 🔖 Selection Focus Transparency 40 🔖 Daily Language Practice Transparencies 56, 57
Teach	SE/TE pp. 660–661, 664 📁 Unit 5 Teaching Resources, Literary History, pp. 20–21 📁 Unit 5 Teaching Resources, Literary Element, p. 29 📁 Unit 5 Teaching Resources, Reading Strategy, p. 30 📁 Unit 5 Teaching Resources, Selection Vocabulary Practice, p. 31 📁 Unit 5 Teaching Resources, Vocabulary Strategy, p. 32 🔖 Literary Elements Transparency 52 💿 Classroom Presentation Toolkit CD-ROM 💿 Listening Library CD, Selection Audio 💿 TeacherWorks Plus CD-ROM 💿 Vocabulary PuzzleMaker CD-ROM
Assess	SE/TE pp. 661, 665 📁 Unit 5 Teaching Resources, Selection Quick Check, p. 33 📁 Unit 5 Teaching Resources, Selection Quick Check (Spanish), p. 34 📁 Assessment Resources, Selection Test, pp. 187–188 💿 ExamView Assessment Suite CD-ROM 💿 Progress Reporter Online Assessment

Differentiated Instruction: English Learners	**TE** English Learner Activities, pp. 659–665 📁 Unit 5 Teaching Resources, English Language Coach, p. 22 📁 Unit 5 Teaching Resources, Selection Summaries: English, Spanish, Vietnamese, Tagalog, Cantonese, Haitian Creole, and Hmong, pp. 23–28 📁 Unit 5 Teaching Resources, Selection Quick Check (Spanish), p. 34 📁 English Language Coach 💿 Glencoe Interactive Vocabulary CD-ROM 💿 Listening Library Audio CD 📁 Listening Library Sourcebook: Strategies and Activities
Differentiated Instruction: Approaching Level	**TE** Approaching Level Activities, pp. 659–665 💿 Glencoe Interactive Vocabulary CD-ROM 💿 Listening Library Audio CD 📁 Listening Library Sourcebook: Strategies and Activities 💿 Skill Level Up! A Skills-Based Language Arts Game CD-ROM
Differentiated Instruction: Advanced/Pre-AP	📘 Novel Companion SE, pp. 207–250 📘 Novel Companion TG, pp. 45–53 💿 Literature Classics, High School CD-ROM 💿 Skill Level Up! A Skills-Based Language Arts Game CD-ROM
Extension	📘 Grammar and Language Workbook SE 📘 Grammar and Language Workbook TAE 📁 Revising with Style 📘 Spelling Power SE 📘 Spelling Power TAE
Daily Writing	**SE/TE** p. 665
Interdisciplinary Connections	**SE/TE** View the Art, pp. 659, 661 **SE/TE** View the Photograph, p. 660 ▶ glencoe.com
Independent Reading	💿 BookLink K–12 CD-ROM 📖 Ethnic Anthologies 📖 Glencoe Literature Library 💿 Glencoe Literature Library Teacher Resources CD-ROM 📖 inTIME magazine 💿 Literature Classics, High School CD-ROM
Technology and Additional Resources	**Planning and Instruction:** 💿 TeacherWorks Plus CD-ROM 💿 Classroom Presentation Toolkit CD-ROM ▶ Literature Online at **glencoe.com** (QuickPass Code: **GLA9879u5T**) **Students Tools:** 💿 StudentWorks Plus CD-ROM or DVD-ROM 💿 Online Student Edition at **glencoe.com** ▶ Literature Online at **glencoe.com** (QuickPass Code: **GLA9800u5**)

Lesson Plan

Glencoe Literature Essential Course of Study

The Love Song of J. Alfred Prufrock (pp. 666–675)

Lesson Plan and Resource Manager

UNIT FIVE Beginnings of the Modern Age 1910–1930s, Part 1: Modern Poetry

Learning Objectives	**Literary Study:** Analyzing allusion. **Reading:** Connecting to cultural context. **Writing:** Writing a short story. **Grammar:** Correcting run-on sentences.
Lesson Summary	On pages **666–675** of the Student Edition, students will be introduced to the following: • **Big Idea:** New Poetics • **Literary Element:** Allusion • **Reading Strategy:** Connect to Cultural Context • **Writing Activities/Grammar:** Short Story, Run-on Sentences • **Vocabulary:** Antonyms, Academic Vocabulary
Lesson Duration	One to five 45–50 minute sessions
Readability Scores	Dale-Chall: N/A DRP: N/A Lexile: N/A
Focus	**SE/TE** pp. 666–667 Selection Focus Transparency 41 Daily Language Practice Transparency 58 Literature Launchers: Pre-Reading Videos DVD, Selection Launcher Literature Launchers Teacher Guide
Teach	**SE/TE** pp. 668–672 Interactive Read and Write SE, pp. 179–188 Interactive Read and Write TE, pp. 179–188 Unit 5 Teaching Resources, Literary Element, p. 41 Unit 5 Teaching Resources, Reading Strategy, p. 42 Unit 5 Teaching Resources, Selection Vocabulary Practice, p. 43 Unit 5 Teaching Resources, Vocabulary Strategy, p. 44 Literary Elements Transparency 3 Classroom Presentation Toolkit CD-ROM Listening Library CD, Selection Audio TeacherWorks Plus CD-ROM Vocabulary PuzzleMaker CD-ROM
Assess	**SE/TE** pp. 673–675 Unit 5 Teaching Resources, Selection Quick Check, p. 45 Unit 5 Teaching Resources, Selection Quick Check (Spanish), p. 46 Assessment Resources, Selection Test, pp. 189–190 ExamView Assessment Suite CD-ROM Progress Reporter Online Assessment

Differentiated Instruction: English Learners	Interactive Read and Write (EL) SE, pp. 179–188 Interactive Read and Write (EL) TE, pp. 179–188 Unit 5 Teaching Resources, English Language Coach, p. 22 Unit 5 Teaching Resources, Selection Summaries: English, Spanish, Vietnamese, Tagalog, Cantonese, Haitian Creole, and Hmong, pp. 35–40 Unit 5 Teaching Resources, Selection Quick Check (Spanish), p. 46 English Language Coach Glencoe Interactive Vocabulary CD-ROM Listening Library Audio CD Listening Library Sourcebook: Strategies and Activities
Differentiated Instruction: Approaching Level	**TE** Approaching Level Activities, pp. 666–675 Interactive Read and Write (Approaching) SE, pp. 179–188 Interactive Read and Write (Approaching) TE, pp. 179–188 Glencoe Interactive Vocabulary CD-ROM Listening Library Audio CD Listening Library Sourcebook: Strategies and Activities Skill Level Up! A Skills-Based Language Arts Game CD-ROM
Differentiated Instruction: Advanced/Pre-AP	**TE** Advanced Learner Activities, pp. 666–675 Novel Companion SE, pp. 207–250 Novel Companion TG, pp. 45–53 Literature Classics, High School CD-ROM Skill Level Up! A Skills-Based Language Arts Game CD-ROM
Extension	Grammar and Language Workbook SE/TAE Revising with Style Spelling Power SE/TAE
Daily Writing	**SE/TE** p. 675
Interdisciplinary Connections	**SE/TE** View the Art, pp. 668, 671 **TE** Literary History: *Poetry*, p. 666 **glencoe.com**
Independent Reading	BookLink K–12 CD-ROM Ethnic Anthologies Glencoe Literature Library Glencoe Literature Library Teacher Resources CD-ROM *inTIME* magazine Literature Classics, High School CD-ROM
Technology and Additional Resources	**Planning and Instruction:** TeacherWorks Plus CD-ROM Classroom Presentation Toolkit CD-ROM Literature Online at **glencoe.com** (QuickPass Code: **GLA9879u5T**) **Students Tools:** StudentWorks Plus CD-ROM or DVD-ROM Online Student Edition at **glencoe.com** Literature Online at **glencoe.com** (QuickPass Code: **GLA9800u5**)

Lesson Plan

Glencoe Literature

The Red Wheelbarrow, This Is Just to Say, and Vocabulary Workshop (pp. 676–681)

Lesson Plan and Resource Manager

UNIT FIVE Beginnings of the Modern Age 1910–1930s, Part 1: Modern Poetry

Learning Objectives	**Literary Study:** Analyzing form. **Reading:** Recognizing author's purpose. **Writing:** Writing a list. **Vocabulary:** Understanding compound words. Understanding language resources.
Lesson Summary	On pages **676–681** of the Student Edition, students will be introduced to the following: • **Big Idea:** New Poetics • **Literary Element:** Form • **Reading Strategy:** Recognize Author's Purpose • **Writing Activity/Grammar:** Write a List • **Vocabulary:** Synonyms, Roots and Affixes, Compound Words
Lesson Duration	One 45–50 minute session
Readability Scores	Dale-Chall: N/A DRP: N/A Lexile: N/A
Focus	**SE/TE** pp. pp. 676–677, 681 Selection Focus Transparency 42 Daily Language Practice Transparency 59
Teach	**SE/TE** pp. 678–679, 681 Unit 5 Teaching Resources, Literary Element, p. 53 Unit 5 Teaching Resources, Reading Strategy, p. 54 Unit 5 Teaching Resources, Vocabulary Strategy, p. 55 Literary Elements Transparencies 33, 97 Classroom Presentation Toolkit CD-ROM Listening Library CD, Selection Audio TeacherWorks Plus CD-ROM Vocabulary PuzzleMaker CD-ROM
Assess	**SE/TE** pp. 680, 681 Unit 5 Teaching Resources, Selection Quick Check, p. 56 Unit 5 Teaching Resources, Selection Quick Check (Spanish), p. 57 Assessment Resources, Selection Test, pp. 191–192 ExamView Assessment Suite CD-ROM Progress Reporter Online Assessment
Differentiated Instruction: English Learners	**TE** English Learner Activities, pp. 676–681 Unit 5 Teaching Resources, English Language Coach, p. 22 Unit 5 Teaching Resources, Selection Summaries: English, Spanish, Vietnamese, Tagalog, Cantonese, Haitian Creole, and Hmong, pp. 47–52 Unit 5 Teaching Resources, Selection Quick Check (Spanish), p. 57 English Language Coach

Differentiated Instruction: English Learners (continued)	Glencoe Interactive Vocabulary CD-ROM
	Listening Library Audio CD
	Listening Library Sourcebook: Strategies and Activities
Differentiated Instruction: Approaching Level	**TE** Approaching Level Activities, pp. 676–681
	Glencoe Interactive Vocabulary CD-ROM
	Listening Library Audio CD
	Listening Library Sourcebook: Strategies and Activities
	Skill Level Up! A Skills-Based Language Arts Game CD-ROM
Differentiated Instruction: Advanced/Pre-AP	Novel Companion SE, pp. 207–250
	Novel Companion TG, pp. 45–53
	Literature Classics, High School CD-ROM
	Skill Level Up! A Skills-Based Language Arts Game CD-ROM
Extension	Grammar and Language Workbook SE
	Grammar and Language Workbook TAE
	Revising with Style
	Spelling Power SE
	Spelling Power TAE
Daily Writing	**SE/TE** p. 680
Interdisciplinary Connections	**SE/TE** View the Art, p. 679
	glencoe.com
Independent Reading	BookLink K–12 CD-ROM
	Ethnic Anthologies
	Glencoe Literature Library
	Glencoe Literature Library Teacher Resources CD-ROM
	inTIME magazine
	Literature Classics, High School CD-ROM
Technology and Additional Resources	**Planning and Instruction:**
	TeacherWorks Plus CD-ROM
	Classroom Presentation Toolkit CD-ROM
	Literature Online at **glencoe.com** (QuickPass Code: **GLA9879u5T**)
	Students Tools:
	StudentWorks Plus CD-ROM or DVD-ROM
	Online Student Edition at **glencoe.com**
	Literature Online at **glencoe.com** (QuickPass Code: **GLA9800u5**)

Lesson Plan

Glencoe Literature

Summer Rain and Fireworks (pp. 682–686)

Lesson Plan and Resource Manager

UNIT FIVE Beginnings of the Modern Age 1910–1930s, Part 1: Modern Poetry

Learning Objectives	**Literary Study:** Analyzing structure. **Reading:** Interpreting imagery. **Writing:** Writing a dialogue.
Lesson Summary	On pages **682–686** of the Student Edition, students will be introduced to the following: • **Big Idea:** New Poetics • **Literary Element:** Structure • **Reading Strategy:** Interpret Imagery • **Writing Activity/Grammar:** Dialogue • **Vocabulary:** Context Clues
Lesson Duration	One 45–50 minute session
Readability Scores	Dale-Chall: N/A DRP: N/A Lexile: N/A
Focus	**SE/TE** pp. 682–683 📖 Daily Language Practice Transparency 60
Teach	**SE/TE** pp. 684–685 📁 Unit 5 Teaching Resources, Literary Element, p. 64 📁 Unit 5 Teaching Resources, Reading Strategy, p. 65 📁 Unit 5 Teaching Resources, Selection Vocabulary Practice, p. 66 📁 Unit 5 Teaching Resources, Vocabulary Strategy, p. 67 📖 Literary Elements Transparency 97 💿 Classroom Presentation Toolkit CD-ROM 💿 Listening Library CD, Selection Audio 💿 TeacherWorks Plus CD-ROM 💿 ▶ Vocabulary PuzzleMaker CD-ROM
Assess	**SE/TE** p. 686 📁 Unit 5 Teaching Resources, Selection Quick Check, p. 68 📁 Unit 5 Teaching Resources, Selection Quick Check (Spanish), p. 69 📁 Assessment Resources, Selection Test, pp. 193–194 💿 ExamView Assessment Suite CD-ROM 💿 Progress Reporter Online Assessment
Differentiated Instruction: English Learners	**TE** English Learner Activities, pp. 682–686 📁 Unit 5 Teaching Resources, English Language Coach, p. 22 📁 Unit 5 Teaching Resources, Selection Summaries: English, Spanish, Vietnamese, Tagalog, Cantonese, Haitian Creole, and Hmong, pp. 58–63 📁 Unit 5 Teaching Resources, Selection Quick Check (Spanish), p. 69 📁 English Language Coach 💿 Glencoe Interactive Vocabulary CD-ROM 💿 Listening Library Audio CD 📁 Listening Library Sourcebook: Strategies and Activities

Differentiated Instruction: Approaching Level	**TE** Approaching Level Activities, pp. 682–686 ⊙ Glencoe Interactive Vocabulary CD-ROM ⊙ Listening Library Audio CD 📁 Listening Library Sourcebook: Strategies and Activities ⊙ Skill Level Up! A Skills-Based Language Arts Game CD-ROM
Differentiated Instruction: Advanced/Pre-AP	📕 Novel Companion SE, pp. 207–250 📕 Novel Companion TG, pp. 45–53 ⊙ ▶ Literature Classics, High School CD-ROM ⊙ Skill Level Up! A Skills-Based Language Arts Game CD-ROM
Extension	📕 Grammar and Language Workbook SE 📕 Grammar and Language Workbook TAE 📁 Revising with Style 📕 Spelling Power SE 📕 Spelling Power TAE
Daily Writing	**SE/TE** p. 686
Interdisciplinary Connections	▶ **glencoe.com**
Independent Reading	⊙ BookLink K–12 CD-ROM 📖 Ethnic Anthologies 📖 Glencoe Literature Library ⊙ Glencoe Literature Library Teacher Resources CD-ROM 📖 *inTIME* magazine ⊙ ▶ Literature Classics, High School CD-ROM
Technology and Additional Resources	**Planning and Instruction:** ⊙ TeacherWorks Plus CD-ROM ⊙ Classroom Presentation Toolkit CD-ROM ▶ Literature Online at **glencoe.com** (QuickPass Code: **GLA9879u5T**) **Students Tools:** ⊙ StudentWorks Plus CD-ROM or DVD-ROM ▶ Online Student Edition at **glencoe.com** ▶ Literature Online at **glencoe.com** (QuickPass Code: **GLA9800u5**)

Lesson Plan

Comparing Literature: *Ars Poetica*, from *Letters to a Young Poet*, *Eating Poetry*, and *beware: do not read this poem* (pp. 687–698)

Lesson Plan and Resource Manager

UNIT FIVE Beginnings of the Modern Age 1910–1930s, Part 1: Modern Poetry

Learning Objectives	**Literary Study:** Comparing cultural context. Comparing historical context. Comparing themes.
Lesson Summary	On pages **687–698** of the Student Edition, students will be introduced to the following: ▪ **Big Idea:** New Poetics ▪ **Literary Element:** Theme ▪ **Reading Strategy:** Analyze Style ▪ **Writing Activity/Grammar:** Compare Literary Trends ▪ **Vocabulary:** Analogies
Lesson Duration	One 45–50 minute session
Readability Scores	"Ars Poetica" Dale-Chall: N/A DRP: N/A Lexile: N/A "Letters to a Young Poet" Dale-Chall: 8.3 DRP: 59 Lexile: 860 "Eating Poetry" Dale-Chall: N/A DRP: N/A Lexile: N/A "beware: do not read this poem" Dale-Chall: N/A DRP: N/A Lexile: N/A
Focus	**SE/TE** pp. 687–689, 692, 694, 696 📷 Selection Focus Transparency 43 📷 Daily Language Practice Transparency 61
Teach	**SE/TE** pp. 690, 693, 695, 697 📁 Unit 5 Teaching Resources, Comparing Literature: Graphic Organizer, p. 70 📁 Unit 5 Teaching Resources, Literary Element, p. 77 📁 Unit 5 Teaching Resources, Reading Strategy, p. 78 📁 Unit 5 Teaching Resources, Vocabulary Strategy, p. 79 📷 Literary Elements Transparency 103 💿 Classroom Presentation Toolkit CD-ROM 💿 Listening Library CD, Selection Audio 💿 TeacherWorks Plus CD-ROM 💿 Vocabulary PuzzleMaker CD-ROM
Assess	**SE/TE** pp. 691, 698 📁 Unit 5 Teaching Resources, Selection Quick Check, p. 80 📁 Unit 5 Teaching Resources, Selection Quick Check (Spanish), p. 81 📁 Assessment Resources, Selection Test, pp. 195–196 💿 ExamView Assessment Suite CD-ROM ▶ Progress Reporter Online Assessment
Differentiated Instruction: English Learners	**TE** English Learner Activities, pp. 687–698 📁 Unit 5 Teaching Resources, English Language Coach, p. 22

Differentiated Instruction: English Learners *(continued)*	📁 Unit 5 Teaching Resources, Selection Summaries: English, Spanish, Vietnamese, Tagalog, Cantonese, Haitian Creole, and Hmong, pp. 71–76 📁 Unit 5 Teaching Resources, Selection Quick Check (Spanish), p. 71 📁 English Language Coach 💿 Glencoe Interactive Vocabulary CD-ROM 💿 Listening Library Audio CD 📁 Listening Library Sourcebook: Strategies and Activities
Differentiated Instruction: Approaching Level	**TE** Approaching Level Activities, pp. 687–698 💿 Glencoe Interactive Vocabulary CD-ROM 💿 Listening Library Audio CD 📁 Listening Library Sourcebook: Strategies and Activities 💿 Skill Level Up! A Skills-Based Language Arts Game CD-ROM
Differentiated Instruction: Advanced/Pre-AP	📕 Novel Companion SE, pp. 207–250 📕 Novel Companion TG, pp. 45–53 💿 Literature Classics, High School CD-ROM 💿 Skill Level Up! A Skills-Based Language Arts Game CD-ROM
Extension	📕 Grammar and Language Workbook SE 📕 Grammar and Language Workbook TAE 📁 Revising with Style 📕 Spelling Power SE 📕 Spelling Power TAE
Daily Writing	**SE/TE** p. 698
Interdisciplinary Connections	**SE/TE** View the Art, pp. 693 **TE** Cultural History, p. 688 **TE** Literary History, p. 692 ▶ glencoe.com
Independent Reading	💿 BookLink K–12 CD-ROM 📖 Ethnic Anthologies 📖 Glencoe Literature Library 💿 Glencoe Literature Library Teacher Resources CD-ROM 📖 *inTIME* magazine 💿 Literature Classics, High School CD-ROM
Technology and Additional Resources	**Planning and Instruction:** 💿 TeacherWorks Plus CD-ROM 💿 Classroom Presentation Toolkit CD-ROM ▶ Literature Online at **glencoe.com** (QuickPass Code: **GLA9879u5T**) **Students Tools:** 💿 StudentWorks Plus CD-ROM or DVD-ROM ▶ Online Student Edition at **glencoe.com** ▶ Literature Online at **glencoe.com** (QuickPass Code: **GLA9800u5**)

Lesson Plan

Glencoe Literature

Study of Two Pears, from The Man with the Blue Guitar, somewhere i have never traveled, gladly beyond, and anyone lived in a pretty how town (pp. 699–708)

Lesson Plan and Resource Manager

UNIT FIVE Beginnings of the Modern Age 1910–1930s, Part 1: Modern Poetry

Learning Objectives	**Literary Study:** Analyzing tone. Analyzing rhythm. **Reading:** Recognizing author's purpose. Analyzing style. **Writing:** Writing a journal entry. Writing a character sketch.
Lesson Summary	On pages **699–708** of the Student Edition, students will be introduced to the following: • **Big Idea:** New Poetics • **Literary Elements:** Tone, Rhythm • **Reading Strategies:** Recognize Author's Purpose, Analyze Style • **Writing Activities/Grammar:** Journal, Character Sketch • **Vocabulary:** Word Origins, Analogies • **Listening/Speaking/Viewing Skill:** Analyze Art
Lesson Duration	One 45–50 minute session
Readability Scores	Dale-Chall: N/A DRP: N/A Lexile: N/A
Focus	**SE/TE** pp. 699–700, 704–705 🖐 Daily Language Practice Transparencies 62–63
Teach	**SE/TE** pp. 701–702, 706–707 📁 Unit 5 Teaching Resources, Literary Element, pp. 88, 99 📁 Unit 5 Teaching Resources, Reading Strategy, pp. 89, 100 📁 Unit 5 Teaching Resources, Vocabulary Strategy, pp. 90, 101 🖐 Literary Elements Transparencies 89, 105 💿 Classroom Presentation Toolkit CD-ROM 💿 Listening Library CD, Selection Audio 💿 TeacherWorks Plus CD-ROM 💿 Vocabulary PuzzleMaker CD-ROM
Assess	**SE/TE** pp. 703, 708 📁 Unit 5 Teaching Resources, Selection Quick Check, pp. 91, 102 📁 Unit 5 Teaching Resources, Selection Quick Check (Spanish), pp. 92, 103 📁 Assessment Resources, Selection Test, pp. 197–198, 199–200 💿 ExamView Assessment Suite CD-ROM 💿 Progress Reporter Online Assessment
Differentiated Instruction: English Learners	**TE** English Learner Activities, pp. 699–708 📁 Unit 5 Teaching Resources, English Language Coach, p. 22 📁 Unit 5 Teaching Resources, Selection Summaries: English, Spanish, Vietnamese, Tagalog, Cantonese, Haitian Creole, and Hmong, pp. 82–87, 93–98 📁 Unit 5 Teaching Resources, Selection Quick Check (Spanish), pp. 92, 103

Differentiated Instruction: English Learners *(continued)*	📁 English Language Coach 💿 Glencoe Interactive Vocabulary CD-ROM 💿 Listening Library Audio CD 📁 Listening Library Sourcebook: Strategies and Activities
Differentiated Instruction: Approaching Level	**TE** Approaching Level Activities, pp. 699–708 💿 Glencoe Interactive Vocabulary CD-ROM 💿 Listening Library Audio CD 📁 Listening Library Sourcebook: Strategies and Activities 💿 Skill Level Up! A Skills-Based Language Arts Game CD-ROM
Differentiated Instruction: Advanced/Pre-AP	**TE** Advanced Learner Activities, pp. 699–708 📖 Novel Companion SE, pp. 207–250 📖 Novel Companion TG, pp. 45–53 💿 ▶ Literature Classics, High School CD-ROM 💿 Skill Level Up! A Skills-Based Language Arts Game CD-ROM
Extension	📖 Grammar and Language Workbook SE 📖 Grammar and Language Workbook TAE 📁 Revising with Style 📖 Spelling Power SE 📖 Spelling Power TAE
Daily Writing	**SE/TE** p. 708
Interdisciplinary Connections	**SE/TE** View the Art, pp. 701, 702, 706 ▶ glencoe.com
Independent Reading	💿 BookLink K–12 CD-ROM 📖 Ethnic Anthologies 📖 Glencoe Literature Library 💿 Glencoe Literature Library Teacher Resources CD-ROM 📖 *inTIME* magazine 💿 ▶ Literature Classics, High School CD-ROM
Technology and Additional Resources	**Planning and Instruction:** 💿 TeacherWorks Plus CD-ROM 💿 Classroom Presentation Toolkit CD-ROM ▶ Literature Online at **glencoe.com** (QuickPass Code: **GLA9879u5T**) **Students Tools:** 💿 StudentWorks Plus CD-ROM or DVD-ROM ▶ Online Student Edition at **glencoe.com** ▶ Literature Online at **glencoe.com** (QuickPass Code: **GLA9800u5**)

Lesson Plan

Glencoe Literature

Chicago and Grass (pp. 709–713)

Lesson Plan and Resource Manager

UNIT FIVE Beginnings of the Modern Age 1910–1930s, Part 1: Modern Poetry

Learning Objectives	**Literary Study:** Analyzing apostrophe. **Reading:** Making inferences about theme. **Writing:** Writing a poem.
Lesson Summary	On pages **709–713** of the Student Edition, students will be introduced to the following: • **Big Idea:** New Poetics • **Literary Element:** Apostrophe • **Reading Strategy:** Make Inferences About Theme • **Writing Activity/Grammar:** Poem • **Vocabulary:** Denotation and Connotation
Lesson Duration	One 45–50 minute session
Readability Scores	Dale-Chall: N/A DRP: N/A Lexile: N/A
Focus	**SE/TE** pp. 709–710 📖 Daily Language Practice Transparency 64
Teach	**SE/TE** pp. 711–712 📁 Unit 5 Teaching Resources, Literary Element, p. 110 📁 Unit 5 Teaching Resources, Reading Strategy, p. 111 📁 Unit 5 Teaching Resources, Vocabulary Strategy, p. 112 📖 Literary Elements Transparency 9 💿 Classroom Presentation Toolkit CD-ROM 💿 Listening Library CD, Selection Audio 💿 TeacherWorks Plus CD-ROM 💿 Vocabulary PuzzleMaker CD-ROM
Assess	**SE/TE** p. 713 📁 Unit 5 Teaching Resources, Selection Quick Check, p. 113 📁 Unit 5 Teaching Resources, Selection Quick Check (Spanish), p. 114 📁 Assessment Resources, Selection Test, pp. 201–202 💿 ExamView Assessment Suite CD-ROM 💿 Progress Reporter Online Assessment
Differentiated Instruction: English Learners	📁 Unit 5 Teaching Resources, English Language Coach, p. 22 📁 Unit 5 Teaching Resources, Selection Summaries: English, Spanish, Vietnamese, Tagalog, Cantonese, Haitian Creole, and Hmong, pp. 104–109 📁 Unit 5 Teaching Resources, Selection Quick Check (Spanish), p. 114 📁 English Language Coach 💿 Glencoe Interactive Vocabulary CD-ROM 💿 Listening Library Audio CD 📁 Listening Library Sourcebook: Strategies and Activities

Differentiated Instruction: Approaching Level	**TE** Approaching Level Activities, pp. 709–713 🌐 Glencoe Interactive Vocabulary CD-ROM 🌐 Listening Library Audio CD 📁 Listening Library Sourcebook: Strategies and Activities 🌐 Skill Level Up! A Skills-Based Language Arts Game CD-ROM
Differentiated Instruction: Advanced/Pre-AP	📗 Novel Companion SE, pp. 207–250 📗 Novel Companion TG, pp. 45–53 🌐 ▶ Literature Classics, High School CD-ROM 🌐 Skill Level Up! A Skills-Based Language Arts Game CD-ROM
Extension	📗 Grammar and Language Workbook SE 📗 Grammar and Language Workbook TAE 📁 Revising with Style 📗 Spelling Power SE 📗 Spelling Power TAE
Daily Writing	**SE/TE** p. 713
Interdisciplinary Connections	**SE/TE** View the Art, p. 712 **TE** Cultural History, p. 711 ▶ glencoe.com
Independent Reading	🌐 BookLink K–12 CD-ROM 📖 Ethnic Anthologies 📖 Glencoe Literature Library 🌐 Glencoe Literature Library Teacher Resources CD-ROM 📖 inTIME magazine 🌐 ▶ Literature Classics, High School CD-ROM
Technology and Additional Resources	**Planning and Instruction:** 🌐 TeacherWorks Plus CD-ROM 🌐 Classroom Presentation Toolkit CD-ROM ▶ Literature Online at **glencoe.com** (QuickPass Code: **GLA9879u5T**) **Students Tools:** 🌐 StudentWorks Plus CD-ROM or DVD-ROM ▶ Online Student Edition at **glencoe.com** ▶ Literature Online at **glencoe.com** (QuickPass Code: **GLA9800u5**)

Lesson Plan

Glencoe Literature

Mending Wall, Birches, and Stopping by Woods on a Snowy Evening (pp. 714–722)

Lesson Plan and Resource Manager

UNIT FIVE Beginnings of the Modern Age 1910–1930s, Part 1: Modern Poetry

Learning Objectives	**Literary Study:** Analyzing blank verse. Analyzing narrative poetry. **Reading:** Comparing and contrasting speakers. Evaluating Characterization. **Writing:** Writing a dialogue. Writing a list.
Lesson Summary	On pages **714–722** of the Student Edition, students will be introduced to the following: • Big Idea: New Poetics • Literary Element: Blank Verse • Reading Strategy: Compare and Contrast Speakers • Writing Activities/Grammar: Dialogue • Vocabulary: Synonyms, Academic Vocabulary • Listening/Speaking/Viewing Skills: Analyze Art
Lesson Duration	One 45–50 minute session
Readability Scores	Dale-Chall: N/A DRP: N/A Lexile: N/A
Focus	**SE/TE** pp. 714–715 Selection Focus Transparency 44 Daily Language Practice Transparency 65
Teach	**SE/TE** pp. 716–719 Unit 5 Teaching Resources, Literary Element, pp. 121, 131 Unit 5 Teaching Resources, Reading Strategy, pp. 122, 132 Literary Elements Transparencies 17 Classroom Presentation Toolkit CD-ROM Listening Library CD, Selection Audio TeacherWorks Plus CD-ROM Vocabulary PuzzleMaker CD-ROM
Assess	**SE/TE** pp. 720, 722 Unit 5 Teaching Resources, Selection Quick Check, pp. 123, 133 Unit 5 Teaching Resources, Selection Quick Check (Spanish), pp. 124, 134 Assessment Resources, Selection Test, pp. 203–204, 205–206 ExamView Assessment Suite CD-ROM Progress Reporter Online Assessment

Differentiated Instruction: English Learners	**TE** English Learner Activities, pp. 714–722
	Unit 5 Teaching Resources, English Language Coach, p. 22
	Unit 5 Teaching Resources, Selection Summaries: English, Spanish, Vietnamese, Tagalog, Cantonese, Haitian Creole, and Hmong, pp. 115–120, 125–130
	Unit 5 Teaching Resources, Selection Quick Check (Spanish), pp. 124, 134
	English Language Coach
	Glencoe Interactive Vocabulary CD-ROM
	Listening Library Audio CD
	Listening Library Sourcebook: Strategies and Activities
Differentiated Instruction: Approaching Level	**TE** Approaching Level Activities, pp. 714–722
	Glencoe Interactive Vocabulary CD-ROM
	Listening Library Audio CD
	Listening Library Sourcebook: Strategies and Activities
	Skill Level Up! A Skills-Based Language Arts Game CD-ROM
Differentiated Instruction: Advanced/Pre-AP	**TE** Advanced Learner Activities, pp. 714–722
	Novel Companion SE, pp. 207–250
	Novel Companion TG, pp. 45–53
	Literature Classics, High School CD-ROM
	Skill Level Up! A Skills-Based Language Arts Game CD-ROM
Extension	Grammar and Language Workbook SE
	Grammar and Language Workbook TAE
	Revising with Style
	Spelling Power SE
	Spelling Power TAE
Daily Writing	**SE/TE** p. 722
Interdisciplinary Connections	**SE/TE** View the Art, pp. 716, 721
	SE/TE View the Photograph, p. 718
	TE Cultural History, p. 719
	TE Literary History, p. 714
	glencoe.com
Independent Reading	BookLink K–12 CD-ROM
	Ethnic Anthologies
	Glencoe Literature Library
	Glencoe Literature Library Teacher Resources CD-ROM
	inTIME magazine
	Literature Classics, High School CD-ROM
Technology and Additional Resources	**Planning and Instruction:**
	TeacherWorks Plus CD-ROM
	Classroom Presentation Toolkit CD-ROM
	Literature Online at **glencoe.com** (QuickPass Code: **GLA9879u5T**)
	Students Tools:
	StudentWorks Plus CD-ROM or DVD-ROM
	Online Student Edition at **glencoe.com**
	Literature Online at **glencoe.com** (QuickPass Code: **GLA9800u5**)

Glencoe Literature

Acquainted with the Night, The Death of the Hired Man, and Political Perspective: Remarks at Amherst College (pp. 723–738)

Lesson Plan and Resource Manager

UNIT FIVE Beginnings of the Modern Age 1910–1930s, Part 1: Modern Poetry

Learning Objectives	**Literary Study:** Making connections across literature. **Reading:** Analyzing informational text. Analyzing philosophical assumptions. **Writing:** Applying characterization in a biographical narrative. **Grammar:** Correcting misplaced modifiers.
Lesson Summary	On pages **723–738** of the Student Edition, students will be introduced to the following: • **Big Idea:** New Poetics • **Literary Elements:** Rhyme Scheme, Narrative Poetry, Blank Verse • **Reading Strategies:** Compare and Contrast Speakers, Evaluate Characterization, Analyze Philosophical Assumptions • **Writing Activities/Grammar:** Write a List, Biographical Narrative, Misplaced Modifiers • **Vocabulary:** Academic Vocabulary, Word Usage • **Listening/Speaking/Viewing Skills:** Analyze Art
Lesson Duration	One 45–50 minute session
Readability Scores	"Acquainted with the Night" Dale-Chall: N/A DRP: N/A Lexile: N/A "The Death of the Hired Man" Dale-Chall: N/A DRP: N/A Lexile: N/A "Remarks at Amherst College" Dale-Chall: 9.7 DRP: 6.5 Lexile: 1270
Focus	**SE/TE** pp. 725, 735
Teach	**SE/TE** pp. 723, 725–731, 735–738 📁 Unit 5 Teaching Resources, Literary Element, pp. 141, 151 📁 Unit 5 Teaching Resources, Reading Strategy, pp. 142, 152, 162 📁 Unit 5 Teaching Resources, Vocabulary Strategy, p. 153 🖾 Literary Elements Transparencies 66, 88 💿 Classroom Presentation Toolkit CD-ROM 💿 Listening Library CD, Selection Audio 💿 TeacherWorks Plus CD-ROMs 💿 Vocabulary PuzzleMaker CD-ROM
Assess	**SE/TE** pp. 724, 732–734, 738 📁 Unit 5 Teaching Resources, Selection Quick Check, pp. 143, 154, 163 📁 Unit 5 Teaching Resources, Selection Quick Check (Spanish), pp. 144, 155, 164 📁 Assessment Resources, Selection Test, pp. 207–208, 209–210, 211–212 💿 ExamView Assessment Suite CD-ROM 💿 Progress Reporter Online Assessment
Differentiated Instruction: English Learners	**TE** English Learner Activities, pp. 723–738 📁 Unit 5 Teaching Resources, English Language Coach, p. 22

Differentiated Instruction: English Learners *(continued)*	📁 Unit 5 Teaching Resources, Selection Summaries: English, Spanish, Vietnamese, Tagalog, Cantonese, Haitian Creole, and Hmong, pp. 135–140, 145–150, 156–161
	📁 Unit 5 Teaching Resources, Selection Quick Check (Spanish), pp. 144, 155, 164
	📁 English Language Coach
	💿 Glencoe Interactive Vocabulary CD-ROM
	💿 Listening Library Audio CD
	📁 Listening Library Sourcebook: Strategies and Activities
Differentiated Instruction: Approaching Level	**TE** Approaching Level Activities, pp. 723–738
	💿 Glencoe Interactive Vocabulary CD-ROM
	💿 Listening Library Audio CD
	📁 Listening Library Sourcebook: Strategies and Activities
	💿 Skill Level Up! A Skills-Based Language Arts Game CD-ROM
Differentiated Instruction: Advanced/Pre-AP	**TE** Advanced Learner Activities, pp. 723–738
	📗 Novel Companion SE, pp. 207–250
	📗 Novel Companion TE, pp. 45–53
	💿 Literature Classics, High School CD-ROM
	💿 Skill Level Up! A Skills-Based Language Arts Game CD-ROM
Extension	📗 Grammar and Language Workbook SE
	📗 Grammar and Language Workbook TAE
	📁 Revising with Style
	📗 Spelling Power SE
	📗 Spelling Power TAE
Daily Writing	**SE/TE** p. 734
Interdisciplinary Connections	**SE/TE** View the Art, pp. 723, 730
	SE/TE View the Photograph, p. 726
	TE Political History, p. 736
	TE Cultural History, p. 735
	TE Literary History, p. 737
	TE Daily Life & Culture, p. 732
	💿 glencoe.com
Independent Reading	📖 Ethnic Anthologies; Glencoe Literature Library; *inTIME* magazine
	💿 BookLink K–12 CD-ROM
	💿 Glencoe Literature Library Teacher Resources CD-ROM
	💿 Literature Classics, High School CD-ROM
Technology and Additional Resources	**Planning and Instruction:**
	💿 TeacherWorks Plus CD-ROM
	💿 Classroom Presentation Toolkit CD-ROM
	💿 Literature Online at **glencoe.com** (QuickPass Code: **GLA9879u5T**)
	Students Tools:
	💿 StudentWorks Plus CD-ROM or DVD-ROM
	💿 Online Student Edition at **glencoe.com**
	💿 Literature Online at **glencoe.com** (QuickPass Code: **GLA9800u5**)

Lesson Plan

Glencoe Literature

Part 2 Opener and Literary History: The Modern American Short Story (pp. 739–741)

Lesson Plan and Resource Manager

UNIT FIVE Beginnings of the Modern Age 1910–1930s, Part 2: Modern Fiction

Learning Objectives	**Literary Study:** Analyzing literary periods. Analyzing literary genres. Evaluating historical influences. Connecting to the literature.
Lesson Summary	On pages **739–741** of the Student Edition, students will be introduced to the following: • **Big Idea:** Modern Fiction • **Literary Element:** Antihero
Lesson Duration	One 45–50 minute session
Readability Scores	Dale-Chall: N/A DRP: N/A Lexile: N/A
Focus	SE/TE p. 740 Daily Language Practice Transparency 66
Teach	SE/TE pp. 740–741 Unit 5 Teaching Resources, Literary History, pp. 166–167 Classroom Presentation Toolkit CD-ROM Listening Library CD, Selection Audio TeacherWorks Plus CD-ROM Vocabulary PuzzleMaker CD-ROM
Assess	SE/TE p. 741 ExamView Assessment Suite CD-ROM Progress Reporter Online Assessment
Differentiated Instruction: English Learners	TE English Learner Activities, pp. 739–741 Unit 5 Teaching Resources, English Language Coach, p. 168 Glencoe Interactive Vocabulary CD-ROM Listening Library Audio CD Listening Library Sourcebook: Strategies and Activities
Differentiated Instruction: Approaching Level	TE Approaching Level Activities, pp. 739–741 Glencoe Interactive Vocabulary CD-ROM Listening Library Audio CD Listening Library Sourcebook: Strategies and Activities Skill Level Up! A Skills-Based Language Arts Game CD-ROM
Differentiated Instruction: Advanced/Pre-AP	Novel Companion SE, pp. 207–250 Novel Companion TG, pp. 45–53 Literature Classics, High School CD-ROM Skill Level Up! A Skills-Based Language Arts Game CD-ROM

Extension	■ Grammar and Language Workbook SE
	■ Grammar and Language Workbook TAE
	🗁 Revising with Style
	■ Spelling Power SE
	■ Spelling Power TAE
Daily Writing	**SE/TE** p. 741
Interdisciplinary Connections	**SE/TE** View the Art, pp. 739, 740
	▶ glencoe.com
Independent Reading	🌐 BookLink K–12 CD-ROM
	📖 Ethnic Anthologies
	📖 Glencoe Literature Library
	💿 Glencoe Literature Library Teacher Resources CD-ROM
	📖 inTIME magazine
	💿 ▶ Literature Classics, High School CD-ROM
Technology and Additional Resources	**Planning and Instruction:**
	💿 TeacherWorks Plus CD-ROM
	💿 Classroom Presentation Toolkit CD-ROM
	▶ Literature Online at **glencoe.com** (QuickPass Code: **GLA9879u5T**)
	Students Tools:
	💿 StudentWorks Plus CD-ROM or DVD-ROM
	▶ Online Student Edition at **glencoe.com**
	▶ Literature Online at **glencoe.com** (QuickPass Code: **GLA9800u5**)

Lesson Plan

In Another Country and Grammar Workshop (pp. 742–751)

Lesson Plan and Resource Manager

UNIT FIVE Beginnings of the Modern Age 1910–1930s, Part 2: Modern Fiction

Learning Objectives	**Literary Study:** Analyzing style. **Reading:** Recognizing author's purpose. **Writing:** Applying diction in a brief narrative. **Grammar:** Understanding how to use coordinating conjunctions. Understanding how to use commas with coordinating conjunctions.
Lesson Summary	On pages **742–751** of the Student Edition, students will be introduced to the following: ▪ **Big Idea:** Modern Fiction ▪ **Literary Element:** Style ▪ **Reading Strategy:** Recognize Author's Purpose ▪ **Writing Activities/Grammar:** Apply Diction, Coordinating Conjunctions ▪ **Vocabulary:** Antonyms, Academic Vocabulary ▪ **Listening/Speaking/Viewing Skill:** Analyze Art
Lesson Duration	One 45–50 minute session
Readability Scores	Dale-Chall: 4.7 DRP: 54 Lexile: 1050
Focus	**SE/TE** pp. 742–743, 751 ⬢ Selection Focus Transparency 45 ⬢ Daily Language Practice Transparency 67
Teach	**SE/TE** pp. 744–748, 751 📁 Unit 5 Teaching Resources, Literary Element, p. 175 📁 Unit 5 Teaching Resources, Reading Strategy, p. 176 📁 Unit 5 Teaching Resources, Selection Vocabulary Practice, p. 177 📁 Unit 5 Teaching Resources, Vocabulary Strategy, p. 178 📁 Unit 5 Teaching Resources, Grammar Practice, p. 179 📁 Unit 5 Teaching Resources, Grammar Workshop, p. 182 ⬢ Grammar and Language Transparency 10 ⬢ Literary Elements Transparencies 98 💿 Classroom Presentation Toolkit CD-ROM 💿 Listening Library CD, Selection Audio 💿 TeacherWorks Plus CD-ROM 💿 ▶ Vocabulary PuzzleMaker CD-ROM
Assess	**SE/TE** pp. 749–750, 751 📁 Unit 5 Teaching Resources, Selection Quick Check, p. 180 📁 Unit 5 Teaching Resources, Selection Quick Check (Spanish), p. 181 📁 Assessment Resources, Selection Test, pp. 213–214 💿 ExamView Assessment Suite CD-ROM ▶ Progress Reporter Online Assessment

Differentiated Instruction: English Learners	**TE** English Learner Activities, pp. 742–751 📁 Unit 5 Teaching Resources, English Language Coach, p. 168 📁 Unit 5 Teaching Resources, Selection Summaries: English, Spanish, Vietnamese, Tagalog, Cantonese, Haitian Creole, and Hmong, pp. 169–174 📁 Unit 5 Teaching Resources, Selection Quick Check (Spanish), p. 181 📁 English Language Coach 💿 Glencoe Interactive Vocabulary CD-ROM 💿 Listening Library Audio CD 📁 Listening Library Sourcebook: Strategies and Activities
Differentiated Instruction: Approaching Level	**TE** Approaching Level Activities, pp. 742–751 💿 Glencoe Interactive Vocabulary CD-ROM 💿 Listening Library Audio CD 📁 Listening Library Sourcebook: Strategies and Activities 💿 Skill Level Up! A Skills-Based Language Arts Game CD-ROM
Differentiated Instruction: Advanced/Pre-AP	📗 Novel Companion SE, pp. 207–250 📗 Novel Companion TG, pp. 45–53 💿 ▶ Literature Classics, High School CD-ROM 💿 Skill Level Up! A Skills-Based Language Arts Game CD-ROM
Extension	📗 Grammar and Language Workbook SE 📗 Grammar and Language Workbook TAE 📁 Revising with Style 📗 Spelling Power SE 📗 Spelling Power TAE
Daily Writing	**SE/TE** p. 750
Interdisciplinary Connections	**SE/TE** View the Art, pp. 744, 747 **TE** Cultural History, p. 748 ▶ glencoe.com
Independent Reading	💿 BookLink K–12 CD-ROM 📖 Ethnic Anthologies 📖 Glencoe Literature Library 💿 Glencoe Literature Library Teacher Resources CD-ROM 📖 *inTIME* magazine 💿 ▶ Literature Classics, High School CD-ROM
Technology and Additional Resources	**Planning and Instruction:** 💿 TeacherWorks Plus CD-ROM 💿 Classroom Presentation Toolkit CD-ROM ▶ Literature Online at **glencoe.com** (QuickPass Code: **GLA9879u5T**) **Students Tools:** 💿 StudentWorks Plus CD-ROM or DVD-ROM ▶ Online Student Edition at **glencoe.com** ▶ Literature Online at **glencoe.com** (QuickPass Code: **GLA9800u5**)

Lesson Plan

Winter Dreams (pp. 752–772)

Lesson Plan and Resource Manager

UNIT FIVE Beginnings of the Modern Age 1910–1930s, Part 2: Modern Fiction

Learning Objectives	**Literary Study:** Analyzing motivation. **Reading:** Evaluating sensory details. **Writing:** Writing short story. **Grammar:** Using pronouns to maintain consistent point of view.
Lesson Summary	On pages **752–772** of the Student Edition, students will be introduced to the following: ▪ **Big Idea:** Modern Fiction ▪ **Literary Element:** Motivation ▪ **Reading Strategy:** Evaluate Sensory Details ▪ **Writing Activity/Grammar:** Short Story ▪ **Vocabulary:** Synonyms, Academic Vocabulary ▪ **Listening/Speaking/Viewing Skills:** Analyze Art, Discussion
Lesson Duration	Two 45–50 minute sessions
Readability Scores	Dale-Chall: 7.9 DRP: 60 Lexile: 1080
Focus	**SE/TE** pp. 752–753 Selection Focus Transparency 46 Daily Language Practice Transparencies 68, 69
Teach	**SE/TE** pp. 754–769 Unit 5 Teaching Resources, Literary Element, p. 189 Unit 5 Teaching Resources, Reading Strategy, p. 190 Unit 5 Teaching Resources, Selection Vocabulary Practice, p. 191 Unit 5 Teaching Resources, Vocabulary Strategy, p. 192 Unit 5 Teaching Resources, Grammar Practice, p. 193 Literary Elements Transparency 65 Classroom Presentation Toolkit CD-ROM Listening Library CD, Selection Audio TeacherWorks Plus CD-ROMs Vocabulary PuzzleMaker CD-ROM
Assess	**SE/TE** pp. 770–772 Unit 5 Teaching Resources, Selection Quick Check, p. 194 Unit 5 Teaching Resources, Selection Quick Check (Spanish), p. 195 Assessment Resources, Selection Test, pp. 215–216 ExamView Assessment Suite CD-ROM Progress Reporter Online Assessment
Differentiated Instruction: English Learners	**TE** English Learner Activities, pp. 752–772 Unit 5 Teaching Resources, English Language Coach, p. 168 Unit 5 Teaching Resources, Selection Summaries: English, Spanish, Vietnamese, Tagalog, Cantonese, Haitian Creole, and Hmong, pp. 183–188

Differentiated Instruction: English Learners *(continued)*	📁 Unit 5 Teaching Resources, Selection Quick Check (Spanish), p. 195 📁 English Language Coach 💿 Glencoe Interactive Vocabulary CD-ROM 💿 Listening Library Audio CD 📁 Listening Library Sourcebook: Strategies and Activities
Differentiated Instruction: Approaching Level	**TE** Approaching Level Activities, pp. 752–772 💿 Glencoe Interactive Vocabulary CD-ROM 💿 Listening Library Audio CD 📁 Listening Library Sourcebook: Strategies and Activities 💿 Skill Level Up! A Skills-Based Language Arts Game CD-ROM
Differentiated Instruction: Advanced/Pre-AP	**TE** Advanced Learner Activities, pp. 752–772 📕 Novel Companion SE, pp. 207–250 📕 Novel Companion TG, pp. 45–53 💿▶ Literature Classics, High School CD-ROM 💿 Skill Level Up! A Skills-Based Language Arts Game CD-ROM
Extension	📕 Grammar and Language Workbook SE/TAE 📁 Revising with Style 📕 Spelling Power SE/TAE
Daily Writing	**TE** p. 756 **SE/TE** p. 772
Interdisciplinary Connections	**SE/TE** View the Art, pp. 756, 759, 760, 764, 766 **TE** Language History, p. 765 **TE** Cultural History, pp. 757, 767 **TE** Daily Life & Culture, p. 770 ▶ glencoe.com
Independent Reading	💿 BookLink K–12 CD-ROM 📖 Ethnic Anthologies 📖 Glencoe Literature Library 💿 Glencoe Literature Library Teacher Resources CD-ROM 📖 *inTIME* magazine 💿▶ Literature Classics, High School CD-ROM
Technology and Additional Resources	**Planning and Instruction:** 💿 TeacherWorks Plus CD-ROM 💿 Classroom Presentation Toolkit CD-ROM ▶ Literature Online at **glencoe.com** (QuickPass Code: **GLA9879u5T**) **Students Tools:** 💿 StudentWorks Plus CD-ROM or DVD-ROM ▶ Online Student Edition at **glencoe.com** ▶ Literature Online at **glencoe.com** (QuickPass Code: **GLA9800u5**)

Lesson Plan

The Jilting of Granny Weatherall (pp. 773–784)

Lesson Plan and Resource Manager

UNIT FIVE Beginnings of the Modern Age 1910–1930s, Part 2: Modern Fiction

Learning Objectives	**Literary Study:** Analyzing stream of consciousness. **Reading:** Drawing conclusions about the protagonist. **Speaking and Listening:** Performing a monologue.
Lesson Summary	On pages **773–784** of the Student Edition, students will be introduced to the following: • **Big Idea:** Modern Fiction • **Literary Element:** Stream of Consciousness • **Reading Strategy:** Draw Conclusions About the Protagonist • **Writing Activity/Grammar:** Monologue • **Listening/Speaking/Viewing Skills:** Analyze Art, Monologue
Lesson Duration	One to five 45–50 minute sessions
Readability Scores	Dale-Chall: 4.6 DRP: 50 Lexile: 820
Focus	**SE/TE** pp. 773–774 Selection Focus Transparency 47 Daily Language Practice Transparency 70 Literature Launchers: Pre-Reading Videos DVD, Selection Launcher Literature Launchers Teacher Guide
Teach	**SE/TE** pp. 775–782 Interactive Read and Write SE/TE, pp. 189–202 Unit 5 Teaching Resources, Literary Element, p. 202 Unit 5 Teaching Resources, Reading Strategy, p. 203 Unit 5 Teaching Resources, Selection Vocabulary Practice, p. 204 Unit 5 Teaching Resources, Vocabulary Strategy, p. 205 Unit 5 Teaching Resources, Grammar Practice, p. 206 Read Aloud, Think Aloud Transparencies 25–27 Literary Elements Transparency 96 Classroom Presentation Toolkit CD-ROM Listening Library CD, Selection Audio TeacherWorks Plus CD-ROM Vocabulary PuzzleMaker CD-ROM
Assess	**SE/TE** pp. 783–784 Unit 5 Teaching Resources, Selection Quick Check, p. 207 Unit 5 Teaching Resources, Selection Quick Check (Spanish), p. 208 Assessment Resources, Selection Test, pp. 217–218 ExamView Assessment Suite CD-ROM Progress Reporter Online Assessment

Differentiated Instruction: English Learners	**TE** English Learner Activities, pp. 773–784 ■ Interactive Read and Write (EL) SE/TE, pp. 189–202 📁 Unit 5 Teaching Resources, English Language Coach, p. 168 📁 Unit 5 Teaching Resources, Selection Summaries: English, Spanish, Vietnamese, Tagalog, Cantonese, Haitian Creole, and Hmong, pp. 196–201 📁 Unit 5 Teaching Resources, Selection Quick Check (Spanish), p. 208 📁 English Language Coach 💿 Glencoe Interactive Vocabulary CD-ROM 💿 Listening Library Audio CD 📁 Listening Library Sourcebook: Strategies and Activities
Differentiated Instruction: Approaching Level	**TE** Approaching Level Activities, pp. 773–784 ■ Interactive Read and Write (Approaching) SE/TE, pp. 189–202 💿 Glencoe Interactive Vocabulary CD-ROM 💿 Listening Library Audio CD 📁 Listening Library Sourcebook: Strategies and Activities 💿 Skill Level Up! A Skills-Based Language Arts Game CD-ROM
Differentiated Instruction: Advanced/Pre-AP	**TE** Advanced Learner Activities, pp. 773–784 ■ Novel Companion SE, pp. 207–250 ■ Novel Companion TG, pp. 45–53 💿 Literature Classics, High School CD-ROM 💿 Skill Level Up! A Skills-Based Language Arts Game CD-ROM
Extension	■ Grammar and Language Workbook SE/TAE 📁 Revising with Style ■ Spelling Power SE/TAE
Daily Writing	**TE** p. 776 **SE/TE** p. 784
Interdisciplinary Connections	**SE/TE** View the Art, pp. 775, 779 **TE** Cultural History, pp. 773, 782 **TE** Language History, p. 777 💿 glencoe.com
Independent Reading	💿 BookLink K–12 CD-ROM 📖 Ethnic Anthologies 📖 Glencoe Literature Library 💿 Glencoe Literature Library Teacher Resources CD-ROM 📖 inTIME magazine 💿 Literature Classics, High School CD-ROM
Technology and Additional Resources	**Planning and Instruction:** 💿 TeacherWorks Plus CD-ROM 💿 Classroom Presentation Toolkit CD-ROM 💿 Literature Online at **glencoe.com** (QuickPass Code: **GLA9879u5T**) **Students Tools:** 💿 StudentWorks Plus CD-ROM or DVD-ROM 💿 Online Student Edition at **glencoe.com** 💿 Literature Online at **glencoe.com** (QuickPass Code: **GLA9800u5**)

Lesson Plan

Glencoe Literature

Part 3 Opener, My City, from *Dust Tracks on a Road*, and Vocabulary Workshop (pp. 785–800)

Lesson Plan and Resource Manager

UNIT FIVE Beginnings of the Modern Age 1910–1930s, Part 3: The Harlem Renaissance

Learning Objectives	**Literary Study:** Analyzing a sonnet. Analyzing voice. **Reading:** Interpreting imagery. Analyzing language. **Writing:** Writing a brochure. Applying allusion in a paragraph. **Vocabulary:** Understanding homonyms.
Lesson Summary	On pages **785–800** of the Student Edition, students will be introduced to the following: • **Big Idea:** The Harlem Renaissance • **Literary Elements:** Sonnet, Voice • **Reading Strategies:** Interpret Imagery, Analyze Language • **Writing Activities/Grammar:** Write a Brochure, Apply Allusion • **Vocabulary:** Antonyms, Analogies, Academic Vocabulary • **Listening/Speaking/Viewing Skill:** Analyze Art
Lesson Duration	Two 45–50 minute sessions
Readability Scores	"My City" Dale-Chall: N/A DRP: N/A Lexile: N/A "Dust Tracks on a Road" Dale-Chall: 5.1 DRP: 53 Lexile: 920
Focus	**SE/TE** pp. 786–787, 790–791, 800 🖳 Selection Focus Transparencies 48–49 🖳 Daily Language Practice Transparencies 71–72
Teach	**SE/TE** pp. 788, 792–797, 800 📁 Unit 5 Teaching Resources, Literary Element, pp. 217, 228 📁 Unit 5 Teaching Resources, Reading Strategy, pp. 218, 229 📁 Unit 5 Teaching Resources, Selection Vocabulary Practice, p. 230 📁 Unit 5 Teaching Resources, Vocabulary Strategy, pp. 219, 231 📁 Unit 5 Teaching Resources, Grammar Practice, p. 232 🖳 Read Aloud, Think Aloud Transparency 28 🖳 Literary Elements Transparencies 94, 107 💿 Classroom Presentation Toolkit CD-ROM 💿 Listening Library CD, Selection Audio 💿 TeacherWorks Plus CD-ROM 💿 ▶ Vocabulary PuzzleMaker CD-ROM
Assess	**SE/TE** pp. 789, 798–799, 800 📁 Unit 5 Teaching Resources, Selection Quick Check, pp. 220, 233 📁 Unit 5 Teaching Resources, Selection Quick Check (Spanish), pp. 221, 234 📁 Assessment Resources, Selection Test, pp. 219–220, 221–222 💿 ExamView Assessment Suite CD-ROM ▶ Progress Reporter Online Assessment

Differentiated Instruction: English Learners	**TE** English Learner Activities, pp. 785–800 📁 Unit 5 Teaching Resources, English Language Coach, p. 210 📁 Unit 5 Teaching Resources, Selection Summaries: English, Spanish, Vietnamese, Tagalog, Cantonese, Haitian Creole, and Hmong, pp. 211–216, 222–227 📁 Unit 5 Teaching Resources, Selection Quick Check (Spanish), pp. 221, 234 📁 English Language Coach 💿 Glencoe Interactive Vocabulary CD-ROM 💿 Listening Library Audio CD 📁 Listening Library Sourcebook: Strategies and Activities
Differentiated Instruction: Approaching Level	**TE** Approaching Level Activities, pp. 785–800 💿 Glencoe Interactive Vocabulary CD-ROM 💿 Listening Library Audio CD 📁 Listening Library Sourcebook: Strategies and Activities 💿 Skill Level Up! A Skills-Based Language Arts Game CD-ROM
Differentiated Instruction: Advanced/Pre-AP	**TE** Advanced Learner Activities, pp. 785–800 📗 Novel Companion SE, pp. 207–250 📗 Novel Companion TG, pp. 45–53 💿 Literature Classics, High School CD-ROM 💿 Skill Level Up! A Skills-Based Language Arts Game CD-ROM
Extension	📗 Grammar and Language Workbook SE 📗 Grammar and Language Workbook TAE 📁 Revising with Style 📗 Spelling Power SE 📗 Spelling Power TAE
Daily Writing	**SE/TE** pp. 789, 799
Interdisciplinary Connections	**SE/TE** View the Art, pp. 785, 788, 792, 795 **TE** Literary History, pp. 796, 797 💿 glencoe.com
Independent Reading	💿 BookLink K–12 CD-ROM 📖 Ethnic Anthologies 📖 Glencoe Literature Library 💿 Glencoe Literature Library Teacher Resources CD-ROM 📖 inTIME magazine 💿 Literature Classics, High School CD-ROM
Technology and Additional Resources	**Planning and Instruction:** 💿 TeacherWorks Plus CD-ROM 💿 Classroom Presentation Toolkit CD-ROM 💿 Literature Online at **glencoe.com** (QuickPass Code: **GLA9879u5T**) **Students Tools:** 💿 StudentWorks Plus CD-ROM or DVD-ROM 💿 Online Student Edition at **glencoe.com** 💿 Literature Online at **glencoe.com** (QuickPass Code: **GLA9800u5**)

Lesson Plan

Glencoe Literature

If We Must Die, The Tropics in New York, and TIME: *Stanzas from a Black Epic* (pp. 801–809)

Lesson Plan and Resource Manager

UNIT FIVE Beginnings of the Modern Age 1910–1930s, Part 3: The Harlem Renaissance

Learning Objectives	**Literary Study:** Analyzing meter. **Reading:** Analyzing tone. Using text features. Analyzing informational text. Scanning text. **Writing:** Writing a poem.
Lesson Summary	On pages **801–809** of the Student Edition, students will be introduced to the following: • **Big Idea:** The Harlem Renaissance • **Literary Element:** Meter • **Reading Strategies:** Analyze Tone, Scan Text to Find Specific Information • **Writing Activity/Grammar:** Write a Poem • **Vocabulary:** Word Origins
Lesson Duration	One 45–50 minute session
Readability Scores	"If We Must Die" Dale-Chall: N/A DRP: N/A Lexile: N/A "The Tropics in New York" Dale-Chall: N/A DRP: N/A Lexile: N/A "Stanzas from a Black Epic" Dale-Chall: 9.8 DRP: 68 Lexile: 1240
Focus	**SE/TE** pp. 801–802, 806 ✎ Selection Focus Transparency 50 ✎ Daily Language Practice Transparency 73
Teach	**SE/TE** pp. 803–804, 806–808 📁 Unit 5 Teaching Resources, Literary Element, p. 241 📁 Unit 5 Teaching Resources, Reading Strategy, pp. 242, 253 📁 Unit 5 Teaching Resources, Selection Vocabulary Practice, p. 243 📁 Unit 5 Teaching Resources, Vocabulary Strategy, p. 244 ✎ Literary Elements Transparency 61 💿 Classroom Presentation Toolkit CD-ROM 💿 Listening Library CD, Selection Audio 💿 TeacherWorks Plus CD-ROM 💿 Vocabulary PuzzleMaker CD-ROM
Assess	**SE/TE** pp. 805, 809 📁 Unit 5 Teaching Resources, Selection Quick Check, pp. 245, 254 📁 Unit 5 Teaching Resources, Selection Quick Check (Spanish), pp. 246, 255 📁 Assessment Resources, Selection Test, pp. 223–224, 225–226 💿 ExamView Assessment Suite CD-ROM 💿 Progress Reporter Online Assessment

Differentiated Instruction: English Learners	**TE** English Learner Activities, pp. 801–809
	Unit 5 Teaching Resources, English Language Coach, p. 210
	Unit 5 Teaching Resources, Selection Summaries: English, Spanish, Vietnamese, Tagalog, Cantonese, Haitian Creole, and Hmong, pp. 235–240, 247–252
	Unit 5 Teaching Resources, Selection Quick Check (Spanish), pp. 246, 255
	English Language Coach
	Glencoe Interactive Vocabulary CD-ROM
	Listening Library Audio CD
	Listening Library Sourcebook: Strategies and Activities
Differentiated Instruction: Approaching Level	**TE** Approaching Level Activities, pp. 801–809
	Glencoe Interactive Vocabulary CD-ROM
	Listening Library Audio CD
	Listening Library Sourcebook: Strategies and Activities
	Skill Level Up! A Skills-Based Language Arts Game CD-ROM
Differentiated Instruction: Advanced/Pre-AP	**TE** Advanced Learner Activities, pp. 801–809
	Novel Companion SE, pp. 207–250
	Novel Companion TG, pp. 45–53
	Literature Classics, High School CD-ROM
	Skill Level Up! A Skills-Based Language Arts Game CD-ROM
Extension	Grammar and Language Workbook SE
	Grammar and Language Workbook TAE
	Revising with Style
	Spelling Power SE
	Spelling Power TAE
Daily Writing	**SE/TE** p. 805
Interdisciplinary Connections	**SE/TE** View the Art, p. 804
	TE Historical Note, p. 806
	TE Cultural History, p. 808
	TE Literary History, p. 807
	glencoe.com
Independent Reading	BookLink K–12 CD-ROM
	Ethnic Anthologies
	Glencoe Literature Library
	Glencoe Literature Library Teacher Resources CD-ROM
	inTIME magazine
	Literature Classics, High School CD-ROM
Technology and Additional Resources	**Planning and Instruction:**
	TeacherWorks Plus CD-ROM
	Classroom Presentation Toolkit CD-ROM
	Literature Online at **glencoe.com** (QuickPass Code: **GLA9879u5T**)
	Students Tools:
	StudentWorks Plus CD-ROM or DVD-ROM
	Online Student Edition at **glencoe.com**
	Literature Online at **glencoe.com** (QuickPass Code: **GLA9800u5**)

Lesson Plan

Glencoe Literature

I, Too and *The Negro Speaks of Rivers* (pp. 810–814)

Lesson Plan and Resource Manager

UNIT FIVE Beginnings of the Modern Age 1910–1930s, Part 3: The Harlem Renaissance

Learning Objectives	**Literary Study:** Analyzing repetition. **Reading:** Making predictions about theme. **Writing:** Writing an essay.

Lesson Summary	On pages **810–814** of the Student Edition, students will be introduced to the following:
	    ▪ **Big Idea:** The Harlem Renaissance
	    ▪ **Literary Element:** Repetition
	    ▪ **Reading Strategy:** Make Predictions About Theme
	    ▪ **Writing Activity/Grammar:** Essay
	    ▪ **Vocabulary:** Analogies

Lesson Duration	One 20–25 minute session
Readability Scores	Dale-Chall: N/A DRP: N/A Lexile: N/A
Focus	**SE/TE** pp. 810–811 📠 Selection Focus Transparency 51 📠 Daily Language Practice Transparency 74
Teach	**SE/TE** pp. 812–813 📁 Unit 5 Teaching Resources, Literary Element, p. 262 📁 Unit 5 Teaching Resources, Reading Strategy, p. 263 📁 Unit 5 Teaching Resources, Vocabulary Strategy, p. 264 📠 Literary Elements Transparencies 56, 85 💿 Classroom Presentation Toolkit CD-ROM 💿 Listening Library CD, Selection Audio 💿 TeacherWorks Plus CD-ROM 💿 Vocabulary PuzzleMaker CD-ROM
Assess	**SE/TE** pp. 814 📁 Unit 5 Teaching Resources, Selection Quick Check, p. 265 📁 Unit 5 Teaching Resources, Selection Quick Check (Spanish), p. 266 📁 Assessment Resources, Selection Test, pp. 227–228 💿 ExamView Assessment Suite CD-ROM 💿 Progress Reporter Online Assessment
Differentiated Instruction: English Learners	**TE** English Learner Activities, pp. 810–814 📁 Unit 5 Teaching Resources, Selection Summaries: English, Spanish, Vietnamese, Tagalog, Cantonese, Haitian Creole, and Hmong, pp. 256–261 📁 Unit 5 Teaching Resources, Selection Quick Check (Spanish), p. 266 📁 English Language Coach 💿 Glencoe Interactive Vocabulary CD-ROM 💿 Listening Library Audio CD 📁 Listening Library Sourcebook: Strategies and Activities

Differentiated Instruction: Approaching Level	**TE** Approaching Level Activities, pp. 810–814 ⊙ Glencoe Interactive Vocabulary CD-ROM ⊙ Listening Library Audio CD 📁 Listening Library Sourcebook: Strategies and Activities ⊙ Skill Level Up! A Skills-Based Language Arts Game CD-ROM
Differentiated Instruction: Advanced/Pre-AP	**TE** Advanced Learner Activities, pp. 810–814 📘 Novel Companion SE, pp. 207–250 📘 Novel Companion TG, pp. 45–53 ⊙ ▶ Literature Classics, High School CD-ROM ⊙ Skill Level Up! A Skills-Based Language Arts Game CD-ROM
Extension	📘 Grammar and Language Workbook SE 📘 Grammar and Language Workbook TAE 📁 Revising with Style 📘 Spelling Power SE 📘 Spelling Power TAE
Daily Writing	**SE/TE** p. 814
Interdisciplinary Connections	⊙ glencoe.com
Independent Reading	⊙ BookLink K–12 CD-ROM 📖 Ethnic Anthologies 📖 Glencoe Literature Library ⊙ Glencoe Literature Library Teacher Resources CD-ROM 📖 *inTIME* magazine ⊙ ▶ Literature Classics, High School CD-ROM
Technology and Additional Resources	**Planning and Instruction:** ⊙ TeacherWorks Plus CD-ROM ⊙ Classroom Presentation Toolkit CD-ROM ▶ Literature Online at **glencoe.com** (QuickPass Code: **GLA9879u5T**) **Students Tools:** ⊙ StudentWorks Plus CD-ROM or DVD-ROM ▶ Online Student Edition at **glencoe.com** ▶ Literature Online at **glencoe.com** (QuickPass Code: **GLA9800u5**)

Lesson Plan

Glencoe Literature Essential Course of Study

When the Negro Was in Vogue (pp. 815–823)

Lesson Plan and Resource Manager

UNIT FIVE Beginnings of the Modern Age 1910–1930s, Part 3: The Harlem Renaissance

Learning Objectives	**Literary Study:** Analyzing juxtaposition. **Reading:** Analyzing concrete details. **Writing:** Writing a persuasive essay. **Grammar:** Using ellipses in quotations.
Lesson Summary	On pages **815–823** of the Student Edition, students will be introduced to the following: • **Big Idea:** The Harlem Renaissance • **Literary Element:** Juxtaposition • **Reading Strategy:** Analyze Concrete Details • **Writing Activities/Grammar:** Persuasive Essay, Ellipses • **Vocabulary:** Synonyms, Academic Vocabulary
Lesson Duration	One to five 20–25 minute sessions
Readability Scores	Dale-Chall: 6.1 DRP: 64 Lexile: 1290
Focus	SE/TE p. 815 Daily Language Practice Transparency 75 Literature Launchers: Pre-Reading Videos DVD, Selection Launcher Literature Launchers Teacher Guide
Teach	SE/TE pp. 816–820 Interactive Read and Write SE, pp. 203–212 Interactive Read and Write TE, pp. 203–212 Unit 5 Teaching Resources, Literary Element, p. 273 Unit 5 Teaching Resources, Reading Strategy, p. 274 Unit 5 Teaching Resources, Selection Vocabulary Practice, p. 275 Unit 5 Teaching Resources, Vocabulary Strategy, p. 276 Unit 5 Teaching Resources, Grammar Practice, p. 277 Literary Elements Transparencies 56, 85 Classroom Presentation Toolkit CD-ROM Listening Library CD, Selection Audio TeacherWorks Plus CD-ROM Vocabulary PuzzleMaker CD-ROM
Assess	SE/TE pp. 821–823 Unit 5 Teaching Resources, Selection Quick Check, p. 278 Unit 5 Teaching Resources, Selection Quick Check (Spanish), p. 279 Assessment Resources, Selection Test, pp. 229–230 ExamView Assessment Suite CD-ROM Progress Reporter Online Assessment

Differentiated Instruction: English Learners	**TE** English Learner Activities, pp. 815–823 📖 Interactive Read and Write (EL) SE, pp. 203–212 📖 Interactive Read and Write (EL) TE, pp. 203–212 📁 Unit 5 Teaching Resources, Selection Summaries: English, Spanish, Vietnamese, Tagalog, Cantonese, Haitian Creole, and Hmong, pp. 267–272 📁 Unit 5 Teaching Resources, Selection Quick Check (Spanish), p. 279 📁 English Language Coach 💿 Glencoe Interactive Vocabulary CD-ROM 💿 Listening Library Audio CD 📁 Listening Library Sourcebook: Strategies and Activities
Differentiated Instruction: Approaching Level	**TE** Approaching Level Activities, pp. 815–823 📖 Interactive Read and Write (Approaching) SE, pp. 203–212 📖 Interactive Read and Write (Approaching) TE, pp. 203–212 💿 Glencoe Interactive Vocabulary CD-ROM 💿 Listening Library Audio CD 📁 Listening Library Sourcebook: Strategies and Activities 💿 Skill Level Up! A Skills-Based Language Arts Game CD-ROM
Differentiated Instruction: Advanced/Pre-AP	**TE** Advanced Learner Activities, pp. 815–823 📖 Novel Companion SE, pp. 207–250 📖 Novel Companion TG, pp. 45–53 💿 ▶ Literature Classics, High School CD-ROM 💿 Skill Level Up! A Skills-Based Language Arts Game CD-ROM
Extension	📖 Grammar and Language Workbook SE 📖 Grammar and Language Workbook TAE 📁 Revising with Style 📖 Spelling Power SE 📖 Spelling Power TAE
Daily Writing	**SE/TE** pp. 820, 823
Interdisciplinary Connections	**SE/TE** View the Art, p. 816 **TE** Cultural History, p. 817 **SE/TE** View the Photograph, p. 818 **SE/TE** Daily Life & Culture: Harlem, p. 821 ▶ glencoe.com
Independent Reading	💿 BookLink K–12 CD-ROM 📖 Ethnic Anthologies 📖 Glencoe Literature Library 💿 Glencoe Literature Library Teacher Resources CD-ROM 📖 inTIME magazine 💿 ▶ Literature Classics, High School CD-ROM
Technology and Additional Resources	**Planning and Instruction:** 💿 TeacherWorks Plus CD-ROM 💿 Classroom Presentation Toolkit CD-ROM ▶ Literature Online at **glencoe.com** (QuickPass Code: **GLA9879u5T**) **Students Tools:** 💿 StudentWorks Plus CD-ROM or DVD-ROM ▶ Online Student Edition at **glencoe.com** ▶ Literature Online at **glencoe.com** (QuickPass Code: **GLA9800u5**)

Lesson Plan

Glencoe Literature

A black man talks of reaping (pp. 824–827)

Lesson Plan and Resource Manager

UNIT FIVE Beginnings of the Modern Age 1910–1930s, Part 3: The Harlem Renaissance

Learning Objectives	**Literary Study:** Analyzing metaphors. **Reading:** Connecting to personal experience. **Writing:** Writing a letter.

Lesson Summary	On pages **824–827** of the Student Edition, students will be introduced to the following:
	   • **Big Idea:** The Harlem Renaissance
	   • **Literary Element:** Metaphor
	   • **Reading Strategy:** Connect to Personal Experience
	   • **Vocabulary:** Context Clues
	   • **Writing Activity/Grammar:** Write a Poem

Lesson Duration	One 20–25 minute session
Readability Scores	Dale-Chall: N/A DRP: N/A Lexile: N/A
Focus	**SE/TE** pp. 824–825 Daily Language Practice Transparency 76
Teach	**SE/TE** pp. 826 Unit 5 Teaching Resources, Literary Element, p. 286 Unit 5 Teaching Resources, Reading Strategy, p. 287 Unit 5 Teaching Resources, Vocabulary Strategy, p. 288 Literary Elements Transparencies 60, 97 Classroom Presentation Toolkit CD-ROM Listening Library CD, Selection Audio TeacherWorks Plus CD-ROM Vocabulary PuzzleMaker CD-ROM
Assess	**SE/TE** p. 827 Unit 5 Teaching Resources, Selection Quick Check, p. 289 Unit 5 Teaching Resources, Selection Quick Check (Spanish), p. 290 Assessment Resources, Selection Test, pp. 231–232 ExamView Assessment Suite CD-ROM Progress Reporter Online Assessment
Differentiated Instruction: English Learners	Unit 5 Teaching Resources, Selection Summaries: English, Spanish, Vietnamese, Tagalog, Cantonese, Haitian Creole, and Hmong, pp. 280–285 Unit 5 Teaching Resources, Selection Quick Check (Spanish), p. 290 English Language Coach Glencoe Interactive Vocabulary CD-ROM Listening Library Audio CD Listening Library Sourcebook: Strategies and Activities

Differentiated Instruction: Approaching Level	**TE** Approaching Level Activities, pp. 824–827 ⊙ Glencoe Interactive Vocabulary CD-ROM ⊙ Listening Library Audio CD 🗀 Listening Library Sourcebook: Strategies and Activities ⊙ Skill Level Up! A Skills-Based Language Arts Game CD-ROM
Differentiated Instruction: Advanced/Pre-AP	**TE** Advanced Learner Activities, pp. 824–827 ▮ Novel Companion SE, pp. 207–250 ▮ Novel Companion TG, pp. 45–53 ⊙ ▶ Literature Classics, High School CD-ROM ⊙ Skill Level Up! A Skills-Based Language Arts Game CD-ROM
Extension	▮ Grammar and Language Workbook SE ▮ Grammar and Language Workbook TAE 🗀 Revising with Style ▮ Spelling Power SE ▮ Spelling Power TAE
Daily Writing	**SE/TE** p. 827
Interdisciplinary Connections	**SE/TE** View the Art, p. 826 ▶ glencoe.com
Independent Reading	⊙ BookLink K–12 CD-ROM 📖 Ethnic Anthologies 📖 Glencoe Literature Library ⊙ Glencoe Literature Library Teacher Resources CD-ROM 📖 *inTIME* magazine ⊙ ▶ Literature Classics, High School CD-ROM
Technology and Additional Resources	**Planning and Instruction:** ⊙ TeacherWorks Plus CD-ROM ⊙ Classroom Presentation Toolkit CD-ROM ▶ Literature Online at **glencoe.com** (QuickPass Code: **GLA9879u5T**) **Students Tools:** ⊙ StudentWorks Plus CD-ROM or DVD-ROM ▶ Online Student Edition at **glencoe.com** ▶ Literature Online at **glencoe.com** (QuickPass Code: **GLA9800u5**)

Lesson Plan

Any Human to Another (pp. 828–831)

Lesson Plan and Resource Manager

UNIT FIVE Beginnings of the Modern Age 1910–1930s, Part 3: The Harlem Renaissance

Learning Objectives	**Literary Study:** Analyzing stanzas. **Reading:** Connecting to contemporary issues. **Writing:** Writing a journal entry.
Lesson Summary	On pages **828–831** of the Student Edition, students will be introduced to the following: ▪ **Big Idea:** The Harlem Renaissance ▪ **Literary Element:** Stanza ▪ **Reading Strategy:** Connect to Contemporary Issues ▪ **Writing Activity/Grammar:** Journal Entry ▪ **Vocabulary:** Antonyms
Lesson Duration	One 20–25 minute session
Readability Scores	Dale-Chall: N/A DRP: N/A Lexile: N/A
Focus	SE/TE pp. 828–829 📖 Selection Focus Transparency 52 📖 Daily Language Practice Transparency 77
Teach	SE/TE p. 830 📁 Unit 5 Teaching Resources, Literary Element, p. 297 📁 Unit 5 Teaching Resources, Reading Strategy, p. 298 📁 Unit 5 Teaching Resources, Selection Vocabulary Practice, p. 299 📁 Unit 5 Teaching Resources, Vocabulary Strategy, p. 300 📖 Literary Elements Transparencies 60, 97 💿 Classroom Presentation Toolkit CD-ROM 💿 Listening Library CD, Selection Audio 💿 TeacherWorks Plus CD-ROM 💿 Vocabulary PuzzleMaker CD-ROM
Assess	SE/TE p. 831 📁 Unit 5 Teaching Resources, Selection Quick Check, p. 301 📁 Unit 5 Teaching Resources, Selection Quick Check (Spanish), p. 302 📁 Assessment Resources, Selection Test, pp. 233–234 💿 ExamView Assessment Suite CD-ROM 💿 Progress Reporter Online Assessment
Differentiated Instruction: English Learners	TE English Learner Activities, pp. 828–831 📁 Unit 5 Teaching Resources, Selection Summaries: English, Spanish, Vietnamese, Tagalog, Cantonese, Haitian Creole, and Hmong, pp. 291–296 📁 Unit 5 Teaching Resources, Selection Quick Check (Spanish), p. 302 📁 English Language Coach 💿 Glencoe Interactive Vocabulary CD-ROM 💿 Listening Library Audio CD 📁 Listening Library Sourcebook: Strategies and Activities

Differentiated Instruction: Approaching Level	**TE** Approaching Level Activities, pp. 828–831
	Glencoe Interactive Vocabulary CD-ROM
	Listening Library Audio CD
	Listening Library Sourcebook: Strategies and Activities
	Skill Level Up! A Skills-Based Language Arts Game CD-ROM
Differentiated Instruction: Advanced/Pre-AP	Novel Companion SE, pp. 207–250
	Novel Companion TG, pp. 45–53
	Literature Classics, High School CD-ROM
	Skill Level Up! A Skills-Based Language Arts Game CD-ROM
Extension	Grammar and Language Workbook SE
	Grammar and Language Workbook TAE
	Revising with Style
	Spelling Power SE
	Spelling Power TAE
Daily Writing	**SE/TE** p. 831
Interdisciplinary Connections	**SE/TE** View the Art, p. 830
	glencoe.com
Independent Reading	BookLink K–12 CD-ROM
	Ethnic Anthologies
	Glencoe Literature Library
	Glencoe Literature Library Teacher Resources CD-ROM
	inTIME magazine
	Literature Classics, High School CD-ROM
Technology and Additional Resources	**Planning and Instruction:**
	TeacherWorks Plus CD-ROM
	Classroom Presentation Toolkit CD-ROM
	Literature Online at **glencoe.com** (QuickPass Code: **GLA9879u5T**)
	Students Tools:
	StudentWorks Plus CD-ROM or DVD-ROM
	Online Student Edition at **glencoe.com**
	Literature Online at **glencoe.com** (QuickPass Code: **GLA9800u5**)

Glencoe Literature

Writing Workshop: Literary Analysis (pp. 832–839)

Lesson Plan and Resource Manager

UNIT FIVE Beginnings of the Modern Age 1910–1930s

Learning Objectives	**Writing:** Analyzing a poem to demonstrate understanding of the poem's meaning and appreciation of the effects that create that meaning.
Lesson Duration	Two 45–50 minute sessions
Writing Prompt	Analyze a poem to interpret its meaning and write a response to literature of about 1,500 words that explains how various techniques help create that meaning. Write with audience and purpose in mind.
Focus	**SE/TE** p. 832
Teach	**SE/TE** pp. 833–839 📁 Writing Resources: Writing Process Strategies 1–23 📁 Writing Resources: Response to Literary Text 1–13 ✎ Writing Workshop Transparencies 21–25 📁 Unit 5 Teaching Resources, Writing Workshop Graphic Organizer, p. 304
Assess	📁 Unit 5 Teaching Resources, Writing Workshop Rubric, pp. 305–306 📁 Rubrics for Assessing Writing, Listening and Speaking, High School, Response to Literature, pp. 4–5 ▶ Glencoe Online Essay Grader at **glencoewriting.com**
Differentiated Instruction: English Learners	**TE** English Learner Activities, pp. 832–839
Differentiated Instruction: Approaching Level	**TE** Approaching Level Activities, pp. 832–839
Differentiated Instruction: Advanced/Pre-AP	**TE** Advanced Learner Activities, pp. 832–839
Extension	▌Grammar and Language Workbook SE ▌Grammar and Language Workbook TAE 📁 Revising with Style ▌Spelling Power SE ▌Spelling Power TAE
Daily Writing	**SE/TE** pp. 835, 839
Interdisciplinary Connections	**TE** Literary History, pp. 833, 835 **TE** Language History, p. 839 ▶ **glencoe.com**

| **Technology and Additional Resources** | **Planning and Instruction:**
📖 Grammar and Composition Handbook
📁 Success in Writing: Research and Reports
📁 Writing Constructed Responses
💿 TeacherWorks Plus CD-ROM
💿 Classroom Presentation Toolkit CD-ROM
▶ Glencoe Online Essay Grader at **glencoewriting.com**
▶ Literature Online at **glencoe.com** (QuickPass Code: **GLA9879u5T**)
Students Tools:
💿 StudentWorks Plus CD-ROM or DVD-ROM
▶ Online Student Edition at **glencoe.com**
▶ Glencoe Online Essay Grader at **glencoewriting.com**
▶ Literature Online at **glencoe.com** (QuickPass Code: **GLA9800u5**) |

Lesson Plan

Glencoe Literature

Speaking, Listening, and Viewing Workshop: Oral Interpretation of a Poem (pp. 840–841)

Lesson Plan and Resource Manager

UNIT FIVE Beginnings of the Modern Age 1910–1930s

Learning Objectives	**Speaking and Listening:** Delivering an oral interpretation of a poem.
Lesson Duration	One 45–50 minute session
Assignment	Plan and deliver an oral interpretation of the subject of your literary analysis or another poem from this unit.
Focus	**SE/TE** p. 840
Teach	**SE/TE** pp. 840–841 Unit 5 Teaching Resources, SLV Activity, pp. 307–308 TeacherWorks Plus CD-ROM Classroom Presentation Toolkit CD-ROM Student Presentation Builder on StudentWorks Plus CD-ROM or DVD-ROM
Assess	Unit 5 Teaching Resources, SLV Workshop Rubrics, pp. 309–310 Rubrics for Assessing Writing, Listening, and Speaking: Presenting an Oral Response to Literature, pp. 48–49
Differentiated Instruction: English Learners	**TE** English Learner Activities, pp. 840–841
Extension	Grammar and Language Workbook SE Grammar and Language Workbook TAE Revising with Style Spelling Power SE Spelling Power TAE
Daily Writing	**TE** p. 841
Interdisciplinary Connections	glencoe.com
Technology and Additional Resources	**Planning and Instruction:** TeacherWorks Plus CD-ROM Classroom Presentation Toolkit CD-ROM Literature Online at **glencoe.com** (QuickPass Code: **GLA9879u5T**) **Students Tools:** StudentWorks Plus CD-ROM or DVD-ROM Online Student Edition at **glencoe.com** Literature Online at **glencoe.com** (QuickPass Code: **GLA9800u5**)

Lesson Plan

Unit 5 Wrap-Up (pp. 842–849)

Lesson Plan and Resource Manager

UNIT FIVE Beginnings of the Modern Age 1910–1930s

Lesson Summary	On pages **842–849** of the Student Edition, students will: ▪ Read independently ▪ Complete the end-of-unit assessment
Lesson Duration	Two 45–50 minute sessions
Focus	**SE/TE** pp. 842, 844
Teach	**SE/TE** pp. 842–843, 844–846
Assess	**SE/TE** pp. 847–849 📁 Assessment Resources, Unit 5 Summative Assessment, pp. 339–340 📘 ACT/SAT Preparation and Practice SE/ATE 💿 ExamView Assessment Suite CD-ROM ▶ Progress Reporter Online Assessment
Differentiated Instruction: English Learners	**TE** English Learner Activities, pp. 842–849
Differentiated Instruction: Approaching Level	**TE** Approaching Level Activities, pp. 842–849
Differentiated Instruction: Advanced/Pre-AP	📘 Novel Companion SE, pp. 207–250/TG, pp. 45–53 💿▶ Literature Classics, High School CD-ROM 💿 Skill Level Up! A Skills-Based Language Arts Game CD-ROM
Extension	📘 Grammar and Language Workbook SE/TAE; Spelling Power SE/TAE 📁 Revising with Style
Daily Writing	**SE/TE** pp. 843, 849
Interdisciplinary Connections	**TE** Cultural History, p. 842 **TE** Literary History, p. 843 **TE** Language History, p. 845
Independent Reading	💿 BookLink K–12 CD-ROM; Glencoe Literature Library Teacher Resources CD-ROM 📖 Ethnic Anthologies; Glencoe Literature Library; *inTIME* magazine 💿▶ Literature Classics, High School CD-ROM
Technology and Additional Resources	**Planning and Instruction:** 💿 TeacherWorks Plus CD-ROM; Classroom Presentation Toolkit CD-ROM ▶ Literature Online at **glencoe.com** (QuickPass Code: **GLA9879u5T**) **Students Tools:** 💿 StudentWorks Plus CD-ROM or DVD-ROM ▶ Online Student Edition at **glencoe.com** ▶ Glencoe Online Essay Grader at **glencoewriting.com** ▶ Literature Online at **glencoe.com** (QuickPass Code: **GLA9800u5**)

Lesson Plan

Glencoe Literature

Unit 6 Introduction (pp. 850–864)

Lesson Plan and Resource Manager

UNIT SIX From Depression to Cold War, 1930s–1960s

Learning Objectives	**Literary Studies:** Analyzing literary periods. Evaluating historical influences. Connecting to the literature.
Unit Summary	In this unit, students will be introduced to the following: • **Big Ideas:** Return to Regionalism, Life in the City, The United States and the World • **Reading Strategies:** Analyze Graphic Information, Make Inferences, Analyze Cause and Effect, Use Timelines, Summarize • **Writing Activities/Grammar:** Graph Migration, Organize and Support, Present Research • **Listening/Speaking/Viewing Skills:** Presentation on Music, Photograph Murals, Analyze Art
Lesson Duration	Two 45–50 minute sessions
Focus	**SE/TE** pp. 850–851 Daily Language Practice Transparency 78 Literature Launchers: Pre-Reading Videos DVD, Unit 6 Launcher Literature Launchers Teacher Guide
Teach	**SE/TE** pp. 852–863 Unit 6 Teaching Resources, Unit Introduction, pp. 1–2 Unit 6 Teaching Resources, Big Idea Foldable, pp. 3–4 Unit 6 Teaching Resources, Big Idea School-to-Home Connection, p. 5 Unit 6 Teaching Resources, Unit Challenge Planner, pp. 12–15 Unit 6 Teaching Resources: Academic Vocabulary Development, pp. 16–17 Classroom Presentation Toolkit CD-ROM TeacherWorks Plus CD-ROM
Assess	**SE/TE** p. 864 Assessment Resources, Unit 6 Diagnostic Assessment, pp. 41–48 ACT/SAT Preparation and Practice SE/ATE ExamView Assessment Suite CD-ROM Progress Reporter Online Assessment
Differentiated Instruction: English Learners	**TE** English Learner Activities, pp. 850–864 Unit 6 Teaching Resources, Big Idea School-to-Home Connections: English, Spanish, Vietnamese, Tagalog, Cantonese, Haitian Creole, and Hmong, pp. 6–11
Differentiated Instruction: Approaching Level	**TE** Approaching Level Activities, pp. 850–864 Skill Level Up! A Skills-Based Language Arts Game CD-ROM
Differentiated Instruction: Advanced/Pre-AP	Novel Companion SE, pp. 251–294 Novel Companion TG, pp. 54–61 Literature Classics, High School CD-ROM Skill Level Up! A Skills-Based Language Arts Game CD-ROM

Copyright © by The McGraw-Hill Companies, Inc.

Extension	▐ Grammar and Language Workbook SE ▐ Grammar and Language Workbook TAE 📁 Revising with Style ▐ Spelling Power SE ▐ Spelling Power TAE
Daily Writing	**TE** p. 860 **SE/TE** SE p. 864
Interdisciplinary Connections	**SE/TE** View the Art, pp. 850–851, 859, 861 **SE/TE** View the Photograph, pp. 855, 856, 863 **TE** Cultural History, pp. 852, 857, 860 **TE** Literary History, pp. 853, 858, 862 ⊙ glencoe.com
Independent Reading	⊙ BookLink K–12 CD-ROM ▥ Ethnic Anthologies ⊙ Glencoe Literature Library ⊙ Glencoe Literature Library Teacher Resources CD-ROM ▥ *inTIME* magazine ⊙ ⊙ Literature Classics, High School CD-ROM
Technology and Additional Resources	**Planning and Instruction:** ⊙ TeacherWorks Plus CD-ROM ⊙ Classroom Presentation Toolkit CD-ROM ⊙ Literature Online at **glencoe.com** (QuickPass Code: **GLA9879u6T**) **Students Tools:** ⊙ StudentWorks Plus CD-ROM or DVD-ROM ⊙ Online Student Edition at **glencoe.com** ⊙ Literature Online at **glencoe.com** (QuickPass Code: **GLA9800u6**)

Lesson Plan

Part 1 Opener, *Breakfast*, and Vocabulary Workshop (pp. 866–873)

Lesson Plan and Resource Manager

UNIT SIX From Depression to Cold War 1930s–1960s, Part 1: The New Regionalism and the City

Learning Objectives	**Literary Study:** Analyzing theme. **Reading:** Connecting to personal experience. **Writing:** Writing a report. **Vocabulary:** Understanding word parts: roots, prefixes, and suffixes.
Lesson Summary	On pages **866–873** of the Student Edition, students will be introduced to the following: ▪ **Big Idea:** Return to Regionalism ▪ **Literary Element:** Implied Theme ▪ **Reading Strategy:** Connect to Personal Experience ▪ **Vocabulary:** Word Usage, Academic Vocabulary, Roots, Prefixes, and Suffixes ▪ **Writing Activity/Grammar:** Report
Lesson Duration	One 45–50 minute session
Readability Scores	Dale-Chall: 6.7 DRP: 52 Lexile: 950
Focus	SE/TE pp. 866–867, 873 Selection Focus Transparency 53 Daily Language Practice Transparency 79
Teach	SE/TE pp. 868–870, 873 Unit 6 Teaching Resources, Literary Element, p. 26 Unit 6 Teaching Resources, Reading Strategy, p. 27 Unit 6 Teaching Resources, Vocabulary Strategy, p. 28 Unit 6 Teaching Resources, Grammar Practice, p. 29 Grammar and Language Transparency 53 Literary Elements Transparency 103 Classroom Presentation Toolkit CD-ROM Listening Library CD, Selection Audio TeacherWorks Plus CD-ROM Vocabulary PuzzleMaker CD-ROM
Assess	SE/TE pp. 871–872, 873 Unit 6 Teaching Resources, Selection Quick Check, p. 30 Unit 6 Teaching Resources, Selection Quick Check (Spanish), p. 31 Assessment Resources, Selection Test, pp. 235–236 ExamView Assessment Suite CD-ROM Progress Reporter Online Assessment
Differentiated Instruction: English Learners	TE English Learner Activities, pp. 866–873 Unit 6 Teaching Resources, English Language Coach, p. 19 Unit 6 Teaching Resources, Selection Summaries: English, Spanish, Vietnamese, Tagalog, Cantonese, Haitian Creole, and Hmong, pp. 20–25

Differentiated Instruction: English Learners *(continued)*	📁 Unit 6 Teaching Resources, Selection Quick Check (Spanish), p. 31 📁 English Language Coach 💿 Glencoe Interactive Vocabulary CD-ROM 💿 Listening Library Audio CD 📁 Listening Library Sourcebook: Strategies and Activities
Differentiated Instruction: Approaching Level	**TE** Approaching Level Activities, pp. 866–873 💿 Glencoe Interactive Vocabulary CD-ROM 💿 Listening Library Audio CD 📁 Listening Library Sourcebook: Strategies and Activities 💿 Skill Level Up! A Skills-Based Language Arts Game CD-ROM
Differentiated Instruction: Advanced/Pre-AP	📘 Novel Companion SE, pp. 251–294 📘 Novel Companion TG, pp. 54–61 💿 Literature Classics, High School CD-ROM 💿 Skill Level Up! A Skills-Based Language Arts Game CD-ROM
Extension	📘 Grammar and Language Workbook SE 📘 Grammar and Language Workbook TAE 📁 Revising with Style 📘 Spelling Power SE 📘 Spelling Power TAE
Daily Writing	**SE/TE** p. 872
Interdisciplinary Connections	**TE** Cultural History, p. 686 **TE** Connect to Math, p. 872 💿 **glencoe.com**
Independent Reading	💿 BookLink K–12 CD-ROM 📖 Ethnic Anthologies 📖 Glencoe Literature Library 💿 Glencoe Literature Library Teacher Resources CD-ROM 📖 *inTIME* magazine 💿 Literature Classics, High School CD-ROM
Technology and Additional Resources	**Planning and Instruction:** 💿 TeacherWorks Plus CD-ROM 💿 Classroom Presentation Toolkit CD-ROM 💿 Literature Online at **glencoe.com** (QuickPass Code: **GLA9879u6T**) **Students Tools:** 💿 StudentWorks Plus CD-ROM or DVD-ROM 💿 Online Student Edition at **glencoe.com** 💿 Literature Online at **glencoe.com** (QuickPass Code: **GLA9800u6**)

Lesson Plan

A Rose for Emily and Address upon Receiving the Nobel Prize in Literature (pp. 874–887)

Lesson Plan and Resource Manager

UNIT SIX From Depression to Cold War 1930s–1960s, Part 1: The New Regionalism and the City

Learning Objectives	**Literary Study:** Analyzing foreshadowing. **Reading:** Identifying sequence. **Writing:** Writing an expository essay.
Lesson Summary	On pages **874–887** of the Student Edition, students will be introduced to the following: • **Big Idea:** Return to Regionalism • **Literary Element:** Foreshadowing • **Reading Strategy:** Identify Sequence • **Vocabulary:** Denotation and Connotation • **Writing Activities/Grammar:** Expository Essay, Degrees of Comparison, Use Adjectives • **Listening/Speaking/Viewing Skills:** Analyze Art, Oral Presentation
Lesson Duration	Two 45–50 minute sessions
Readability Scores	"A Rose for Emily" Dale-Chall: 5.9 DRP: 60 Lexile: 1120 "Address upon Receiving the Nobel Prize in Literature" Dale-Chall: 8.4 DRP: 62 Lexile: 1170
Focus	**SE/TE** pp. 874–875 Selection Focus Transparency 54 Daily Language Practice Transparency 80
Teach	**SE/TE** pp. 876–884 Unit 6 Teaching Resources, Literary Element, p. 38 Unit 6 Teaching Resources, Reading Strategy, p. 39 Unit 6 Teaching Resources, Selection Vocabulary Practice, p. 40 Unit 6 Teaching Resources, Vocabulary Strategy, p. 41 Unit 6 Teaching Resources, Grammar Practice, p. 42 Grammar and Language Transparency 6 Literary Elements Transparency 44 Classroom Presentation Toolkit CD-ROM Listening Library CD, Selection Audio TeacherWorks Plus CD-ROM Vocabulary PuzzleMaker CD-ROM
Assess	**SE/TE** pp. 885–887 Unit 6 Teaching Resources, Selection Quick Check, p. 43 Unit 6 Teaching Resources, Selection Quick Check (Spanish), p. 44 Assessment Resources, Selection Test, pp. 237–238 ExamView Assessment Suite CD-ROM Progress Reporter Online Assessment

Differentiated Instruction: English Learners	**TE** English Learner Activities, pp. 874–887 📁 Unit 6 Teaching Resources, English Language Coach, p. 19 📁 Unit 6 Teaching Resources, Selection Summaries: English, Spanish, Vietnamese, Tagalog, Cantonese, Haitian Creole, and Hmong, pp. 32–37 📁 Unit 6 Teaching Resources, Selection Quick Check (Spanish), p. 44 📁 English Language Coach 💿 Glencoe Interactive Vocabulary CD-ROM 💿 Listening Library Audio CD 📁 Listening Library Sourcebook: Strategies and Activities
Differentiated Instruction: Approaching Level	**TE** Approaching Level Activities, pp. 874–887 💿 Glencoe Interactive Vocabulary CD-ROM 💿 Listening Library Audio CD 📁 Listening Library Sourcebook: Strategies and Activities 💿 Skill Level Up! A Skills-Based Language Arts Game CD-ROM
Differentiated Instruction: Advanced/Pre-AP	**TE** Advanced Learner Activities, pp. 874–887 📖 Novel Companion SE, pp. 251–294 📖 Novel Companion TG, pp. 54–61 💿 Literature Classics, High School CD-ROM 💿 Skill Level Up! A Skills-Based Language Arts Game CD-ROM
Extension	📖 Grammar and Language Workbook SE 📖 Grammar and Language Workbook TAE 📁 Revising with Style 📖 Spelling Power SE 📖 Spelling Power TAE
Daily Writing	**TE** p. 884 **SE/TE** p. 887
Interdisciplinary Connections	**SE/TE** View the Art, pp. 879, 881, 883 **TE** Language History, p. 878 ▶ glencoe.com
Independent Reading	💿 BookLink K–12 CD-ROM 📖 Ethnic Anthologies; Glencoe Literature Library; *inTIME* magazine 💿 Glencoe Literature Library Teacher Resources CD-ROM 💿 Literature Classics, High School CD-ROM
Technology and Additional Resources	**Planning and Instruction:** 💿 TeacherWorks Plus CD-ROM 💿 Classroom Presentation Toolkit CD-ROM ▶ Literature Online at **glencoe.com** (QuickPass Code: **GLA9879u6T**) **Students Tools:** 💿 StudentWorks Plus CD-ROM or DVD-ROM ▶ Online Student Edition at **glencoe.com** ▶ Literature Online at **glencoe.com** (QuickPass Code: **GLA9800u6**)

Lesson Plan

Glencoe Literature

A Worn Path (pp. 888–898)

Lesson Plan and Resource Manager

UNIT SIX From Depression to Cold War 1930s–1960s, Part 1: The New Regionalism and the City

Learning Objectives	**Literary Study:** Analyzing description. **Reading:** Visualizing. **Writing:** Applying dialogue.
Lesson Summary	On pages **888–898** of the Student Edition, students will be introduced to the following: • **Big Idea:** Return to Regionalism • **Literary Element:** Description • **Reading Strategy:** Visualize • **Vocabulary:** Analogies, Academic Vocabulary • **Writing:** Apply Dialogue • **Listening/Speaking/Viewing Skills:** Analyze Art, Readers Theater
Lesson Duration	One 45–50 minute session
Readability Scores	Dale-Chall: 3.4 DRP: 52 Lexile: 780
Focus	**SE/TE** pp. 888–889 Selection Focus Transparency 55 Daily Language Practice Transparency 81
Teach	**SE/TE** pp. 890–896 Unit 6 Teaching Resources, Literary Element, p. 51 Unit 6 Teaching Resources, Reading Strategy, p. 52 Unit 6 Teaching Resources, Selection Vocabulary Practice, p. 53 Unit 6 Teaching Resources, Vocabulary Strategy, p. 54 Unit 6 Teaching Resources, Grammar Practice, p. 55 Literary Elements Transparency 24 Classroom Presentation Toolkit CD-ROM Listening Library CD, Selection Audio TeacherWorks Plus CD-ROM Vocabulary PuzzleMaker CD-ROM
Assess	**SE/TE** pp. 897–898 Unit 6 Teaching Resources, Selection Quick Check, p. 56 Unit 6 Teaching Resources, Selection Quick Check (Spanish), p. 57 Assessment Resources, Selection Test, pp. 239–240 ExamView Assessment Suite CD-ROM Progress Reporter Online Assessment
Differentiated Instruction: English Learners	**TE** English Learner Activities, pp. 888–898 Unit 6 Teaching Resources, English Language Coach, p. 19 Unit 6 Teaching Resources, Selection Summaries: English, Spanish, Vietnamese, Tagalog, Cantonese, Haitian Creole, and Hmong, pp. 45–50

Differentiated Instruction: English Learners *(continued)*	📁 Unit 6 Teaching Resources, Selection Quick Check (Spanish), p. 57
	📁 English Language Coach
	💿 Glencoe Interactive Vocabulary CD-ROM
	💿 Listening Library Audio CD
	📁 Listening Library Sourcebook: Strategies and Activities
Differentiated Instruction: Approaching Level	**TE** Approaching Level Activities, pp. 888–898
	💿 Glencoe Interactive Vocabulary CD-ROM
	💿 Listening Library Audio CD
	📁 Listening Library Sourcebook: Strategies and Activities
	💿 Skill Level Up! A Skills-Based Language Arts Game CD-ROM
Differentiated Instruction: Advanced/Pre-AP	📗 Novel Companion SE, pp. 251–294
	📗 Novel Companion TG, pp. 54–61
	💿 ▶ Literature Classics, High School CD-ROM
	💿 Skill Level Up! A Skills-Based Language Arts Game CD-ROM
Extension	📗 Grammar and Language Workbook SE
	📗 Grammar and Language Workbook TAE
	📁 Revising with Style
	📗 Spelling Power SE
	📗 Spelling Power TAE
Daily Writing	**SE/TE** p. 898
Interdisciplinary Connections	**SE/TE** View the Photograph, pp. 890, 892, 895
	▶ glencoe.com
Independent Reading	💿 BookLink K–12 CD-ROM
	📖 Ethnic Anthologies
	📖 Glencoe Literature Library
	💿 Glencoe Literature Library Teacher Resources CD-ROM
	📖 *inTIME* magazine
	💿 ▶ Literature Classics, High School CD-ROM
Technology and Additional Resources	**Planning and Instruction:**
	💿 TeacherWorks Plus CD-ROM
	💿 Classroom Presentation Toolkit CD-ROM
	▶ Literature Online at **glencoe.com** (QuickPass Code: **GLA9879u6T**)
	Students Tools:
	💿 StudentWorks Plus CD-ROM or DVD-ROM
	💿 Online Student Edition at **glencoe.com**
	▶ Literature Online at **glencoe.com** (QuickPass Code: **GLA9800u6**)

Lesson Plan

Glencoe Literature

from *Black Boy* (pp. 899–908)

Lesson Plan and Resource Manager

UNIT SIX From Depression to Cold War 1930s–1960s, Part 1: The New Regionalism and the City

Learning Objectives	**Literary Study:** Analyzing sequence. **Reading:** Comparing and contrasting characters. **Speaking and Listening:** Delivering a speech.
Lesson Summary	On pages **899–908** of the Student Edition, students will be introduced to the following: ▪ **Big Idea:** Life in the City ▪ **Literary Element:** Flash-forward ▪ **Reading Strategy:** Compare and Contrast Characters ▪ **Vocabulary:** Context Clues, Academic Vocabulary ▪ **Writing:** Letter ▪ **Study Skills/Research/Assessment:** Short-Answer Questions ▪ **Listening/Speaking/Viewing Skills:** Analyze Art, Speech
Lesson Duration	One 20–25 minute session
Readability Scores	Dale-Chall: 5.6 DRP: 57 Lexile: 970
Focus	**TE** pp. 899–900 🔦 Selection Focus Transparency 56 🔦 Daily Language Practice Transparency 82
Teach	**TE** pp. 901–906 📁 Unit 6 Teaching Resources, Literary Element, p. 64 📁 Unit 6 Teaching Resources, Reading Strategy, p. 65 📁 Unit 6 Teaching Resources, Selection Vocabulary Practice, p. 66 📁 Unit 6 Teaching Resources, Vocabulary Strategy, p. 67 📁 Unit 6 Teaching Resources, Grammar Practice, p. 68 🔦 Literary Elements Transparency 42 💿 Classroom Presentation Toolkit CD-ROM 💿 Listening Library CD, Selection Audio 💿 TeacherWorks Plus CD-ROM 💿 ▶ Vocabulary PuzzleMaker CD-ROM
Assess	**TE** pp. 907–908 📁 Unit 6 Teaching Resources, Selection Quick Check, p. 69 📁 Unit 6 Teaching Resources, Selection Quick Check (Spanish), p. 70 📁 Assessment Resources, Selection Test, pp. 241–242 💿 ExamView Assessment Suite CD-ROM ▶ Progress Reporter Online Assessment
Differentiated Instruction: English Learners	**TE** English Learner Activities, pp. 899–908 📁 Unit 6 Teaching Resources, Selection Summaries: English, Spanish, Vietnamese, Tagalog, Cantonese, Haitian Creole, and Hmong, pp. 58–63 📁 Unit 6 Teaching Resources, Selection Quick Check (Spanish), p. 70

Differentiated Instruction: English Learners *(continued)*	📁 English Language Coach 💿 Glencoe Interactive Vocabulary CD-ROM 💿 Listening Library Audio CD 📁 Listening Library Sourcebook: Strategies and Activities
Differentiated Instruction: Approaching Level	**TE** Approaching Level Activities, pp. 899–908 💿 Glencoe Interactive Vocabulary CD-ROM 💿 Listening Library Audio CD 📁 Listening Library Sourcebook: Strategies and Activities 💿 Skill Level Up! A Skills-Based Language Arts Game CD-ROM
Differentiated Instruction: Advanced/Pre-AP	📘 Novel Companion SE, pp. 251–294 📘 Novel Companion TG, pp. 54–61 💿 ▶ Literature Classics, High School CD-ROM 💿 Skill Level Up! A Skills-Based Language Arts Game CD-ROM
Extension	📘 Grammar and Language Workbook SE 📘 Grammar and Language Workbook TAE 📁 Revising with Style 📘 Spelling Power SE 📘 Spelling Power TAE
Daily Writing	**TE** p. 902
Interdisciplinary Connections	**SE/TE** View the Art, pp. 903, 905 ▶ glencoe.com
Independent Reading	💿 BookLink K–12 CD-ROM 📖 Ethnic Anthologies 📖 Glencoe Literature Library 💿 Glencoe Literature Library Teacher Resources CD-ROM 📖 *inTIME* magazine 💿 ▶ Literature Classics, High School CD-ROM
Technology and Additional Resources	**Planning and Instruction:** 💿 TeacherWorks Plus CD-ROM 💿 Classroom Presentation Toolkit CD-ROM ▶ Literature Online at **glencoe.com** (QuickPass Code: **GLA9879u6T**) **Students Tools:** 💿 StudentWorks Plus CD-ROM or DVD-ROM ▶ Online Student Edition at **glencoe.com** ▶ Literature Online at **glencoe.com** (QuickPass Code: **GLA9800u6**)

Lesson Plan

Glencoe Literature

from *You Have Seen Their Faces* (pp. 909–912)

Lesson Plan and Resource Manager

UNIT SIX From Depression to Cold War 1930s–1960s, Part 1: The New Regionalism and the City

Learning Objectives	**Reading:** Making connections across literature. Analyzing historical texts and photographs. Analyzing informational text.
Lesson Summary	On pages **909–912** of the Student Edition, students will be introduced to the following: • **Big Idea:** Return to Regionalism • **Reading Strategy:** Analyze the Purpose of Historical Texts and Photographs
Lesson Duration	One 20–25 minute session
Readability Scores	Dale-Chall: 11.7 DRP: 63 Lexile: 1210
Focus	**TE** p. 909
Teach	**TE** pp. 909–911 📁 Unit 6 Teaching Resources, Reading Strategy, p. 77 💿 Classroom Presentation Toolkit CD-ROM 💿 Listening Library CD, Selection Audio 💿 TeacherWorks Plus CD-ROM 💿 ▶ Vocabulary PuzzleMaker CD-ROM
Assess	**TE** p. 912 📁 Unit 6 Teaching Resources, Selection Quick Check, p. 78 📁 Unit 6 Teaching Resources, Selection Quick Check (Spanish), p. 79 📁 Assessment Resources, Selection Test, pp. 243–244 💿 ExamView Assessment Suite CD-ROM ▶ Progress Reporter Online Assessment
Differentiated Instruction: English Learners	**TE** English Learner Activities, pp. 909–912 📁 Unit 6 Teaching Resources, Selection Summaries: English, Spanish, Vietnamese, Tagalog, Cantonese, Haitian Creole, and Hmong, pp. 71–76 📁 English Language Coach 💿 Glencoe Interactive Vocabulary CD-ROM 💿 Listening Library Audio CD 📁 Listening Library Sourcebook: Strategies and Activities
Differentiated Instruction: Approaching Level	**TE** Approaching Level Activities, pp. 909–912 💿 Glencoe Interactive Vocabulary CD-ROM 💿 Listening Library Audio CD 📁 Listening Library Sourcebook: Strategies and Activities 💿 Skill Level Up! A Skills-Based Language Arts Game CD-ROM
Differentiated Instruction: Advanced/Pre-AP	**TE** Advanced Learner Activities, pp. 909–912 📘 Novel Companion SE, pp. 251–294 📘 Novel Companion TG, pp. 54–61 💿 ▶ Literature Classics, High School CD-ROM 💿 Skill Level Up! A Skills-Based Language Arts Game CD-ROM

Extension	▪ Grammar and Language Workbook SE ▪ Grammar and Language Workbook TAE ▢ Revising with Style ▪ Spelling Power SE ▪ Spelling Power TAE
Interdisciplinary Connections	**SE/TE** View the Art, p. 909 **SE/TE** View the Photograph, p. 911 ▶ glencoe.com
Independent Reading	◉ BookLink K–12 CD-ROM ▢ Ethnic Anthologies ▢ Glencoe Literature Library ◉ Glencoe Literature Library Teacher Resources CD-ROM ▢ *inTIME* magazine ◉ ▶ Literature Classics, High School CD-ROM
Technology and Additional Resources	**Planning and Instruction:** ◉ TeacherWorks Plus CD-ROM ◉ Classroom Presentation Toolkit CD-ROM ▶ Literature Online at **glencoe.com** (QuickPass Code: **GLA9879u6T**) **Students Tools:** ◉ StudentWorks Plus CD-ROM or DVD-ROM ▶ Online Student Edition at **glencoe.com** ▶ Literature Online at **glencoe.com** (QuickPass Code: **GLA9800u6**)

Lesson Plan

Glencoe Literature

The Life You Save May Be Your Own and Grammar Workshop (pp. 913–927)

Lesson Plan and Resource Manager

UNIT SIX From Depression to Cold War 1930s–1960s, Part 1: The New Regionalism and the City

Learning Objectives	**Literary Study:** Analyzing dialogue. **Reading:** Applying background knowledge. **Writing:** Writing a persuasive essay. Writing a review. **Grammar:** Understanding how to use introductory phrases and clauses.

Lesson Summary	On pages **913–927** of the Student Edition, students will be introduced to the following:
	  ▪ **Big Idea:** Return to Regionalism
	  ▪ **Literary Element:** Dialogue
	  ▪ **Reading Strategy:** Apply Background Knowledge
	  ▪ **Vocabulary:** Word Usage, Academic Vocabulary
	  ▪ **Writing Activities/Grammar:** Write a Review, Introductory Phrases and Clauses

Lesson Duration	One 45–50 minute session
Readability Scores	Dale-Chall: 6.1 DRP: 54 Lexile: 970
Focus	**TE** pp. 913–914, 927 ⬛ Selection Focus Transparency 57 ⬛ Daily Language Practice Transparency 83
Teach	**TE** pp. 915–923, 927 📁 Unit 6 Teaching Resources, Literary Element, p. 86 📁 Unit 6 Teaching Resources, Reading Strategy, p. 87 📁 Unit 6 Teaching Resources, Selection Vocabulary Practice, p. 88 📁 Unit 6 Teaching Resources, Vocabulary Strategy, p. 89 📁 Unit 6 Teaching Resources, Grammar Practice, p. 90 ⬛ Grammar and Language Transparencies 8, 67 ⬛ Literary Elements Transparency 26 ⬤ Classroom Presentation Toolkit CD-ROM ⬤ Listening Library CD, Selection Audio ⬤ TeacherWorks Plus CD-ROM ⬤⬤ Vocabulary PuzzleMaker CD-ROM
Assess	**TE** pp. 924–926, 927 📁 Unit 6 Teaching Resources, Selection Quick Check, p. 91 📁 Unit 6 Teaching Resources, Selection Quick Check (Spanish), p. 92 📁 Assessment Resources, Selection Test, pp. 245–246 ⬤ ExamView Assessment Suite CD-ROM ⬤ Progress Reporter Online Assessment

Differentiated Instruction: English Learners	**TE** English Learner Activities, pp. 913–927 📁 Unit 6 Teaching Resources, English Language Coach, p. 19 📁 Unit 6 Teaching Resources, Selection Summaries: English, Spanish, Vietnamese, Tagalog, Cantonese, Haitian Creole, and Hmong, pp. 80–85 📁 Unit 6 Teaching Resources, Selection Quick Check (Spanish), p. 92 📁 English Language Coach 💿 Glencoe Interactive Vocabulary CD-ROM 💿 Listening Library Audio CD 📁 Listening Library Sourcebook: Strategies and Activities
Differentiated Instruction: Approaching Level	**TE** Approaching Level Activities, pp. 913–927 💿 Glencoe Interactive Vocabulary CD-ROM 💿 Listening Library Audio CD 📁 Listening Library Sourcebook: Strategies and Activities 💿 Skill Level Up! A Skills-Based Language Arts Game CD-ROM
Differentiated Instruction: Advanced/Pre-AP	**TE** Advanced Learner Activities, pp. 913–927 📘 Novel Companion SE, pp. 251–294 📘 Novel Companion TG, pp. 54–61 💿 Literature Classics, High School CD-ROM 💿 Skill Level Up! A Skills-Based Language Arts Game CD-ROM
Extension	📘 Grammar and Language Workbook SE 📘 Grammar and Language Workbook TAE 📁 Revising with Style 📘 Spelling Power SE 📘 Spelling Power TAE
Daily Writing	**SE/TE** p. 926
Interdisciplinary Connections	**SE/TE** View the Art, p. 915 **SE/TE** View the Photograph, pp. 917, 921 **TE** Cultural History, pp. 916, 919, 920 💿 glencoe.com
Independent Reading	💿 BookLink K–12 CD-ROM 📖 Ethnic Anthologies; Glencoe Literature Library; *inTIME* magazine 💿 Glencoe Literature Library Teacher Resources CD-ROM 💿 Literature Classics, High School CD-ROM
Technology and Additional Resources	**Planning and Instruction:** 💿 TeacherWorks Plus CD-ROM 💿 Classroom Presentation Toolkit CD-ROM 💿 Literature Online at **glencoe.com** (QuickPass Code: **GLA9879u6T**) **Students Tools:** 💿 StudentWorks Plus CD-ROM or DVD-ROM 💿 Online Student Edition at **glencoe.com** 💿 Literature Online at **glencoe.com** (QuickPass Code: **GLA9800u6**)

Lesson Plan

Glencoe Literature

The Second Tree from the Corner (pp. 928–936)

Lesson Plan and Resource Manager

UNIT SIX From Depression to Cold War 1930s–1960s, Part 1: The New Regionalism and the City

Learning Objectives	**Literary Study:** Analyzing plot. **Reading:** Analyzing text structure.
Lesson Summary	On pages **928–936** of the Student Edition, students will be introduced to the following: • **Big Idea:** Life in the City • **Literary Element:** Plot • **Reading Strategy:** Analyze Text Structure • **Vocabulary:** Word Parts, Academic Vocabulary • **Writing Activity/Grammar:** Apply Irony
Lesson Duration	One 45–50 minute session
Readability Scores	Dale-Chall: 5.7 DRP: 57 Lexile: 1110
Focus	**TE** pp. 928–929 Selection Focus Transparency 58 Daily Language Practice Transparency 84
Teach	**TE** pp. 930–934 Unit 6 Teaching Resources, Literary Element, p. 100 Unit 6 Teaching Resources, Reading Strategy, p. 101 Unit 6 Teaching Resources, Selection Vocabulary Practice, p. 102 Unit 6 Teaching Resources, Vocabulary Strategy, p. 103 Unit 6 Teaching Resources, Grammar Practice, p. 104 Literary Elements Transparency 78 Classroom Presentation Toolkit CD-ROM Listening Library CD, Selection Audio TeacherWorks Plus CD-ROM Vocabulary PuzzleMaker CD-ROM
Assess	**TE** pp. 935–936 Unit 6 Teaching Resources, Selection Quick Check, p. 105 Unit 6 Teaching Resources, Selection Quick Check (Spanish), p. 106 Assessment Resources, Selection Test, pp. 247–248 ExamView Assessment Suite CD-ROM Progress Reporter Online Assessment

Copyright © by The McGraw-Hill Companies, Inc.

Differentiated Instruction: English Learners	**TE** English Learner Activities, pp. 928–936
	📁 Unit 6 Teaching Resources, English Language Coach, p. 19
	📁 Unit 6 Teaching Resources, Selection Summaries: English, Spanish, Vietnamese, Tagalog, Cantonese, Haitian Creole, and Hmong, pp. 94–99
	📁 Unit 6 Teaching Resources, Selection Quick Check (Spanish), p. 106
	📁 English Language Coach
	💿 Glencoe Interactive Vocabulary CD-ROM
	💿 Listening Library Audio CD
	📁 Listening Library Sourcebook: Strategies and Activities
Differentiated Instruction: Approaching Level	**TE** Approaching Level Activities, pp. 928–936
	💿 Glencoe Interactive Vocabulary CD-ROM
	💿 Listening Library Audio CD
	📁 Listening Library Sourcebook: Strategies and Activities
	💿 Skill Level Up! A Skills-Based Language Arts Game CD-ROM
Differentiated Instruction: Advanced/Pre-AP	**TE** Advanced Learner Activities, pp. 928–936
	📓 Novel Companion SE, pp. 251–294
	📓 Novel Companion TG, pp. 54–61
	💿 ▶ Literature Classics, High School CD-ROM
	💿 Skill Level Up! A Skills-Based Language Arts Game CD-ROM
Extension	📓 Grammar and Language Workbook SE
	📓 Grammar and Language Workbook TAE
	📁 Revising with Style
	📓 Spelling Power SE
	📓 Spelling Power TAE
Daily Writing	**SE/TE** p. 936
Interdisciplinary Connections	**SE/TE** View the Art, pp. 930, 933
	TE Cultural History, p. 932
	▶ glencoe.com
Independent Reading	💿 BookLink K–12 CD-ROM
	📖 Ethnic Anthologies
	📖 Glencoe Literature Library
	💿 Glencoe Literature Library Teacher Resources CD-ROM
	📖 inTIME magazine
	💿 ▶ Literature Classics, High School CD-ROM
Technology and Additional Resources	**Planning and Instruction:**
	💿 TeacherWorks Plus CD-ROM
	💿 Classroom Presentation Toolkit CD-ROM
	▶ Literature Online at **glencoe.com** (QuickPass Code: **GLA9879u6T**)
	Students Tools:
	💿 StudentWorks Plus CD-ROM or DVD-ROM
	▶ Online Student Edition at **glencoe.com**
	▶ Literature Online at **glencoe.com** (QuickPass Code: **GLA9800u6**)

Lesson Plan

To Don at Salaam and The Bean Eaters (pp. 937–941)

Lesson Plan and Resource Manager

UNIT SIX From Depression to Cold War 1930s–1960s, Part 1: The New
Regionalism and the City

Learning Objectives	**Literary Study:** Analyzing rhyme and rhyme scheme. **Reading:** Evaluating diction. **Writing:** Writing an essay.
Lesson Summary	On pages **937–941** of the Student Edition, students will be introduced to the following: • **Big Idea:** Life in the City • **Literary Element:** Rhyme Scheme • **Reading Strategy:** Evaluate Diction • **Vocabulary:** Context Clues • **Writing Activity/Grammar:** Essay
Lesson Duration	One 45–50 minute session
Readability Scores	Dale-Chall: N/A DRP: N/A Lexile: N/A
Focus	**TE** pp. 937–938 ✎ Daily Language Practice Transparency 85
Teach	**TE** pp. 939–940 📁 Unit 6 Teaching Resources, Literary Element, p. 113 📁 Unit 6 Teaching Resources, Reading Strategy, p. 114 📁 Unit 6 Teaching Resources, Selection Vocabulary Practice, p. 115 📁 Unit 6 Teaching Resources, Vocabulary Strategy, p. 116 ✎ Literary Elements Transparency 88 💿 Classroom Presentation Toolkit CD-ROM 💿 Listening Library CD, Selection Audio 💿 TeacherWorks Plus CD-ROM 💿 ▶ Vocabulary PuzzleMaker CD-ROM
Assess	**TE** p. 941 📁 Unit 6 Teaching Resources, Selection Quick Check, p. 117 📁 Unit 6 Teaching Resources, Selection Quick Check (Spanish), p. 118 📁 Assessment Resources, Selection Test, pp. 249–250 💿 ExamView Assessment Suite CD-ROM ▶ Progress Reporter Online Assessment
Differentiated Instruction: English Learners	📁 Unit 6 Teaching Resources, English Language Coach, p. 19 📁 Unit 6 Teaching Resources, Selection Summaries: English, Spanish, Vietnamese, Tagalog, Cantonese, Haitian Creole, and Hmong, pp. 107–112 📁 Unit 6 Teaching Resources, Selection Quick Check (Spanish), p. 118 📁 English Language Coach 💿 Listening Library Audio CD 📁 Listening Library Sourcebook: Strategies and Activities

Differentiated Instruction: Approaching Level	TE Approaching Level Activities, pp. 937–941
	Glencoe Interactive Vocabulary CD-ROM
	Listening Library Audio CD
	Listening Library Sourcebook: Strategies and Activities
	Skill Level Up! A Skills-Based Language Arts Game CD-ROM
Differentiated Instruction: Advanced/Pre-AP	Novel Companion SE, pp. 251–294
	Novel Companion TG, pp. 54–61
	Literature Classics, High School CD-ROM
	Skill Level Up! A Skills-Based Language Arts Game CD-ROM
Extension	Grammar and Language Workbook SE
	Grammar and Language Workbook TAE
	Revising with Style
	Spelling Power SE
	Spelling Power TAE
Daily Writing	SE/TE p. 941
Interdisciplinary Connections	SE/TE View the Art, p. 939
	TE Cultural History, p. 937
	glencoe.com
Independent Reading	BookLink K–12 CD-ROM
	Ethnic Anthologies
	Glencoe Literature Library
	Glencoe Literature Library Teacher Resources CD-ROM
	inTIME magazine
	Literature Classics, High School CD-ROM
Technology and Additional Resources	**Planning and Instruction:**
	TeacherWorks Plus CD-ROM
	Classroom Presentation Toolkit CD-ROM
	Literature Online at **glencoe.com** (QuickPass Code: **GLA9879u6T**)
	Students Tools:
	StudentWorks Plus CD-ROM or DVD-ROM
	Online Student Edition at **glencoe.com**
	Literature Online at **glencoe.com** (QuickPass Code: **GLA9800u6**)

Lesson Plan

Glencoe Literature

The Magic Barrel (pp. 942–958)

Lesson Plan and Resource Manager

UNIT SIX From Depression to Cold War 1930s–1960s, Part 1: The New Regionalism and the City

Learning Objectives	**Literary Study:** Analyzing dialect. **Reading:** Analyzing characterization. **Speaking and Listening:** Debating.

Lesson Summary	On pages **942–958** of the Student Edition, students will be introduced to the following:
	    ▪ **Big Idea:** Life in the City
	    ▪ **Literary Element:** Dialect
	    ▪ **Reading Strategy:** Analyze Characterization
	    ▪ **Vocabulary:** Word Origins
	    ▪ **Writing Activities/Grammar:** Evaluate, Journal Entry
	    ▪ **Listening/Speaking/Viewing Skills:** Debate, Analyze Art

Lesson Duration	One 45–50 minute session
Readability Scores	Dale-Chall: 6.3 DRP: 62 Lexile: 1010
Focus	**TE** pp. 942–943 Selection Focus Transparency 59 Daily Language Practice Transparency 86
Teach	**TE** pp. 944–956 Unit 6 Teaching Resources, Literary Element, p. 125 Unit 6 Teaching Resources, Reading Strategy, p. 126 Unit 6 Teaching Resources, Selection Vocabulary Practice, p. 127 Unit 6 Teaching Resources, Vocabulary Strategy, p. 128 Unit 6 Teaching Resources, Grammar Practice, p. 129 Literary Elements Transparency 25 Classroom Presentation Toolkit CD-ROM Listening Library CD, Selection Audio TeacherWorks Plus CD-ROM Vocabulary PuzzleMaker CD-ROM
Assess	**TE** pp. 957–958 Unit 6 Teaching Resources, Selection Quick Check, p. 130 Unit 6 Teaching Resources, Selection Quick Check (Spanish), p. 131 Assessment Resources, Selection Test, pp. 251–252 ExamView Assessment Suite CD-ROM Progress Reporter Online Assessment

Copyright © by The McGraw-Hill Companies, Inc.

Differentiated Instruction: English Learners	**TE** English Learner Activities, pp. 942–958
	📁 Unit 6 Teaching Resources, English Language Coach, p. 19
	📁 Unit 6 Teaching Resources, Selection Summaries: English, Spanish, Vietnamese, Tagalog, Cantonese, Haitian Creole, and Hmong, pp. 119–124
	📁 Unit 6 Teaching Resources, Selection Quick Check (Spanish), p. 131
	📁 English Language Coach
	💿 Glencoe Interactive Vocabulary CD-ROM
	💿 Listening Library Audio CD
	📁 Listening Library Sourcebook: Strategies and Activities
Differentiated Instruction: Approaching Level	**TE** Approaching Level Activities, pp. 942–958
	💿 Glencoe Interactive Vocabulary CD-ROM
	💿 Listening Library Audio CD
	📁 Listening Library Sourcebook: Strategies and Activities
	💿 Skill Level Up! A Skills-Based Language Arts Game CD-ROM
Differentiated Instruction: Advanced/Pre-AP	**TE** Advanced Learner Activities, pp. 942–958
	📖 Novel Companion SE, pp. 251–294
	📖 Novel Companion TG, pp. 54–61
	💿 ▶ Literature Classics, High School CD-ROM
	💿 Skill Level Up! A Skills-Based Language Arts Game CD-ROM
Extension	📖 Grammar and Language Workbook SE
	📖 Grammar and Language Workbook TAE
	📁 Revising with Style
	📖 Spelling Power SE
	📖 Spelling Power TAE
Daily Writing	**SE/TE** p. 948
Interdisciplinary Connections	**SE/TE** View the Art, pp. 944, 946, 949, 954
	TE Political History, p. 942
	TE Cultural History, pp. 952, 956
	TE Literary History, p. 947
	🌐 **glencoe.com**
Independent Reading	💿 BookLink K–12 CD-ROM
	📕 Ethnic Anthologies
	📕 Glencoe Literature Library
	💿 Glencoe Literature Library Teacher Resources CD-ROM
	📘 *inTIME* magazine
	💿 ▶ Literature Classics, High School CD-ROM
Technology and Additional Resources	**Planning and Instruction:**
	💿 TeacherWorks Plus CD-ROM
	💿 Classroom Presentation Toolkit CD-ROM
	▶ Literature Online at **glencoe.com** (QuickPass Code: **GLA9879u6T**)
	Students Tools:
	💿 StudentWorks Plus CD-ROM or DVD-ROM
	▶ Online Student Edition at **glencoe.com**
	▶ Literature Online at **glencoe.com** (QuickPass Code: **GLA9800u6**)

Lesson Plan

Glencoe Literature Essential Course of Study

The Rockpile (pp. 959–968)

Lesson Plan and Resource Manager

UNIT SIX From Depression to Cold War 1930s–1960s, Part 1: The New Regionalism and the City

Learning Objectives	**Literary Study:** Analyzing a foil character. **Reading:** Making generalizations about characters. **Writing:** Writing a character sketch.
Lesson Summary	On pages **959–968** of the Student Edition, students will be introduced to the following: • **Big Idea:** Life in the City • **Literary Element:** Foil • **Reading Strategy:** Make Generalizations About Characters • **Vocabulary:** Analogies • **Writing Activity/Grammar:** Character Sketch • **Listening/Speaking/Viewing Skill:** Analyze Art
Lesson Duration	One to five 45–50 minute sessions
Readability Scores	Dale-Chall: 4.6　　　DRP: 59　　　Lexile: 850
Focus	**TE** pp. 959–960 Selection Focus Transparency 60 Daily Language Practice Transparency 87 Literature Launchers: Pre-Reading Videos DVD, Selection Launcher Literature Launchers Teacher Guide
Teach	**TE** pp. 961–967 Interactive Read and Write SE/TE, pp. 213–226 Unit 6 Teaching Resources, Literary Element, p. 138 Unit 6 Teaching Resources, Reading Strategy, p. 139 Unit 6 Teaching Resources, Selection Vocabulary Practice, p. 140 Unit 6 Teaching Resources, Vocabulary Strategy, p. 141 Unit 6 Teaching Resources, Grammar Practice, p. 142 Literary Elements Transparency 43 Classroom Presentation Toolkit CD-ROM Listening Library CD, Selection Audio TeacherWorks Plus CD-ROM Vocabulary PuzzleMaker CD-ROM
Assess	**TE** p. 968 Unit 6 Teaching Resources, Selection Quick Check, p. 143 Unit 6 Teaching Resources, Selection Quick Check (Spanish), p. 144 Assessment Resources, Selection Test, pp. 253–254 ExamView Assessment Suite CD-ROM Progress Reporter Online Assessment

Differentiated Instruction: English Learners	**TE** English Learner Activities, pp. 959–968 📖 Interactive Read and Write (EL) SE/TE, pp. 213–226 📁 Unit 6 Teaching Resources, English Language Coach, p. 19 📁 Unit 6 Teaching Resources, Selection Summaries: English, Spanish, Vietnamese, Tagalog, Cantonese, Haitian Creole, and Hmong, pp. 132–137 📁 Unit 6 Teaching Resources, Selection Quick Check (Spanish), p. 144 📁 English Language Coach 💿 Glencoe Interactive Vocabulary CD-ROM 💿 Listening Library Audio CD 📁 Listening Library Sourcebook: Strategies and Activities
Differentiated Instruction: Approaching Level	**TE** Approaching Level Activities, pp. 959–968 📖 Interactive Read and Write (Approaching) SE/TE, pp. 213–226 💿 Glencoe Interactive Vocabulary CD-ROM 💿 Listening Library Audio CD 📁 Listening Library Sourcebook: Strategies and Activities 💿 Skill Level Up! A Skills-Based Language Arts Game CD-ROM
Differentiated Instruction: Advanced/Pre-AP	**TE** Advanced Learner Activities, pp. 959–968 📖 Novel Companion SE, pp. 251–294 📖 Novel Companion TG, pp. 54–61 💿 ▶ Literature Classics, High School CD-ROM 💿 Skill Level Up! A Skills-Based Language Arts Game CD-ROM
Extension	📖 Grammar and Language Workbook SE 📖 Grammar and Language Workbook TAE 📁 Revising with Style 📖 Spelling Power SE 📖 Spelling Power TAE
Daily Writing	**SE/TE** p. 968
Interdisciplinary Connections	**SE/TE** View the Art, pp. 961, 963, 965, 966 **TE** Cultural History, pp. 962, 967 ▶ glencoe.com
Independent Reading	💿 BookLink K–12 CD-ROM 📙 Ethnic Anthologies 📙 Glencoe Literature Library 💿 Glencoe Literature Library Teacher Resources CD-ROM 📙 inTIME magazine 💿 ▶ Literature Classics, High School CD-ROM
Technology and Additional Resources	**Planning and Instruction:** 💿 TeacherWorks Plus CD-ROM 💿 Classroom Presentation Toolkit CD-ROM ▶ Literature Online at **glencoe.com** (QuickPass Code: **GLA9879u6T**) **Students Tools:** 💿 StudentWorks Plus CD-ROM or DVD-ROM ▶ Online Student Edition at **glencoe.com** ▶ Literature Online at **glencoe.com** (QuickPass Code: **GLA9800u6**)

Lesson Plan

Part 2 Opener, *War Message to Congress*, and Vocabulary Workshop (pp. 969–975)

Lesson Plan and Resource Manager

UNIT SIX From Depression to Cold War 1930s–1960s, Part 2: The United States and the World

Learning Objectives	**Literary Study:** Analyzing author's purpose. **Reading:** Distinguishing fact and opinion. **Writing:** Writing a press release. **Vocabulary:** Understanding word origins.
Lesson Summary	On pages **969–975** of the Student Edition, students will be introduced to the following: • **Big Idea:** The United States and the World • **Literary Element:** Author's Purpose • **Reading Strategy:** Distinguish Fact and Opinion • **Vocabulary:** Denotation and Connotation, Word Origins • **Writing Activity/Grammar:** Press Release
Lesson Duration	One 20–25 minute session
Readability Scores	Dale-Chall: 8.9 DRP: 66 Lexile: 1280
Focus	**TE** pp. 970–971, 975 Daily Language Practice Transparency 88
Teach	**TE** pp. 972–973, 975 Unit 6 Teaching Resources, Literary Element, p. 153 Unit 6 Teaching Resources, Reading Strategy, p. 154 Unit 6 Teaching Resources, Selection Vocabulary Practice, p. 155 Unit 6 Teaching Resources, Vocabulary Strategy, p. 156 Unit 6 Teaching Resources, Grammar Practice, p. 157 Literary Elements Transparencies 14, 52 Classroom Presentation Toolkit CD-ROM Listening Library CD, Selection Audio TeacherWorks Plus CD-ROM Vocabulary PuzzleMaker CD-ROM
Assess	**TE** pp. 974, 975 Unit 6 Teaching Resources, Selection Quick Check, p. 158 Unit 6 Teaching Resources, Selection Quick Check (Spanish), p. 159 Assessment Resources, Selection Test, pp. 255–256 ExamView Assessment Suite CD-ROM Progress Reporter Online Assessment

Differentiated Instruction: English Learners	**TE** English Learner Activities, pp. 969–975 📁 Unit 6 Teaching Resources, English Language Coach, Part 2, p. 146 📁 Unit 6 Teaching Resources, Selection Summaries: English, Spanish, Vietnamese, Tagalog, Cantonese, Haitian Creole, and Hmong, pp. 147–152 📁 Unit 6 Teaching Resources, Selection Quick Check (Spanish), p. 159 📁 English Language Coach 💿 Glencoe Interactive Vocabulary CD-ROM 💿 Listening Library Audio CD 📁 Listening Library Sourcebook: Strategies and Activities
Differentiated Instruction: Approaching Level	**TE** Approaching Level Activities, pp. 969–975 💿 Glencoe Interactive Vocabulary CD-ROM 💿 Listening Library Audio CD 📁 Listening Library Sourcebook: Strategies and Activities 💿 Skill Level Up! A Skills-Based Language Arts Game CD-ROM
Differentiated Instruction: Advanced/Pre-AP	**TE** Advanced Learner Activities, pp. 969–975 📘 Novel Companion SE, pp. 251–294 📘 Novel Companion TG, pp. 54–61 💿 Literature Classics, High School CD-ROM 💿 Skill Level Up! A Skills-Based Language Arts Game CD-ROM
Extension	📘 Grammar and Language Workbook SE 📘 Grammar and Language Workbook TAE 📁 Revising with Style 📘 Spelling Power SE 📘 Spelling Power TAE
Daily Writing	**SE/TE** p. 974
Interdisciplinary Connections	**SE/TE** View the Art, p. 969 **TE** Political History, pp. 970, 972 ▶ glencoe.com
Independent Reading	💿 BookLink K–12 CD-ROM 📖 Ethnic Anthologies 📖 Glencoe Literature Library 💿 Glencoe Literature Library Teacher Resources CD-ROM 📖 inTIME magazine 💿 Literature Classics, High School CD-ROM
Technology and Additional Resources	**Planning and Instruction:** 💿 TeacherWorks Plus CD-ROM 💿 Classroom Presentation Toolkit CD-ROM ▶ Literature Online at **glencoe.com** (QuickPass Code: **GLA9879u6T**) **Students Tools:** 💿 StudentWorks Plus CD-ROM or DVD-ROM ▶ Online Student Edition at **glencoe.com** ▶ Literature Online at **glencoe.com** (QuickPass Code: **GLA9800u6**)

Lesson Plan

Glencoe Literature

The Death of the Ball Turret Gunner (pp. 976–979)

Lesson Plan and Resource Manager

UNIT SIX From Depression to Cold War 1930s–1960s, Part 2: The United States and the World

Learning Objectives	**Literary Study:** Analyzing imagery. **Reading:** Visualizing setting, characters, and action. **Writing:** Writing a journal entry.

Lesson Summary	On pages **975–979** of the Student Edition, students will be introduced to the following:
	  • **Big Idea:** The United States and the World
	  • **Literary Element:** Imagery
	  • **Reading Strategy:** Visualize
	  • **Vocabulary:** Context Clues
	  • **Writing Activity/Grammar:** Journal Entry

Lesson Duration	One 20–25 minute session
Readability Scores	Dale-Chall: N/A DRP: N/A Lexile: N/A
Focus	**TE** pp. 976–977 📽 Selection Focus Transparency 61 📽 Daily Language Practice Transparency 89
Teach	**TE** p. 978 📁 Unit 6 Teaching Resources, Literary Element, p. 166 📁 Unit 6 Teaching Resources, Reading Strategy, p. 167 📁 Unit 6 Teaching Resources, Selection Vocabulary Practice, p. 168 📁 Unit 6 Teaching Resources, Vocabulary Strategy, p. 169 📽 Literary Elements Transparencies 14, 52 💿 Classroom Presentation Toolkit CD-ROM 💿 Listening Library CD, Selection Audio 💿 TeacherWorks Plus CD-ROM 💿 Vocabulary PuzzleMaker CD-ROM
Assess	**TE** p. 979 📁 Unit 6 Teaching Resources, Selection Quick Check, p. 170 📁 Unit 6 Teaching Resources, Selection Quick Check (Spanish), p. 171 📁 Assessment Resources, Selection Test, pp. 257–258 💿 ExamView Assessment Suite CD-ROM 💿 Progress Reporter Online Assessment
Differentiated Instruction: English Learners	**TE** English Learner Activities, pp. 976–979 📁 Unit 6 Teaching Resources, Selection Summaries: English, Spanish, Vietnamese, Tagalog, Cantonese, Haitian Creole, and Hmong, pp. 160–165 📁 Unit 6 Teaching Resources, Selection Quick Check (Spanish), p. 171 📁 English Language Coach 💿 Glencoe Interactive Vocabulary CD-ROM 💿 Listening Library Audio CD 📁 Listening Library Sourcebook: Strategies and Activities

Copyright © by The McGraw-Hill Companies, Inc.

Differentiated Instruction: Approaching Level	💿 Glencoe Interactive Vocabulary CD-ROM 💿 Listening Library Audio CD 📁 Listening Library Sourcebook: Strategies and Activities 💿 Skill Level Up! A Skills-Based Language Arts Game CD-ROM
Differentiated Instruction: Advanced/Pre-AP	📕 Novel Companion SE, pp. 251–294 📕 Novel Companion TG, pp. 54–61 💿 ▶ Literature Classics, High School CD-ROM 💿 Skill Level Up! A Skills-Based Language Arts Game CD-ROM
Extension	📕 Grammar and Language Workbook SE 📕 Grammar and Language Workbook TAE 📁 Revising with Style 📕 Spelling Power SE 📕 Spelling Power TAE
Interdisciplinary Connections	**TE** Cultural History, p. 976 ▶ glencoe.com
Independent Reading	💿 BookLink K–12 CD-ROM 📖 Ethnic Anthologies 📖 Glencoe Literature Library 💿 Glencoe Literature Library Teacher Resources CD-ROM 📖 *inTIME* magazine 💿 ▶ Literature Classics, High School CD-ROM
Technology and Additional Resources	**Planning and Instruction:** 💿 TeacherWorks Plus CD-ROM 💿 Classroom Presentation Toolkit CD-ROM ▶ Literature Online at **glencoe.com** (QuickPass Code: **GLA9879u6T**) **Students Tools:** 💿 StudentWorks Plus CD-ROM or DVD-ROM 💿 Online Student Edition at **glencoe.com** ▶ Literature Online at **glencoe.com** (QuickPass Code: **GLA9800u6**)

Lesson Plan

Glencoe Literature

Comparing Literature: from *All Rivers Run to the Sea*, from *Kubota*, and from *Maus: A Survivor's Tale* (pp. 980–1001)

Lesson Plan and Resource Manager

UNIT SIX From Depression to Cold War 1930s–1960s, Part 2: The United States and the World

Learning Objectives	**Literary Study:** Comparing cultural context. Comparing historical context. Comparing themes.
Lesson Summary	On pages **980–1001** of the Student Edition, students will be introduced to the following: - **Big Idea:** The United States and the World - **Literary Element:** Narrator - **Reading Strategy:** Activate Prior Knowledge - **Vocabulary:** Denotation and Connotation, Academic Vocabulary - **Writing Activities/Grammar:** Essay, Character Sketch - **Listening/Speaking/Viewing Skills:** Analyze Art, Oral Report
Lesson Duration	Two 45–50 minute sessions
Readability Scores	from "All Rivers Run to the Sea" Dale-Chall: 6.1 DRP: 53 Lexile: 860 from "Kubota" Dale-Chall: 9.0 DRP: 63 Lexile: 1180
Focus	**TE** pp. 980–982, 993, 998 📖 Daily Language Practice Transparency 90
Teach	**TE** pp. 983–990, 993–997, 999–1000 📁 Unit 6 Teaching Resources, Comparing Literature Graphic Organizer, p. 172 📁 Unit 6 Teaching Resources, Literary Element, p. 179 📁 Unit 6 Teaching Resources, Reading Strategy, p. 180 📁 Unit 6 Teaching Resources, Selection Vocabulary Practice, p. 181 📁 Unit 6 Teaching Resources, Vocabulary Strategy, p. 182 📁 Unit 6 Teaching Resources, Grammar Practice, p. 183 📖 Read Aloud, Think Aloud Transparencies 29–32 📖 Literary Elements Transparency 67 💿 Classroom Presentation Toolkit CD-ROM 💿 Listening Library CD, Selection Audio 💿 TeacherWorks Plus CD-ROM 💿▶ Vocabulary PuzzleMaker CD-ROM
Assess	**TE** pp. 991–992, 1001 📁 Unit 6 Teaching Resources, Selection Quick Check, p. 184 📁 Unit 6 Teaching Resources, Selection Quick Check (Spanish), p. 186 📁 Assessment Resources, Selection Test, pp. 259–260 💿 ExamView Assessment Suite CD-ROM ▶ Progress Reporter Online Assessment

Differentiated Instruction: English Learners	**TE** English Learner Activities, pp. 980–1001 📁 Unit 6 Teaching Resources, English Language Coach, p. 146 📁 Unit 6 Teaching Resources, Selection Summaries: English, Spanish, Vietnamese, Tagalog, Cantonese, Haitian Creole, and Hmong, pp. 173–178 📁 Unit 6 Teaching Resources, Selection Quick Check (Spanish), p. 185 📁 English Language Coach 💿 Glencoe Interactive Vocabulary CD-ROM 💿 Listening Library Audio CD 💿 Listening Library Sourcebook: Strategies and Activities
Differentiated Instruction: Approaching Level	**TE** Approaching Level Activities, pp. 980–1001 💿 Glencoe Interactive Vocabulary CD-ROM 💿 Listening Library Audio CD 📁 Listening Library Sourcebook: Strategies and Activities 💿 Skill Level Up! A Skills-Based Language Arts Game CD-ROM
Differentiated Instruction: Advanced/Pre-AP	**TE** Advanced Learner Activities, pp. 980–1001 📕 Novel Companion SE, pp. 251–294 📕 Novel Companion TG, pp. 54–61 💿 ▶ Literature Classics, High School CD-ROM 💿 Skill Level Up! A Skills-Based Language Arts Game CD-ROM
Extension	📕 Grammar and Language Workbook SE 📕 Grammar and Language Workbook TAE 📁 Revising with Style 📕 Spelling Power SE 📕 Spelling Power TAE
Daily Writing	**TE** p. 994, **SE** p. 1001
Interdisciplinary Connections	**SE/TE** View the Art, p. 997 **SE/TE** View the Photograph, pp. 983, 986, 995 **TE** Cultural History, pp. 984, 987, 998 **TE** Political History, pp. 989, 990, 994, 1000 **TE** Language History, p. 985 ▶ glencoe.com
Independent Reading	💿 BookLink K–12 CD-ROM 📖 Ethnic Anthologies; Glencoe Literature Library; *inTIME* magazine 💿 Glencoe Literature Library Teacher Resources CD-ROM 💿 ▶ Literature Classics, High School CD-ROM
Technology and Additional Resources	**Planning and Instruction:** 💿 TeacherWorks Plus CD-ROM 💿 Classroom Presentation Toolkit CD-ROM ▶ Literature Online at **glencoe.com** (QuickPass Code: **GLA9879u6T**) **Students Tools:** 💿 StudentWorks Plus CD-ROM or DVD-ROM ▶ Online Student Edition at **glencoe.com** ▶ Literature Online at **glencoe.com** (QuickPass Code: **GLA9800u6**)

Lesson Plan

Glencoe Literature

from *Hiroshima* (pp. 1002–1016)

Lesson Plan and Resource Manager

UNIT SIX From Depression to Cold War 1930s–1960s, Part 2: The United States and the World

Learning Objectives	**Literary Study:** Analyzing point of view. **Reading:** Drawing conclusions about author's beliefs. **Writing:** Writing an expository essay.
Lesson Summary	On pages **1002–1016** of the Student Edition, students will be introduced to the following: ▪ **Big Idea:** The United States and the World ▪ **Literary Element:** Point of View ▪ **Reading Strategy:** Draw Conclusions About Author's Beliefs ▪ **Vocabulary:** Word Origins, Academic Vocabulary ▪ **Writing Activities/Grammar:** Expository Essay, Editorial ▪ **Listening/Speaking/Viewing Skill:** Analyze Art
Lesson Duration	One 45–50 minute session
Readability Scores	Dale-Chall: 9.9 DRP: 64 Lexile: 1260
Focus	**TE** pp. 1002–1003 Selection Focus Transparency 62 Daily Language Practice Transparency 91
Teach	**TE** pp. 1004–1013 Unit 6 Teaching Resources, Literary Element, p. 192 Unit 6 Teaching Resources, Reading Strategy, p. 193 Unit 6 Teaching Resources, Selection Vocabulary Practice, p. 194 Unit 6 Teaching Resources, Vocabulary Strategy, p. 195 Unit 6 Teaching Resources, Grammar Practice, p. 196 Grammar and Language Transparency 72 Literary Elements Transparency 80 Classroom Presentation Toolkit CD-ROM Listening Library CD, Selection Audio TeacherWorks Plus CD-ROM Vocabulary PuzzleMaker CD-ROM
Assess	**TE** pp. 1014–1016 Unit 6 Teaching Resources, Selection Quick Check, p. 197 Unit 6 Teaching Resources, Selection Quick Check (Spanish), p. 198 Assessment Resources, Selection Test, pp. 261–262 ExamView Assessment Suite CD-ROM Progress Reporter Online Assessment
Differentiated Instruction: English Learners	**TE** English Learner Activities, pp. 1002–1016 Unit 6 Teaching Resources, English Language Coach, p. 146 Unit 6 Teaching Resources, Selection Summaries: English, Spanish, Vietnamese, Tagalog, Cantonese, Haitian Creole, and Hmong, pp. 186–191

Differentiated Instruction: English Learners *(continued)*	📁 Unit 6 Teaching Resources, Selection Quick Check (Spanish), p. 198 📁 English Language Coach 💿 Glencoe Interactive Vocabulary CD-ROM 💿 Listening Library Audio CD 📁 Listening Library Sourcebook: Strategies and Activities
Differentiated Instruction: Approaching Level	**TE** Approaching Level Activities, pp. 1002–1016 💿 Glencoe Interactive Vocabulary CD-ROM 💿 Listening Library Audio CD 📁 Listening Library Sourcebook: Strategies and Activities 💿 Skill Level Up! A Skills-Based Language Arts Game CD-ROM
Differentiated Instruction: Advanced/Pre-AP	**TE** Advanced Learner Activities, pp. 1002–1016 📘 Novel Companion SE, pp. 251–294 📘 Novel Companion TG, pp. 54–61 💿 Literature Classics, High School CD-ROM 💿 Skill Level Up! A Skills-Based Language Arts Game CD-ROM
Extension	📘 Grammar and Language Workbook SE 📘 Grammar and Language Workbook TAE 📁 Revising with Style 📘 Spelling Power SE 📘 Spelling Power TAE
Daily Writing	**SE/TE** p. 1016
Interdisciplinary Connections	**TE** Political History, p. 1007 **SE/TE** View the Photograph, pp. 1008, 1010, 1013 💿 glencoe.com
Independent Reading	💿 BookLink K–12 CD-ROM 📖 Ethnic Anthologies 📖 Glencoe Literature Library 💿 Glencoe Literature Library Teacher Resources CD-ROM 📖 *inTIME* magazine 💿 Literature Classics, High School CD-ROM
Technology and Additional Resources	**Planning and Instruction:** 💿 TeacherWorks Plus CD-ROM 💿 Classroom Presentation Toolkit CD-ROM 💿 Literature Online at **glencoe.com** (QuickPass Code: **GLA9879u6T**) **Students Tools:** 💿 StudentWorks Plus CD-ROM or DVD-ROM 💿 Online Student Edition at **glencoe.com** 💿 Literature Online at **glencoe.com** (QuickPass Code: **GLA9800u6**)

Lesson Plan

The Portrait and Literary History: Cultural Rebels: Writers of the Beat Generation (pp. 1017–1025)

Lesson Plan and Resource Manager

UNIT SIX From Depression to Cold War 1930s–1960s, Part 2: The United States and the World

Learning Objectives	**Literary Study:** Analyzing idiom. **Reading:** Responding to plot and characters. Analyzing cultural context. Analyzing literary periods. Evaluating historical influences. **Writing:** Writing a report.
Lesson Summary	On pages **1017–1025** of the Student Edition, students will be introduced to the following: • **Big Idea:** The United States and the World • **Literary Element:** Idiom • **Reading Strategy:** Respond to Plot and Characters • **Vocabulary:** Context Clues • **Writing Activity/Grammar:** Report • **Listening/Speaking/Viewing Skill:** Analyze Art
Lesson Duration	One 45–50 minute session
Readability Scores	Dale-Chall: 4.5 DRP: 47 Lexile: 760
Focus	**TE** pp. 1017–1018, 1024 Selection Focus Transparency 63 Daily Language Practice Transparencies 92–93
Teach	**TE** pp. 1019–1021, 1024–1025 Unit 6 Teaching Resources, Literary Element, p. 205 Unit 6 Teaching Resources, Reading Strategy, p. 206 Unit 6 Teaching Resources, Vocabulary Strategy, p. 207 Unit 6 Teaching Resources, Grammar Practice, p. 208 Unit 6 Teaching Resources, Literary History: Cultural Rebels, pp. 211–212 Literary Elements Transparency 51 Classroom Presentation Toolkit CD-ROM Listening Library CD, Selection Audio TeacherWorks Plus CD-ROM Vocabulary PuzzleMaker CD-ROM
Assess	**TE** pp. 1022–1023, 1025 Unit 6 Teaching Resources, Selection Quick Check, p. 209 Unit 6 Teaching Resources, Selection Quick Check (Spanish), p. 210 Assessment Resources, Selection Test, pp. 263–264 ExamView Assessment Suite CD-ROM Progress Reporter Online Assessment

Differentiated Instruction: English Learners	**TE** English Learner Activities, pp. 1017–1025 📁 Unit 6 Teaching Resources, English Language Coach, p. 146 📁 Unit 6 Teaching Resources, Selection Summaries: English, Spanish, Vietnamese, Tagalog, Cantonese, Haitian Creole, and Hmong, pp. 199–204 📁 Unit 6 Teaching Resources, Selection Quick Check (Spanish), p. 210 📁 English Language Coach 💿 Glencoe Interactive Vocabulary CD-ROM 💿 Listening Library Audio CD 📁 Listening Library Sourcebook: Strategies and Activities
Differentiated Instruction: Approaching Level	**TE** Approaching Level Activities, pp. 1017–1025 💿 Glencoe Interactive Vocabulary CD-ROM 💿 Listening Library Audio CD 📁 Listening Library Sourcebook: Strategies and Activities 💿 Skill Level Up! A Skills-Based Language Arts Game CD-ROM
Differentiated Instruction: Advanced/Pre-AP	**TE** Advanced Learner Activities, pp. 1017–1025 📕 Novel Companion SE, pp. 251–294 📕 Novel Companion TG, pp. 54–61 💿 ▶ Literature Classics, High School CD-ROM 💿 Skill Level Up! A Skills-Based Language Arts Game CD-ROM
Extension	📕 Grammar and Language Workbook SE 📕 Grammar and Language Workbook TAE 📁 Revising with Style 📕 Spelling Power SE 📕 Spelling Power TAE
Daily Writing	**SE/TE** p. 1023
Interdisciplinary Connections	**SE/TE** View the Photograph, pp. 1020 ▶ glencoe.com
Independent Reading	💿 BookLink K–12 CD-ROM 📖 Ethnic Anthologies 📖 Glencoe Literature Library 💿 Glencoe Literature Library Teacher Resources CD-ROM 📖 *inTIME* magazine 💿 ▶ Literature Classics, High School CD-ROM
Technology and Additional Resources	**Planning and Instruction:** 💿 TeacherWorks Plus CD-ROM 💿 Classroom Presentation Toolkit CD-ROM ▶ Literature Online at **glencoe.com** (QuickPass Code: **GLA9879u6T**) **Students Tools:** 💿 StudentWorks Plus CD-ROM or DVD-ROM ▶ Online Student Edition at **glencoe.com** ▶ Literature Online at **glencoe.com** (QuickPass Code: **GLA9800u6**)

Lesson Plan

Glencoe Literature Essential Course of Study

The Crucible, Act One (pp. 1026–1050)

Lesson Plan and Resource Manager

UNIT SIX From Depression to Cold War 1930s–1960s, Part 2: The United States and the World

Learning Objectives	**Literary Study:** Analyzing dialogue. **Reading:** Drawing conclusions about characters. **Writing:** Writing a dialogue.
Lesson Summary	On pages **1026–1050** of the Student Edition, students will be introduced to the following: • **Big Idea:** The United States and the World • **Literary Element:** Dialogue • **Reading Strategy:** Draw Conclusions About Characters • **Vocabulary:** Word Parts • **Writing Activity/Grammar:** Dialogue • **Listening/Speaking/Viewing Skills:** Analyze Art, Relate Art to Text, Readers Theater
Lesson Duration	One to five 45–50 minute sessions
Readability Scores	Dale-Chall: N/A DRP: N/A Lexile: N/A
Focus	**TE** pp. 1026–1027 ⚑ Selection Focus Transparency 64 ⚑ Daily Language Practice Transparency 94 💿 Literature Launchers: Pre-Reading Videos DVD, Selection Launcher 📁 Literature Launchers Teacher Guide
Teach	**TE** pp. 1028–1049 📕 Interactive Read and Write SE/TE, pp. 227–254 📁 Unit 6 Teaching Resources, Literary Element, p. 219 📁 Unit 6 Teaching Resources, Reading Strategy, p. 220 📁 Unit 6 Teaching Resources, Selection Vocabulary Practice, p. 221 📁 Unit 6 Teaching Resources, Vocabulary Strategy, p. 222 📁 Unit 6 Teaching Resources, Grammar Practice, p. 223 ⚑ Read Aloud, Think Aloud Transparencies 33–36 ⚑ Literary Elements Transparency 26 💿 Classroom Presentation Toolkit CD-ROM 💿 Listening Library CD, Selection Audio 💿 TeacherWorks Plus CD-ROM 💿▶ Vocabulary PuzzleMaker CD-ROM
Assess	**TE** p. 1050 📁 Unit 6 Teaching Resources, Selection Quick Check, p. 224 📁 Unit 6 Teaching Resources, Selection Quick Check (Spanish), p. 225 📁 Assessment Resources, Selection Test, pp. 265–267 💿 ExamView Assessment Suite CD-ROM ▶ Progress Reporter Online Assessment

Differentiated Instruction: English Learners	**TE** English Learner Activities, pp. 1026–1050 📓 Interactive Read and Write (EL) SE/TE, pp. 227–254 📁 Unit 6 Teaching Resources, English Language Coach, p. 146 📁 Unit 6 Teaching Resources, Selection Summaries: English, Spanish, Vietnamese, Tagalog, Cantonese, Haitian Creole, and Hmong, pp. 213–218 📁 Unit 6 Teaching Resources, Selection Quick Check (Spanish), p. 225 📁 English Language Coach 💿 Glencoe Interactive Vocabulary CD-ROM 💿 Listening Library Audio CD 📁 Listening Library Sourcebook: Strategies and Activities
Differentiated Instruction: Approaching Level	**TE** Approaching Level Activities, pp. 1026–1050 📓 Interactive Read and Write (Approaching) SE/TE, pp. 227–254 💿 Glencoe Interactive Vocabulary CD-ROM 💿 Listening Library Audio CD 📁 Listening Library Sourcebook: Strategies and Activities 💿 Skill Level Up! A Skills-Based Language Arts Game CD-ROM
Differentiated Instruction: Advanced/Pre-AP	**TE** Advanced Learner Activities, pp. 1026–1050 📓 Novel Companion SE, pp. 251–294 📓 Novel Companion TG, pp. 54–61 💿 Literature Classics, High School CD-ROM 💿 Skill Level Up! A Skills-Based Language Arts Game CD-ROM
Extension	📓 Grammar and Language Workbook SE 📓 Grammar and Language Workbook TAE 📁 Revising with Style 📓 Spelling Power SE 📓 Spelling Power TAE
Daily Writing	**SE/TE** p. 1050
Interdisciplinary Connections	**SE/TE** View the Art, pp. 1039, 1046, 1049 **SE/TE** View the Photograph, p. 1028 **TE** Cultural History, pp. 1029, 1031, 1033, 1035, 1040, 1046 **TE** Literary History, p. 1032 **TE** Political History, p. 1036 ▶ glencoe.com
Independent Reading	💿 BookLink K–12 CD-ROM 📖 Ethnic Anthologies; Glencoe Literature Library; *inTIME* magazine 💿 Glencoe Literature Library Teacher Resources CD-ROM 💿 Literature Classics, High School CD-ROM
Technology and Additional Resources	**Planning and Instruction:** 💿 TeacherWorks Plus CD-ROM 💿 Classroom Presentation Toolkit CD-ROM ▶ Literature Online at **glencoe.com** (QuickPass Code: **GLA9879u6T**) **Students Tools:** 💿 StudentWorks Plus CD-ROM or DVD-ROM ▶ Online Student Edition at **glencoe.com** ▶ Literature Online at **glencoe.com** (QuickPass Code: **GLA9800u6**)

Lesson Plan

Glencoe Literature

The Crucible, Act Two (pp. 1051–1072)

Lesson Plan and Resource Manager

UNIT SIX From Depression to Cold War 1930s–1960s, Part 2: The United States and the World

Learning Objectives	**Literary Study:** Analyzing stage directions. **Reading:** Analyzing historical context. **Writing:** Writing stage directions.
Lesson Summary	On pages **1051–1072** of the Student Edition, students will be introduced to the following: • **Big Idea:** The United States and the World • **Literary Element:** Stage Directions • **Reading Strategy:** Analyze Historical Context • **Vocabulary:** Analogies • **Writing Activity/Grammar:** Stage Directions • **Listening/Speaking/Viewing Skills:** Analyze Art, Mock Newscast, Debate
Lesson Duration	One 45–50 minute session
Readability Scores	Dale-Chall: N/A DRP: N/A Lexile: N/A
Focus	TE p. 1051 📖 Selection Focus Transparency 64
Teach	TE pp. 1052–1071 📁 Unit 6 Teaching Resources, Literary Element, p. 232 📁 Unit 6 Teaching Resources, Reading Strategy, p. 233 📁 Unit 6 Teaching Resources, Selection Vocabulary Practice, p. 234 📁 Unit 6 Teaching Resources, Vocabulary Strategy, p. 235 📁 Unit 6 Teaching Resources, Grammar Practice, p. 236 📖 Literary Elements Transparency 95 💿 Classroom Presentation Toolkit CD-ROM 💿 Listening Library CD, Selection Audio 💿 TeacherWorks Plus CD-ROM 💿 ▶ Vocabulary PuzzleMaker CD-ROM
Assess	TE p. 1072 📁 Unit 6 Teaching Resources, Selection Quick Check, p. 237 📁 Unit 6 Teaching Resources, Selection Quick Check (Spanish), p. 238 📁 Assessment Resources, Selection Test, pp. 267–268 💿 ExamView Assessment Suite CD-ROM ▶ Progress Reporter Online Assessment
Differentiated Instruction: English Learners	TE English Learner Activities, pp. 1051–1072 📁 Unit 6 Teaching Resources, English Language Coach, p. 146 📁 Unit 6 Teaching Resources, Selection Summaries: English, Spanish, Vietnamese, Tagalog, Cantonese, Haitian Creole, and Hmong, pp. 226–231

Differentiated Instruction: English Learners *(continued)*	📁 Unit 6 Teaching Resources, Selection Quick Check (Spanish), p. 238 📁 English Language Coach 💿 Glencoe Interactive Vocabulary CD-ROM 💿 Listening Library Audio CD 📁 Listening Library Sourcebook: Strategies and Activities
Differentiated Instruction: Approaching Level	**TE** Approaching Level Activities, pp. 1051–1072 💿 Glencoe Interactive Vocabulary CD-ROM 💿 Listening Library Audio CD 📁 Listening Library Sourcebook: Strategies and Activities 💿 Skill Level Up! A Skills-Based Language Arts Game CD-ROM
Differentiated Instruction: Advanced/Pre-AP	**TE** Advanced Learner Activities, pp. 1051–1072 📓 Novel Companion SE, pp. 251–294 📓 Novel Companion TG, pp. 54–61 💿 ▶ Literature Classics, High School CD-ROM 💿 Skill Level Up! A Skills-Based Language Arts Game CD-ROM
Extension	📓 Grammar and Language Workbook SE 📓 Grammar and Language Workbook TAE 📁 Revising with Style 📓 Spelling Power SE 📓 Spelling Power TAE
Daily Writing	**SE/TE** p. 1072
Interdisciplinary Connections	**SE/TE** View the Art, pp. 1053, 1064, 1067, 1068 **TE** Cultural History, pp. 1062, 1067 **TE** Political History, p. 1054 ▶ glencoe.com
Independent Reading	💿 BookLink K–12 CD-ROM 📖 Ethnic Anthologies 📖 Glencoe Literature Library 💿 Glencoe Literature Library Teacher Resources CD-ROM 📖 *inTIME* magazine 💿 ▶ Literature Classics, High School CD-ROM
Technology and Additional Resources	**Planning and Instruction:** 💿 TeacherWorks Plus CD-ROM 💿 Classroom Presentation Toolkit CD-ROM ▶ Literature Online at **glencoe.com** (QuickPass Code: **GLA9879u6T**) **Students Tools:** 💿 StudentWorks Plus CD-ROM or DVD-ROM ▶ Online Student Edition at **glencoe.com** ▶ Literature Online at **glencoe.com** (QuickPass Code: **GLA9800u6**)

Lesson Plan

The Crucible, Act Three (pp. 1073–1095)

Lesson Plan and Resource Manager

UNIT SIX From Depression to Cold War 1930s–1960s, Part 2: The United States and the World

Learning Objectives	**Literary Study:** Analyzing plot. **Reading:** Evaluating argument. **Writing:** Writing a summary.
Lesson Summary	On pages **1071–1095** of the Student Edition, students will be introduced to the following: • **Big Idea:** The United States and the World • **Literary Element:** Plot • **Reading Strategy:** Evaluate Argument • **Vocabulary:** Context Clues • **Writing Activity/Grammar:** Summary • **Listening/Speaking/Viewing Skills:** Analyze Art, Dramatic Reading
Lesson Duration	One to five 45–50 minute sessions
Readability Scores	Dale-Chall: N/A DRP: N/A Lexile: N/A
Focus	**TE** p. 1073 📖 Selection Focus Transparency 64
Teach	**TE** pp. 1074–1094 📁 Unit 6 Teaching Resources, Literary Element, p. 245 📁 Unit 6 Teaching Resources, Reading Strategy, p. 246 📁 Unit 6 Teaching Resources, Selection Vocabulary Practice, p. 247 📁 Unit 6 Teaching Resources, Vocabulary Strategy, p. 248 📁 Unit 6 Teaching Resources, Grammar Practice, p. 249 📖 Literary Elements Transparency 78 💿 Classroom Presentation Toolkit CD-ROM 💿 Listening Library CD, Selection Audio 💿 TeacherWorks Plus CD-ROM 💿 Vocabulary PuzzleMaker CD-ROM
Assess	**TE** p. 1095 📁 Unit 6 Teaching Resources, Selection Quick Check, p. 250 📁 Unit 6 Teaching Resources, Selection Quick Check (Spanish), p. 251 📁 Assessment Resources, Selection Test, pp. 269–270 💿 ExamView Assessment Suite CD-ROM 💿 Progress Reporter Online Assessment
Differentiated Instruction: English Learners	**TE** English Learner Activities, pp. 1073–1095 📁 Unit 6 Teaching Resources, English Language Coach, p. 146 📁 Unit 6 Teaching Resources, Selection Summaries: English, Spanish, Vietnamese, Tagalog, Cantonese, Haitian Creole, and Hmong, pp. 239–244

Differentiated Instruction: English Learners *(continued)*	📁 Unit 6 Teaching Resources, Selection Quick Check (Spanish), p. 251 📁 English Language Coach 💿 Glencoe Interactive Vocabulary CD-ROM 💿 Listening Library Audio CD 📁 Listening Library Sourcebook: Strategies and Activities
Differentiated Instruction: Approaching Level	**TE** Approaching Level Activities, pp. 1073–1095 💿 Glencoe Interactive Vocabulary CD-ROM 💿 Listening Library Audio CD 📁 Listening Library Sourcebook: Strategies and Activities 💿 Skill Level Up! A Skills-Based Language Arts Game CD-ROM
Differentiated Instruction: Advanced/Pre-AP	**TE** Advanced Learner Activities, pp. 1073–1095 📘 Novel Companion SE, pp. 251–294 📘 Novel Companion TG, pp. 54–61 💿 ▶ Literature Classics, High School CD-ROM 💿 Skill Level Up! A Skills-Based Language Arts Game CD-ROM
Extension	📘 Grammar and Language Workbook SE 📘 Grammar and Language Workbook TAE 📁 Revising with Style 📘 Spelling Power SE 📘 Spelling Power TAE
Daily Writing	**SE/TE** p. 1096
Interdisciplinary Connections	**SE/TE** View the Art, pp. 1081, 1089 **TE** Cultural History, p. 1085 **TE** Language History, p. 1082 ▶ glencoe.com
Independent Reading	💿 BookLink K–12 CD-ROM 📖 Ethnic Anthologies 📖 Glencoe Literature Library 💿 Glencoe Literature Library Teacher Resources CD-ROM 📖 *inTIME* magazine 💿 ▶ Literature Classics, High School CD-ROM
Technology and Additional Resources	**Planning and Instruction:** 💿 TeacherWorks Plus CD-ROM 💿 Classroom Presentation Toolkit CD-ROM ▶ Literature Online at **glencoe.com** (QuickPass Code: **GLA9879u6T**) **Students Tools:** 💿 StudentWorks Plus CD-ROM or DVD-ROM ▶ Online Student Edition at **glencoe.com** ▶ Literature Online at **glencoe.com** (QuickPass Code: **GLA9800u6**)

Lesson Plan

Glencoe Literature

The Crucible, Act Four and Literary History: Modern American Drama (pp. 1096–1117)

....

Lesson Plan and Resource Manager

UNIT SIX From Depression to Cold War 1930s–1960s, Part 2: The United States and the World

Learning Objectives	**Literary Study:** Analyzing tragedy. **Reading:** Analyzing theme. Analyzing cultural context. Analyzing literary periods. Evaluating historical influences. **Writing:** Writing an editorial. **Grammar:** Using comparative and superlative forms of adjectives.
Lesson Summary	On pages **1096–1117** of the Student Edition, students will be introduced to the following: • **Big Idea:** The United States and the World • **Literary Element:** Tragedy • **Reading Strategy:** Analyze Theme • **Vocabulary:** Word Usage, Academic Vocabulary • **Writing Activity/Grammar:** Editorial • **Listening/Speaking/Viewing Skill:** Analyze Art
Lesson Duration	One 45–50 minute session
Readability Scores	Dale-Chall: N/A DRP: N/A Lexile: N/A
Focus	**TE** pp. 1096, 1116 🕯 Selection Focus Transparency 64 🕯 Daily Language Practice Transparency 95
Teach	**TE** pp. 1097–1112, 1116–1117 📁 Unit 6 Teaching Resources, Literary Element, p. 258 📁 Unit 6 Teaching Resources, Reading Strategy, p. 259 📁 Unit 6 Teaching Resources, Selection Vocabulary Practice, p. 260 📁 Unit 6 Teaching Resources, Vocabulary Strategy, p. 261 📁 Unit 6 Teaching Resources, Grammar Practice, p. 262 📁 Unit 6 Teaching Resources, Literary History: Modern American Drama, pp. 265–266 🕯 Literary Elements Transparency 106 💿 Classroom Presentation Toolkit CD-ROM 💿 Listening Library CD, Selection Audio 💿 TeacherWorks Plus CD-ROM 💿 ▶ Vocabulary PuzzleMaker CD-ROM
Assess	**TE** pp. 1113–1115, 1117 📁 Unit 6 Teaching Resources, Selection Quick Check, p. 263 📁 Unit 6 Teaching Resources, Selection Quick Check (Spanish), p. 264 📁 Assessment Resources, Selection Test, pp. 271–272 💿 ExamView Assessment Suite CD-ROM ▶ Progress Reporter Online Assessment

Differentiated Instruction: English Learners	**TE** English Learner Activities, pp. 1096–1117 📁 Unit 6 Teaching Resources, English Language Coach, p. 146 📁 Unit 6 Teaching Resources, Selection Summaries: English, Spanish, Vietnamese, Tagalog, Cantonese, Haitian Creole, and Hmong, pp. 252–257 📁 Unit 6 Teaching Resources, Selection Quick Check (Spanish), p. 264 📁 English Language Coach 💿 Glencoe Interactive Vocabulary CD-ROM 💿 Listening Library Audio CD 📁 Listening Library Sourcebook: Strategies and Activities
Differentiated Instruction: Approaching Level	**TE** Approaching Level Activities, pp. 1096–1117 💿 Glencoe Interactive Vocabulary CD-ROM 💿 Listening Library Audio CD 📁 Listening Library Sourcebook: Strategies and Activities 💿 Skill Level Up! A Skills-Based Language Arts Game CD-ROM
Differentiated Instruction: Advanced/Pre-AP	**TE** Advanced Learner Activities, pp. 1096–1117 📖 Novel Companion SE, pp. 251–294 📖 Novel Companion TG, pp. 54–61 💿 ▶ Literature Classics, High School CD-ROM 💿 Skill Level Up! A Skills-Based Language Arts Game CD-ROM
Extension	📖 Grammar and Language Workbook SE 📖 Grammar and Language Workbook TAE 📁 Revising with Style 📖 Spelling Power SE 📖 Spelling Power TAE
Daily Writing	**SE/TE** p. 1115
Interdisciplinary Connections	**SE/TE** View the Art, p. 1101, 1103 **SE/TE** View the Photograph, p. 1107 **TE** Cultural History, pp. 1099, 1111 **TE** Literary History, p. 1102 ▶ **glencoe.com**
Independent Reading	💿 BookLink K–12 CD-ROM 📕 Ethnic Anthologies 📕 Glencoe Literature Library 💿 Glencoe Literature Library Teacher Resources CD-ROM 📕 inTIME magazine 💿 ▶ Literature Classics, High School CD-ROM
Technology and Additional Resources	**Planning and Instruction:** 💿 TeacherWorks Plus CD-ROM 💿 Classroom Presentation Toolkit CD-ROM ▶ Literature Online at **glencoe.com** (QuickPass Code: **GLA9879u6T**) **Students Tools:** 💿 StudentWorks Plus CD-ROM or DVD-ROM ▶ Online Student Edition at **glencoe.com** ▶ Literature Online at **glencoe.com** (QuickPass Code: **GLA9800u6**)

Lesson Plan

Writing Workshop: Creative Nonfiction (pp. 1118–1125)

Lesson Plan and Resource Manager

UNIT SIX From Depression to Cold War 1930s–1960s

Learning Objectives	**Writing:** Writing creative nonfiction using the writing process.
Lesson Duration	Two 45–50 minute sessions
Writing Prompt	Write a creative nonfiction essay of about 1,500 words to describe a personal or other experience and to show how the experience was meaningful. As you work, keep your audience and purpose in mind.
Focus	TE p. 1118
Teach	TE pp. 1119–1125 📁 Writing Resources: Writing Process Strategies 1–23 📁 Writing Resources: Narrative Writing 1–15 ✍ Writing Workshop Transparencies 31–35 📁 Unit 6 Teaching Resources, Writing Workshop Graphic Organizer, p. 268
Assess	📁 Unit 6 Teaching Resources, Writing Workshop Rubric, pp. 269–270 📁 Rubrics for Assessing Writing, Listening and Speaking, High School, Autobiographical Narrative, pp. 6–7 ▶ Glencoe Online Essay Grader at **glencoewriting.com**
Differentiated Instruction: English Learners	TE English Learner Activities, pp. 1118–1125
Differentiated Instruction: Approaching Level	TE Approaching Level Activities, pp. 1118–1125
Extension	📘 Grammar and Language Workbook SE 📘 Grammar and Language Workbook TAE 📁 Revising with Style 📘 Spelling Power SE 📘 Spelling Power TAE
Daily Writing	TE p. 1120 SE/TE p. 1125
Interdisciplinary Connections	TE Literary History, p. 1119 🔘 glencoe.com

Technology and Additional Resources	**Planning and Instruction:**
	📁 Grammar and Composition Handbook
	📁 Success in Writing: Research and Reports
	📁 Writing Constructed Responses
	💿 TeacherWorks Plus CD-ROM
	💿 Classroom Presentation Toolkit CD-ROM
	▶ Glencoe Online Essay Grader at **glencoewriting.com**
	▶ Literature Online at **glencoe.com** (QuickPass Code: **GLA9879u6T**)
	Students Tools:
	💿 StudentWorks Plus CD-ROM or DVD-ROM
	▶ Online Student Edition at **glencoe.com**
	▶ Glencoe Online Essay Grader at **glencoewriting.com**
	▶ Literature Online at **glencoe.com** (QuickPass Code: **GLA9800u6**)

Lesson Plan

Glencoe Literature

Speaking, Listening, and Viewing Workshop: Photo Essay (pp. 1126–1127)

Lesson Plan and Resource Manager

UNIT SIX From Depression to Cold War 1930s–1960s

Learning Objectives	**Speaking, Listening, and Viewing:** Creating a photo essay.
Lesson Duration	One 45–50 minute session
Assignment	Plan and deliver a photo essay.
Focus	**TE** p. 1126
Teach	**TE** pp. 1126–1127 📁 Unit 6 Teaching Resources, SLV Activity, pp. 271–272 💿 TeacherWorks Plus CD-ROM 💿 Classroom Presentation Toolkit CD-ROM 💿 Student Presentation Builder on StudentWorks Plus CD-ROM or DVD-ROM
Assess	📁 Unit 6 Teaching Resources, SLV Workshop Rubrics, pp. 273–274 📁 Rubrics for Assessing Writing, Listening, and Speaking: Presenting a Photo Essay, pp. 44–45
Differentiated Instruction: English Learners	**TE** English Learner Activities, pp. 1126–1127
Daily Writing	**SE/TE** p. 1127
Interdisciplinary Connections	▶ glencoe.com
Technology and Additional Resources	**Planning and Instruction:** 💿 TeacherWorks Plus CD-ROM 💿 Classroom Presentation Toolkit CD-ROM ▶ Glencoe Online Essay Grader at **glencoewriting.com** ▶ Literature Online at **glencoe.com** (QuickPass Code: **GLA9879u6T**) **Students Tools:** 💿 Student Presentation Builder on StudentWorks Plus CD-ROM or DVD-ROM 💿 StudentWorks Plus CD-ROM or DVD-ROM ▶ Online Student Edition at **glencoe.com** ▶ Glencoe Online Essay Grader at **glencoewriting.com** ▶ Literature Online at **glencoe.com** (QuickPass Code: **GLA9800u6**)

Lesson Plan

Glencoe Literature

Unit 6 Wrap-Up (pp. 1128–1135)

Lesson Plan and Resource Manager

UNIT SIX From Depression to Cold War 1930s–1960s

Lesson Summary	On pages **1128–1135** of the Student Edition, students will: • Read independently • Complete the end-of-unit assessment
Lesson Duration	Two 45–50 minute sessions
Focus	**TE** pp. 1128, 1130
Teach	**TE** pp. 1128–1129, 1130
Assess	**TE** pp. 1131–1135 📁 Assessment Resources, Unit 6 Summative Assessment, pp. 341–342 📘 ACT/SAT Preparation and Practice SE/ATE 💿 ExamView Assessment Suite CD-ROM ▶ Progress Reporter Online Assessment
Differentiated Instruction: Approaching Level	**TE** Approaching Level Activities, pp. 1128–1135
Differentiated Instruction: Advanced/Pre-AP	📘 Novel Companion SE, pp. 251–294 📘 Novel Companion TG, pp. 54–61 💿 ▶ Literature Classics, High School CD-ROM
Extension	📘 Grammar and Language Workbook SE/TAE 📁 Revising with Style 📘 Spelling Power SE/TAE
Daily Writing	**SE/TE** pp. 1129, 1135
Interdisciplinary Connections	**TE** Literary History, p. 1128
Independent Reading	💿 BookLink K–12 CD-ROM 📖 Ethnic Anthologies; Glencoe Literature Library; *inTIME* magazine 💿 Glencoe Literature Library Teacher Resources CD-ROM 💿 ▶ Literature Classics, High School CD-ROM
Technology and Additional Resources	**Planning and Instruction:** 💿 TeacherWorks Plus CD-ROM 💿 Classroom Presentation Toolkit CD-ROM ▶ Literature Online at **glencoe.com** (QuickPass Code: **GLA9879u6T**) **Students Tools:** 💿 StudentWorks Plus CD-ROM or DVD-ROM ▶ Online Student Edition at **glencoe.com** ▶ Glencoe Online Essay Grader at **glencoewriting.com** ▶ Literature Online at **glencoe.com** (QuickPass Code: **GLA9800u6)**

Lesson Plan

Unit 7 Introduction (pp. 1136–1150)

Lesson Plan and Resource Manager

UNIT SEVEN Into the 21st Century 1960s–Present

Learning Objectives	**Literary Studies:** Analyzing literary periods. Analyzing literary genres. Evaluating historical influences. Connecting to the literature.
Unit Summary	In this unit, students will be introduced to the following: ▪ **Big Ideas:** An Era of Protest, Nature and Technology, Extending and Remaking Traditions ▪ **Literary Elements:** Allusion, Style ▪ **Reading Strategies:** Analyze Graphic Information, Analyze Cause and Effect, Interpret, Evaluate, Create Graphic Organizers ▪ **Writing Activity/Grammar:** Persuasive Essay ▪ **Listening/Speaking/Viewing Skills:** Analyze Art, Presentation on Postmodernist Literature, Visual Literacy: Timeline
Lesson Duration	Two 45–50 minute sessions
Focus	**TE** pp. 1136–1137 Daily Language Practice Transparency 96 Literature Launchers: Pre-Reading Videos DVD, Unit 7 Launcher Literature Launchers Teacher Guide
Teach	**TE** pp. 1138–1149 Unit 7 Teaching Resources, Unit Introduction, pp. 1–2 Unit 7 Teaching Resources, Big Idea Foldable, pp. 3–4 Unit 7 Teaching Resources, Big Idea School-to-Home Connection, p. 5 Unit 7 Teaching Resources, Unit Challenge Planner, pp. 12–15 Unit 7 Teaching Resources: Academic Vocabulary Development, pp. 16–18 Classroom Presentation Toolkit CD-ROM TeacherWorks Plus CD-ROM
Assess	**TE** p. 1150 Assessment Resources, Unit 7 Diagnostic Assessment, pp. 49–55 ACT/SAT Preparation and Practice SE/ATE ExamView Assessment Suite CD-ROM Progress Reporter Online Assessment
Differentiated Instruction: English Learners	**TE** English Learner Activities, pp. 1136–1150 Unit 7 Teaching Resources, Big Idea School-to-Home Connections: English, Spanish, Vietnamese, Tagalog, Cantonese, Haitian Creole, and Hmong, pp. 6–11 English Language Coach
Differentiated Instruction: Approaching Level	**TE** Approaching Level Activities, pp. 1136–1150 Skill Level Up! A Skills-Based Language Arts Game CD-ROM

Differentiated Instruction: Advanced/Pre-AP	**TE** Advanced Learner Activities, pp. 1136–1150 📘 Novel Companion SE, pp. 295–338 📘 Novel Companion TG, pp. 62–70 💿▶ Literature Classics, High School CD-ROM 💿 Skill Level Up! A Skills-Based Language Arts Game CD-ROM
Extension	📘 Grammar and Language Workbook SE 📘 Grammar and Language Workbook TAE 📁 Revising with Style 📘 Spelling Power SE 📘 Spelling Power TAE
Daily Writing	**TE** p. 1144 **SE/TE** SE p. 1150
Interdisciplinary Connections	**SE/TE** View the Art, pp. 1136, 1149 **SE/TE** View the Photograph, pp. 1141, 1142, 1145, 1147 **TE** Language History, Personal Computer, p. 1137 **TE** Political History, Three Mile Island, p. 1138 **TE** Political History, Kent State, p. 1143 **TE** Political History, The Space Race, p. 1146 **TE** Cultural History, Cell Phones, p. 1140 **TE** Cultural History, NOW (The National Organization for Women), p. 1144 **TE** Literary History, The Joy Luck Club, p. 1139 **TE** Literary History, Rita Dove, p. 1148 ▶ **glencoe.com**
Independent Reading	💿 BookLink K–12 CD-ROM 📖 Ethnic Anthologies 📖 Glencoe Literature Library 💿 Glencoe Literature Library Teacher Resources CD-ROM 📖 *inTIME* magazine 💿▶ Literature Classics, High School CD-ROM
Technology and Additional Resources	**Planning and Instruction:** 💿 TeacherWorks Plus CD-ROM 💿 Classroom Presentation Toolkit CD-ROM ▶ Literature Online at **glencoe.com** (QuickPass Code: **GLA9879u7T**) **Students Tools:** 💿 StudentWorks Plus CD-ROM or DVD-ROM ▶ Online Student Edition at **glencoe.com** ▶ Literature Online at **glencoe.com** (QuickPass Code: **GLA9800u7**)

Lesson Plan

Glencoe Literature

Part 1 Opener and TIME: *The Torchbearer* (pp. 1151–1154)

Lesson Plan and Resource Manager

UNIT SEVEN Into the 21st Century 1960s–Present, Part 1: An Era of Protest

Learning Objectives	**Reading:** Analyzing text structure.
Lesson Summary	On pages **1151–1154** of the Student Edition, students will be introduced to the following: • **Big Idea:** An Era of Protest • **Reading Strategy:** Analyze Text Structure
Lesson Duration	One 20–25 minute session
Readability Scores	Dale-Chall: 8.2 DRP: 61 Lexile: 1060
Focus	**SE/TE** p. 1152
Teach	**SE/TE** pp. 1152–1154 📁 Unit 7 Teaching Resources, Reading Strategy, p. 27 🔖 Read Aloud, Think Aloud Transparencies 37–40 🔖 Literary Elements Transparencies 5, 101 💿 Classroom Presentation Toolkit CD-ROM 💿 Listening Library CD, Selection Audio 💿 TeacherWorks Plus CD-ROM 💿▶ Vocabulary PuzzleMaker CD-ROM
Assess	**SE/TE** p. 1154 📁 Unit 7 Teaching Resources, Selection Quick Check, p. 28 📁 Unit 7 Teaching Resources, Selection Quick Check (Spanish), p. 29 📁 Assessment Resources, Selection Test, pp. 273–274 💿 ExamView Assessment Suite CD-ROM ▶ Progress Reporter Online Assessment
Differentiated Instruction: English Learners	**TE** English Learner Activities, pp. 1151–1154 📁 Unit 7 Teaching Resources, English Language Coach, Part 1, p. 20 📁 Unit 7 Teaching Resources, Selection Summaries: English, Spanish, Vietnamese, Tagalog, Cantonese, Haitian Creole, and Hmong, pp. 21–26 📁 Unit 7 Teaching Resources, Selection Quick Check (Spanish), p. 29 📁 English Language Coach 💿 Glencoe Interactive Vocabulary CD-ROM 💿 Listening Library Audio CD 📁 Listening Library Sourcebook: Strategies and Activities
Differentiated Instruction: Approaching Level	**TE** Approaching Level Activities, pp. 1151–1154 💿 Glencoe Interactive Vocabulary CD-ROM 💿 Listening Library Audio CD 📁 Listening Library Sourcebook: Strategies and Activities 💿 Skill Level Up! A Skills-Based Language Arts Game CD-ROM

Copyright © by The McGraw-Hill Companies, Inc.

Glencoe Literature, American Literature 235

Differentiated Instruction: Advanced/Pre-AP	▮ Novel Companion SE, pp. 295–338 ▮ Novel Companion TG, pp. 62–70 ◉ ▷ Literature Classics, High School CD-ROM ◉ Skill Level Up! A Skills-Based Language Arts Game CD-ROM
Extension	▮ Grammar and Language Workbook SE ▮ Grammar and Language Workbook TAE 📁 Revising with Style ▮ Spelling Power SE ▮ Spelling Power TAE
Interdisciplinary Connections	**SE/TE** View the Art, p. 1151 **TE** Cultural History: Rosa Parks, p. 1154 ▷ glencoe.com
Independent Reading	◉ BookLink K–12 CD-ROM 📖 Ethnic Anthologies 📖 Glencoe Literature Library ◉ Glencoe Literature Library Teacher Resources CD-ROM 📖 *inTIME* magazine ◉ ▷ Literature Classics, High School CD-ROM
Technology and Additional Resources	**Planning and Instruction:** ◉ TeacherWorks Plus CD-ROM ◉ Classroom Presentation Toolkit CD-ROM ▷ Literature Online at **glencoe.com** (QuickPass Code: **GLA9879u7T**) **Students Tools:** ◉ StudentWorks Plus CD-ROM or DVD-ROM ▷ Online Student Edition at **glencoe.com** ▷ Literature Online at **glencoe.com** (QuickPass Code: **GLA9800u7**)

Lesson Plan

Glencoe Literature

from *Stride Toward Freedom* (pp. 1155–1160)

Lesson Plan and Resource Manager

UNIT SEVEN Into the 21st Century 1960s–Present, Part 1: An Era of Protest

Learning Objectives	**Literary Study:** Analyzing structure. **Reading:** Paraphrasing.
Lesson Summary	On pages **1155–1160** of the Student Edition, students will be introduced to the following: • **Big Idea:** An Era of Protest • **Literary Element:** Structure • **Reading Strategies:** Paraphrase, Analyze Arguments • **Vocabulary:** Word Usage, Cognates • **Writing Activity/Grammar:** Write a Summary
Lesson Duration	One 20–25 minute session
Readability Scores	Dale-Chall: 11.2 DRP: 67 Lexile: 1040
Focus	**SE/TE** pp. 1155–1156 Selection Focus Transparency 65 Daily Language Practice Transparency 97
Teach	**SE/TE** pp. 1157–1159 Unit 7 Teaching Resources, Literary Element, p. 36 Unit 7 Teaching Resources, Reading Strategy, p. 37 Unit 7 Teaching Resources, Selection Vocabulary Practice, p. 38 Unit 7 Teaching Resources, Vocabulary Strategy, p. 39 Unit 7 Teaching Resources, Grammar Practice, p. 40 Read Aloud, Think Aloud Transparencies 37–40 Literary Elements Transparencies 5, 101 Classroom Presentation Toolkit CD-ROM Listening Library CD, Selection Audio TeacherWorks Plus CD-ROM Vocabulary PuzzleMaker CD-ROM
Assess	**SE/TE** p. 1160 Unit 7 Teaching Resources, Selection Quick Check, p. 41 Unit 7 Teaching Resources, Selection Quick Check (Spanish), p. 42 Assessment Resources, Selection Test, pp. 275–276 ExamView Assessment Suite CD-ROM Progress Reporter Online Assessment
Differentiated Instruction: English Learners	**TE** English Learner Activities, pp. 1155–1160 Unit 7 Teaching Resources, Selection Summaries: English, Spanish, Vietnamese, Tagalog, Cantonese, Haitian Creole, and Hmong, pp. 30–35 Unit 7 Teaching Resources, Selection Quick Check (Spanish), p. 42 English Language Coach Glencoe Interactive Vocabulary CD-ROM Listening Library Audio CD Listening Library Sourcebook: Strategies and Activities

Differentiated Instruction: Approaching Level	**TE** Approaching Level Activities, pp. 1155–1160
	Glencoe Interactive Vocabulary CD-ROM
	Listening Library Audio CD
	Listening Library Sourcebook: Strategies and Activities
	Skill Level Up! A Skills-Based Language Arts Game CD-ROM
Differentiated Instruction: Advanced/Pre-AP	Novel Companion SE, pp. 295–338
	Novel Companion TG, pp. 62–70
	Literature Classics, High School CD-ROM
	Skill Level Up! A Skills-Based Language Arts Game CD-ROM
Extension	Grammar and Language Workbook SE
	Grammar and Language Workbook TAE
	Revising with Style
	Spelling Power SE
	Spelling Power TAE
Daily Writing	**SE/TE** p. 1160
Interdisciplinary Connections	**SE/TE** View the Photograph, p. 1159
	TE Political History: Segregation, p. 1155
	glencoe.com
Independent Reading	BookLink K–12 CD-ROM
	Ethnic Anthologies
	Glencoe Literature Library
	Glencoe Literature Library Teacher Resources CD-ROM
	inTIME magazine
	Literature Classics, High School CD-ROM
Technology and Additional Resources	**Planning and Instruction:**
	TeacherWorks Plus CD-ROM
	Classroom Presentation Toolkit CD-ROM
	Literature Online at **glencoe.com** (QuickPass Code: **GLA9879u7T**)
	Students Tools:
	StudentWorks Plus CD-ROM or DVD-ROM
	Online Student Edition at **glencoe.com**
	Literature Online at **glencoe.com** (QuickPass Code: **GLA9800u7**)

Lesson Plan

Choice: A Tribute to Dr. Martin Luther King Jr. and Vocabulary Workshop (pp. 1161–1166)

Lesson Plan and Resource Manager

UNIT SEVEN Into the 21st Century 1960s–Present, Part 1: An Era of Protest

Learning Objectives	**Literary Study:** Analyzing anecdote. **Reading:** Activating prior knowledge. **Vocabulary:** Understanding how to recognize loaded words.
Lesson Summary	On pages **1161–1166** of the Student Edition, students will be introduced to the following: • **Big Idea:** An Era of Protest • **Literary Element:** Anecdote • **Reading Strategy:** Activate Prior Knowledge • **Vocabulary:** Analogies • **Writing Activities/Grammar:** Write a Speech, Tribute, Past Perfect Tense
Lesson Duration	One 20–25 minute session
Readability Scores	Dale-Chall: 7.3 DRP: 60 Lexile: 1170
Focus	SE/TE pp. 1161–1162, 1166 Selection Focus Transparency 66 Daily Language Practice Transparency 98
Teach	SE/TE pp. 1163–1164, 1166 Unit 7 Teaching Resources, Literary Element, p. 49 Unit 7 Teaching Resources, Reading Strategy, p. 50 Unit 7 Teaching Resources, Selection Vocabulary Practice, p. 51 Unit 7 Teaching Resources, Vocabulary Strategy, p. 52 Unit 7 Teaching Resources, Grammar Practice, p. 53 Read Aloud, Think Aloud Transparencies 37–40 Literary Elements Transparencies 5, 101 Classroom Presentation Toolkit CD-ROM Listening Library CD, Selection Audio TeacherWorks Plus CD-ROM Vocabulary PuzzleMaker CD-ROM
Assess	SE/TE p. 1165, 1166 Unit 7 Teaching Resources, Selection Quick Check, p. 54 Unit 7 Teaching Resources, Selection Quick Check (Spanish), p. 55 Assessment Resources, Selection Test, pp. 277–278 ExamView Assessment Suite CD-ROM Progress Reporter Online Assessment

Differentiated Instruction: English Learners	**TE** English Learner Activities, pp. 1161–1166
	📁 Unit 7 Teaching Resources, Selection Summaries: English, Spanish, Vietnamese, Tagalog, Cantonese, Haitian Creole, and Hmong, pp. 43–48
	📁 Unit 7 Teaching Resources, Selection Quick Check (Spanish), p. 55
	📁 English Language Coach
	💿 Glencoe Interactive Vocabulary CD-ROM
	💿 Listening Library Audio CD
	📁 Listening Library Sourcebook: Strategies and Activities
Differentiated Instruction: Approaching Level	**TE** Approaching Level Activities, pp. 1161–1166
	💿 Glencoe Interactive Vocabulary CD-ROM
	💿 Listening Library Audio CD
	📁 Listening Library Sourcebook: Strategies and Activities
	💿 Skill Level Up! A Skills-Based Language Arts Game CD-ROM
Differentiated Instruction: Advanced/Pre-AP	📘 Novel Companion SE, pp. 295–338
	📘 Novel Companion TG, pp. 62–70
	💿 ▶ Literature Classics, High School CD-ROM
	💿 Skill Level Up! A Skills-Based Language Arts Game CD-ROM
Extension	📘 Grammar and Language Workbook SE
	📘 Grammar and Language Workbook TAE
	📁 Revising with Style
	📘 Spelling Power SE
	📘 Spelling Power TAE
Interdisciplinary Connections	▶ **glencoe.com**
Independent Reading	💿 BookLink K–12 CD-ROM
	📖 Ethnic Anthologies
	📖 Glencoe Literature Library
	💿 Glencoe Literature Library Teacher Resources CD-ROM
	📖 *inTIME* magazine
	💿 ▶ Literature Classics, High School CD-ROM
Technology and Additional Resources	**Planning and Instruction:**
	💿 TeacherWorks Plus CD-ROM
	💿 Classroom Presentation Toolkit CD-ROM
	▶ Literature Online at **glencoe.com** (QuickPass Code: **GLA9879u7T**)
	Students Tools:
	💿 StudentWorks Plus CD-ROM or DVD-ROM
	▶ Online Student Edition at **glencoe.com**
	▶ Literature Online at **glencoe.com** (QuickPass Code: **GLA9800u7**)

Lesson Plan

from *Working: Roberto Acuna, Farm Worker*; and Grammar Workshop (pp. 1167–1179)

Lesson Plan and Resource Manager

UNIT SEVEN Into the 21st Century 1960s–Present, Part 1: An Era of Protest

Learning Objectives	**Literary Study:** Evaluating oral history. **Reading:** Analyzing cause-and-effect relationships. **Grammar:** Understanding how to avoid run-on sentences.
Lesson Summary	On pages **1166–1179** of the Student Edition, students will be introduced to the following: ▪ **Big Idea:** An Era of Protest ▪ **Literary Elements:** Oral History, Structure ▪ **Reading Strategies:** Analyze Cause-and-Effect Relationships, Review ▪ **Vocabulary:** Loaded Words, Context Clues, Academic Vocabulary ▪ **Writing Activities/Grammar:** Evaluate an Interview, Using Good and Well, Avoid Run-On Sentences ▪ **Listening/Speaking/Viewing Skills:** Conduct an Interview, Interview Practice, Analyze Art
Lesson Duration	One 45–50 minute session
Readability Scores	"Working" Dale-Chall: 4.8 DRP: 52 Lexile: 720
Focus	**SE/TE** pp. 1167–1168, 1179 Daily Language Practice Transparency 99
Teach	**SE/TE** pp. 1169–1176, 1179 Unit 7 Teaching Resources, Literary Element, p. 62 Unit 7 Teaching Resources, Reading Strategy, p. 63 Unit 7 Teaching Resources, Selection Vocabulary Practice, p. 64 Unit 7 Teaching Resources, Vocabulary Strategy, p. 65 Unit 7 Teaching Resources, Grammar Practice, p. 66 Grammar and Language Transparency 35 Literary Elements Transparency 70 Classroom Presentation Toolkit CD-ROM Listening Library CD, Selection Audio TeacherWorks Plus CD-ROM Vocabulary PuzzleMaker CD-ROM
Assess	**SE/TE** pp. 1177–1178, 1179 Unit 7 Teaching Resources, Selection Quick Check, p. 67 Unit 7 Teaching Resources, Selection Quick Check (Spanish), p. 68 Assessment Resources, Selection Test, pp. 279–280 ExamView Assessment Suite CD-ROM Progress Reporter Online Assessment

Differentiated Instruction: English Learners	**TE** English Learner Activities, pp. 1167–1179 📁 Unit 7 Teaching Resources, English Language Coach, p. 20 📁 Unit 7 Teaching Resources, Selection Summaries: English, Spanish, Vietnamese, Tagalog, Cantonese, Haitian Creole, and Hmong, pp. 56–61 📁 Unit 7 Teaching Resources, Selection Quick Check (Spanish), p. 68 📁 English Language Coach 💿 Glencoe Interactive Vocabulary CD-ROM 💿 Listening Library Audio CD 📁 Listening Library Sourcebook: Strategies and Activities
Differentiated Instruction: Approaching Level	**TE** Approaching Level Activities, pp. 1167–1179 💿 Glencoe Interactive Vocabulary CD-ROM 💿 Listening Library Audio CD 📁 Listening Library Sourcebook: Strategies and Activities 💿 Skill Level Up! A Skills-Based Language Arts Game CD-ROM
Differentiated Instruction: Advanced/Pre-AP	**TE** Advanced Learner Activities, pp. 1167–1179 📗 Novel Companion SE, pp. 295–338 📗 Novel Companion TG, pp. 62–70 💿 ▶ Literature Classics, High School CD-ROM 💿 Skill Level Up! A Skills-Based Language Arts Game CD-ROM
Extension	📗 Grammar and Language Workbook SE 📗 Grammar and Language Workbook TAE 📁 Revising with Style 📗 Spelling Power SE 📗 Spelling Power TAE
Daily Writing	**SE/TE** p. 1178
Interdisciplinary Connections	**SE/TE** View the Photograph, pp. 1169, 1171, 1172, 1173 **TE** Cultural History: Imperial Valley, p. 1170 **TE** Political History: Political Protests, p. 1167 **TE** Political History: Cesar Chavez and the UFW, p. 1175 ▶ glencoe.com
Independent Reading	💿 BookLink K–12 CD-ROM 📖 Ethnic Anthologies 📖 Glencoe Literature Library; *inTIME* magazine 💿 Glencoe Literature Library Teacher Resources CD-ROM 💿 ▶ Literature Classics, High School CD-ROM
Technology and Additional Resources	**Planning and Instruction:** 💿 TeacherWorks Plus CD-ROM 💿 Classroom Presentation Toolkit CD-ROM ▶ Literature Online at **glencoe.com** (QuickPass Code: **GLA9879u7T**) **Students Tools:** 💿 StudentWorks Plus CD-ROM or DVD-ROM 💿 Online Student Edition at **glencoe.com** ▶ Literature Online at **glencoe.com** (QuickPass Code: **GLA9800u7**)

Lesson Plan

Comparing Literature: *Ambush; The Gift in Wartime;* from *Stay Alive, My Son;* and *Camouflaging the Chimera* (pp. 1180–1191)

Lesson Plan and Resource Manager

UNIT SEVEN Into the 21ˢᵗ Century 1960s–Present, Part 1: An Era of Protest

Learning Objectives	**Literary Study:** Analyzing mood. **Reading:** Analyzing concrete details.
Lesson Summary	On pages **1180–1191** of the Student Edition, students will be introduced to the following: • **Big Idea:** An Era of Protest • **Literary Elements:** Mood, Theme • **Reading Strategies:** Analyze Concrete Details, Make Predictions • **Vocabulary:** Word Origins • **Writing Activities/Grammar:** Journal Entry, Contrast Images, Visual Display • **Listening/Speaking/Viewing Skills:** Small-Group Discussion, Prepare an Oral Report
Lesson Duration	One to five 45–50 minute sessions
Readability Scores	"Ambush"　　　　　　　　　Dale-Chall: 5.8　　DRP: 53　　Lexile: 650 "The Gift in Wartime"　　Dale-Chall: N/A　　DRP: N/A　　Lexile: N/A "Stay Alive, My Son"　　　Dale-Chall: 6.5　　DRP: 49　　Lexile: 650 "Camouflaging the Chimera"　Dale-Chall: N/A　　DRP: N/A　　Lexile: N/A
Focus	**SE/TE** pp. 1180–1182, 1186, 1187 Selection Focus Transparency 67; Daily Language Practice Transparency 100 Literature Launchers: Pre-Reading Videos DVD, Selection Launcher Literature Launchers Teacher Guide
Teach	**SE/TE** pp. 1183–1184, 1186, 1188–1189, 1190 Interactive Read and Write SE/TE, pp. 255–268 Unit 7 Teaching Resources, Comparing Literature Graphic Organizer, p. 70 Unit 7 Teaching Resources, Literary Element, p. 77 Unit 7 Teaching Resources, Reading Strategy, p. 78 Unit 7 Teaching Resources, Selection Vocabulary Practice, p. 79 Unit 7 Teaching Resources, Vocabulary Strategy, p. 80 Unit 7 Teaching Resources, Grammar Practice, p. 81 Literary Elements Transparency 63 Classroom Presentation Toolkit CD-ROM Listening Library CD, Selection Audio; TeacherWorks Plus CD-ROM Vocabulary PuzzleMaker CD-ROM
Assess	**SE/TE** pp. 1185, 1186, 1189, 1191 Unit 7 Teaching Resources, Selection Quick Check, p. 82 Unit 7 Teaching Resources, Selection Quick Check (Spanish), p. 83

Assess (continued)	📁 Assessment Resources, Selection Test, pp. 281–282
	💿 ExamView Assessment Suite CD-ROM
	▶️ Progress Reporter Online Assessment
Differentiated Instruction: English Learners	**TE** English Learner Activities, pp. 1180–1191
	📘 Interactive Read and Write (EL) SE, pp. 255–268
	📘 Interactive Read and Write (EL) TE
	📁 Unit 7 Teaching Resources, English Language Coach, p. 20
	📁 Unit 7 Teaching Resources, Selection Summaries: English, Spanish, Vietnamese, Tagalog, Cantonese, Haitian Creole, and Hmong, pp. 71–76
	📁 Unit 7 Teaching Resources, Selection Quick Check (Spanish), p. 83
	📁 English Language Coach
	💿 Glencoe Interactive Vocabulary CD-ROM
	💿 Listening Library Audio CD
	📁 Listening Library Sourcebook: Strategies and Activities
Differentiated Instruction: Approaching Level	**TE** Approaching Level Activities, pp. 1180–1191
	📘 Interactive Read and Write (Approaching) SE, pp. 255–268
	📘 Interactive Read and Write (Approaching) TE, pp. 255–268
	💿 Glencoe Interactive Vocabulary CD-ROM
	💿 Listening Library Audio CD
	📁 Listening Library Sourcebook: Strategies and Activities
	💿 Skill Level Up! A Skills-Based Language Arts Game CD-ROM
Differentiated Instruction: Advanced/Pre-AP	**TE** Advanced Learner Activities, pp. 1180–1191
	📘 Novel Companion SE, pp. 295–338
	📘 Novel Companion TG, pp. 62–70
	💿 ▶️ Literature Classics, High School CD-ROM
	💿 Skill Level Up! A Skills-Based Language Arts Game CD-ROM
Extension	📘 Grammar and Language Workbook SE/TAE
	📁 Revising with Style
	📘 Spelling Power SE/TAE
Daily Writing	**SE/TE** p. 1185
Interdisciplinary Connections	**TE** Political History: The Vietnam War, p. 1181
	TE Political History: Guerrilla Warfare, p. 1184
	TE Political History: Pin Yathay, p. 1189
	SE/TE View the Art, p. 1183
	TE Literary History: Khmer Rouge, p. 1188
	▶️ **glencoe.com**
Independent Reading	💿 BookLink K–12 CD-ROM
	📖 Ethnic Anthologies; Glencoe Literature Library; *inTIME* magazine
	💿 Glencoe Literature Library Teacher Resources CD-ROM
	💿 ▶️ Literature Classics, High School CD-ROM
Technology and Additional Resources	**Planning and Instruction:**
	💿 TeacherWorks Plus CD-ROM
	💿 Classroom Presentation Toolkit CD-ROM
	▶️ Literature Online at **glencoe.com** (QuickPass Code: **GLA9879u7T**)
	Students Tools:
	💿 StudentWorks Plus CD-ROM or DVD-ROM
	▶️ Online Student Edition at **glencoe.com**
	▶️ Literature Online at **glencoe.com** (QuickPass Code: **GLA9800u7**)

Lesson Plan

Glencoe Literature

The Asians Dying, Separation, and When You Go Away (pp. 1192–1197)

Lesson Plan and Resource Manager

UNIT SEVEN Into the 21st Century 1960s–Present, Part 1: An Era of Protest

Learning Objectives	**Literary Study:** Analyzing figurative language. **Reading:** Clarifying meaning.
Lesson Summary	On pages **1192–1197** of the Student Edition, students will be introduced to the following: ▪ **Big Idea:** An Era of Protest ▪ **Literary Elements:** Figurative Language, Free Verse ▪ **Reading Strategy:** Clarify Meaning, Make Critical Judgments ▪ **Vocabulary:** Analogies, Academic Vocabulary ▪ **Listening/Speaking/Viewing Skill:** Literature Groups
Lesson Duration	One 45–50 minute session
Focus	**SE/TE** pp. 1192–1193 Daily Language Practice Transparency 101
Teach	**SE/TE** pp. 1194–1195 Unit 7 Teaching Resources, Literary Element, p. 90 Unit 7 Teaching Resources, Reading Strategy, p. 91 Unit 7 Teaching Resources, Vocabulary Strategy, p. 92 Literary Elements Transparency 41 Classroom Presentation Toolkit CD-ROM Listening Library CD, Selection Audio TeacherWorks Plus CD-ROM Vocabulary PuzzleMaker CD-ROM
Assess	**SE/TE** pp. 1196–1197, 1201 Unit 7 Teaching Resources, Selection Quick Check, p. 93 Unit 7 Teaching Resources, Selection Quick Check (Spanish), p. 94 Assessment Resources, Selection Test, pp. 283–284 ExamView Assessment Suite CD-ROM Progress Reporter Online Assessment
Differentiated Instruction: English Learners	**TE** English Learner Activities, pp. 1192–1197 Unit 7 Teaching Resources, Selection Summaries: English, Spanish, Vietnamese, Tagalog, Cantonese, Haitian Creole, and Hmong, pp. 84–89 Unit 7 Teaching Resources, Selection Quick Check (Spanish), p. 94 English Language Coach Glencoe Interactive Vocabulary CD-ROM Listening Library Audio CD Listening Library Sourcebook: Strategies and Activities

Differentiated Instruction: Approaching Level	**TE** Approaching Level Activities, pp. 1192–1197 ◉ Glencoe Interactive Vocabulary CD-ROM ◉ Listening Library Audio CD 📁 Listening Library Sourcebook: Strategies and Activities ◉ Skill Level Up! A Skills-Based Language Arts Game CD-ROM
Differentiated Instruction: Advanced/Pre-AP	📘 Novel Companion SE, pp. 295–338 📘 Novel Companion TG, pp. 62–70 ◉ ▶ Literature Classics, High School CD-ROM ◉ Skill Level Up! A Skills-Based Language Arts Game CD-ROM
Extension	📗 Grammar and Language Workbook SE 📗 Grammar and Language Workbook TAE 📁 Revising with Style 📗 Spelling Power SE 📗 Spelling Power TAE
Interdisciplinary Connections	**TE** Cultural History: War Protests, p. 1192 ▶ **glencoe.com**
Independent Reading	💿 BookLink K–12 CD-ROM 📖 Ethnic Anthologies 📖 Glencoe Literature Library ◉ Glencoe Literature Library Teacher Resources CD-ROM 📖 *inTIME* magazine ◉ ▶ Literature Classics, High School CD-ROM
Technology and Additional Resources	**Planning and Instruction:** ◉ TeacherWorks Plus CD-ROM ◉ Classroom Presentation Toolkit CD-ROM ▶ Literature Online at **glencoe.com** (QuickPass Code: **GLA9879u7T**) **Students Tools:** ◉ StudentWorks Plus CD-ROM or DVD-ROM ▶ Online Student Edition at **glencoe.com** ▶ Literature Online at **glencoe.com** (QuickPass Code: **GLA9800u7**)

Lesson Plan

Glencoe Literature

Artistic Perspective: *Proposal for the Vietnam Veterans Memorial* (pp. 1198–1201)

Lesson Plan and Resource Manager

UNIT SEVEN Into the 21ˢᵗ Century 1960s–Present, Part 1: An Era of Protest

Learning Objectives	**Reading:** Analyzing political assumptions.
Lesson Summary	On pages **1198–1201** of the Student Edition, students will be introduced to the following: • **Big Idea:** An Era of Protest • **Reading Strategy:** Analyze Political Assumptions • **Listening/Speaking/Viewing Skill:** Literature Groups
Lesson Duration	One 20–25 minute session
Readability Scores	Dale-Chall: 13 DRP: 66 Lexile: 1310
Focus	**SE/TE** p. 1198
Teach	**SE/TE** pp. 1198–1201 📁 Unit 7 Teaching Resources, Reading Strategy, p. 101 💿 Classroom Presentation Toolkit CD-ROM 💿 Listening Library CD, Selection Audio 💿 TeacherWorks Plus CD-ROM 💿 Vocabulary PuzzleMaker CD-ROM
Assess	**SE/TE** p. 1201 📁 Unit 7 Teaching Resources, Selection Quick Check, p. 102 📁 Unit 7 Teaching Resources, Selection Quick Check (Spanish), p. 103 📁 Assessment Resources, Selection Test, pp. 285–286 💿 ExamView Assessment Suite CD-ROM 💿 Progress Reporter Online Assessment
Differentiated Instruction: English Learners	**TE** English Learner Activities, pp. 1198–1201 📁 Unit 7 Teaching Resources, Selection Summaries: English, Spanish, Vietnamese, Tagalog, Cantonese, Haitian Creole, and Hmong, pp. 95–100 📁 Unit 7 Teaching Resources, Selection Quick Check (Spanish), p. 103 📁 English Language Coach 💿 Glencoe Interactive Vocabulary CD-ROM 💿 Listening Library Audio CD 📁 Listening Library Sourcebook: Strategies and Activities
Differentiated Instruction: Approaching Level	💿 Glencoe Interactive Vocabulary CD-ROM 💿 Listening Library Audio CD 📁 Listening Library Sourcebook: Strategies and Activities 💿 Skill Level Up! A Skills-Based Language Arts Game CD-ROM

Differentiated Instruction: Advanced/Pre-AP	**TE** Advanced Learner Activities, pp. 1198–1201 Novel Companion SE, pp. 295–338 Novel Companion TG, pp. 62–70 Literature Classics, High School CD-ROM Skill Level Up! A Skills-Based Language Arts Game CD-ROM
Extension	Grammar and Language Workbook SE Grammar and Language Workbook TAE Revising with Style Spelling Power SE Spelling Power TAE
Daily Writing	**SE/TE** p. 1201
Interdisciplinary Connections	**SE/TE** View the Photograph, p. 1200 **TE** Political History: Controversial Design, p. 1199 glencoe.com
Independent Reading	BookLink K–12 CD-ROM Ethnic Anthologies Glencoe Literature Library Glencoe Literature Library Teacher Resources CD-ROM *inTIME* magazine Literature Classics, High School CD-ROM
Technology and Additional Resources	**Planning and Instruction:** TeacherWorks Plus CD-ROM Classroom Presentation Toolkit CD-ROM Literature Online at **glencoe.com** (QuickPass Code: **GLA9879u7T**) **Students Tools:** StudentWorks Plus CD-ROM or DVD-ROM Online Student Edition at **glencoe.com** Literature Online at **glencoe.com** (QuickPass Code: **GLA9800u7**)

Lesson Plan

A Hard Rain's A-Gonna Fall (pp. 1202–1207)

Lesson Plan and Resource Manager

UNIT SEVEN Into the 21st Century 1960s–Present, Part 1: An Era of Protest

Learning Objectives	**Literary Study:** Analyzing rhythm. **Reading:** Analyzing rhetorical devices.
Lesson Summary	On pages **1202–1207** of the Student Edition, students will be introduced to the following: • **Big Idea:** An Era of Protest • **Literary Elements:** Rhythm, Mood • **Reading Strategy:** Analyze Rhetorical Devices • **Vocabulary:** Academic Vocabulary • **Writing Activities/Grammar:** Assess Oral Interpretation, Simple and Compound Sentences • **Listening/Speaking/Viewing Skill:** Oral Interpretation
Lesson Duration	One 20–25 minute session
Readability Scores	Dale-Chall: N/A DRP: N/A Lexile: N/A
Focus	**SE/TE** pp. 1202–1203 🖋 Daily Language Practice Transparency 103
Teach	**SE/TE** pp. 1204–1205 📁 Unit 7 Teaching Resources, Literary Element, p. 110 📁 Unit 7 Teaching Resources, Reading Strategy, p. 111 📁 Unit 7 Teaching Resources, Vocabulary Strategy, p. 112 🖋 Literary Elements Transparencies 46, 89 💿 Classroom Presentation Toolkit CD-ROM 💿 Listening Library CD, Selection Audio 💿 TeacherWorks Plus CD-ROM 💿 ▶ Vocabulary PuzzleMaker CD-ROM
Assess	**SE/TE** pp. 1206–1207 📁 Unit 7 Teaching Resources, Selection Quick Check, p. 113 📁 Unit 7 Teaching Resources, Selection Quick Check (Spanish), p. 114 📁 Assessment Resources, Selection Test, pp. 287–288 💿 ExamView Assessment Suite CD-ROM ▶ Progress Reporter Online Assessment
Differentiated Instruction: English Learners	**TE** English Learner Activities, pp. 1202–1207 📁 Unit 7 Teaching Resources, Selection Summaries: English, Spanish, Vietnamese, Tagalog, Cantonese, Haitian Creole, and Hmong, pp. 104–109 📁 Unit 7 Teaching Resources, Selection Quick Check (Spanish), p. 114 📁 English Language Coach 💿 Glencoe Interactive Vocabulary CD-ROM 💿 Listening Library Audio CD 📁 Listening Library Sourcebook: Strategies and Activities

Differentiated Instruction: Approaching Level	**TE** Approaching Level Activities, pp. 1202–1207 ◉ Glencoe Interactive Vocabulary CD-ROM ◉ Listening Library Audio CD 📁 Listening Library Sourcebook: Strategies and Activities ◉ Skill Level Up! A Skills-Based Language Arts Game CD-ROM
Differentiated Instruction: Advanced/Pre-AP	**TE** Advanced Learner Activities, pp. 1202–1207 📕 Novel Companion SE, pp. 295–338 📕 Novel Companion TG, pp. 62–70 ◉ ▶ Literature Classics, High School CD-ROM ◉ Skill Level Up! A Skills-Based Language Arts Game CD-ROM
Extension	📕 Grammar and Language Workbook SE 📕 Grammar and Language Workbook TAE 📁 Revising with Style 📕 Spelling Power SE 📕 Spelling Power TAE
Interdisciplinary Connections	**TE** Cultural History: Protest Songs, p. 1203 ▶ **glencoe.com**
Independent Reading	◉ BookLink K–12 CD-ROM 📖 Ethnic Anthologies 📖 Glencoe Literature Library ◉ Glencoe Literature Library Teacher Resources CD-ROM 📖 *inTIME* magazine ◉ ▶ Literature Classics, High School CD-ROM
Technology and Additional Resources	**Planning and Instruction:** ◉ TeacherWorks Plus CD-ROM ◉ Classroom Presentation Toolkit CD-ROM ▶ Literature Online at **glencoe.com** (QuickPass Code: **GLA9879u7T**) **Students Tools:** ◉ StudentWorks Plus CD-ROM or DVD-ROM ▶ Online Student Edition at **glencoe.com** ▶ Literature Online at **glencoe.com** (QuickPass Code: **GLA9800u7**)

Lesson Plan

Glencoe Literature

Courage (pp. 1208–1212)

Lesson Plan and Resource Manager

UNIT SEVEN Into the 21st Century 1960s–Present, Part 1: An Era of Protest

Learning Objectives	**Literary Study:** Analyzing verse paragraph. **Reading:** Examining connotation and denotation.
Lesson Summary	On pages **1208–1212** of the Student Edition, students will be introduced to the following: • **Big Idea:** An Era of Protest • **Literary Element:** Verse Paragraph • **Reading Strategy:** Examine Denotation and Connotation, Make Predictions • **Vocabulary:** Synonyms, Verb Power • **Writing Activity/Grammar:** Write a Letter
Lesson Duration	One 20–25 minute session
Readability Scores	Dale-Chall: N/A DRP: N/A Lexile: N/A
Focus	**SE/TE** pp. 1208–1209 Daily Language Practice Transparency 104
Teach	**SE/TE** pp. 1210–1211 Unit 7 Teaching Resources, Literary Element, p. 121 Unit 7 Teaching Resources, Reading Strategy, p. 122 Unit 7 Teaching Resources, Selection Vocabulary Practice, p. 123 Unit 7 Teaching Resources, Vocabulary Strategy, p. 124 Literary Elements Transparencies 46, 89 Classroom Presentation Toolkit CD-ROM Listening Library CD, Selection Audio TeacherWorks Plus CD-ROM Vocabulary PuzzleMaker CD-ROM
Assess	**SE/TE** p. 1212 Unit 7 Teaching Resources, Selection Quick Check, p. 125 Unit 7 Teaching Resources, Selection Quick Check (Spanish), p. 126 Assessment Resources, Selection Test, pp. 289–290 ExamView Assessment Suite CD-ROM Progress Reporter Online Assessment
Differentiated Instruction: English Learners	**TE** English Learner Activities, pp. 1208–1212 Unit 7 Teaching Resources, Selection Summaries: English, Spanish, Vietnamese, Tagalog, Cantonese, Haitian Creole, and Hmong, pp. 115–120 Unit 7 Teaching Resources, Selection Quick Check (Spanish), p. 126 English Language Coach Glencoe Interactive Vocabulary CD-ROM Listening Library Audio CD Listening Library Sourcebook: Strategies and Activities

Differentiated Instruction: Approaching Level	**TE** Approaching Level Activities, pp. 1208–1212 ⊙ Glencoe Interactive Vocabulary CD-ROM ⊙ Listening Library Audio CD 📁 Listening Library Sourcebook: Strategies and Activities ⊙ Skill Level Up! A Skills-Based Language Arts Game CD-ROM
Differentiated Instruction: Advanced/Pre-AP	▮ Novel Companion SE, pp. 295–338 ▮ Novel Companion TG, pp. 62–70 ⊙ ⊙ Literature Classics, High School CD-ROM ⊙ Skill Level Up! A Skills-Based Language Arts Game CD-ROM
Extension	▮ Grammar and Language Workbook SE ▮ Grammar and Language Workbook TAE 📁 Revising with Style ▮ Spelling Power SE ▮ Spelling Power TAE
Daily Writing	**SE/TE** p. 1212
Interdisciplinary Connections	⊙ glencoe.com
Independent Reading	⊙ BookLink K–12 CD-ROM ▥ Ethnic Anthologies ▥ Glencoe Literature Library ⊙ Glencoe Literature Library Teacher Resources CD-ROM ▥ *inTIME* magazine ⊙ ⊙ Literature Classics, High School CD-ROM
Technology and Additional Resources	**Planning and Instruction:** ⊙ TeacherWorks Plus CD-ROM ⊙ Classroom Presentation Toolkit CD-ROM ⊙ Literature Online at **glencoe.com** (QuickPass Code: **GLA9879u7T**) **Students Tools:** ⊙ StudentWorks Plus CD-ROM or DVD-ROM ⊙ Online Student Edition at **glencoe.com** ⊙ Literature Online at **glencoe.com** (QuickPass Code: **GLA9800u7**)

Lesson Plan

Glencoe Literature

Part 2 Opener, *The Fish*, and *Filling Station* (pp. 1213–1221)

Lesson Plan and Resource Manager

UNIT SEVEN Into the 21st Century 1960s–Present, Part 2: Nature and Technology

Learning Objectives	**Literary Study:** Analyzing tone. **Reading:** Evaluating sensory details.
Lesson Summary	On pp. **1213–1221** of the Student Edition, students will be introduced to the following: • **Big Idea:** Nature and Technology • **Literary Elements:** Tone, Setting • **Reading Strategies:** Evaluate Sensory Details, Monitor Comprehension • **Vocabulary:** Context Clues, Academic Vocabulary, Parts of Speech • **Writing Activity/Grammar:** Write a Report, Punctuation
Lesson Duration	One 20–25 minute session
Readability Scores	Dale-Chall: N/A DRP: N/A Lexile: N/A
Focus	**SE/TE** pp. 1214–1215 📖 Selection Focus Transparency 68 📖 Daily Language Practice Transparency 105
Teach	**SE/TE** pp. 1216–1219 📁 Unit 7 Teaching Resources, Literary Element, p. 135 📁 Unit 7 Teaching Resources, Reading Strategy, p. 136 📁 Unit 7 Teaching Resources, Vocabulary Strategy, p. 137 📖 Literary Elements Transparencies 92, 105 💿 Classroom Presentation Toolkit CD-ROM 💿 Listening Library CD, Selection Audio 💿 TeacherWorks Plus CD-ROM 💿 Vocabulary PuzzleMaker CD-ROM
Assess	**SE/TE** pp. 1220–1221 📁 Unit 7 Teaching Resources, Selection Quick Check, p. 138 📁 Unit 7 Teaching Resources, Selection Quick Check (Spanish), p. 139 📁 Assessment Resources, Selection Test, pp. 291–292 💿 ExamView Assessment Suite CD-ROM 💿 Progress Reporter Online Assessment
Differentiated Instruction: English Learners	**TE** English Learner Activities, pp. 1213–1221 📁 Unit 7 Teaching Resources, English Language Coach, Part 2, p. 128 📁 Unit 7 Teaching Resources, Selection Summaries: English, Spanish, Vietnamese, Tagalog, Cantonese, Haitian Creole, and Hmong, pp. 129–134 📁 Unit 7 Teaching Resources, Selection Quick Check (Spanish), p. 139 📁 English Language Coach 💿 Glencoe Interactive Vocabulary CD-ROM 💿 Listening Library Audio CD 📁 Listening Library Sourcebook: Strategies and Activities

Differentiated Instruction: Approaching Level	**TE** Approaching Level Activities, pp. 1213–1221 ● Glencoe Interactive Vocabulary CD-ROM ● Listening Library Audio CD 📁 Listening Library Sourcebook: Strategies and Activities ● Skill Level Up! A Skills-Based Language Arts Game CD-ROM
Differentiated Instruction: Advanced/Pre-AP	**TE** Advanced Learner Activities, pp. 1213–1221 📕 Novel Companion SE, pp. 295–338 📕 Novel Companion TG, pp. 62–70 ● ▶ Literature Classics, High School CD-ROM ● Skill Level Up! A Skills-Based Language Arts Game CD-ROM
Extension	📕 Grammar and Language Workbook SE 📕 Grammar and Language Workbook TAE 📁 Revising with Style 📕 Spelling Power SE 📕 Spelling Power TAE
Daily Writing	**SE/TE** p. 1221
Interdisciplinary Connections	**SE/TE** View the Art, pp. 1213, 1216 ▶ glencoe.com
Independent Reading	● BookLink K–12 CD-ROM 📖 Ethnic Anthologies 📖 Glencoe Literature Library ● Glencoe Literature Library Teacher Resources CD-ROM 📖 *inTIME* magazine ● ▶ Literature Classics, High School CD-ROM
Technology and Additional Resources	**Planning and Instruction:** ● TeacherWorks Plus CD-ROM ● Classroom Presentation Toolkit CD-ROM ▶ Literature Online at **glencoe.com** (QuickPass Code: **GLA9879u7T**) **Students Tools:** ● StudentWorks Plus CD-ROM or DVD-ROM ▶ Online Student Edition at **glencoe.com** ▶ Literature Online at **glencoe.com** (QuickPass Code: **GLA9800u7**)

Copyright © by The McGraw-Hill Companies, Inc.

Lesson Plan

Root Cellar (pp. 1222–1225)

Lesson Plan and Resource Manager

UNIT SEVEN Into the 21st Century 1960s–Present, Part 2: Nature and Technology

Learning Objectives	**Literary Study:** Analyzing simile. **Reading:** Interpreting imagery.
Lesson Summary	On pp. **1222–1225** of the Student Edition, students will be introduced to the following: • **Big Idea:** Nature and Technology • **Literary Elements:** Simile, Figurative Language • **Reading Strategy:** Interpret Imagery • **Vocabulary:** Synonyms • **Writing Activity/Grammar:** Write a Poem
Lesson Duration	One 25–30 minute session
Readability Scores	Dale-Chall: N/A DRP: N/A Lexile: N/A
Focus	**SE/TE** pp. 1222–1223 📖 Daily Language Practice Transparency 106
Teach	**SE/TE** p. 1224 📁 Unit 7 Teaching Resources, Literary Element, p. 146 📁 Unit 7 Teaching Resources, Reading Strategy, p. 147 📁 Unit 7 Teaching Resources, Vocabulary Strategy, p. 148 📖 Literary Elements Transparencies 92, 105 💿 Classroom Presentation Toolkit CD-ROM 💿 Listening Library CD, Selection Audio 💿 TeacherWorks Plus CD-ROM 💿 ▶ Vocabulary PuzzleMaker CD-ROM
Assess	**SE/TE** p. 1225 📁 Unit 7 Teaching Resources, Selection Quick Check, p. 149 📁 Unit 7 Teaching Resources, Selection Quick Check (Spanish), p. 150 📁 Assessment Resources, Selection Test, pp. 293–294 💿 ExamView Assessment Suite CD-ROM ▶ Progress Reporter Online Assessment
Differentiated Instruction: English Learners	**TE** English Learner Activities, pp. 1222–1225 📁 Unit 7 Teaching Resources, Selection Summaries: English, Spanish, Vietnamese, Tagalog, Cantonese, Haitian Creole, and Hmong, pp. 140–145 📁 Unit 7 Teaching Resources, Selection Quick Check (Spanish), p. 150 📁 English Language Coach 💿 Glencoe Interactive Vocabulary CD-ROM 💿 Listening Library Audio CD 📁 Listening Library Sourcebook: Strategies and Activities

Differentiated Instruction: Approaching Level	**TE** Approaching Level Activities, pp. 1222–1225 ● Glencoe Interactive Vocabulary CD-ROM ● Listening Library Audio CD 📁 Listening Library Sourcebook: Strategies and Activities ● Skill Level Up! A Skills-Based Language Arts Game CD-ROM
Differentiated Instruction: Advanced/Pre-AP	▌ Novel Companion SE, pp. 295–338 ▌ Novel Companion TG, pp. 62–70 ● Literature Classics, High School CD-ROM ● Skill Level Up! A Skills-Based Language Arts Game CD-ROM
Extension	▌ Grammar and Language Workbook SE ▌ Grammar and Language Workbook TAE 📁 Revising with Style ▌ Spelling Power SE ▌ Spelling Power TAE
Daily Writing	**SE/TE** p. 1225
Interdisciplinary Connections	**SE/TE** View the Art, p. 1224 **TE** Literary History: Transcendentalism, p. 1222 ▶ glencoe.com
Independent Reading	● BookLink K–12 CD-ROM 📖 Ethnic Anthologies 📖 Glencoe Literature Library ● Glencoe Literature Library Teacher Resources CD-ROM 📖 *inTIME* magazine ● ▶ Literature Classics, High School CD-ROM
Technology and Additional Resources	**Planning and Instruction:** ● TeacherWorks Plus CD-ROM ● Classroom Presentation Toolkit CD-ROM ▶ Literature Online at **glencoe.com** (QuickPass Code: **GLA9879u7T**) **Students Tools:** ● StudentWorks Plus CD-ROM or DVD-ROM ▶ Online Student Edition at **glencoe.com** ▶ Literature Online at **glencoe.com** (QuickPass Code: **GLA9800u7**)

Lesson Plan

Glencoe Literature

Sleep in the Mojave Desert and Crossing the Water (pp. 1226–1231)

Lesson Plan and Resource Manager

UNIT SEVEN Into the 21ˢᵗ Century 1960s–Present, Part 2: Nature and Technology

Learning Objectives	**Literary Study:** Analyzing mood. **Reading:** Analyzing voice.
Lesson Summary	On pages **1226–1231** of the Student Edition, students will be introduced to the following: • **Big Idea:** Nature and Technology • **Literary Elements:** Mood, Figurative Language • **Reading Strategy:** Analyze Voice, Predict • **Vocabulary:** Word Origins • **Writing Activity/Grammar:** Compare and Contrast Setting • **Listening/Speaking/Viewing Skill:** Oral Interpretation of Literature
Lesson Duration	One 20 minute session
Readability Scores	Dale-Chall: N/A DRP: N/A Lexile: N/A
Focus	**TE** pp. 1226–1227 📖 Daily Language Practice Transparency 107
Teach	**TE** pp. 1228–1229 📁 Unit 7 Teaching Resources, Literary Element, p. 157 📁 Unit 7 Teaching Resources, Reading Strategy, p. 158 📁 Unit 7 Teaching Resources, Selection Vocabulary Practice, p. 159 📁 Unit 7 Teaching Resources, Vocabulary Strategy, p. 160 📖 Read Aloud, Think Aloud Transparencies, pp. 41–43 📖 Literary Elements Transparencies, pp. 63, 77 💿 Classroom Presentation Toolkit CD-ROM 💿 Listening Library CD, Selection Audio 💿 TeacherWorks Plus CD-ROM 💿 Vocabulary PuzzleMaker CD-ROM
Assess	**TE** pp. 1230–1231 📁 Unit 7 Teaching Resources, Selection Quick Check, p. 161 📁 Unit 7 Teaching Resources, Selection Quick Check (Spanish), p. 162 📁 Assessment Resources, Selection Test, pp. 295–296 💿 ExamView Assessment Suite CD-ROM 💿 Progress Reporter Online Assessment
Differentiated Instruction: English Learners	**TE** English Learner Activities, pp. 1226–1231 📁 Unit 7 Teaching Resources, Selection Summaries: English, Spanish, Vietnamese, Tagalog, Cantonese, Haitian Creole, and Hmong, pp. 151–156 📁 Unit 7 Teaching Resources, Selection Quick Check (Spanish), p. 162 📁 English Language Coach

Differentiated Instruction: English Learners *(continued)*	● Glencoe Interactive Vocabulary CD-ROM ● Listening Library Audio CD 📁 Listening Library Sourcebook: Strategies and Activities
Differentiated Instruction: Approaching Level	**TE** Approaching Level Activities, pp. 1226–1231 ● Glencoe Interactive Vocabulary CD-ROM ● Listening Library Audio CD 📁 Listening Library Sourcebook: Strategies and Activities ● Skill Level Up! A Skills-Based Language Arts Game CD-ROM
Differentiated Instruction: Advanced/Pre-AP	▌ Novel Companion SE, pp. 295–338 ▌ Novel Companion TG, pp. 62–70 ● Literature Classics, High School CD-ROM ● Skill Level Up! A Skills-Based Language Arts Game CD-ROM
Extension	▌ Grammar and Language Workbook SE ▌ Grammar and Language Workbook TAE 📁 Revising with Style ▌ Spelling Power SE ▌ Spelling Power TAE
Daily Writing	**SE/TE** p. 1231
Interdisciplinary Connections	**TE** Literary History: The Bell Jar, p. 1226 **SE/TE** View the Art, p. 1228 ▶ glencoe.com
Independent Reading	● BookLink K–12 CD-ROM 📖 Ethnic Anthologies 📖 Glencoe Literature Library ● Glencoe Literature Library Teacher Resources CD-ROM 📖 *inTIME* magazine ● ▶ Literature Classics, High School CD-ROM
Technology and Additional Resources	**Planning and Instruction:** ● TeacherWorks Plus CD-ROM ● Classroom Presentation Toolkit CD-ROM ▶ Literature Online at **glencoe.com** (QuickPass Code: **GLA9879u7T**) **Students Tools:** ● StudentWorks Plus CD-ROM or DVD-ROM ▶ Online Student Edition at **glencoe.com** ▶ Literature Online at **glencoe.com** (QuickPass Code: **GLA9800u7**)

Lesson Plan

Glencoe Literature

The War Against the Trees (pp. 1232–1235)

Lesson Plan and Resource Manager

UNIT SEVEN Into the 21st Century 1960s–Present, Part 2: Nature and Technology

Learning Objectives	**Literary Study:** Analyzing personification. **Reading:** Evaluating figures of speech.
Lesson Summary	On pages **1232–1235** of the Student Edition, students will be introduced to the following: ▪ **Big Idea:** Nature and Technology ▪ **Literary Elements:** Personification, Slant Rhymes ▪ **Reading Strategy:** Evaluate Figures of Speech ▪ **Vocabulary:** Analogies ▪ **Writing Activity/Grammar:** Dialogue
Lesson Duration	One 20 minute session
Readability Scores	Dale-Chall: N/A DRP: N/A Lexile: N/A
Focus	**TE** pp. 1232–1233 🔖 Daily Language Practice Transparency 108
Teach	**TE** p. 1234 📁 Unit 7 Teaching Resources, Literary Element, p. 169 📁 Unit 7 Teaching Resources, Reading Strategy, p. 170 📁 Unit 7 Teaching Resources, Selection Vocabulary Practice, p. 171 📁 Unit 7 Teaching Resources, Vocabulary Strategy, p. 172 🔖 Read Aloud, Think Aloud Transparencies, pp. 41–43 🔖 Literary Elements Transparencies, pp. 63, 77 💿 Classroom Presentation Toolkit CD-ROM 💿 Listening Library CD, Selection Audio 💿 TeacherWorks Plus CD-ROM 💿 Vocabulary PuzzleMaker CD-ROM
Assess	**TE** p. 1235 📁 Unit 7 Teaching Resources, Selection Quick Check, p. 173 📁 Unit 7 Teaching Resources, Selection Quick Check (Spanish), p. 174 📁 Assessment Resources, Selection Test, pp. 297–298 💿 ExamView Assessment Suite CD-ROM ▶ Progress Reporter Online Assessment
Differentiated Instruction: English Learners	**TE** English Learner Activities, pp. 1232–1235 📁 Unit 7 Teaching Resources, Selection Summaries: English, Spanish, Vietnamese, Tagalog, Cantonese, Haitian Creole, and Hmong, pp. 163–168 📁 Unit 7 Teaching Resources, Selection Quick Check (Spanish), p. 174 📁 English Language Coach 💿 Glencoe Interactive Vocabulary CD-ROM 💿 Listening Library Audio CD 📁 Listening Library Sourcebook: Strategies and Activities

Differentiated Instruction: Approaching Level	⊙ Glencoe Interactive Vocabulary CD-ROM
	⊙ Listening Library Audio CD
	📁 Listening Library Sourcebook: Strategies and Activities
	⊙ Skill Level Up! A Skills-Based Language Arts Game CD-ROM
Differentiated Instruction: Advanced/Pre-AP	**TE** Advanced Learner Activities, pp. 1232–1235
	📕 Novel Companion SE, pp. 295–338
	📕 Novel Companion TG, pp. 62–70
	⊙ ▶ Literature Classics, High School CD-ROM
	⊙ Skill Level Up! A Skills-Based Language Arts Game CD-ROM
Extension	📕 Grammar and Language Workbook SE
	📕 Grammar and Language Workbook TAE
	📁 Revising with Style
	📕 Spelling Power SE
	📕 Spelling Power TAE
Daily Writing	**SE/TE** SE, p. 1235
Interdisciplinary Connections	**TE** Literary History: Poet Laureate, p. 1232
	▶ **glencoe.com**
Independent Reading	⊙ BookLink K–12 CD-ROM
	📖 Ethnic Anthologies
	📖 Glencoe Literature Library
	⊙ Glencoe Literature Library Teacher Resources CD-ROM
	📖 *inTIME* magazine
	⊙ ▶ Literature Classics, High School CD-ROM
Technology and Additional Resources	**Planning and Instruction:**
	⊙ TeacherWorks Plus CD-ROM
	⊙ Classroom Presentation Toolkit CD-ROM
	▶ Literature Online at **glencoe.com** (QuickPass Code: **GLA9879u7T**)
	Students Tools:
	⊙ StudentWorks Plus CD-ROM or DVD-ROM
	▶ Online Student Edition at **glencoe.com**
	▶ Literature Online at **glencoe.com** (QuickPass Code: **GLA9800u7**)

Lesson Plan

Glencoe Literature

Scientific Perspective: from *Silent Spring* (pp. 1236–1238)

Lesson Plan and Resource Manager

UNIT SEVEN Into the 21ˢᵗ Century 1960s–Present, Part 2: Nature and Technology

Learning Objectives	**Reading:** Recognizing author's purpose. Analyzing informational text.
Lesson Summary	On pages **1236–1238** of the Student Edition, students will be introduced to the following: • **Big Idea:** Nature and Technology • **Reading Strategies:** Recognize author's purpose, Predict
Lesson Duration	One 20 minute session
Readability Scores	Dale-Chall: 7.4 DRP: 62 Lexile: 1150
Focus	**TE** p. 1236
Teach	**TE** pp. 1236–1237 📁 Unit 7 Teaching Resources, Reading Strategy, p. 181 💿 Classroom Presentation Toolkit CD-ROM 💿 Listening Library CD, Selection Audio 💿 TeacherWorks Plus CD-ROM 💿 Vocabulary PuzzleMaker CD-ROM
Assess	**TE** p. 1238 📁 Unit 7 Teaching Resources, Selection Quick Check, p. 182 📁 Unit 7 Teaching Resources, Selection Quick Check (Spanish), p. 183 📁 Assessment Resources, Selection Test, pp. 299–300 💿 ExamView Assessment Suite CD-ROM ▶ Progress Reporter Online Assessment
Differentiated Instruction: English Learners	**TE** English Learner Activities, pp. 1236–1238 📁 Unit 7 Teaching Resources, Selection Summaries: English, Spanish, Vietnamese, Tagalog, Cantonese, Haitian Creole, and Hmong, pp. 175–180 📁 Unit 7 Teaching Resources, Selection Quick Check (Spanish), p. 183 📁 English Language Coach 💿 Glencoe Interactive Vocabulary CD-ROM 💿 Listening Library Audio CD 📁 Listening Library Sourcebook: Strategies and Activities
Differentiated Instruction: Approaching Level	**TE** Approaching Level Activities, pp. 1236–1238 💿 Glencoe Interactive Vocabulary CD-ROM 💿 Listening Library Audio CD 📁 Listening Library Sourcebook: Strategies and Activities 💿 Skill Level Up! A Skills-Based Language Arts Game CD-ROM
Differentiated Instruction: Advanced/Pre-AP	📘 Novel Companion SE, pp. 295–338 📘 Novel Companion TG, pp. 62–70 💿▶ Literature Classics, High School CD-ROM 💿 Skill Level Up! A Skills-Based Language Arts Game CD-ROM

Extension	▮ Grammar and Language Workbook SE ▮ Grammar and Language Workbook TAE 📁 Revising with Style ▮ Spelling Power SE ▮ Spelling Power TAE
Interdisciplinary Connections	**SE/TE** View the Photograph, p. 1237 ▶ **glencoe.com**
Independent Reading	🌐 BookLink K–12 CD-ROM 📖 Ethnic Anthologies 📖 Glencoe Literature Library 🌐 Glencoe Literature Library Teacher Resources CD-ROM 📖 *inTIME* magazine 🌐 ▶ Literature Classics, High School CD-ROM
Technology and Additional Resources	**Planning and Instruction:** 🌐 TeacherWorks Plus CD-ROM 🌐 Classroom Presentation Toolkit CD-ROM ▶ Literature Online at **glencoe.com** (QuickPass Code: **GLA9879u7T**) **Students Tools:** 🌐 StudentWorks Plus CD-ROM or DVD-ROM ▶ Online Student Edition at **glencoe.com** ▶ Literature Online at **glencoe.com** (QuickPass Code: **GLA9800u7**)

Lesson Plan

Glencoe Literature

SQ (pp. 1239–1252)

Lesson Plan and Resource Manager

UNIT SEVEN Into the 21st Century 1960s–Present, Part 2: Nature and Technology

Learning Objectives	**Literary Study:** Analyzing satire. **Reading:** Identifying genre. **Writing:** Evaluating satire in an expository essay. Using brackets in quotations.
Lesson Summary	On pages **1239–1252** of the Student Edition, students will be introduced to the following: • **Big Idea:** Nature and Technology • **Literary Elements:** Satire, Narrator • **Reading Strategies:** Identify Genre, Use Graphic Organizers, Predict • **Vocabulary:** Analogies, Academic Vocabulary • **Writing Activities/Grammar:** Expository Essay, Science Fiction • **Listening/Speaking/Viewing Skill:** Analyze Art
Lesson Duration	One 45–50 minute session
Readability Scores	Dale-Chall: 8.3 DRP: 58 Lexile: 1120
Focus	TE pp. 1239–1240 Daily Language Practice Transparency 109
Teach	TE pp. 1241–1249 Unit 7 Teaching Resources, Literary Element, p. 190 Unit 7 Teaching Resources, Reading Strategy, p. 191 Unit 7 Teaching Resources, Selection Vocabulary Practice, p. 192 Unit 7 Teaching Resources, Vocabulary Strategy, p. 193 Unit 7 Teaching Resources, Grammar Practice, p. 194 Literary Elements Transparency, p. 90 Classroom Presentation Toolkit CD-ROM Listening Library CD, Selection Audio TeacherWorks Plus CD-ROM Vocabulary PuzzleMaker CD-ROM
Assess	TE pp. 1250-1252 Unit 7 Teaching Resources, Selection Quick Check, p. 195 Unit 7 Teaching Resources, Selection Quick Check (Spanish), p. 196 Assessment Resources, Selection Test, pp. 301–302 ExamView Assessment Suite CD-ROM Progress Reporter Online Assessment
Differentiated Instruction: English Learners	TE English Learner Activities, pp. 1239–1252 Unit 7 Teaching Resources, English Language Coach, p. 126 Unit 7 Teaching Resources, Selection Summaries: English, Spanish, Vietnamese, Tagalog, Cantonese, Haitian Creole, and Hmong, pp. 184–189

Differentiated Instruction: English Learners (continued)	📁 Unit 7 Teaching Resources, Selection Quick Check (Spanish), p. 196 📁 English Language Coach 💿 Glencoe Interactive Vocabulary CD-ROM 💿 Listening Library Audio CD 📁 Listening Library Sourcebook: Strategies and Activities
Differentiated Instruction: Approaching Level	**TE** Approaching Level Activities, pp. 1239–1252 💿 Glencoe Interactive Vocabulary CD-ROM 💿 Listening Library Audio CD 📁 Listening Library Sourcebook: Strategies and Activities 💿 Skill Level Up! A Skills-Based Language Arts Game CD-ROM
Differentiated Instruction: Advanced/Pre-AP	**TE** Advanced Learner Activities, pp. 1239–1252 📘 Novel Companion SE, pp. 295–338 📘 Novel Companion TG, pp. 62–70 💿 ▶ Literature Classics, High School CD-ROM 💿 Skill Level Up! A Skills-Based Language Arts Game CD-ROM
Extension	📘 Grammar and Language Workbook SE 📘 Grammar and Language Workbook TAE 📁 Revising with Style 📘 Spelling Power SE 📘 Spelling Power TAE
Daily Writing	**SE/TE** p. 1252
Interdisciplinary Connections	**SE/TE** View the Art, pp. 1241, 1243, 1244 **TE** Political History: The United Nations, p. 1242 **TE** Cultural History: Measuring Intelligence, p. 1249 ▶ glencoe.com
Independent Reading	💿 BookLink K–12 CD-ROM 📖 Ethnic Anthologies 📖 Glencoe Literature Library 💿 Glencoe Literature Library Teacher Resources CD-ROM 📖 *inTIME* magazine 💿 ▶ Literature Classics, High School CD-ROM
Technology and Additional Resources	**Planning and Instruction:** 💿 TeacherWorks Plus CD-ROM 💿 Classroom Presentation Toolkit CD-ROM 💿 ▶ Literature Online at **glencoe.com** (QuickPass Code: **GLA9879u7T**) **Students Tools:** 💿 StudentWorks Plus CD-ROM or DVD-ROM 💿 Online Student Edition at **glencoe.com** ▶ Literature Online at **glencoe.com** (QuickPass Code: **GLA9800u7**)

Lesson Plan

Glencoe Literature Essential Course of Study

Snow (pp. 1253–1256)

Lesson Plan and Resource Manager

UNIT SEVEN Into the 21st Century 1960s–Present, Part 2: Nature and Technology

Learning Objectives	**Literary Study:** Analyzing indirect characterization. **Reading:** Connecting to contemporary issues.
Lesson Summary	On pages **1253–1256** of the Student Edition, students will be introduced to the following: • **Big Idea:** Nature and Technology • **Literary Element:** Indirect Characterization • **Reading Strategy:** Connect to Contemporary Issues • **Vocabulary:** Word Parts, Suffixes • **Writing Activity/Grammar:** Journal Entry
Lesson Duration	One to five 45–50 minute sessions
Readability Scores	Dale-Chall: 5.2 DRP: 56 Lexile: 980
Focus	**TE** pp. 1253–1254 Selection Focus Transparency 69 Daily Language Practice Transparency 110 Literature Launchers: Pre-Reading Videos DVD, Selection Launcher Literature Launchers Teacher Guide
Teach	**TE** p. 1255 Interactive Read and Write SE, pp. 269–276 Interactive Read and Write TE, pp. 269–276 Unit 7 Teaching Resources, Literary Element, p. 203 Unit 7 Teaching Resources, Reading Strategy, p. 204 Unit 7 Teaching Resources, Selection Vocabulary Practice, p. 205 Unit 7 Teaching Resources, Vocabulary Strategy, p. 206 Unit 7 Teaching Resources, Grammar Practice, p. 207 Literary Elements Transparencies, p. 21, 46 Classroom Presentation Toolkit CD-ROM Listening Library CD, Selection Audio TeacherWorks Plus CD-ROM Vocabulary PuzzleMaker CD-ROM
Assess	**TE** pp. 1256 Unit 7 Teaching Resources, Selection Quick Check, p. 208 Unit 7 Teaching Resources, Selection Quick Check (Spanish), p. 209 Assessment Resources, Selection Test, pp. 303–304 ExamView Assessment Suite CD-ROM Progress Reporter Online Assessment
Differentiated Instruction: English Learners	Interactive Read and Write (EL) SE, pp. 269–276 Interactive Read and Write (EL) TE, pp. 269–276 Unit 7 Teaching Resources, Selection Summaries: English, Spanish, Vietnamese, Tagalog, Cantonese, Haitian Creole, and Hmong, pp. 197–202 Unit 7 Teaching Resources, Selection Quick Check (Spanish), p. 209

Differentiated Instruction: English Learners *(continued)*	📁 English Language Coach 💿 Glencoe Interactive Vocabulary CD-ROM 💿 Listening Library Audio CD 📁 Listening Library Sourcebook: Strategies and Activities
Differentiated Instruction: Approaching Level	**TE** Approaching Level Activities, pp. 1253–1256 📘 Interactive Read and Write (Approaching) SE, pp. 269–276 📘 Interactive Read and Write (Approaching) TE, pp. 269–276 💿 Glencoe Interactive Vocabulary CD-ROM 💿 Listening Library Audio CD 📁 Listening Library Sourcebook: Strategies and Activities 💿 Skill Level Up! A Skills-Based Language Arts Game CD-ROM
Differentiated Instruction: Advanced/Pre-AP	📘 Novel Companion SE, pp. 295–338 📘 Novel Companion TG, pp. 62–70 💿 Literature Classics, High School CD-ROM 💿 Skill Level Up! A Skills-Based Language Arts Game CD-ROM
Extension	📘 Grammar and Language Workbook SE 📘 Grammar and Language Workbook TAE 📁 Revising with Style 📘 Spelling Power SE 📘 Spelling Power TAE
Daily Writing	**SE/TE** p. 1256
Interdisciplinary Connections	**TE** Political History, The Mirabel Sisters, p. 1253 ▶ glencoe.com
Independent Reading	💿 BookLink K–12 CD-ROM 📖 Ethnic Anthologies 📖 Glencoe Literature Library 💿 Glencoe Literature Library Teacher Resources CD-ROM 📖 *inTIME* magazine 💿 ▶ Literature Classics, High School CD-ROM
Technology and Additional Resources	**Planning and Instruction:** 💿 TeacherWorks Plus CD-ROM 💿 Classroom Presentation Toolkit CD-ROM 💿 ▶ Literature Online at **glencoe.com** (QuickPass Code: **GLA9879u7T**) **Students Tools:** 💿 StudentWorks Plus CD-ROM or DVD-ROM ▶ Online Student Edition at **glencoe.com** ▶ Literature Online at **glencoe.com** (QuickPass Code: **GLA9800u7**)

Lesson Plan

Cottonmouth Country and Daisies (pp. 1257–1262)

Lesson Plan and Resource Manager

UNIT SEVEN Into the 21st Century 1960s–Present, Part 2: Nature and Technology

Learning Objectives	**Literary Study:** Analyzing free verse. **Reading:** Making inferences about theme.

Lesson Summary	On pages **1257–1262** of the Student Edition, students will be introduced to the following:
	  • **Big Idea:** Nature and Technology
	  • **Literary Elements:** Free Verse, Voice
	  • **Reading Strategy:** Make Inferences About Theme
	  • **Vocabulary:** Analogies, Academic Vocabulary
	  • **Writing Activities/Grammar:** Evaluate Interpretation, Free Verse

Lesson Duration	One 20–25 minute session
Readability Scores	Dale-Chall: N/A DRP: N/A Lexile: N/A
Focus	**TE** pp. 1257–1258 📖 Daily Language Practice Transparency 111
Teach	**TE** pp. 1259–1260 📁 Unit 7 Teaching Resources, Literary Element, p. 216 📁 Unit 7 Teaching Resources, Reading Strategy, p. 217 📁 Unit 7 Teaching Resources, Selection Vocabulary Practice, p. 218 📁 Unit 7 Teaching Resources, Vocabulary Strategy, p. 219 📖 Literary Elements Transparencies, pp. 21, 46 💿 Classroom Presentation Toolkit CD-ROM 💿 Listening Library CD, Selection Audio 💿 TeacherWorks Plus CD-ROM 💿 ▶ Vocabulary PuzzleMaker CD-ROM
Assess	**TE** pp. 1261–1262 📁 Unit 7 Teaching Resources, Selection Quick Check, p. 220 📁 Unit 7 Teaching Resources, Selection Quick Check (Spanish), p. 221 📁 Assessment Resources, Selection Test, pp. 305–306 💿 ExamView Assessment Suite CD-ROM ▶ Progress Reporter Online Assessment
Differentiated Instruction: English Learners	**TE** English Learner Activities, pp. 1257–1262 📁 Unit 7 Teaching Resources, Selection Summaries: English, Spanish, Vietnamese, Tagalog, Cantonese, Haitian Creole, and Hmong, pp. 210–215 📁 Unit 7 Teaching Resources, Selection Quick Check (Spanish), p. 221 📁 English Language Coach 💿 Glencoe Interactive Vocabulary CD-ROM 💿 Listening Library Audio CD 📁 Listening Library Sourcebook: Strategies and Activities

Differentiated Instruction: Approaching Level	**TE** Approaching Level Activities, pp. 1257–1262 ⊙ Glencoe Interactive Vocabulary CD-ROM ⊙ Listening Library Audio CD 📁 Listening Library Sourcebook: Strategies and Activities ⊙ Skill Level Up! A Skills-Based Language Arts Game CD-ROM
Differentiated Instruction: Advanced/Pre-AP	**TE** Advanced Learner Activities, pp. 1257–1262 📕 Novel Companion SE, pp. 295–338 📕 Novel Companion TG, pp. 62–70 ⊙ Literature Classics, High School CD-ROM ⊙ Skill Level Up! A Skills-Based Language Arts Game CD-ROM
Extension	📕 Grammar and Language Workbook SE 📕 Grammar and Language Workbook TAE 📁 Revising with Style 📕 Spelling Power SE 📕 Spelling Power TAE
Daily Writing	**SE/TE** p. 1262
Interdisciplinary Connections	**TE** Literary History, Averno, p. 1257 **SE/TE** View the Art, p. 1259 ▶ glencoe.com
Independent Reading	⊙ BookLink K–12 CD-ROM 📖 Ethnic Anthologies 📖 Glencoe Literature Library ⊙ Glencoe Literature Library Teacher Resources CD-ROM 📖 inTIME magazine ⊙ ▶ Literature Classics, High School CD-ROM
Technology and Additional Resources	**Planning and Instruction:** ⊙ TeacherWorks Plus CD-ROM ⊙ Classroom Presentation Toolkit CD-ROM ⊙ ▶ Literature Online at **glencoe.com** (QuickPass Code: **GLA9879u7T**) **Students Tools:** ⊙ StudentWorks Plus CD-ROM or DVD-ROM ⊙ Online Student Edition at **glencoe.com** ▶ Literature Online at **glencoe.com** (QuickPass Code: **GLA9800u7**)

Lesson Plan

Part 3 Opener and from *The Woman Warrior* (pp. 1263–1273)

Lesson Plan and Resource Manager

UNIT SEVEN Into the 21st Century 1960s–Present, Part 3: Extending and Remaking Traditions

Learning Objectives	**Literary Study:** Identifying exposition. **Reading:** Making inferences about characters. **Writing:** Applying flashback in an autobiographical narrative.
Lesson Summary	On pages **1263–1273** of the Student Edition, students will be introduced to the following: • **Big Idea:** Extending and Remaking Traditions • **Literary Elements:** Exposition, Dialogue • **Reading Strategy:** Make Inferences About Characters • **Vocabulary:** Synonyms • **Writing Activities/Grammar:** Autobiographical Narrative, Sentence Fragments, Connect • **Study Skill/Research/Assessment:** Short Responses • **Listening/Speaking/Viewing Skill:** Analyze Art
Lesson Duration	One 45–50 minute session
Readability Scores	Dale-Chall: 4.4 DRP: 51 Lexile: 800
Focus	TE pp. 1264–1265 Selection Focus Transparency 70 Daily Language Practice Transparency 112
Teach	TE pp. 1266–1270 Unit 7 Teaching Resources, Literary Element, p. 230 Unit 7 Teaching Resources, Reading Strategy, p. 231 Unit 7 Teaching Resources, Selection Vocabulary Practice, p. 232 Unit 7 Teaching Resources, Vocabulary Strategy, p. 233 Unit 7 Teaching Resources, Grammar Practice, p. 234 Literary Elements Transparency, p. 38 Classroom Presentation Toolkit CD-ROM Listening Library CD, Selection Audio TeacherWorks Plus CD-ROM Vocabulary PuzzleMaker CD-ROM
Assess	TE pp. 1271–1273 Unit 7 Teaching Resources, Selection Quick Check, p. 235 Unit 7 Teaching Resources, Selection Quick Check (Spanish), p. 236 Assessment Resources, Selection Test, pp. 307–308 ExamView Assessment Suite CD-ROM Progress Reporter Online Assessment

Differentiated Instruction: English Learners	**TE** English Learner Activities, pp. 1263–1273 📁 Unit 7 Teaching Resources, English Language Coach, p. 223 📁 Unit 7 Teaching Resources, Selection Summaries: English, Spanish, Vietnamese, Tagalog, Cantonese, Haitian Creole, and Hmong, pp. 224–229 📁 Unit 7 Teaching Resources, Selection Quick Check (Spanish), p. 236 📁 English Language Coach 💿 Glencoe Interactive Vocabulary CD-ROM 💿 Listening Library Audio CD 📁 Listening Library Sourcebook: Strategies and Activities
Differentiated Instruction: Approaching Level	**TE** Approaching Level Activities, pp. 1263–1273 💿 Glencoe Interactive Vocabulary CD-ROM 💿 Listening Library Audio CD 📁 Listening Library Sourcebook: Strategies and Activities 💿 Skill Level Up! A Skills-Based Language Arts Game CD-ROM
Differentiated Instruction: Advanced/Pre-AP	**TE** Advanced Learner Activities, pp. 1263–1273 📘 Novel Companion SE, pp. 295–338 📘 Novel Companion TG, pp. 62–70 💿▶ Literature Classics, High School CD-ROM 💿 Skill Level Up! A Skills-Based Language Arts Game CD-ROM
Extension	📘 Grammar and Language Workbook SE 📘 Grammar and Language Workbook TAE 📁 Revising with Style 📘 Spelling Power SE 📘 Spelling Power TAE
Daily Writing	**SE/TE** p. 1273
Interdisciplinary Connections	**SE/TE** View the Art, pp. 1263, 1266 **TE** Literary History, Port of Entry, p. 1268 💿 glencoe.com
Independent Reading	💿 BookLink K–12 CD-ROM 📖 Ethnic Anthologies 📖 Glencoe Literature Library 💿 Glencoe Literature Library Teacher Resources CD-ROM 📖 inTIME magazine 💿▶ Literature Classics, High School CD-ROM
Technology and Additional Resources	**Planning and Instruction:** 💿 TeacherWorks Plus CD-ROM 💿 Classroom Presentation Toolkit CD-ROM ▶ Literature Online at **glencoe.com** (QuickPass Code: **GLA9879u7T**) **Students Tools:** 💿 StudentWorks Plus CD-ROM or DVD-ROM ▶ Online Student Edition at **glencoe.com** ▶ Literature Online at **glencoe.com** (QuickPass Code: **GLA9800u7**)

Lesson Plan

Glencoe Literature

Everything Stuck to Him (pp. 1274–1281)

Lesson Plan and Resource Manager

UNIT SEVEN Into the 21st Century 1960s–Present, Part 3: Extending and Remaking Traditions

Learning Objectives	**Literary Study:** Understanding frame stories. **Reading:** Questioning. **Listening and Speaking:** Using logical arguments in debates.
Lesson Summary	On pages **1274–1281** of the Student Edition, students will be introduced to the following: ▪ **Big Idea:** Extending and Remaking Traditions ▪ **Literary Elements:** Frame Story, Style ▪ **Reading Strategies:** Question, Connect ▪ **Vocabulary:** Context Clues ▪ **Writing Activity/Grammar:** Evaluate Debate ▪ **Listening/Speaking/Viewing Skill:** Analyze Art
Lesson Duration	One 20–25 minute session
Readability Scores	Dale-Chall: 3.3 DRP: 46 Lexile: 460
Focus	**TE** pp. 1274–1275 📖 Daily Language Practice Transparency 113
Teach	**TE** pp. 1276–1279 📁 Unit 7 Teaching Resources, Literary Element, p. 243 📁 Unit 7 Teaching Resources, Reading Strategy, p. 244 📁 Unit 7 Teaching Resources, Selection Vocabulary Practice, p. 245 📁 Unit 7 Teaching Resources, Vocabulary Strategy, p. 246 📁 Unit 7 Teaching Resources, Grammar Practice, p. 247 📖 Literary Elements Transparencies, pp. 45, 80 💿 Classroom Presentation Toolkit CD-ROM 💿 Listening Library CD, Selection Audio 💿 TeacherWorks Plus CD-ROM 💿 Vocabulary PuzzleMaker CD-ROM
Assess	**TE** pp. 1280–1281 📁 Unit 7 Teaching Resources, Selection Quick Check, p. 248 📁 Unit 7 Teaching Resources, Selection Quick Check (Spanish), p. 249 📁 Assessment Resources, Selection Test, pp. 309–310 💿 ExamView Assessment Suite CD-ROM 💿 Progress Reporter Online Assessment
Differentiated Instruction: English Learners	**TE** English Learner Activities, pp. 1274–1281 📁 Unit 7 Teaching Resources, Selection Summaries: English, Spanish, Vietnamese, Tagalog, Cantonese, Haitian Creole, and Hmong, pp. 237–242 📁 Unit 7 Teaching Resources, Selection Quick Check (Spanish), p. 249 📁 English Language Coach 💿 Glencoe Interactive Vocabulary CD-ROM

Differentiated Instruction: English Learners *(continued)*	◉ Listening Library Audio CD 📁 Listening Library Sourcebook: Strategies and Activities
Differentiated Instruction: Approaching Level	**TE** Approaching Level Activities, pp. 1274–1281 ◉ Glencoe Interactive Vocabulary CD-ROM ◉ Listening Library Audio CD 📁 Listening Library Sourcebook: Strategies and Activities ◉ Skill Level Up! A Skills-Based Language Arts Game CD-ROM
Differentiated Instruction: Advanced/Pre-AP	▮ Novel Companion SE, pp. 295–338 ▮ Novel Companion TG, pp. 62–70 ◉ ▶ Literature Classics, High School CD-ROM ◉ Skill Level Up! A Skills-Based Language Arts Game CD-ROM
Extension	▮ Grammar and Language Workbook SE ▮ Grammar and Language Workbook TAE 📁 Revising with Style ▮ Spelling Power SE ▮ Spelling Power TAE
Interdisciplinary Connections	**SE/TE** View the Art, pp. 1276, 1278 ▶ glencoe.com
Independent Reading	◉ BookLink K–12 CD-ROM 📖 Ethnic Anthologies 📖 Glencoe Literature Library ◉ Glencoe Literature Library Teacher Resources CD-ROM 📖 *inTIME* magazine ◉ ▶ Literature Classics, High School CD-ROM
Technology and Additional Resources	**Planning and Instruction:** ◉ TeacherWorks Plus CD-ROM ◉ Classroom Presentation Toolkit CD-ROM ▶ Literature Online at **glencoe.com** (QuickPass Code: **GLA9879u7T**) **Students Tools:** ◉ StudentWorks Plus CD-ROM or DVD-ROM ▶ Online Student Edition at **glencoe.com** ▶ Literature Online at **glencoe.com** (QuickPass Code: **GLA9800u7**)

Lesson Plan

El Olvido (pp. 1282–1285)

Lesson Plan and Resource Manager

UNIT SEVEN Into the 21st Century 1960s–Present, Part 3: Extending and Remaking Traditions

Learning Objectives	**Literary Study:** Understanding point of view. **Reading:** Examining connotations. **Writing:** Writing a poem.
Lesson Summary	On pages **1282–1285** of the Student Edition, students will be introduced to the following: • **Big Idea:** Extending and Remaking Traditions • **Literary Element:** Point of View • **Reading Strategies:** Examine Connotations, Draw Conclusions • **Vocabulary:** Denotation and Connotation • **Listening/Speaking/Viewing Skill:** Analyze Art
Lesson Duration	One 20–25 minute session
Readability Scores	Dale-Chall: N/A DRP: N/A Lexile: N/A
Focus	**TE** pp. 1282–1283 📖 Daily Language Practice Transparency 114
Teach	**TE** pp. 1284 📁 Unit 7 Teaching Resources, Literary Element, p. 256 📁 Unit 7 Teaching Resources, Reading Strategy, p. 257 📁 Unit 7 Teaching Resources, Vocabulary Strategy, p. 258 📖 Literary Elements Transparencies, pp. 45, 80 💿 Classroom Presentation Toolkit CD-ROM 💿 Listening Library CD, Selection Audio 💿 TeacherWorks Plus CD-ROM 💿 ▶ Vocabulary PuzzleMaker CD-ROM
Assess	**TE** p. 1285 📁 Unit 7 Teaching Resources, Selection Quick Check, p. 259 📁 Unit 7 Teaching Resources, Selection Quick Check (Spanish), p. 260 📁 Assessment Resources, Selection Test, pp. 311–312 💿 ExamView Assessment Suite CD-ROM ▶ Progress Reporter Online Assessment
Differentiated Instruction: English Learners	📁 Unit 7 Teaching Resources, Selection Summaries: English, Spanish, Vietnamese, Tagalog, Cantonese, Haitian Creole, and Hmong, pp. 250–255 📁 Unit 7 Teaching Resources, Selection Quick Check (Spanish), p. 260 📁 English Language Coach 💿 Glencoe Interactive Vocabulary CD-ROM 💿 Listening Library Audio CD 📁 Listening Library Sourcebook: Strategies and Activities

Differentiated Instruction: Approaching Level	**TE** Approaching Level Activities, pp. 1282–1285
	🔘 Glencoe Interactive Vocabulary CD-ROM
	🔘 Listening Library Audio CD
	🗀 Listening Library Sourcebook: Strategies and Activities
	🔘 Skill Level Up! A Skills-Based Language Arts Game CD-ROM
Differentiated Instruction: Advanced/Pre-AP	📙 Novel Companion SE, pp. 295–338
	📙 Novel Companion TG, pp. 62–70
	🔘 ▶ Literature Classics, High School CD-ROM
	🔘 Skill Level Up! A Skills-Based Language Arts Game CD-ROM
Extension	📗 Grammar and Language Workbook SE
	📗 Grammar and Language Workbook TAE
	🗀 Revising with Style
	📗 Spelling Power SE
	📗 Spelling Power TAE
Daily Writing	**SE/TE** p. 1285
Interdisciplinary Connections	**SE/TE** View the Art, p. 1284
	🔘 glencoe.com
Independent Reading	🔘 BookLink K–12 CD-ROM
	📖 Ethnic Anthologies
	📖 Glencoe Literature Library
	🔘 Glencoe Literature Library Teacher Resources CD-ROM
	📖 *inTIME* magazine
	🔘 ▶ Literature Classics, High School CD-ROM
Technology and Additional Resources	**Planning and Instruction:**
	🔘 TeacherWorks Plus CD-ROM
	🔘 Classroom Presentation Toolkit CD-ROM
	🔘 Literature Online at **glencoe.com** (QuickPass Code: **GLA9879u7T**)
	Students Tools:
	🔘 StudentWorks Plus CD-ROM or DVD-ROM
	🔘 Online Student Edition at **glencoe.com**
	🔘 Literature Online at **glencoe.com** (QuickPass Code: **GLA9800u7**)

Lesson Plan

My Father and the Figtree (pp. 1286–1290)

Lesson Plan and Resource Manager

UNIT SEVEN Into the 21st Century 1960s–Present, Part 3: Extending and Remaking Traditions

Learning Objectives	**Literary Study:** Analyzing symbols. **Reading:** Summarizing. **Writing:** Writing a list.
Lesson Summary	On pages **1286–1290** of the Student Edition, students will be introduced to the following: ▪ **Big Idea:** Extending and Remaking Traditions ▪ **Literary Element:** Symbol ▪ **Reading Strategies:** Summarize, Scan ▪ **Vocabulary:** Context Clues ▪ **Writing Activity/Grammar:** Write a List
Lesson Duration	One 20–25 minute session
Readability Scores	Dale-Chall: N/A DRP: N/A Lexile: N/A
Focus	**TE** pp. 1286–1287 ✋ Daily Language Practice Transparency 115
Teach	**TE** pp. 1288–1289 📁 Unit 7 Teaching Resources, Literary Element, p. 267 📁 Unit 7 Teaching Resources, Reading Strategy, p. 268 📁 Unit 7 Teaching Resources, Selection Vocabulary Practice, p. 269 📁 Unit 7 Teaching Resources, Vocabulary Strategy, p. 270 ✋ Literary Elements Transparencies, p. 77, 100 💿 Classroom Presentation Toolkit CD-ROM 💿 Listening Library CD, Selection Audio 💿 TeacherWorks Plus CD-ROM 💿 ▶ Vocabulary PuzzleMaker CD-ROM
Assess	**TE** p. 1290 📁 Unit 7 Teaching Resources, Selection Quick Check, p. 271 📁 Unit 7 Teaching Resources, Selection Quick Check (Spanish), p. 272 📁 Assessment Resources, Selection Test, pp. 313–314 💿 ExamView Assessment Suite CD-ROM ▶ Progress Reporter Online Assessment
Differentiated Instruction: English Learners	**TE** English Learner Activities, pp. 1286–1290 📁 Unit 7 Teaching Resources, Selection Summaries: English, Spanish, Vietnamese, Tagalog, Cantonese, Haitian Creole, and Hmong, pp. 261–266 📁 Unit 7 Teaching Resources, Selection Quick Check (Spanish), p. 272 📁 English Language Coach 💿 Glencoe Interactive Vocabulary CD-ROM 💿 Listening Library Audio CD 📁 Listening Library Sourcebook: Strategies and Activities

Differentiated Instruction: Approaching Level	**TE** Approaching Level Activities, pp. 1286–1290
	🖭 Glencoe Interactive Vocabulary CD-ROM
	🖭 Listening Library Audio CD
	📁 Listening Library Sourcebook: Strategies and Activities
	🖭 Skill Level Up! A Skills-Based Language Arts Game CD-ROM
Differentiated Instruction: Advanced/Pre-AP	📕 Novel Companion SE, pp. 295–338
	📕 Novel Companion TG, pp. 62–70
	🖭 ▶ Literature Classics, High School CD-ROM
	🖭 Skill Level Up! A Skills-Based Language Arts Game CD-ROM
Extension	📕 Grammar and Language Workbook SE
	📕 Grammar and Language Workbook TAE
	📁 Revising with Style
	📕 Spelling Power SE
	📕 Spelling Power TAE
Daily Writing	**SE/TE** p. 1290
Interdisciplinary Connections	▶ **glencoe.com**
Independent Reading	🖭 BookLink K–12 CD-ROM
	📖 Ethnic Anthologies
	📖 Glencoe Literature Library
	🖭 Glencoe Literature Library Teacher Resources CD-ROM
	📖 *inTIME* magazine
	🖭 ▶ Literature Classics, High School CD-ROM
Technology and Additional Resources	**Planning and Instruction:**
	🖭 TeacherWorks Plus CD-ROM
	🖭 Classroom Presentation Toolkit CD-ROM
	▶ Literature Online at **glencoe.com** (QuickPass Code: **GLA9879u7T**)
	Students Tools:
	🖭 StudentWorks Plus CD-ROM or DVD-ROM
	▶ Online Student Edition at **glencoe.com**
	▶ Literature Online at **glencoe.com** (QuickPass Code: **GLA9800u7**)

Lesson Plan

Glencoe Literature

I Chop Some Parsley While Listening to Art Blakey's Version of "Three Blind Mice" (pp. 1291–1295)

Lesson Plan and Resource Manager

UNIT SEVEN Into the 21st Century 1960s–Present, Part 3: Extending and Remaking Traditions

Learning Objectives	**Literary Study:** Identifying personification. **Reading:** Connecting to personal experience. **Writing:** Writing a journal entry.
Lesson Summary	On pages **1291–1295** of the Student Edition, students will be introduced to the following: • **Big Idea:** Extending and Remaking Traditions • **Literary Element:** Personification • **Reading Strategies:** Connect to Personal Experience, Tone • **Vocabulary:** Word Usage • **Writing Activities/Grammar:** Journal Entry, Subject Complements
Lesson Duration	One 20–25 minute session
Readability Scores	Dale-Chall: N/A DRP: N/A Lexile: N/A
Focus	TE pp. 1291–1292 🔖 Daily Language Practice Transparency 116
Teach	TE pp. 1293-1294 📁 Unit 7 Teaching Resources, Literary Element, p. 279 📁 Unit 7 Teaching Resources, Reading Strategy, p. 280 📁 Unit 7 Teaching Resources, Selection Vocabulary Practice, p. 281 📁 Unit 7 Teaching Resources, Vocabulary Strategy, p. 282 🔖 Literary Elements Transparencies, p. 77, 100 💿 Classroom Presentation Toolkit CD-ROM 💿 Listening Library CD, Selection Audio 💿 TeacherWorks Plus CD-ROM 💿 Vocabulary PuzzleMaker CD-ROM
Assess	TE p. 1295 📁 Unit 7 Teaching Resources, Selection Quick Check, p. 283 📁 Unit 7 Teaching Resources, Selection Quick Check (Spanish), p. 284 📁 Assessment Resources, Selection Test, pp. 315–316 💿 ExamView Assessment Suite CD-ROM 💿 Progress Reporter Online Assessment

Differentiated Instruction: English Learners	**TE** English Learner Activities, pp. 1291–1295 📁 Unit 7 Teaching Resources, Selection Summaries: English, Spanish, Vietnamese, Tagalog, Cantonese, Haitian Creole, and Hmong, pp. 273–278 📁 Unit 7 Teaching Resources, Selection Quick Check (Spanish), p. 284 📁 English Language Coach 💿 Glencoe Interactive Vocabulary CD-ROM 💿 Listening Library Audio CD 📁 Listening Library Sourcebook: Strategies and Activities
Differentiated Instruction: Approaching Level	💿 Glencoe Interactive Vocabulary CD-ROM 💿 Listening Library Audio CD 📁 Listening Library Sourcebook: Strategies and Activities 💿 Skill Level Up! A Skills-Based Language Arts Game CD-ROM
Differentiated Instruction: Advanced/Pre-AP	📘 Novel Companion SE, pp. 295–338 📘 Novel Companion TG, pp. 62–70 💿 ▶ Literature Classics, High School CD-ROM 💿 Skill Level Up! A Skills-Based Language Arts Game CD-ROM
Extension	📘 Grammar and Language Workbook SE 📘 Grammar and Language Workbook TAE 📁 Revising with Style 📘 Spelling Power SE 📘 Spelling Power TAE
Daily Writing	**SE/TE** p. 1295
Interdisciplinary Connections	**SE/TE** View the Art, p. 1293 ▶ glencoe.com
Independent Reading	💿 BookLink K–12 CD-ROM 📖 Ethnic Anthologies 📖 Glencoe Literature Library 💿 Glencoe Literature Library Teacher Resources CD-ROM 📖 *inTIME* magazine 💿 ▶ Literature Classics, High School CD-ROM
Technology and Additional Resources	**Planning and Instruction:** 💿 TeacherWorks Plus CD-ROM 💿 Classroom Presentation Toolkit CD-ROM ▶ Literature Online at **glencoe.com** (QuickPass Code: **GLA9879u7T**) **Students Tools:** 💿 StudentWorks Plus CD-ROM or DVD-ROM ▶ Online Student Edition at **glencoe.com** ▶ Literature Online at **glencoe.com** (QuickPass Code: **GLA9800u7**)

Lesson Plan

Glencoe Literature

The Names of Women (pp. 1296–1303)

Lesson Plan and Resource Manager

UNIT SEVEN Into the 21st Century 1960s–Present, Part 3: Extending and Remaking Traditions

Learning Objectives	**Literary Study:** Analyzing rhetorical devices. **Reading:** Distinguishing fact and opinion. **Writing:** Applying symbolism.
Lesson Summary	On pages **1296–1303** of the Student Edition, students will be introduced to the following: • **Big Idea:** Extending and Remaking Traditions • **Literary Elements:** Catalog, Symbol • **Reading Strategies:** Distinguish Fact and Opinion, Analyze Sections • **Vocabulary:** Word Parts, Academic Vocabulary • **Writing Activities/Grammar:** Apply Symbolism, Apostrophes
Lesson Duration	One 45–50 minute session
Readability Scores	Dale-Chall: 7.3 DRP: 62 Lexile: 1300
Focus	**TE** pp. 1296–1297 📖 Selection Focus Transparency 71 📖 Daily Language Practice Transparency 117
Teach	**TE** pp. 1298–1301 📁 Unit 7 Teaching Resources, Literary Element, p. 291 📁 Unit 7 Teaching Resources, Reading Strategy, p. 292 📁 Unit 7 Teaching Resources, Selection Vocabulary Practice, p. 293 📁 Unit 7 Teaching Resources, Vocabulary Strategy, p. 294 📁 Unit 7 Teaching Resources, Grammar Practice, p. 295 📖 Literary Elements Transparencies, p. 19, 52 💿 Classroom Presentation Toolkit CD-ROM 💿 Listening Library CD, Selection Audio 💿 TeacherWorks Plus CD-ROM 💿 Vocabulary PuzzleMaker CD-ROM
Assess	**TE** pp. 1302–1303 📁 Unit 7 Teaching Resources, Selection Quick Check, p. 296 📁 Unit 7 Teaching Resources, Selection Quick Check (Spanish), p. 297 📁 Assessment Resources, Selection Test, pp. 317–318 💿 ExamView Assessment Suite CD-ROM 💿 Progress Reporter Online Assessment

Differentiated Instruction: English Learners	**TE** English Learner Activities, pp. 1296–1303 📁 Unit 7 Teaching Resources, Selection Summaries: English, Spanish, Vietnamese, Tagalog, Cantonese, Haitian Creole, and Hmong, pp. 285–290 📁 Unit 7 Teaching Resources, Selection Quick Check (Spanish), p. 297 📁 English Language Coach 💿 Glencoe Interactive Vocabulary CD-ROM 💿 Listening Library Audio CD 📁 Listening Library Sourcebook: Strategies and Activities
Differentiated Instruction: Approaching Level	**TE** Approaching Level Activities, pp. 1296–1303 💿 Glencoe Interactive Vocabulary CD-ROM 💿 Listening Library Audio CD 📁 Listening Library Sourcebook: Strategies and Activities 💿 Skill Level Up! A Skills-Based Language Arts Game CD-ROM
Differentiated Instruction: Advanced/Pre-AP	📘 Novel Companion SE, pp. 295–338 📘 Novel Companion TG, pp. 62–70 💿 ▶ Literature Classics, High School CD-ROM 💿 Skill Level Up! A Skills-Based Language Arts Game CD-ROM
Extension	📘 Grammar and Language Workbook SE 📘 Grammar and Language Workbook TAE 📁 Revising with Style 📘 Spelling Power SE 📘 Spelling Power TAE
Daily Writing	**SE/TE** p. 1303
Interdisciplinary Connections	▶ **glencoe.com**
Independent Reading	💿 BookLink K–12 CD-ROM 📖 Ethnic Anthologies 📖 Glencoe Literature Library 💿 Glencoe Literature Library Teacher Resources CD-ROM 📖 *inTIME* magazine 💿 ▶ Literature Classics, High School CD-ROM
Technology and Additional Resources	**Planning and Instruction:** 💿 TeacherWorks Plus CD-ROM 💿 Classroom Presentation Toolkit CD-ROM ▶ Literature Online at **glencoe.com** (QuickPass Code: **GLA9879u7T**) **Students Tools:** 💿 StudentWorks Plus CD-ROM or DVD-ROM ▶ Online Student Edition at **glencoe.com** ▶ Literature Online at **glencoe.com** (QuickPass Code: **GLA9800u7**)

Lesson Plan

Glencoe Literature Essential Course of Study

Salvador Late or Early (pp. 1304–1307)

Lesson Plan and Resource Manager

UNIT SEVEN Into the 21st Century 1960s–Present, Part 3: Extending and Remaking Traditions

Learning Objectives	**Literary Study:** Analyzing imagery. **Reading:** Analyzing sound devices. **Writing:** Writing an essay.
Lesson Summary	On pages **1304–1307** of the Student Edition, students will be introduced to the following: • **Big Idea:** Extending and Remaking Traditions • **Literary Element:** Imagery • **Reading Strategies:** Analyze Sound Devices, Identify Sequence • **Vocabulary:** Academic Vocabulary • **Writing Activity/Grammar:** Write an Essay
Lesson Duration	One to five 45–50 minute sessions
Readability Scores	Dale-Chall: 5.5 DRP: 63 Lexile: (not testable due to length)
Focus	TE pp. 1304–1305 Selection Focus Transparency 72 Daily Language Practice Transparency 118 Literature Launchers: Pre-Reading Videos DVD, Selection Launcher Literature Launchers Teacher Guide
Teach	TE p. 1306 Interactive Read and Write SE, pp. 277–282 Interactive Read and Write TE, pp. 277–282 Unit 7 Teaching Resources, Literary Element, p. 304 Unit 7 Teaching Resources, Reading Strategy, p. 305 Unit 7 Teaching Resources, Vocabulary Strategy, p. 306 Unit 7 Teaching Resources, Grammar Practice, p. 307 Literary Elements Transparencies pp. 19, 52 Classroom Presentation Toolkit CD-ROM Listening Library CD, Selection Audio TeacherWorks Plus CD-ROM Vocabulary PuzzleMaker CD-ROM
Assess	TE p. 1307 Unit 7 Teaching Resources, Selection Quick Check, p. 308 Unit 7 Teaching Resources, Selection Quick Check (Spanish), p. 309 Assessment Resources, Selection Test, pp. 319–320 ExamView Assessment Suite CD-ROM Progress Reporter Online Assessment

Differentiated Instruction: English Learners	**TE** English Learner Activities, pp. 1304–1307
	Interactive Read and Write (EL) SE, pp. 277–282
	Interactive Read and Write (EL) TE, pp. 277–282
	Unit 7 Teaching Resources, Selection Summaries: English, Spanish, Vietnamese, Tagalog, Cantonese, Haitian Creole, and Hmong, pp. 298–303
	Unit 7 Teaching Resources, Selection Quick Check (Spanish), p. 309
	English Language Coach
	Glencoe Interactive Vocabulary CD-ROM
	Listening Library Audio CD
	Listening Library Sourcebook: Strategies and Activities
Differentiated Instruction: Approaching Level	Interactive Read and Write (Approaching) SE, pp. 277–282
	Interactive Read and Write (Approaching) TE, pp. 277–282
	Glencoe Interactive Vocabulary CD-ROM
	Listening Library Audio CD
	Listening Library Sourcebook: Strategies and Activities
	Skill Level Up! A Skills-Based Language Arts Game CD-ROM
Differentiated Instruction: Advanced/Pre-AP	Novel Companion SE, pp. 295–338
	Novel Companion TG, pp. 62–70
	Literature Classics, High School CD-ROM
	Skill Level Up! A Skills-Based Language Arts Game CD-ROM
Extension	Grammar and Language Workbook SE
	Grammar and Language Workbook TAE
	Revising with Style
	Spelling Power SE
	Spelling Power TAE
Daily Writing	**SE/TE** p. 1307
Interdisciplinary Connections	glencoe.com
Independent Reading	BookLink K–12 CD-ROM
	Ethnic Anthologies
	Glencoe Literature Library
	Glencoe Literature Library Teacher Resources CD-ROM
	inTIME magazine
	Literature Classics, High School CD-ROM
Technology and Additional Resources	**Planning and Instruction:**
	TeacherWorks Plus CD-ROM
	Classroom Presentation Toolkit CD-ROM
	Literature Online at **glencoe.com** (QuickPass Code: **GLA9879u7T**)
	Students Tools:
	StudentWorks Plus CD-ROM or DVD-ROM
	Online Student Edition at **glencoe.com**
	Literature Online at **glencoe.com** (QuickPass Code: **GLA9800u7**)

Lesson Plan

Thoughts on the African American Novel and Vocabulary Workshop (pp. 1308–1315)

Lesson Plan and Resource Manager

UNIT SEVEN Into the 21st Century 1960s–Present, Part 3: Extending and Remaking Traditions

Learning Objectives	**Literary Study:** Analyzing essays. **Reading:** Determining main idea and supporting details. **Writing:** Applying parallelism. **Vocabulary:** Using suffixes to form nouns.
Lesson Summary	On pages **1308–1315** of the Student Edition, students will be introduced to the following: • **Big Idea:** Extending and Remaking Traditions • **Literary Elements:** Essay, Parallelism • **Reading Strategies:** Determine Main Idea and Supporting Details, Vary Reading Rate • **Vocabulary:** Word Parts • **Writing Activities/Grammar:** Apply Parallelism, Identify the Thesis • **Listening/Speaking/Viewing Skill:** Analyze Art
Lesson Duration	One to five 45–50 minute sessions
Readability Scores	Dale-Chall: 7.4 DRP: 61 Lexile: 1130
Focus	**TE** pp. 1308–1309, 1315 Selection Focus Transparency 73 Daily Language Practice Transparency 119 Literature Launchers: Pre-Reading Videos DVD, Selection Launcher Literature Launchers Teacher Guide
Teach	**TE** pp. 1310–1312, 1315 Interactive Read and Write SE, pp. 283–294 Interactive Read and Write TE, pp. 283–294 Unit 7 Teaching Resources, Literary Element, p. 316 Unit 7 Teaching Resources, Reading Strategy, p. 317 Unit 7 Teaching Resources, Selection Vocabulary Practice, p. 318 Unit 7 Teaching Resources, Vocabulary Strategy, p. 319 Unit 7 Teaching Resources, Grammar Practice, p. 320 Literary Elements Transparency 37 Classroom Presentation Toolkit CD-ROM Listening Library CD, Selection Audio TeacherWorks Plus CD-ROM Vocabulary PuzzleMaker CD-ROM

Assess	**TE** pp. 1313–1314, 1315
	📁 Unit 7 Teaching Resources, Selection Quick Check, p. 321
	📁 Unit 7 Teaching Resources, Selection Quick Check (Spanish), p. 322
	📁 Assessment Resources, Selection Test, pp. 321–323
	💿 ExamView Assessment Suite CD-ROM
	▶ Progress Reporter Online Assessment
Differentiated Instruction: English Learners	**TE** English Learner Activities, pp. 1308–1315
	📘 Interactive Read and Write (EL) SE, pp. 283–294
	📘 Interactive Read and Write (EL) TE, pp. 283–294
	📁 Unit 7 Teaching Resources, Selection Summaries: English, Spanish, Vietnamese, Tagalog, Cantonese, Haitian Creole, and Hmong, pp. 310–315
	📁 Unit 1 Teaching Resources, Selection Quick Check (Spanish), p. 322
	📁 English Language Coach
	💿 Glencoe Interactive Vocabulary CD-ROM
	💿 Listening Library Audio CD
	📁 Listening Library Sourcebook: Strategies and Activities
Differentiated Instruction: Approaching Level	**TE** Approaching Level Activities, pp. 1308–1315
	📘 Interactive Read and Write (Approaching) SE, pp. 283–294
	📘 Interactive Read and Write (Approaching) TE, pp. 283–294
	💿 Glencoe Interactive Vocabulary CD-ROM
	💿 Listening Library Audio CD
	📁 Listening Library Sourcebook: Strategies and Activities
	💿 Skill Level Up! A Skills-Based Language Arts Game CD-ROM
Differentiated Instruction: Advanced/Pre-AP	📘 Novel Companion SE, pp. 295–338
	📘 Novel Companion TG, pp. 62–70
	💿 ▶ Literature Classics, High School CD-ROM
	💿 Skill Level Up! A Skills-Based Language Arts Game CD-ROM
Extension	📘 Grammar and Language Workbook SE
	📘 Grammar and Language Workbook TAE
	📁 Revising with Style
	📘 Spelling Power SE
	📘 Spelling Power TAE
Daily Writing	**SE/TE** p. 1314
Interdisciplinary Connections	**SE/TE** View the Art, p. 1310
	TE Literary History, Early Novelists, p. 1311
	▶ glencoe.com
Independent Reading	💿 BookLink K–12 CD-ROM
	📖 Ethnic Anthologies
	📖 Glencoe Literature Library
	💿 Glencoe Literature Library Teacher Resources CD-ROM
	📖 *inTIME* magazine
	💿 ▶ Literature Classics, High School CD-ROM
Technology and Additional Resources	**Planning and Instruction:**
	💿 TeacherWorks Plus CD-ROM
	💿 Classroom Presentation Toolkit CD-ROM
	▶ Literature Online at **glencoe.com** (QuickPass Code: **GLA9879u7T**)
	Students Tools:
	💿 StudentWorks Plus CD-ROM or DVD-ROM
	▶ Online Student Edition at **glencoe.com**
	▶ Literature Online at **glencoe.com** (QuickPass Code: **GLA9800u7**)